Introduction to International Human
Resource Management

Introduction to International Human Resource Management

Eileen Crawley

Stephen Swailes

David Walsh

OXFORD

UNIVERSITY PRESS

OXFORD

UNIVERSITY PRESS

Great Clarendon Street, Oxford, OX2 6DP,
United Kingdom

Oxford University Press is a department of the University of Oxford.
It furthers the University's objective of excellence in research, scholarship,
and education by publishing worldwide. Oxford is a registered trade mark of
Oxford University Press in the UK and in certain other countries

British Library Cataloguing in Publication Data

Data available

ISBN 978-0-19-956321-0

Printed in Italy by L.E.G.O. S.p.A.—Lavis TN

Outline contents

Detailed contents

The lead author for each chapter is as follows: Eileen Crawley for chapters 1 to 5, 8, 9, 11 and 14; Stephen Swailes for chapters 6, 7 and 13; and David Walsh for chapters 10 and 12. The authors gratefully acknowledge the many helpful suggestions received from anonymous reviewers during the writing process.

List of figures

List of tables

About the authors

Eileen Crawley has had an international career in business management, corporate training, and academic teaching over the past thirty years.

Eileen graduated from the University of East Anglia with a degree in social studies. She began her career in the UK Department of Employment. However, on moving to Malaysia she developed a career and a business, providing corporate training for leading Malaysian institutions. During this time she completed her MSc in training and human resource management (HRM) with Leicester University's Centre for Labour Market Studies. This stimulated her interest in cross-cultural issues and international HRM.

On moving to Spain she was employed by the Open University Business School and tutored MBA students in Brussels, Vienna, and Munich. She also worked as a corporate trainer for senior managers in leading Spanish organizations and conducted programmes for IEDE and BBVA Business Schools in Madrid.

Following a year teaching in China, she was appointed Senior Lecturer at the University of Bournemouth Business School, where she developed and taught International HRM and other HR/OB courses for five years. She was also a programme leader during this time.

She returned to Malaysia in 2008 and continues to work as a part-time lecturer and dissertation supervisor for British and Australian university partner colleges. Currently she is a part-time lecturer on the University of East London MBA Programme, teaching International HRM at WIM College (Malaysia), and is a coordinating lecturer for the University of Ballarat, Australia, MBA programme, teaching HRM at Stamford College. She also teaches on the Cardiff Metropolitan University BABS programme at Westminster International College. She has recently been an external examiner for Nottingham Trent University in Malaysia. Students in Malaysia come from all over the world and Eileen enjoys the constant challenge of supporting students from different cultures.

Stephen Swailes is Professor of Human Resource Management at the University of Huddersfield. After graduating in chemistry he worked in industry on a range of technical and management projects and after completing his MBA he moved to the University of Northampton. Before joining Huddersfield he was Director of the full-time MBA programme at the University of Hull. In addition to supervising PhD students he delivers a range of HRM modules, including teaching on MBA programmes delivered in Gulf countries.

His research interests include the assessment of management team roles, how organizations can evaluate talent management programmes, and how management in the Gulf States is influenced by local cultural factors. He is co-author of a popular text on organizational change and has written over thirty articles for leading academic journals.

David Walsh is Principal Lecturer in Human Resource Management at Nottingham Trent University in the UK. As Director of the professional HRM programmes at his university, he was instrumental in its being designated a Centre of Research Excellence by the Chartered

Institute of Personnel and Development (CIPD); and also in the establishment of thriving CIPD courses in Moscow and in Baku, Azerbaijan.

David has over thirty years' university teaching experience, including visiting lectureships in Europe and South East Asia. His current teaching in Nottingham is centred on Masters programmes in Management, HRM, and Business Administration, which attract students from all parts of the world.

David's subject specialism is International Human Resource Management (IHRM), alongside the more strategic aspects of HRM, which include his scholarly interests in People and Productivity, Workplace Employment Relations, Exit Management, and Diversity Management.

How to use this book

Learning outcomes

Each chapter opens with a series of learning outcomes which provide a route map through the chapter and the goals of each section, so that you know what you can expect to achieve as you progress through the chapter.

Introduction

At the beginning of each chapter you will find an introductory section offering a brief overview of the subject topic and key issues to be covered in that section of the book.

Discussion activities

Each chapter contains a number of discussion questions and points. These are designed to provide an opportunity for readers to work together and share ideas. This feature will also help you to assess your own understanding of the text and to consider how topics and ideas might be applied to your own country and work experiences.

Case examples

Each chapter includes several cases in order to illustrate the points being made or to show their practical application.

Stop and Think

We have learned that Insure-Co. has employed Ravi and Preethi on identical te employment; and that this is a prerequisite for ensuring the fairness and consi a stable and cooperative employment relationship with each individual. Yet in meeting these essentials, the attitudes of these two employees towards their w

It is the concept of the 'psychological contract' that leads us to stop and thi employment relationship is inherently problematical. Employees should not be of management's directions, but as people with their own distinctive reasons their employment.

Stop and Think

Every chapter features a section that invites you to 'stop and think' about particular points of interest. This encourages personal reflection and offers an additional way to help you learn about aspects of IHRM.

Review questions

1. What is the difference between HRM, Strategic HRM and Intern
2. In what ways may the focus of the study of IHRM differ between
3. What differences might you find between texts originating from Europe, in terms of their approach to IHRM?
4. What does the study of comparative international HRM include
5. What are the main challenges that face MNEs in their m

Review questions

At the end of each chapter there is a list of ten questions which relate to the contents of the chapter. These are designed to help you check your understanding across the breadth of information in the chapter. By focussing attention on the most relevant issues covered in the chapter, these questions will help further develop your learning.

Further reading

FDI Report (2011) Manufacturing makes a comeback, FDI Global Outlo Intelligence, *Financial Times*, April/May, online at http://www.fdiIntel June 2012).
   A useful overview of changes in FDI in different regions and sectors.
OECD (2011) *International Migration Outlook: SOPEMI 2011*, summary i
   This publication analyses recent developments in migration movements and and some non-member countries, including migration of highly qualified an

Further reading

Recommendations are given at the end of each chapter, should you wish to develop your learning through more specialized reading. Each source has a short explanation of its particular relevance and value.

Glossary

360-degree (Three-hundred-and-sixty-degree) or multi-source performance rating system—a performance rating system that uses opinions of not only the line manager but also peers, subordinates, and sometimes customers and suppliers to provide an

Bounded rationali not make perfectly rationality is bound other words there person can have o

Glossary

New terms which are introduced in each chapter have been combined into a final glossary. These terms are identified in **bold** when they appear in the text for the first time. You will also be directed to other chapters where related concepts or topics are developed.

How to use the Online Resource Centre

http://www.oxfordtextbooks.co.uk/orc/crawley/

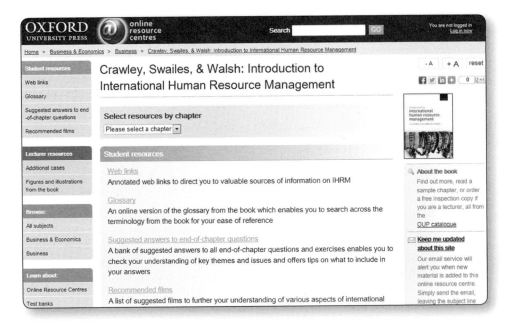

For students:

Brookfield Global Relocation Services
This site provides interesting, free reports on a wide rang[e]
Knowledge Centre. It is an international relocation consul[t]
the USA.
http://www.brookfieldgrs.com/knowledge/grts_research/

The Work Foundation is a UK not for profit organization [y]

Web links

A series of annotated web links will direct you to valuable sources of information on IHRM and specialist forums to further your learning in the field.

A

Agency Theory
Suggests that in the process of internationalization, MNE[s]
MNE headquarters (the principal) and the subsidiaries (th[e]
have different interests and preferences. For example su[ch]
decisions in their own interests (such as retaining inform[a]
control). This might not benefit the headquarters or the o[ther]

Online glossary

The authors have provided an online version of the glossary from the book which enables you to search across the terminology from the book for your ease of reference.

Chapter 1 Review questions

1. What is the difference between HRM, Strategic HF

HRM is the development of policies, and managemer undertaken by a Human Resource Department for an evolved from what used to be called Personnel Mana

Suggested answers to end-of-chapter questions

A bank of suggested answers to all end-of-chapter questions and exercises enables you to check your understanding of key themes and issues and offers tips on what to include in your answer.

The following films illustrate different aspects of cultural d may arise when there is a clash of cultures.

Gran Torino: A recent film that looks at how an elderly A neighbours who are Asian immigrants.

Bend it Like Beckham: A British film which highlights the the UK who wants to have the freedom of her UK friends

Recommended films

The authors have provided a list of suggested films which you may like to watch to further your understanding of various aspects of international human resource management.

For registered adopters:

Case Study and Questions

Introduction to the Chapter 1 Online Resource Ce

While chapter 1 has provided an introduction to the ra

discussed throughout this text and included a variety

Online case study

A detailed online case study is offered for each chapter. The case studies reinforce key issues from the textbook and are accompanied by a series of questions.

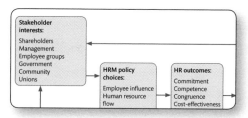

Figures and illustrations from the book

These have been provided for your ease of use – you can insert them into your PowerPoint® slides or simply show them to students on-screen.

Part I

The context of IHRM

What is IHRM? Definitions and perspectives

Learning Outcomes

After reading this chapter you will be able to:

- understand the meaning of Human Resource Management (HRM) and Strategic HRM (SHRM)
- explain the difference between various approaches to International HRM (IHRM)
- make sense of some of the key terminology, concepts, and perspectives in IHRM
- see the relationship between the development of internationalization and IHRM
- appreciate the range of issues that IHRM presents for multinational enterprises (MNEs) and for **small or medium-sized enterprises (SMEs)**.

Introduction

This book provides an introduction to International Human Resource Management (IHRM) and goes on to discuss the major challenges facing multinational organizations in the world-wide management of their human resources. It is particularly useful for those students who are taking an undergraduate or postgraduate course in International HRM, but who may not have previously studied HRM.

First, however, this opening chapter explains how IHRM differs from HRM. Then, key concepts and terminology related to our study of this academic subject are briefly explained. We begin by considering the terms HRM and Strategic HRM, go on to explore the foremost approaches to the study of IHRM, and then provide an introduction to concepts and arguments that underpin both HRM and IHRM. Finally, we briefly consider the role of an IHRM department and its degree of involvement in HR issues across the organization, in the context of the evolving structure of MNEs.

The second part of the chapter presents an overview of the book and an outline of each of the chapters.

What is the study of HRM?

The study of HRM, which has evolved from what used to be called 'Personnel Management', incorporates a consideration of how organizations plan and manage their staff. It is concerned, therefore, with the composition of the organization's workforce and with those processes that incorporate the recruitment and selection of employees, their training and development, the management of their performance and rewards, and finally the termination of their employment. It also involves the management of employment relations, which may include dealing with employee representatives or their trade unions.

In spite of this generally agreed set of management processes, HRM is often examined from the perspective of just one country. So, texts published in the UK, the USA, or India, and so on, tend to use examples local to them and to focus their attention on the way national employment legislation impacts on the practice of HRM in their particular country. By contrast, some texts take a more comparative approach, examining the human resource systems and practices used in different countries. This approach provides a helpful insight into the complexities of managing people in different parts of the world, and a useful guide to the laws and customs that influence how human resource activities are performed. In addition, we can differentiate between texts by the extent to which they adopt an academic or a practitioner focus. From our viewpoint, the latter tend to pay insufficient attention to a critical (i.e. questioning) discussion of theory and the likely implications for HR in practice.

Whereas the concept of Personnel Management is often perceived as a middle management function in which the manager has little influence on strategic decisions, the concept of HRM (derived from the USA in the 1980s) is based on 'the notion that people management can be a key source of competitive advantage' (Tayeb, 2005: 5). As a consequence, HRM is more associated with a senior management role, with its occupant being expected to have direct involvement in strategic decision making.

Storey (2001) has identified twenty-seven differences between Personnel Management and HRM. He then divides these into four broad areas:

- beliefs and assumptions;
- strategic qualities;
- the critical role of managers;
- key levers.

Taking these in turn, Storey suggests that HRM places emphasis on giving the organization a competitive edge through gaining employees' commitment, as opposed to their mere observance or compliance with company rules. Second, HRM is seen as being integrated with an organization's strategic objectives. Third, as a result of this enhanced importance, HRM responsibilities go beyond the specialist personnel manager and involve line managers as drivers of HR policies. Finally, the focus of HRM is on managing organizational culture rather than simply ensuring compliance with procedures.

From the above, it follows that the main functions of HRM (in terms of recruiting, training, and rewarding staff, and so on) also need to be integrated. Moreover, increased significance is given to job redesign and restructuring to allow devolved responsibility and empowerment (Storey, 2001).

Storey's actual definition of HRM (1995: 5) is as follows: 'Human resource management is a distinctive approach to employment management which seeks to achieve competitive advantage through the strategic deployment of a highly committed and capable workforce, using an array of cultural, structural and personnel techniques.'

However, this might be seen as rather idealistic. Redman and Wilkinson (2006), for example, suggest that Storey's definition is associated with what is now known as 'high commitment management' and 'high performance work systems'. These tend to lay down a somewhat prescriptive view of what HRM should look like. Perhaps a more realistic, general, and all-embracing definition of HRM is provided by Boxall and Purcell (2011: 1): 'HRM refers to all those activities associated with the management of work and people in organisations.'

While there has been considerable academic debate concerning the real difference between Personnel Management and HRM, both terms continue to be used and, from a practical perspective, they are generally assumed to mean much the same thing. However, there is a general consensus that the concept of HRM has evolved from Personnel to become more closely linked with the strategy of the firm. This is explored below, and further discussion of the models used in HRM, SHRM, and IHRM can be found throughout Chapter 3, 'Key academic models, theories, and debates'.

Definitions of HRM terms

Strategic HRM

Strategic HRM is the term used to indicate that HRM policies and practices are aligned and developed to support the organization's broad strategy. It is assumed, therefore, that the HR function should be a partner in developing this organizational strategy. In essence this means that business goals and objectives are developed alongside human resource deliberations about the potential availability of employees, who will be required to carry out the tasks and jobs identified.

While there has been some discussion about whether there is a difference between HRM and SHRM, Schuler and Tarique (2007: 720) focus on academic research into the subject and suggest that most scholars would agree that SHRM 'covers research intended to improve our understanding of the relationship between how organisations manage their human resources and their success in implementing business strategies'.

An alternative definition of SHRM, which refers more to its actual practice, is provided by Wright and McMahan (1992: 298): 'SHRM is the pattern of planned Human Resource deployments and activities intended to enable a firm to achieve its goals.'

In simple terms and based upon both definitions, HRM is 'strategic' when all of its functions and elements are directly linked to the pursuit of the organization's strategic corporate objectives. Logically, therefore, when an organization operates overseas and develops an international strategy, Strategic HRM is extended to incorporate international employment policies and practices. In this case the organization would aspire to adopting **Strategic International HRM** (SIHRM) policies and practices.

Strategic HRM and Strategic International HRM have been discussed extensively in the literature (Schuler and Jackson, 1999; Sparrow and Brewster, 2006; Schuler and Tarique, 2007; Morris et al., 2009) and much of our understanding has been 'heavily influenced by thinking in the USA' (Brewster, 2007: 769). With this in mind let us now turn our attention to IHRM.

International HRM

Drawing on the views of Schuler and Tarique (2007: 717–18), 'International HRM is about the worldwide management of human resources' while:

> the *field of IHRM* is about understanding, researching, applying and revising all human resource activities in their internal and external contexts as they impact the processes of managing human resources in organisations throughout the global environment to enhance the experience of multiple stakeholders.

Quite simply, they add, *'the purpose of IHRM* is to enable the firm, multinational enterprise (MNE) to be successful globally' (Schuler and Tarique, 2007: 718), which 'entails being (a) competitive throughout the world; (b) efficient; (c) locally responsive; (d) flexible and adaptable within the shortest of time periods; and (e) capable of transferring knowledge and learning across globally dispersed units' (Sparrow and Brewster, 2006, cited in Schuler and Tarique, 2007: 718).

Such fundamental requirements would seem to present considerable difficulties and complications for MNEs, and Part I of this book considers the wider international context of these challenges. Part II then explores the practicalities of managing employees who are employed to work towards their MNE's strategic and international goals.

Contextual or Comparative HRM

Contextual or Comparative HRM is the term used to describe the study of HRM as it is practised within different countries, primarily in their domestic organizations. It considers the extent to which different national institutions may impact on employment conditions and HR activities, paying particular attention to the historical, legal, and institutional context of the country in which organizations operate. Hence it seeks to compare different countries by focusing on those institutions that affect employment, including labour markets, education, and political systems. This approach also seeks to make national comparisons by looking at differences and similarities in the practice and methods used in, for example, recruitment and selection, training and development, rewards and performance management, and relationships with trade unions.

Since any organization planning to set up its business in another country needs to work within the target country's domestic framework, contextual or comparative HRM is an important area for an MNE's research and understanding. However, as well as considering national institutions, comparative HRM also includes the study of how national culture such as legislation and education impacts on human resource practices and on aspects of institutions.

International HRM in MNEs

MNEs have to manage their human resources in many different national environments. The study of IHRM takes account of this and considers the added complexities that face MNEs in managing their employees, who need to be recruited for different subsidiary companies in a variety of countries.

Invariably, local people are employed in the overseas subsidiaries of an MNE. This type of employee is a **Host Country National** or **HCN**. Typically, HCNs are managed locally, with little interference from headquarters. Thus, while many MNEs would like to pursue common HR practices throughout their global organization, the local environments in which they operate, with the cultural and institutional differences this implies, often make this problematic.

Certainly, IHRM is thought to be more complex than domestic HRM, in that it needs to consider the management of a wider range of employees, who support the MNE's corporate strategy in a variety of national cultural contexts. Most frequently, the study of IHRM focuses on the particular problems associated with employing more senior, **expatriate** staff overseas. Expatriates can be drawn from the parent company and are known as a **Parent Country**

National or **PCN**. Alternatively, they could be a **Third Country National** or **TCN**, in that they come neither from the company's home base nor from the host country location of its overseas subsidiary. From this perspective, IHRM examines the practical issues concerning an expatriate's adaptation to each new environment and role. These issues are addressed in Part Two of the book.

One of the major concerns of the management of expatriates and IHRM is *cultural difference* and the issues that arise because of this. This topic is discussed in detail in Chapter 4. Consequently, many authors suggest the need for *cross-cultural training* to help expatriate managers acclimatize to their foreign posting; this is explored in Chapter 9. Combining these two points, one practical issue that may well arise is the relationship between expatriate managers and their host country staff—and the behaviours adopted, particularly in *managing conflict*.

The following case study, 1.1, which has been adapted from Chen Yi-Feng and Tjosvold (2007), summarizes the results of interviews between American and Japanese managers and their Chinese host country employees regarding the handling of conflict. It also produces a framework for overcoming obstacles to working together.

 Case Study 1.1 Co-operative conflict management: An approach aimed at strengthening relationships between expatriate managers and their Chinese host country employees

Expatriate managers working in countries in Asia are faced with a culture where harmony is highly regarded. Consequently conflict is invariably avoided. However, this study questions the traditional assumption of the value of avoiding conflict.

First, the authors suggest that difficulties can arise when working across cultural boundaries because people from 'other cultures' are perceived as adversaries with different values, beliefs, and styles of interacting. Their study goes on to recommend the selection and training of expatriate managers, who are willing to practise cooperative rather than competitive or avoidance approaches to managing conflict. They also reassert the importance of facilitating mutual trust and commitment. This helps to promote team performance, inter-organizational partnerships, and effective leadership.

Based on interviews with mainland Chinese employees on their interactions with their Japanese and American managers, and using the 'critical incident technique', the study was able to evaluate the effectiveness of three approaches to conflict management: *competitive, avoidance,* and *cooperative*.

Utilizing Deutsche's (1973, cited in Chen and Tjosvold, 2007, p. 275) theory of cooperation and conflicts, the authors focus on the importance of cooperative goals. They view conflict as a 'joint problem', which needs to be discussed openly until a mutually acceptable solution results. Applied to this particular international context, they suggest that expatriate managers who approach conflict in a cooperative, mutually beneficial way are likely to strengthen their relationship with Chinese employees and help them develop trust and commitment.

However, the authors also recognize that developing such an interpersonal relationship is challenging, in view of the Chinese tendency to want to avoid potential conflict. The authors recommend, therefore, that managers link their cooperative approach to conflict to the organization's reward and task systems. In this way Chinese employees can be made aware that conflicts are to be seen as 'common problems', which they will want to resolve for the mutual benefits that will be the outcome.

Ideally, therefore, expatriate managers and local employees will together develop shared goals, integrated roles, common tasks, team identity, personal relationships, and shared reward distributions, which should reinforce their cooperative behaviour.

Adapted from: Chen Yi-Feng and Tjosvold (2007)

Discussion Activity 1.1

Discuss how you like to deal with conflict.

Are there occasions when you would rather ignore the problem than face the unpleasant situation of discussing it openly? Or would you prefer to ensure that the other party fully understands your point of view by arguing in favour of it?

Is it better to have harmony rather than bringing conflict to the surface?

Two important debates of IHRM

Convergence versus divergence

The role of many senior expatriates has traditionally included both a management and a control function. Thus a major concern for international managers includes the difficulty of balancing local needs ('differentiation') with the integration of company-wide strategy, systems, and processes—for the overall profitability of the organization worldwide. The integrative processes can be said to operate as a force for 'convergence'. This refers to the degree to which there is convergence towards the same way of operating across the world, and the supposed benefits of this. The opposing force for 'differentiation' concerns the extent to which an MNE's operational practices remain 'divergent', largely because of national institutional or cultural differences among its subsidiaries.

The nature and extent of these opposing forces comprises a major ongoing debate in both international management and IHRM: the **convergence/divergence debate**.

Universalist versus contextual approaches

A second area of debate arises from two competing approaches to analysing and understanding IHRM. This is discussed in more detail in Chapter 3 under the section heading *Studying IHRM: universalistic and contextual/comparative approaches*. The **Universalist approach** reflects mainstream thinking from American authors, in which they consider the MNE to be the main focus of research. They constantly look for 'one best way' to manage, which can then be universally applied throughout the MNE.

In contrast, much of the research from UK and European authors adopts a **Contextual approach**. These authors consider that the study of IHRM extends beyond the firm and includes contextual factors: both cultural and institutional. These are thought to be integral to our understanding of IHRM, and not simply contingencies to be managed by the firm. It follows, therefore, that this approach goes beyond looking for '**one best way**'. Rather, it appreciates that 'the best way' to manage will depend on the particular set of circumstances facing the MNE. Consequently, managers should seek to achieve a '**best fit**', which will depend largely on contextual factors that need to be understood.

As a result of this, European research and texts tend to be more exploratory and less prescriptive than American publications. See Chapter 3, in the section *Two different perspectives on IHRM*.

Discussion Activity 1.2

Compare two or three texts on HRM and IHRM, from both European (UK) and American authors. Identify the difference in approach to IHRM issues.

Also, select a textbook that is prescriptive (i.e. one that tells managers what they *should* do) and one that is more discursive or critical, containing more theory and argument. Which will be most useful (a) for academic work; and (b) in the workplace?

Finally, evaluate the above texts and make a list of the most useful, including the authors' names, publisher, library reference numbers, and ISBN number for future use.

The internationalization of organizations and IHRM

While some aspects of the internationalization process are discussed in Chapter 2 in the section *The internationalization process of MNEs*, it is appropriate that this is introduced here. IHRM practices and policies will be affected by the way an organization internationalizes, and by the structural forms the MNE may adopt, including the position of its HR function. The organization may at first not consider how such changes could affect the role of the HR department. However, depending on the *strategy* of the company and the *structure* that evolves, the HR department will certainly need to develop its own IHRM policy and also define the limitations of its control.

The development of an international HR department

The development of an MNE's international HR department is influenced by how the company *evolves* internationally and the various *structures* this may imply. In addition, it will be influenced by the strategic objectives of the MNE and its organizational values. These will help determine the role, policies, activities, and contribution of IHRM to the business.

Since international and multinational organizations take many forms, it is often difficult to ascertain which part of the MNE we are referring to when we discuss IHRM. Which office does the International HR manager report to? What is the extent of his or her span of control? For example is the management of subsidiary employees the responsibility of an International HR manager or of local managements? Is there a central HR function that coordinates the employment of expatriates or are such tasks devolved and decentralized? These issues are discussed throughout the text and it will become evident that the approach differs depending on the MNEs concerned and their relationship with their overseas subsidiaries or partners.

As we have already suggested, MNEs can adopt a variety of *organizational structures*, influenced by factors such as company size and strategic requirements. At the *early stages* of internationalization, when companies are beginning to develop links overseas to market their products or obtain supplies and services, organizations do not need an international HR department. As such they probably send people abroad only for short visits—to establish contacts, evaluate the opportunities, sound out the market, and to meet potential agents or suppliers. Companies who then decide to develop these contacts will normally set up an international section, department, or division to administer these links, but this does not include an international HR function.

Further internationalization may see organizations seeking to establish manufacturing plants, service contracts, or subsidiary companies abroad. It is here that they begin to send employees to work overseas for extended periods of time. As we have implied above, these expatriates or **international assignees** are likely to need special support. For this reason a person responsible for IHRM may be appointed and an international HR department may well evolve.

Organizational structures and IHRM

The structure of an organization is determined by what it does. Hence a company's structure is designed around its main activity and the strategies it adopts to make its operations both efficient and effective. Structures both evolve and are also deliberately changed, to support business operations. Hence the existence and role of IHRM as a functional department will be subject to these same processes. In most cases, however, an IHRM department is responsible mainly for expatriate employees and corporate HR policy. With regard to the degree to which such a department is involved in the activities of overseas subsidiaries, much can depend upon the MNE's dominant orientation. This concept is explained later in this chapter, through our outline of the 'EPRG model' (Chakravarthy and Perlmutter, 1985), in the section *Organizational orientations and IHRM*.

Returning to the way MNEs organize themselves to achieve international business success, the following forms have been identified by Rugman and Hodgetts (2003: 246–54).

International division structure

This structure centralizes all the international operations into one division, a division that has the same status as the MNE's domestic divisions. It makes it easier to manage all international activities and provides the opportunity for developing a cadre of international managers. This is the dominant structure used by US MNEs.

Global product structure

Domestic (e.g. parent country) divisions are given control of worldwide product groups. Each product division is a profit centre and it can focus on the needs of a particular product line across the world. In this case, managers drawn from various countries will need specific product knowledge to manage that product in their own countries.

Global geographic area structure

In this approach responsibility is given to managers of each geographic area. This is applied in MNEs with narrow product lines, such as foods, which might need to be adapted to local tastes. While managers need local knowledge for their roles, they also need to have knowledge of, and conform to, the company's overall strategy.

Global functional structure

This is built around the main functions of the organization. It allows a few managers to maintain tight control over a wide-reaching organization. It is common among MNEs with heavy investment, such as raw materials extractors and energy providers.

Matrix or three-dimensional structure

This is a more complex mix of product, functional, and geographic structures. It is common for employees to report to multiple project managers as well as a line manager. A great deal of coordination and cooperation is needed to make this effective, given the duality of reporting lines and multiple responsibilities.

Network structure

This is a common form for very large transnational organizations. It strives to take advantage of global economies of scale and at the same time be responsive to local customer demands. It is differentiated from the matrix structure (above) by having nodes that are responsible for coordinating product, functional, and geographic information. It is made up of dispersed units (subsidiaries all over the world) alongside specialized operations. The latter are subunits that focus on particular areas, products, research, etc., and which locate expertise to be used throughout the organization. This is a complex form, which is constantly changing.

Organizational orientations and IHRM

The degree to which an IHRM department is required by an MNE will depend partly on the extent to which it is thought necessary to send PCNs and TCNs overseas. Attracting, training, developing, and retaining suitable employees to work on international assignments requires a clearly focused IHRM function that is fully aware of the company's global strategic requirements.

At the same time the remit of an IHRM department will also depend upon the orientation or values of the organization, notably in the MNE's stance towards its subsidiaries. This can take various forms, but has been usefully classified as: ethnocentric, polycentric, regiocentric, and geocentric (EPRG) (Chakravarthy and Perlmutter, 1985). This EPRG model helps explain the degree to which the parent company tries to control its subsidiaries' activities. It also illustrates how different orientations result in a variety of staffing outcomes, in terms of the appointment and development of either expatriate or host country managers. The implications of this are discussed in Chapter 6 in the section *Broad approaches to staffing, corporate approaches*; and in Chapter 8, Table 8.2, *Factors that impact on expatriate adjustment*.

The effects of the EPRG model on strategy, international HR policies, and the structure of the organization are briefly summarized below, noting that each orientation reflects the dominant view of the MNE.

Ethnocentric orientation

Strategy	global integration
HR practices	PCNs are developed for key positions worldwide
Structure	hierarchical product divisions.

Polycentric orientation

Strategy	national responsiveness
HR practices	HCNs are developed for key positions in their own country
Structure	hierarchical area divisions with autonomous national units.

Regiocentric orientation

Strategy	regional integration and national responsiveness
HR practices	people from a region are developed for key positions in that region (e.g. Eastern Europe, Asia-Pacific, etc.)
Structure	product and regional organization tied together through a matrix structure.

Geocentric orientation

Strategy	global integration and national responsiveness
HR practices	the best people (whether PCN, TCN, or HCN) are developed for key positions worldwide
Structure	a network of organizations (in some cases this includes stockholders and competitors).

This model is discussed further in Chapter 3, 'Key academic models, theories, and debates', in the section *Models of human resource management: 3 The 'EPRG' model of mind sets and international strategies (Perlmutter, 1969)*.

The stages of organizational internationalization

Adler and Ghadar (1990, cited in Jackson, 2002: 48) consider how organizations internationalize and identify four sequential stages, with links between culture and human resource responses at each stage. The phases are classified as domestic, international, multinational, and global.

The *domestic* stage sees the organization focusing on its home market and where appropriate on the export of products produced at home. Although there is no need for employees to be recruited to work overseas, visits by sales or technical staff to foreign offices may be required. The *international* stage sees the company developing its presence overseas. Its main focus is on local responsiveness and the transfer of learning from the home base. This approach aligns to a polycentric orientation, mentioned above in the section *Organizational orientations and IHRM*.

The *multinational* form focuses on global strategy, typically governed from headquarters and bolstered by an ethnocentric orientation. Finally, the *global* stage adopts a form that seeks to combine local responsiveness and global integration (Jackson, 2002; Adler and

Ghadar, 1990). As such it shares characteristics associated with a regiocentric orientation. This model is explained in more detail in Chapter 3, in the section *International human resource management (IHRM): 8 Product life cycle model (Adler and Ghadar, 1990)*.

Not all multinational organizations go through these sequential stages. However, as business organizations develop internationally, a key role played by expatriate managers is the transfer of knowledge from the parent company to its overseas subsidiary (Massingham, 2010). It should come as no surprise that, in view of cultural and institutional differences between nations, this process is not without its difficulties. The following case discusses these issues in the context of Australian expatriate managers dealing with six subsidiaries in China, Indonesia, Malaysia, Papua New Guinea, Taiwan, and Vietnam.

 Case Study 1.2   Managing knowledge transfer between PCNs (Australia) and HCNs (Asian countries)

This extract summarizes research into knowledge transfer in an Australian multinational operating in Asia and in particular how the 'knowledge gap' between PCNs and HCNs represents a barrier to the transfer of knowledge. The nature of the knowledge gap is examined, as well as the effect this has on the relationship between PCNs and HCNs. The article also explains how PCNs can adapt their role in response to this knowledge gap.

Multinationals share knowledge mainly between the headquarters parent company and host country subsidiaries, to ensure strategy is implemented, market opportunities are created, and performance is controlled. If any barriers to knowledge transfer exist between the key actors, the PCNs and HCNs, companies need to manage these.

The focus of this research is *tacit* knowledge: the knowledge held in people's heads. Previous research has shown there are barriers to transferring tacit knowledge. These barriers relate to the characteristics of the participants and can include their motivation, their ability to absorb and retain information, and their differences in national culture and language. These might lead to cognitive biases, such as PCN arrogance.

This study shows that in the knowledge transfer relationship, the PCN plays four roles: parent, master, guide, and mentor—defined by the nature of the knowledge being transferred, and by the respective motivation and abilities of the sender and receiver. The study shows that the relationship between PCN and HCN is multidimensional and dynamic. Hence, as the HCN receives and learns new knowledge the PCN's role changes, moving from parent towards mentor.

The article also discusses the significance of the organizational culture, especially as it affects the way in which a PCN's wealth of experience or their most valuable tacit knowledge was hoarded and protected. Because of this, relationships were often ineffective, resulting in the exclusion of HCNs from the PCN's social network and their cherished knowledge. The importance of strategic *consensus* is identified for its impact on relationships, knowledge flows, and the development required of HCNs in their evolving roles.

Finally, having proposed new ways of thinking about knowledge flows and the impact of PCN/HCN relationships, the author provides managerial guidelines in areas of managerial behaviour, human resource strategy, and a framework for understanding and managing PCN and HCN interaction. He also suggests that the role of 'global coach' (akin to guide and mentor) is the most important one for PCNs and should be emphasized in selection decisions and PCN development.

Adapted from: Massingham (2010)

The topic of knowledge management is discussed further throughout the second half of Chapter 9, 'Training, development, and knowledge management', under the heading *Knowledge management in MNEs*.

Discussion Activity 1.3

Discuss your own views on how and why relationships between PCNs and HCNs may prevent the flow of information and knowledge transfer.

What can PCNs and HCNs do, in order to resolve this problem?

(See Chapter 4, 'Understanding IHRM: the cultural approach', in the section *Cultural concepts and the research of key authors: Hofstede: Long- or short-term orientation (LTO)* for discussion of this aspect of culture; and Table 4.1, *Cultural dimensions and resulting HRM practices.*)

International mergers and acquisitions and IHRM

Against a background of businesses facing constant pressure to be more globally competitive, MNEs are often attracted towards expanding through *international mergers and acquisitions*. However, these can create enormous strain on Human Resource departments. As part of the move towards cost controls and efficiencies, employees may have to be relocated or made redundant. More costly expatriate staff may be the first to suffer, in some cases being asked to take local (i.e. host country) salary packages or actually losing their jobs. Similarly, when work is moved overseas to new partner companies, home-based employees may also lose out. Moreover, increasing calls by overseas partners and subsidiaries to utilize local staff also threaten opportunities for overseas assignees.

According to Schuler et al. (2004: 30), mergers can come about for many reasons:

- to promote growth;
- to manage technology;
- as a response to government policy;
- to take advantage of exchange rates;
- as a response to political and economic conditions;
- to reduce labour costs;
- to increase productivity though acquiring a skilled workforce;
- to follow clients;
- to achieve greater vertical integration;
- to diversify the business and manage risk.

Mergers can range from those between equals to those between firms that are unequal in size and market value. Other forms of merger include alliances, partnerships, and joint ventures. On the other hand, acquisitions occur when one company buys another and manages it in its own way. However, whereas some acquisitions can result in integration of the businesses, others may result in separation, where a part (or parts) of the whole entity becomes a new organization (Schuler et al., 2004: 2–5).

Implications for IHRM

Whatever form the merging of two companies takes, there will need to be negotiations over the alignment of all aspects of employment conditions, remuneration, and benefits, as well as a degree of bargaining over reduced head counts. This is because there will now be overlap between certain employees' roles, where efficiencies can readily be made. For these reasons it is important that senior HR managers are included at the start of any strategic decision-making processes concerning mergers and acquisitions. However, a recent survey by the CIPD (2007: 12) on HR in international mergers and acquisitions indicates that:

> Overall, then, the picture that emerges from the UK operations of firms engaging in international M and As is one of a relatively small HR function despite the inherent HR challenges that they bring, and that these challenges are coupled with the requirements of being part of a co-ordinated international function and of being monitored from higher levels that are at least as strong, and maybe stronger, than in firms that either have not grown or which have grown through greenfield investments.

This survey illustrates the fact that human resource decisions are often taken by merger teams with little input from human resource specialists. This is despite the fact that people are supposedly such an important component in strategic decision making. It seems that HR professionals are seldom in senior enough positions to be influential in strategic decision-making activities. As a result, international decisions at both strategic and operational levels are made without consulting HR experts and without sufficient knowledge of the HR consequences of these decisions.

Having provided a brief introduction to the evolution and structure of multinational organizations, we can now go on to consider the IHRM function in more detail.

The difference between HRM and IHRM

Some authors suggest that there is no difference between HRM and IHRM and that the scope of activities is basically the same. However, the complexities of managing employees in other parts of the world, and the problems that can arise, add to, or *extend* the functions of the domestic HR role to include the issues outlined below. This applies most directly to the employment of expatriate staff. Thus, while a domestic HR role is usually concerned only with the employee, IHR may well add to this by taking responsibility for the expatriate's accompanying family and their needs. Further, compared with a domestic employee, an expatriate's career is more complex in terms of distance, circumstances, personal issues, and therefore its management by HR.

We can gauge these additional aspects of IHRM more tangibly through the work of Stone (2008: 802–20), which specifies issues associated with (a) adaptation and family; and (b) expatriate career and compensation.

Adaptation and family issues

location issues climate, living conditions, transport facilities, and availability of food required;

safety and health medical arrangements, hospital facilities, risks, terrorism, and kidnapping;

accommodation assistance with finding and funding appropriate housing, moving, and storage;

travel allowances frequency of paid trips home;

family pre-departure preparation for family, adaptation assistance, spouse's work permission;

children's education advice on schools, allowances for education costs.

Expatriate career and compensation issues

recruitment and selection an understanding of the attributes and characteristics required for international assignees compared with domestic employees;

performance appraisal management key decisions on who will carry out the appraisal, where this will take place (at home or overseas), and what criteria will be used, in view of the different demands placed on expatriates;

compensation type of package for international assignees, covering allowances, pension rights, social security and income tax arrangements, taking account of exchange rates and cost of living issues; special benefits at end of assignment;

training and development cultural adaptation training for expatriates (and their family members), language training, and opportunities for ongoing development while overseas;

career implications combating the likelihood of 'out of sight, out of mind', networking arrangements to keep in touch while away, and career planning for repatriation.

These and similar issues are the concern of Part Two of this book. For now, let us consider some of the current factors behind the rise in importance of IHRM.

The BRIC countries and IHRM

While Brazil, Russia, India, and China (BRIC) share the common feature of undergoing recent and dramatic economic growth resulting in new opportunities for international business, each of these countries has very different institutions, employment regulations, and cultural environments. It is these matters that international investors need to understand when embarking on business overseas.

For example Russia has complex bureaucratic legislation and poses political problems and ethical concerns for business investors. Large organizations with a track record in Russia, such as BP (which has earned one-eighth of its profits from its TNK-BP business), are keen to stay and pursue future benefits. Others, however, may be influenced more by the political and economic risks, which may dictate against any investment. For example commenting on BP's new contract with Rosneft, a Russian state-controlled company, *The Economist* (2011a) asked: 'Should a responsible company climb into bed with a dodgy one?' This is clearly related to ethical concerns, which are considered throughout Chapter 11, 'Corporate social responsibility and ethics'.

The growth of BRIC countries has resulted in the focus of international business moving away from the West to developing countries in other parts of the world. India is one such country, and is especially significant for IHRM in its appeal as an outsourcing location for companies in the UK and the USA. India has a growing economy, a large and educated middle class, and it continues to offer inward investment opportunities to MNEs. Indeed, Russia has traditionally had ties with India in the field of telecommunications and defence technologies and continues this relationship while also providing nuclear technology support. Russia also has a small truck manufacturing company in India (BBC World News, 2011).

Such ties imply the movement of international assignees and the need for considerable learning in terms of expatriates' cultural adaptation. In China expatriates are known as 'foreign experts' and their employment is likely to continue for some time because of the lack of management skills in the local population and the lack of effective management development programmes there (Wang et al., 2009: 208). As a result, McKinsey and Co. (2008, cited in Wang et al., 2009: 216) warns: 'If the current situation continues, the relief of the shortages in management talents will not be in sight any time soon and the talent wars among organisations in China will be likely to continue.'

This same article observes that multinationals are competing for senior management talent in China despite the large numbers of Chinese MBA holders and graduates. This is because there are still insufficient local managers with the requisite type of international expertise or calibre.

A similar shortage of managers, especially those with technical backgrounds, is reported for Brazil (*The Economist*, 2011b). This is attributed to large oil finds and national infrastructure plans, which together have resulted in a soaring demand for labour combined with a limited number of engineering graduates each year: 35,000 compared with 250,000 in India and 400,000 in China. As a result, CEOs and company directors earn more in Sao Paulo than in New York, London, Singapore, or Hong Kong. Yet, although firms are looking outside Brazil to fill their top posts, the high crime rate and a need to master Portuguese are thought to be factors that make it difficult to entice such recruits (*The Economist*, 2011b: 40).

Current trends in IHRM

International talent management

A matter of rising importance in MNEs and international SMEs is international talent management, which concerns how and where to recruit and select the 'best employees'– and how to keep them. While there is a perceived shortage of competent international managers, the traditional approach of recruiting from parent companies is being called into question. Hence, more diverse sources of managers from host countries and third countries are being included in pools of potential recruits. Additionally, alternative methods of managing international work are increasingly being used, both to reduce high expatriate costs and to enable talented individuals to work more effectively. Thus, for example, companies are making increased use of short-term overseas visits, and taking advantage of broadband technologies that permit 'virtual' management communications. These topics are discussed in more detail throughout Chapter 6, 'Global staffing', and Chapter 13, 'Global talent management'.

International reward management

These 'cut price' types of appointment result in a wider range of reward strategies, which are influenced both by the desire to rationalize expatriate staffing costs and to give consideration to issues of equity between expatriates and local staff. Such issues are addressed throughout Chapter 7, 'International reward management', noting the impact of a company's reward strategy and philosophy as well as the influence of factors such as national cultural difference, international labour markets, and performance management practices.

An article published by Baker and Roberts (2006) has considered the real costs of expatriation. The following summary provides some insights.

The article provides insights into the wide range of practical and financial considerations that managing an expatriate assignment implies. It graphically explains the financial issues that an MNE needs to understand, as these are what an expatriate employee and his/her family will consider before accepting an assignment. It is the enormity of these costs that leads multinationals to consider other ways of managing overseas businesses. It explains the trend towards the use of regular short-term visits, which do not require relocation costs, and the attraction of employing TCNs or HCNs, who can be trained in the parent country. These issues are discussed throughout Chapter 7, 'International reward management' and Chapter 13, 'Global talent management'.

Most IHRM literature on expatriates considers managers or specialists travelling either from developed countries to other developed countries, or from developed countries to less-developed countries. Thus, there is an emphasis upon the considerable costs incurred by the MNE because there is a presumption that expatriates will expect to live in comfort that is at

 Case Study 1.3 Managing the costs of expatriation: they may be greater than you think

In this article, the real costs of expatriation are examined from an accountant's point of view. The authors suggest that direct and indirect costs can amount to three to five times the expatriate's base salary, some estimating the costs at more than US$1m per person per assignment.

The costs of expatriation are analysed in detail in terms of:

upstream costs: the costs of selection and training in advance of the appointment;

direct cash-outlay costs: the costs of housing, transport, travel (including home leave, and travel to maintain contacts), salary, benefits, taxation, and the costs for the family (including assistance for spouse with job search, family transportation, shipping of personal effects, visas, medical costs, and education costs);

indirect behavioural costs: the expatriate's feelings of isolation and 'culture shock', which prevent initial optimum performance on the job, so that the expatriate needs to be supported by a regular communication home (unlimited telephone/fax costs);

downstream costs: repatriation (to ensure a smooth transition back into a home country management role), knowledge management (so that the experience gained by the expatriate is shared), and expatriate retention (ensuring the manager stays with the company, through a salary premium and career planning/advancement).

Adapted from: Baker and Roberts (2006)

least equivalent to what they experience at home. However, the reality is increasingly one of expatriates travelling the world in any direction, and this may well lessen the financial consequences for the MNE.

 Stop and Think

Stop and think about your likely reaction to being offered an overseas posting in a country less developed than your own, but at only a local salary. How would you describe your feelings?

How would you justify the view that you should receive more than a local employee?

Finally, would this international appointment, on these terms, be more acceptable to a TCN from a developing country? If so, why?

Having considered a few of the issues that constitute some elements of IHRM, this chapter now continues with a brief introduction to the contents of each chapter.

Overview of the contents of the book

This book has two distinct parts. Part One covers the first five chapters, which consider the global environment within which MNEs operate. These five chapters provide an opportunity to appreciate the broader context that companies need to consider when operating abroad. They pay particular attention to cultural and institutional issues, which may challenge and channel the way that international companies operate. They also provide an introduction to the key concepts and theories used to explain developments in managing people internationally, including expatriate management.

Part Two of the book looks at the *practicalities* of managing people in foreign subsidiaries, including those on overseas assignments. So for example it examines the different ways that expatriates may be recruited and selected. It explores the challenges facing companies with regard to rewards management and the effectiveness of performance management processes. Training and development issues are also considered, alongside the complexities of knowledge sharing. These integrate with Chapter 13, 'Global talent management'.

Other chapters explore the specific international dimensions associated with managing people in MNEs, including managing a diverse workforce, managing the employment relationship, and corporate social responsibility and ethics. The latter topic is significant in view of the particular issues surrounding the fairness of treatment of overseas employees, and the responsibilities of managers to behave in an ethical manner in environments where bribery and corruption are common practices.

 Discussion Activity 1.4

Conduct some research in your library to find HRM textbooks that may have sections on IHRM and on topics that will contribute to your understanding of the context of IHRM, such as culture, globalization, international business, management, etc.

Look for definitions of IHRM from a variety of authors and compare these.

Keep a record of these books and where you can find them for your future reference.

PART ONE　**The Context of IHRM**

··

Chapter 1　What is IHRM? Definitions and perspectives

This chapter provides a brief introduction to the key concepts used in HRM and IHRM, which you will need to understand when you read this book. It explains briefly the various approaches to IHRM and some basic concepts and debates. It introduces some issues and uses short case studies to provide examples of practical considerations in IHRM. The contents of the book are outlined and the Learning Approach used throughout the book is explained.

Chapter 2　The wider context of IHRM

This chapter provides an overview of the changing global environment within which international business takes place. It considers the economic context, the increase in trade, demographic changes, the role of 'supra-national' bodies, and the internationalization of organizations, including the growth of 'off-shoring'. These provide a backdrop for our understanding of IHRM.

Chapter 3　Key academic models, theories, and debates

This chapter provides an explanation of the key concepts, perspectives, models, and theories that guide our understanding of IHRM. The first part is designed to assist those students without a background in HRM. It continues with an explanation of some of the theories associated with IHRM, and includes some activities to help demonstrate their relevance to the subject.

Chapter 4　Understanding IHRM: the cultural approach

This chapter concerns the challenges of operating in countries with different national cultures. Expatriates often face culture shock, have difficulty adapting to their new environment, and, as a result, may fail in their assignments. This chapter explains some key concepts used to evaluate cultural difference and provides examples of problems faced by expatriates—which IHRM managers have to solve.

Chapter 5　Understanding IHRM: the institutional approach

The understanding by MNEs of their host environment, including national legislation and other social, economic, and political institutions, is essential for the success of their business operations. This chapter considers how the institutions of different countries affect HRM policies and practices, and consequently how they can support or limit the success of MNEs.

PART TWO　**The challenges of HRM in MNEs**

··

Chapter 6　Global staffing

This chapter examines the evolution of approaches to international staffing and explains why differences are found in different countries. It also identifies the range of selection methods used internationally, while recognizing the importance of acquiring the right employees for organizational performance and competitive advantage. However, it questions the idea of a universal method of selection, observing how local culture and social systems impact on organizational performance. It concludes that staffing processes must be aligned with an MNE's other HR policies and practices.

Chapter 7 International reward management

This chapter explains the meaning of reward philosophy and strategy, and links this to issues of labour costs. Employee satisfaction with reward packages is examined and related to its impact upon employee performance. The connection between national cultures and reward practices is discussed, in conjunction with the role played by multinationals in spreading different reward practices.

Chapter 8 Performance management

This chapter explains the purpose and elements of performance management in MNEs, while highlighting the added difficulty of managing overseas employees, who typically occupy diverse roles with complicated lines of reporting. In addition, it illustrates the problems caused by local cultural influences on effective performance management.

Chapter 9 Training, development, and knowledge management

This chapter considers the training and development of expatriates, including their preparation for international assignments. It examines the link between their training and their adjustment to a new environment, as well as the reasons why MNE training might not meet expatriates' needs. Finally, it evaluates the role of the expatriate in knowledge transfer and the factors that contribute to effective knowledge management in MNEs.

Chapter 10 Diversity management in an international environment

This chapter evaluates the concept of diversity management and its application to the international workplace. It contrasts this with the traditional approach of MNEs, which is often ethnocentric and discriminatory. It also charts the extent to which changes are taking place to prevent unfair treatment through the provision of equal opportunities, and a move in MNEs towards more inclusive policies. Particular attention is paid to the role of women and the imbalance between men and women in management roles. This develops into a discussion on the degree to which Western views on diversity management may or may not be accepted overseas, in spite of the 'business case' for such an approach.

Chapter 11 Corporate social responsibility and ethics

This chapter offers an overview of the meaning of corporate social responsibility and ethics, as a backdrop to the dilemmas faced by expatriates in their management roles in MNEs. It explains a number of CSR and ethical issues and considers what is understood as right and wrong within different cultural contexts. The chapter contains examples of CSR challenges faced by MNEs and their approach to CSR codes of practice and reporting.

Chapter 12 Managing the employment relationship in international organizations

This chapter considers the employment relationship from an individual and collective perspective, noting the twin elements of conflict and cooperation between employee and employer. The relationship is classified across five key dimensions, including the legal and the psychological. These help form the employment contract, which governs the relationship, and helps to explain the attitude and behaviour of employees and their employers. The principles of good employment relations management, applied across all cultures, are explored. However, attention is also drawn to the alternative approaches of managing the relationship through high or low commitment HR. Finally, the chapter considers the factors that influence the way MNEs manage their overseas employment relations, including the influence of home country policy and host country practices.

Chapter 13 Global talent management

This chapter explains the difference between global talent management and IHRM. It discusses the complexities of identifying talent, different approaches to talent management, and the threats to effective and fair talent management strategies.

Chapter 14 The dark side of international employment

This chapter looks at patterns of migration to and from different regions of the world, the dominant types of migrants, their employment, and the particular problems they encounter, including their exploitation. The extent of an MNE's involvement, often through outsourcing or subcontracting arrangements, is discussed. It is argued that the employment issues of migrant workers cannot be simply pushed aside as something out of reach or beyond the responsibility of MNEs. These issues are an integral element of IHRM.

Learning approach

The book aims to ensure that the reader finds learning about IHRM interesting, relevant, and understandable. IHRM is a complex subject, but we have tried to make even the most complicated ideas clear—and applicable to the practical aspects of managing people in international companies.

Writing style

The authors have attempted to write in a way that is accessible to every reader, including those who may use English as a second language. At the same time, care has been taken not to simplify complex ideas to the extent that they lose their essential meaning.

A glossary

New terms, which are introduced in each chapter, have been combined into a final glossary. These terms are identified in **bold** when they appear in the text for the first time. You will also be directed to other chapters where related concepts or topics are developed.

Case study examples

Each chapter includes several case studies in order to illustrate the points being made or to show their practical application.

Discussion activities

Each chapter contains a number of discussion questions and points. These are designed to provide an opportunity for readers to work together and share ideas. The activities also help students to examine their own understanding of the text and to consider how topics and ideas might apply to their own countries or work experiences.

Stop and think

Every chapter features a section that invites the individual reader to 'stop and think' about particular points of interest. This encourages personal reflection and offers an additional way to help your learning about aspects of IHRM.

Review questions

At the end of each chapter there is a list of ten questions, which relate to the contents of the chapter. These are designed to help the reader check their understanding across the breadth of information in the chapter. Also, by focusing attention on the most relevant issues covered in the chapter, they encourage individuals to further develop their learning.

Further reading

Recommendations are given at the end of each chapter for those who wish to develop their learning through more specialized reading. Each source has a short explanation of its particular relevance and value.

A bibliography

For ease of reference, a list of all the references and sources used by the author follows each chapter.

On-line resources for students

For each of the chapters there is an extended case study, followed by some questions.

On-line resources for teachers

For each chapter there is an additional case study, two seminar activities, and a written assignment idea, which could be considered for use as a longer assignment or in an examination.

Summary

This chapter introduces the subject of IHRM and some of the key terminology and approaches used in its study, as well as explaining the ways in which authors may differ in their conceptualization and writing about the subject. It then goes on to consider some of the key challenges in managing HR in international companies. In particular, it looks at factors that influence approaches to the management of an overseas workforce, including the organization's structure and its dominant orientation. It also briefly explains some of the key differences between international and domestic HRM, and includes case studies that give a flavour of the type of issues faced in IHRM. Finally, the chapter provides an overview of each chapter and the features contained within them.

Review questions

1. What is the difference between HRM, Strategic HRM and International HRM?
2. In what ways may the focus of the study of IHRM differ between authors?
3. What differences might you find between texts originating from the USA and those from Europe, in terms of their approach to IHRM?
4. What does the study of comparative international HRM include?
5. What are the main challenges that face MNEs in their management of overseas operations?
6. What is the significance of the EPRG theory to IHRM?
7. What factors determine the approach of an international HR department to their management of overseas employees?
8. How might the structure of an organization influence the role of an international HR manager?
9. In practical terms, how might the work of an international HR manager differ from that of an HR manager handling only domestic HRM?
10. How and why might the compensation of expatriate employees be more complicated to manage than that of domestic employees?

Further reading

Boxall, P. and Purcell, J. (2011) *Strategy and Human Resource Management*, 3rd edn, Basingstoke: Palgrave Macmillan.
    Chapter 1, 'The goals of human resource management', provides an overview of current issues in HRM.

Chapter 10, 'Human resource strategy in multidivisional and multinational firms', considers the HR implications of organizational structure, and of mergers and acquisitions.

Brewster, C. (2007) Comparative HRM: European views and perspectives, *International Journal of Human Resource Management*, 18(5): 769–87.

This article gives a comprehensive view of the issues in comparative HRM from a European perspective.

Rugman, A. and Hodgetts, R. (2003) *International Business*, Harlow: FT Prentice Hall.

Chapters 1 and 2 provide a very helpful introduction to regional and global strategy and the multinational enterprise.

Bibliography

Baker, W.M. and Roberts, F.D. (2006) Managing the costs of expatriation, they may be greater than you think, *Strategic Finance International*, May: 35–41, online at http://www.imanet.org/PDFs/Public/SF/2006_05/05_06_baker.pdf (accessed 11 May 2012).

BBC World News (2011) *Russia Business Report*, with Tanya Beckett, 29 January.

Boxall, P. and Purcell, J. (2011) *Strategy and Human Resource Management*, 3rd edn, Houndmills: Palgrave Macmillan.

Brewster, C. (2007) Comparative HRM: European views and perspectives, *International Journal of Human Resource Management*, 18(5): 769–87.

Chakravarthy, B.S. and Perlmutter, H.V. (1985) Strategic planning for a global business, *Columbia Journal of World Business*, Summer: 5–6.

Chartered Institute of Personnel and Development (CIPD) (2007) *HR in International Mergers and Acquisitions*, CIPD Survey Report, May, online at http://www.cipd.co.uk/NR/rdonlyres/B29DD027-C12E-4712-923D-5B3C44645D73/0/hrintmergacqu.pdf (accessed 5 May 2012).

Chen Y.-F. and Tjosvold, D. (2007) Co-operative conflict management: An approach to strengthen relationships between foreign managers and Chinese employees, *Asia Pacific Journal of Human Resources*, 45(3): 271–94, online at https://www.ahri.com.au/MMSDocuments/comms/apjhr/apjhr_2007/apjhr_45_3_271.pdf (accessed 11 May 2012).

Deutsche, M. (1973) *The Resolution of Conflict*, New Haven, CT: Yale University Press.

The Economist (2011a) Doing deals in Russia, how bad is BP? Management Thinking, from print edn, 20 January, online at http://www.economist.com/node/17961912?story_id=17961912?fsrc=nlw|mgt|01-26-2011|management_thinking (accessed 5 May 2012).

— (2011b) Top whack. Executive pay in Brazil: Big country, big pay cheques, 29 January, p. 35.

Jackson, T. (2002) *International Human Resource Management: a Cross-cultural Approach*, London: Sage.

McKinsey and Co. (2008) Competition from China, *McKinsey Quarterly*, 17(2): 1–6.

Massingham, P. (2010) Managing knowledge transfer between parent country nationals (Australia) and host country nationals (Asia), *International Journal of Human Resource Management*, 21(9): 1414–35.

Morris, J., Wilkinson, B., and Gamble, J. (2009) Strategic international human resource management or the 'bottom line'? The cases of electronics and garments commodity chains in China, *International Journal of Human Resource Management*, 20(2): 348–71.

Redman, T. and Wilkinson, A. (2006) *Contemporary Human Resource Management*, 2nd edn, Harlow: FT Prentice Hall.

Rugman, A. and Hodgetts, R. (2003) *International Business*, Harlow: FT Prentice Hall.

Schuler, R.S. and Jackson, S.E. (1999) Linking competitive strategies with human resource practices, in R.S. Schuler and S.E. Jackson (eds) *Strategic Human Resource Management*, Oxford: Blackwell, ch. 9, pp. 159–76.

— and Tarique, I. (2007) International human resource management: a North American perspective, a thematic update and suggestions for future research, *International Journal of Human Resource Management*, 18(5): 717–18, 720.

—, Jackson, S.E., and Yadong Luo (2004) *Managing Human Resources in Cross-border Alliances*, London: Routledge.

Sparrow, P. and Brewster, C. (2006) Globalizing HRM: The growing revolution in managing employees internationally, in C. Cooper and R. Burke (eds) *The Human Resources Revolution, Research and Practice*, London: Elsevier.

Sparrow, P., Brewster, C., and Harris, H. (2004) *Globalizing HRM*, London: Routledge.

Stone, R.J. (2008) *Human Resource Management*, 6th edn, Milton, QLD: John Wiley & Sons.

Storey, J. (ed.) (1995) *Human Resource Management, A Critical Text*, London: Routledge.

— (2001) *Human Resource Management, A Critical Text*, 2nd edn, London: Thomson.

Tayeb, M. (2005) *International Human Resource Management: A Multinational Company Perspective*, Oxford: Oxford University Press.

Wang, G.G., Rothwell, W.J., and Sun, J.Y. (2009) Management development in China: a policy analysis, *International Journal of Training and Development*, 13(4): 205–20.

Wright, P.M. and McMahan, G.C. (1992) Theoretical perspectives for strategic human resource management, *Journal of Management*, 18(2): 298.

 Visit the Online Resource Centre for web links, interactive glossary, and more: **http://www.oxfordtextbooks.co.uk/orc/crawley.**

2

The wider context of IHRM

 Learning Outcomes

After reading this chapter you will be able to:

- understand the macroeconomic context of IHRM and the role of supranational organizations in the growth of globalization
- appreciate recent changes in the world economy that impact on IHRM
- understand the factors that encourage **foreign direct investment (FDI)** and recent changes in the direction of investment
- explain the impact of demographic change on labour markets and, as a consequence, the issues that arise for Human Resource (HR) managers
- appreciate the process of internationalization, including the growth of **outsourcing** and **off-shoring**.

Introduction

International Human Resource Management (IHRM) concerns the management of people within the context of international business. It follows, therefore, that a working knowledge of the macroeconomic contexts within which international business is conducted is required by international managers, expatriates, and HR managers. As such, a student of IHRM needs to fully understand the global context within which international organizations operate and to appreciate the challenges faced by international managers when implementing their own organization's worldwide strategy. Such challenges are presented, for example, when firms expand their markets overseas or move their productive capacity or other functions abroad. This will typically involve the processes known as outsourcing or off-shoring. Hence, the management, training, and development of people on such matters will be integral to the success of the organization. Neither is this confined to international managers. HR managers at home are increasingly faced with a more diverse workforce. Yet those with international responsibilities can have the added complexity of dealing with overseas employees from different cultures, who are employed under different legal conditions.

This chapter provides an overview of the changing global environment within which international business takes place. It also explores the factors that continue to stimulate economic growth. It begins with a brief introduction to the organization and its environment. This is followed by a section on those major supranational organizations that have supported the rapid pace of economic growth and international trade over the past twenty years. It then addresses trade and investment issues, and demographic changes that impact on labour markets. Finally, the chapter offers further insights into the internationalization process, including the adoption of off-shoring by organizations seeking to optimize operational effectiveness.

The organization and its environment

A fundamental starting point for learning about IHRM is an understanding about the organization and its environment. The organization is essentially subject to the environment within which it operates. More specifically, the open systems approach (Katz and Khan, 1978) suggests that organizations have a dynamic relationship with their environment. They respond to the pressures the environment presents, which in turn influences their ability to operate effectively.

An open systems model

An open systems model can be used to illustrate the external environment within which organizations operate today. This model (as set out in Figure 2.1) illustrates the influence the external environment has on the organization and also the organization's impact on its environment.

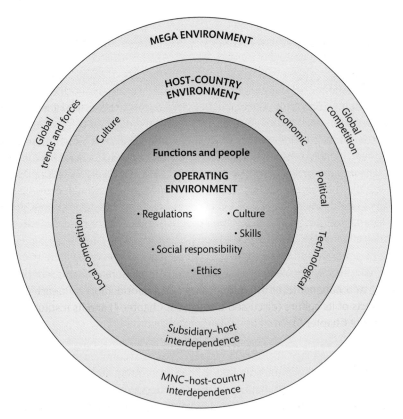

Figure 2.1 An open systems model

Deresky, H. *International Management, Managing across Borders and Cultures*, 6th edn, p. 16. © 2008. Reprinted by permission of Pearson Education Inc., Upper Saddle River, NJ.

The outer circle represents the 'mega environment'. This contains supranational organizations, which themselves influence the international business environment—and are explained in the section *Supranational organizations* in this chapter. The mega environment also includes an organization's worldwide competitors and significant trends in the marketplace. The multinational enterprise (MNE) as a global entity also has a relationship with its host-country subsidiaries. Each influences the other in terms of what they do. For example an MNE's decisions about local HR policy are influenced by policies originating in the parent country. At the same time the MNE may have to adjust its expectations and actions in response to the environment of the host country subsidiary.

The second level is the 'host country environment', which represents the nation states and within these their respective ethnic, religious, social, and cultural groups. It also refers to the factors in a **PESTLE analysis** (political, economic, social, technological, legal, and environmental), which operate at a national and international level. While all the PESTLE factors influence the organization, the organization too has an impact on these same factors—through its interaction with suppliers, customers, employees, and the environment. Last, 'subsidiary-host country interdependence' focuses on the relationship an MNE subsidiary has with its host country, which will incorporate that nation's social institutions, laws, and culture.

Finally, placed at the centre of the inner circle is the organization and its 'operating environment'. Here the organization is subject to all of the *external* factors located in Figure 2.1. At the same time it also operates within the constraints of its own *internal* environment. This consists of the human, financial, technological, and physical resources available to the organization. These will vary in complexity, depending on the size of the organization. As the model combines the external and internal types of environment and because the organization is influenced by and reciprocates to both, the model is described as an 'open system'.

This chapter addresses the *external environment* that managers need to assess and respond to when operating internationally. The organization is influenced by supranational, regional, and national organizations and institutions. *Supranational* organizations include international legal and regulatory bodies such as the United Nations (UN), the World Trade Organisation (WTO), the World Bank, and the International Monetary Fund (IMF). *Regional* organizations that group countries together can be found in bodies such as the European Union (EU), the Association of Southeast Asian Nations (ASEAN), the North American Free Trade Agreement (NAFTA), and MERCOSUR. These provide both support and a regulatory framework, within which groups of countries enter trade agreements and conduct their business. Finally, at a *national* level the nation state has a considerable influence on the firm, through aspects of its culture (discussed throughout Chapter 4) and its institutions (considered throughout Chapter 5).

Factors associated with globalization

In the past twenty years a combination of factors has facilitated the growth of international business and trade worldwide. First, supranational and regional organizations have produced international trade agreements and financial conditions conducive to greater economic cooperation and trade between countries. Second, developments in information and communication technologies (ICT) have contributed to advances in telecommunication systems. The internet, corporate intranet systems, and coordinated administrative processes have together enhanced organizational communication, management, and financial transactions worldwide.

These factors have been supported by the following *global* developments:

1. advances in electronics, which contribute to all aspects of manufacturing, including industrial robotics, process engineering, computerized control systems, and distribution processes;

2. availability and distribution of cheaper energy, notably oil and gas pipelines linked to transportation on super tanker ships, as well as more efficient nuclear and traditional power generation systems;

3. growth in the capacity of global transport systems combining road, rail, air, and sea, including cargo container ships and air freight connecting to container ports and airports worldwide;

4. research and development (R&D), leading to technological and design improvements, as well as productive efficiencies;

5. an extended period of relative world peace and security between the larger economic blocs.

Alongside these contributors to globalization there are *industry level* factors that also help drive globalization, primarily through their association with the competitive and market dynamics that embroil MNEs. These involve MNEs seeking advantages through worldwide economies of scale and sourcing efficiencies, and significant differences in costs between nations, government policies, and environmental factors (Yip et al., 1988, cited in Boddy, 2008: 116, fig. 4.2).

Having examined factors that help to promote the process of globalization, we now turn to the role of the main supranational organizations in that process, and particularly in the development of world trade.

Supranational organizations

The importance of supranational organizations to IHRM may not seem immediately obvious. However, international regulations affect many aspects of business. International HR managers, therefore, need to be aware of how these affect their company's expatriate employees and the staff working in its subsidiary operations.

What follows is a brief overview of a number of supranational organizations, but to obtain more comprehensive details of each one you are advised to access their websites.

The United Nations

The UN was set up in 1945, in the aftermath of the Second World War, by fifty-one countries who were committed to preserving peace through international cooperation and collective security. Today there are 162 members. Through its agencies, the UN works to promote human rights, protect the environment, fight disease, and reduce poverty.

Of particular relevance to MNEs is the research conducted by agencies of the UN. This provides insights into key social issues, which international managers need to understand when they move their business operations to countries with considerable income disparities allied to complex social, educational, and health problems.

Somalia is one such nation. Its political instability and extreme inequalities are thought to have played a major role in the growth of piracy off the Somali coast in recent years. Unsurprisingly, the UN is closely involved in the issue of maritime safety, and this is taken up in Case Study 2.2.

International Labour Organisation

This is a key agency of the UN and one that has direct relevance to IHRM and employment relations. The ILO works to improve labour standards throughout the world. It brings together representatives of governments, employers, and workers, to promote decent work for all. Labour standards, which are listed on the ILO website, cover issues such as freedom of association, wages, employment security, working time, health and safety, maternity protection, and particular provision for specific groups of workers.

United Nations Commission on International Trade Law

This body was established in 1966, to reduce or remove the obstacles to the flow of trade caused by differences in national laws. UNCITRAL works to modernize and harmonize rules and guidelines in order to regulate and facilitate international trade.

The World Trade Organisation

The WTO deals with the rules of trade between nations at a near-global level. It promotes the liberalization of trade and provides a place for governments to negotiate trade agreements and to settle trade disputes. It also operates a system of trade rules and has introduced intellectual property rules into multilateral trading.

Intellectual Property Rights

The intellectual property rules into the multilateral trading system was introduced by the WTO with an agreement known as trade-related aspects of intellectual property rights (TRIPS). The scope of this agreement includes laws related to various types of intellectual property, notably those on patents, copyright, and trademarks.

This is one aspect of international business with which an international traveller or assignee to an Asian country or Russia will soon become familiar. In Asia laws protecting intellectual property rights are routinely ignored, and pirated goods are publicly available. Most DVDs and computer software are pirated. However, as international law is strengthened, MNEs may need to consider how far their business abroad is being conducted within the law and to address their liability if such breaches are discovered, for example, in the use of software.

An excellent overview of intellectual property laws and their widespread infringement across emerging markets is provided by Creer (2004), citing examples from Russia, North Korea, and China, as well as other Asian countries. The 'grey market' goods include 'pirated CDs, DVDs, software, pharmaceuticals, genetic material, and other goods that can be counterfeited or copied in violation of intellectual property law' (Creer, 2004: 213). The scale of the problem is illustrated by the following extract on China:

> Rampant infringement of intellectual property rights persists in China because of few legal redresses. Reforms in China have brought about some protection for intellectual property owners, but United States businesses alone have been reporting an annual loss of $14 billion due to piracy.
>
> (Jen-Sie, 2002; Tiefenbrun, 1998, cited in Creer, 2004: 219)

Continuing with China, Case Study 2.1 offers a practical insight into some of the other challenges faced by the WTO, followed by a discussion on the real implications for international human resource managers. In particular, following its membership of the WTO, China has received a significant amount of FDI. The case study illustrates some of the issues that have arisen.

 Case Study 2.1 China and the WTO

After lengthy negotiations China became the 143rd member of the WTO in 2001 and Taiwan was admitted in 2002. Yet even now the membership of China causes concern among some nations in view of the failure by China to abide by many of the rules set under the conditions for joining the WTO. China is accused of providing subsidies and having tax laws that promote exports and limit imports. Indeed, in 2008, the WTO ruled against China for imposing taxes on imported car components. China's action had resulted in pressure being put on international car part manufacturers to move their production plants to China (Workman, 2008).

China is also accused of complicity in piracy of goods, including designer clothes, medicines, toys, CDs, DVDs, and computer software. A case against China has already been brought to the WTO, and the WTO panel faulted China for not prosecuting pirates who sought to avoid prosecution by copying fewer than the threshold level of 500 copies (Los Angeles Times, 2008). Part of the problem is that China does not have a well-developed legal system to protect against intellectual property theft. This means that international companies are often reluctant to bring R&D projects to China.

In addition to these issues, the lack of ability by the Chinese authorities to monitor the quality of products resulted in a baby milk scandal in 2008. The widely reported scandal occurred when baby milk formula, tainted with melamine, caused at least six deaths and illness in over 294,000 children in China (Internet News Agencies, 2008a, 2008b, 2008c). The implications of this scandal extended throughout South-East Asia and Australasia. As countries that imported milk products from China, they were obliged to remove products from their stores.

Similarly, in 2007 the withdrawal of millions of China-made plastic toys from the shelves of toy shops in Australia, Europe, and the USA arose because of the use of toxic paint in their manufacture. Mattel and Fischer-Price were just two of the many toy manufacturers affected by this issue (Internet News Agencies, 2007a, 2007b, 2007c).

Disputes between the WTO and China are ongoing. Between 2005 and 2010, China was involved in 26 out of the 84 cases filed (Economist, 2011). In July 2009, the WTO's dispute settlement body found against China's policy of restricting the export of some industrial raw materials (rare earths) in three linked cases brought by three different countries. There remains a number of outstanding disputes. A chronological list of these can be found in the dispute settlement section of the WTO website, as well as lists of disputes classified by country (WTO, 2012).

The above case study has implications for HR managers who are required to select employees for jobs that require knowledge and understanding of international regulations regarding the products or services they are manufacturing or selling. They need some system of monitoring employees and their ability to apply regulations efficiently. This implies that the organization must have a legal department or person who is able to advise the HR manager of national and international regulations regarding products and services, as well as the qualifications and training requirements needed by employees tasked with ensuring quality standards and compliance with international standards or overseas customers' requirements.

 ## Discussion Activity 2.1

Research and study recent news articles on the WTO and China.
  Why is it difficult, do you think, for the WTO to supervise member countries' activities?
  What further actions could be taken to ensure that member countries abide by the conditions of their membership?

The World Bank and the International Monetary Fund

The World Bank and the International Monetary Fund (IMF) are collectively known as the Bretton Woods institutions, following an agreement reached in that part of the USA in 1944. The World Bank Group, through its five institutions, today provides financial and technical assistance to developing countries, being concerned with their longer-term development and poverty reduction. Its work is complemented by the IMF, which focuses chiefly on macroeconomic and financial sector issues and which seeks to achieve certain aims. These are to foster global monetary cooperation, secure financial stability, facilitate international trade, create sustainable economic growth, promote high employment, and reduce poverty. It monitors economic and financial developments and provides advice to prevent crises. More specifically, it plays an important role in combating money laundering, which is the practice of passing money that has been illegally acquired through a legitimate business or bank account in order to disguise its dishonest origins.

In spite of their laudable aims, there is increasing criticism of the way in which the World Bank and the IMF operate and the terms of their loans to less developed countries. The World Bank is sometimes criticized for the type of projects it finances, its links to political interests, the harmful environmental consequences of its large-scale projects, the high interest rates on its loans to poor countries, and for the conditions it attaches to such loans.

Additionally, Stein (2004) has criticized the growth of US influence over the World Bank and the IMF alongside the increase in total long-term outstanding debt. With this influence has come more power to dictate the policy agenda through 'loan conditionality'. Furthermore, US-based non-governmental organizations (NGOs) have been able to influence some of the World Bank's agenda through the role of the US Congress in allocating funds every three years for the International Development Association (IDA) (Stein, 2004: 25).

In his criticism of the World Bank and its role in Africa, Stein sees a failed policy agenda for that continent, writing that the strategy adopted:

> [P]re-supposes a base of institutions, organizations, skills and structures that allow free markets to achieve an optimal allocation of resources. These conditions do not exist in any African economies (arguably they don't exist anywhere outside the mind of a neo-classical economist).
>
> (Stein, 2004: 22)

The International Development Association

The IDA is one of the five agencies of the World Bank Group, providing interest-free loans and grants to the poorest countries. This sounds generous, yet Tan (2006) has criticized the World Bank and IDA for their strategy towards low-income borrowing countries. She highlights a continuation of policies that bind 'IDA countries to financing flows and financial discipline' at a time when the institutions are having difficulty 'to maintain their operational relevance and political legitimacy' (2006: 2). She goes on to assert that the measures 'appear to seek to curtail the right of countries to seek alternative sources of financing' ... with the World Bank viewing these lenders not only as potential competitors but also as 'threats to the financial integrity and political hegemony of the Bank' (2006: 32, cited in Tan 2006: 31). Finally, Tan suggests that these organizations are taking measures in the form of loans or grants more focused on preserving their own existence than on the welfare of the countries requiring help.

One source of competition for the World Bank is the government-owned Chinese Development Bank, which 'makes loans to developing countries to secure access, for Chinese companies, to their national resources' (Quirk, 2008: 347). These deals are made 'without the human rights, social and environmental conditions imposed by the IMF and World Bank' (Quirk, 2008: 347). According to the World Bank's Global Financing Development Report (2006, cited in Tan, 2006: 31), China contributed 'more than half of concessional lending from developing countries from 1994–2004'. In Africa, this has resulted in massive investment by Chinese companies, but a failure to improve local human resource conditions. Investment in the construction sector in Africa by Chinese corporations, especially state-owned enterprises, tends to employ mainly Chinese nationals in management roles (see Case Study 10.2 for an example of this). In other sectors, common trends across Chinese companies in Africa are:

> [T]ense labour relations, hostile attitudes by Chinese employers towards trade unions, violation of workers' rights, poor working conditions and unfair labour practices. There is a virtual absence of employment contracts and the Chinese employers unilaterally determine wages and benefits. African workers are often employed as 'casual workers', depriving them of benefits that they are legally entitled to. In addition several ILO conventions such as 'the right to join trade unions, to bargain collectively, to receive equal remuneration and to be protected against discrimination' are violated.
>
> (Yaw Baah and Jauch, 2009: 13)

The ethical issues that surround this topic are mentioned throughout Chapter 11, 'Corporate social responsibility and ethics'. On a wider canvas, the increasing overseas investments by China in recent years, combined with her industrial and economic growth, have resulted in added competition for resources worldwide and a rapidly changing investment landscape. This will be discussed in the subsection headed *What has FDI got to do with IHRM?*.

Regional organizations

Other significant supranational organizations that have an important influence on trade and international business across the world are a number of regional bodies or trading blocs. The most prominent are the Organisation for Economic Co-operation and Development (OECD), the European Union (EU), the North American Free Trade Agreement (NAFTA), the Association of Southeast Asian Nations (ASEAN), Asia-Pacific Economic Cooperation (APEC) and MERCOSUR, which is the 'common market' for South American nations. Information on these groupings can be found on their respective websites.

International risk

International risk is a supranational, cross-border issue of concern. It encompasses national security, risks of terrorism, and financial instability caused by, among other things, white-collar crime and money laundering. Risk situated in a nation can have international repercussions. Recent terrorist attacks on centres of international business, such as that in Mumbai in 2008, create ripples far beyond national boundaries. The 'sub-prime' crisis in the USA, in 2008 also, extended into a world economic crisis that has continued for years. It is within this broad international context that organizations operate.

International risk includes piracy on the sea, causing concern for all organizations that ship goods across the world. Despite the existence of supranational and regional agencies, as well as navy patrols of key shipping lanes, the incidence of piracy and kidnappings appears to be increasing. Not only is there a threat to lives, there are also increased costs as firms employ security firms or pay higher insurance premiums against such risks. More precisely, piracy affects all international business navigating through the major trade routes of the South China Sea, Straits of Malacca, Indian Ocean, and particularly routes passing Somalia and the Gulf of Aden to the Suez Canal. Case Study 2.2 shows how the prevalence of piracy off the coast of Somalia is now a matter of pressing international concern.

Please see the ORC for a link to maps of the areas affected by maritime piracy.

International risk and IHRM

The international HR manager might indeed have to consider the company's responsibilities and policies for emergency scenarios, such as those described above, as well as kidnapping and robbery. Other countries with a reputation for personal safety and kidnapping for ransom include the Philippines and parts of South America. Terrorism is another source of risk to employees and the impact of terrorism on business activity and supply-chain disruption is well documented (Suder, 2006, cited in Reade, 2009: 470).

The psychological effects of terrorism have been shown in research carried out following the 11 September attacks in the USA. More applicable to IHRM, recent research has been conducted into the relationship between terrorism and employees' work attitudes, examining supply-chain firms in Sri Lanka, which is an important off-shoring and outsourcing destination and supplier of raw materials for use in global supply chains (Reade, 2009: 471). It is a country with a history of civil war, ethnic conflict, and terrorist attacks. Despite being based on a small sample in a very specific geographic area, the results are interesting and valuable for IHRM. In private sector organizations they show support for hypotheses that link employees' sensitivity to terrorism with negative attitudes towards the organization. These include:

- reduced organizational commitment;
- greater organizational frustration;
- having less trust in top management;
- diminished perception of supervisory leadership and support.

Case Study 2.2 Why piracy off the coast of Somalia matters

A significant threat

According to the website of the US Department of State, developments are a threat to maritime commerce, humanitarian assistance, disaster relief, regional security, and regional development. It continues:

> Recent attacks by pirates operating from the waters adjoining the Horn of Africa region, including on USA-flagged commercial vessels, threaten international security, the global economy, and American citizens and commercial interests. These attacks have hindered both US and US-supported, UN World Food Program transports delivering aid to some of the world's most vulnerable populations.
>
> This piracy has endangered innocent mariners from countries around the world and jeopardized commercial shipping interests. The attacks also pose an environmental hazard as ships may be damaged or purposely run aground by the pirates, thereby contaminating the seas, reefs, and coastal areas with dangerous pollutants.

A spreading threat

> The piracy in this region occurred originally off Somalia's east coast for several years. In August 2009, the pirates extended their attacks to the Gulf of Aden, between Yemen and Somalia's north coast. Subsequently, the pirates have been ranging farther out to sea—up to 600 miles—and now affect over 1 million square miles (2.59 million square kilometres) in the Gulf of Aden, the west Indian Ocean, and the Red Sea.

(US Department of State, 2010)

According to a special report for the US Bureau of Transportation Statistics:

> Pirates prey upon targets of opportunity. Given optimal conditions (e.g. calm weather, slow cruising speed, and daylight, relatively small, fast vessels (e.g. containerships) may be no less at risk than large, slower vessels (e.g. crude carriers). The vessels held by pirates can range from 2,000 to 100,000 deadweight tons.

(Chambers, 2010: 3)

Despite increased patrols, there were 445 pirate attacks in 2010, a rise of 10% from 2009. In 2010 pirates took a record 1181 hostages and of 53 ships hijacked worldwide, 49 were off Somalia's coast (BBC News, Asia Pacific, 2011). Unsurprisingly, international shipping companies increasingly need to use the services of armed private security contractors to protect their vessels off Somalia (BBC News Africa, 2012). National forces can also be mobilized. In January 2011, Malaysian naval commandos foiled an attempted hijacking of a Malaysian-flagged chemical tanker in the Gulf of Aden, rescuing the 23 crew and capturing 7 Somali pirates (BBC News, Asia Pacific, 2011).

However, in public sector organizations, the opposite findings were revealed. This was because, in the context of civil war, employees perceived attacks to be against their employer, the government. As a consequence, the more their employer was threatened by the terrorist group, the more trusting and supportive employees became of management and their government organization (Reade, 2009: 481).

The conclusions from this study are that HRM needs to introduce initiatives that will address problems associated with employees' frustration with the organization, distrust in top management, and scepticism about support from supervisors and peers, as well as evidence of decreased extrinsic job satisfaction. Suggestions to management include employee assistance programmes, counselling, and staffing changes.

This timely article also offers suggestions regarding multinationals' responsibilities concerning international risk. These include, for example, disaster planning and management, the need for different responses to terrorist attack in different cultural environments, and a 'labour-chain management strategy'. This last idea means 'matching available people with openings across functions, countries and regions' in the form of short-term assignments to 'invigorate employees' and 'enhance positive attitudes' across the organization (Panchak, 2005, cited in Reade, 2009: 480).

Since terrorism appears to be an increasing worldwide threat, it is an aspect of the international context for which IHRM needs to be prepared. IHRM has to take seriously its responsibility for managing and ensuring the health, safety, and welfare of its international workforce.

Another, albeit less dramatic, area of risk that we must now consider is the concept of the MNE's geographic homes. This is an essential feature of international business and provides a helpful background to discussing MNEs' and their employees' responses to internationalization activities.

The organization and its geographic home

The organization may be seen from a geographic perspective, especially when identifying its relationships with its main stakeholders. In geographic terms the organization is first of all a *local* firm. It responds and interacts with people in its vicinity, providing jobs for the local labour market, while complying with the regulations or norms of the national and local government and the industrial sector to which it belongs. Second, the firm may have a wider, *regional* identity. This may be derived from a traditional availability of raw materials, typically linked to an agricultural, mining, or industrial base, and supported by specialist skilled labour. Third, most organizations are perceived as being associated primarily with a particular *country*, normally the one in which the firm originated. Thus, in spite of globalization, it remains true that the distinctive organizational culture of an MNE is strongly influenced by features of its home country: national culture, institutions, legal processes, and trades union regulations (*The Economist*, 2000). Finally, as an organization begins to venture into overseas markets or to place production overseas, it joins the group of internationalized organizations, defined as multinational corporations (MNCs) or MNEs.

A more recent term to define those organizations with multiple overseas operations and a less defined focus on one parent country, is that of the 'transnational' or 'global' organization. However, some writers suggest that there may never be such a thing as a truly global or stateless organization, since in reality they are no more than national firms with international operations (Hu, 1992). However, this assertion is placed in doubt by the pervasive, global actions of international companies. More specifically, the question of whether multinationals have any 'national' loyalty arises when jobs are lost as a result of decisions to move operations to more cost-effective locations, as Case Study 2.3 illustrates.

Case Study 2.3   International business and national loyalty

The relationship between an organization and its local community is a significant factor when expansion and/or cost considerations result in the movement of productive or non-core service activities abroad, resulting in local job losses or worse, complete factory closures. Employers are often accused of displaying a lack of corporate social responsibility when such decisions are made, though a company's senior decision makers are typically motivated by a perceived need to ensure their organization remains profitable and competitive in a global context.

In 2008, Barclays Bank decided to move many of its IT operations from Poole, Dorset in the UK to Singapore, resulting in the loss of 2000 jobs. As its reasons, the company cited cost savings, technical expertise of Singaporean staff, and the need to be more global and operational 24/7 (Computing News, 2008; Connect, 2008).

Similarly, Burberry's decision in 2007 to move some of its productive capacity away from Wales to China was justified by cost considerations and in providing a productive unit closer to its growing Asian marketplace. Given the brand's association with everything British, as well as its Royal Family endorsement, not surprisingly this decision produced an emotive response in the UK. However, cost considerations won the day (BBC News, 2006; Fuller, 2007).

Western multinationals have often relocated their production units to Asia in order to take advantage of cheap labour, while perhaps not fully considering the consequences in terms of national interest and potential job losses at home. This has led to accusations of a lack of morality on the part of the multinationals, which are perceived as contributing to the exploitation of overseas workers who are unprotected by trade unions, thus creating unfair competition and endangering the economies of the West.

This is an ongoing issue for discussion, as unemployment figures in Western countries remain high, while business in Asia seems set for a faster recovery. Austerity measures in Europe are criticized by trades unions (BBC News Europe, 2012) as they appear to do little for the unemployed or to create employment. At the same time the cost of labour in Asia continues to be more competitive.

However, many factors in addition to labour costs are considered by international organizations when deciding where to locate their operations. It is these other aspects of strategic IHRM that particularly test the national loyalty of IHRM managers.

 Discussion Activity 2.2

Name three MNEs and try to identify their geographic homes. (This information may be quite difficult to untangle.)

Where does each MNE have its headquarters and the majority of its operations, and why?

The macroeconomic context

From our discussion so far it has become clear that MNEs face local, regional, national, and international pressures in their attempts to become globally competitive. Compelled to internationalize, organizations will inevitably have to invest in overseas countries, a process that is reflected in national statistics related to foreign investment. Hence, the scale of a nation's achievements in international business can be derived from levels of inward FDI. This is in addition to the amount of business being transacted between countries in terms of both imports and exports.

More generally, the macroeconomic context of a nation can be understood by considering the economy and its main indicators. Thus, as well as levels of FDI, we can include the balance of payments, unemployment, growth, and inflation. The macroeconomic context also considers the structure and institutions of a national economy and how these impact on its performance. Observed from this perspective, the contrasting and changing fortunes of European and BRIC countries, for example, reveal how national economies can grow or decline. In turn, as their relative strength changes, their attraction as investment destinations may increase or contract. Parallel to these trends, countries usually try to attract foreign investment in order to enhance economic achievement through the creation of new business and the enhancement of productive capacity, technology, and employment.

What has FDI got to do with IHRM?

FDI implies interaction and cooperation with people in other countries through the creation of new overseas businesses or via mergers and alliances. As a consequence, inward FDI generates more business and employment opportunities for the home population. Initially the MNE's management of its international business operations may be directly controlled by parent country managers, who may also wish to introduce their ways of working to the local population of Host Country Nationals (HCNs). As a consequence, systems of work and ways of managing may be experienced by HCNs as a different and 'imported' cultural framework. Hence, it is important that line and HR managers, both at home and overseas, have a good understanding of managing and working with people from diverse backgrounds. Moreover, international HR managers will need to be consulted about the strategic HR requirements of the MNE as a result of its plans to operate overseas, whether through direct investment, the outsourcing of activities, or within the context of mergers, acquisitions, or joint ventures.

As well as the amount of capital invested, a nation's FDI can be measured by the number of projects or by the number of jobs created. The FDI Global Outlook Report (2011) states that in 2010 the top five regions for FDI were Asia Pacific, Western Europe, the rest of Europe, North America, and finally Latin America and the Caribbean. Measured by capital expenditure the scale for these regions was almost the same. However, in terms of project numbers the leading destinations were USA, China, UK, India, and Germany. In relation to the number of jobs created the foremost cities were Shanghai, Singapore, St Petersburg, Bangalore, and Tianjin in China (FDI Report, 2011).

Factors that influence FDI locations

According to the Economist Intelligence Unit (EIU) report (2007), ongoing prospects for FDI worldwide are good because of better business environments and technological change. However, the essential impetus for FDI comes from sharper global competition pushing companies to seek lower-cost destinations, combined with their search for competitively priced skills. At the same time, the report acknowledges the risks attached to FDI, which are associated with global financial turbulence and political instability.

The EIU (2007) report indicated that MNEs would prefer to invest in East Asia rather than in Eastern European countries, based upon a consideration of skills levels, the cost of labour, and opportunities for R&D in the potential location. On the other hand, *The Economist* (2008) observed a shared advantage of doing business in Eastern Europe and Central Asia, in that it takes less time to register a business. However, in Asia taxes are lower and it is cheaper to move goods across borders. More specifically, Singapore is singled out as the best country in which to do business, in contrast to Japan, where a relatively low level of FDI is a result of a complex regulatory environment, high labour costs, weak economic growth, and cultural barriers.

Until recently, however, it was the EU region that dominated global FDI flows, both as a recipient of FDI, receiving more than the USA, and also as a source of FDI (EIU, 2007). While European investment has been largely within the EU, it still involves cross-border acquisitions, which have often been controversial and raised nationalistic sentiments. Examples include the Spanish acquisition of two large UK companies, O^2 in 2005 by Telfonica, and the British Airports Authority (BAA) in 2006 by Ferrovial. Examples beyond the EU boundaries are French Alcatel's purchase of the USA technology giant Lucent, and the French AXA takeover of the Swiss Wintherhur Insurance Group. Perhaps an even greater public outcry comes from the foreign takeover of utility companies. In the UK, 2006 saw the Australian takeover of two such companies: Thames Water, and Anglian Water Group.

In view of ongoing economic and financial issues one might expect European FDI to have faltered over recent years. Yet in 2010 Europe attracted 35% of global FDI projects, more than the Asia-Pacific region. The lead was taken by Western Europe, which attracted 21% of global FDI projects and created over 170,000 jobs (FDI Report, 2011). London was the leading city in this region.

However, FDI flows are changing and they are unlikely to remain dominated by Western developed countries. 'Indian, South Korean, Japanese and Chinese companies were among the fastest growing investors overseas in 2010' (FDI Report 2011: 3). The report singles out China as a growing source of substantial investment across the world, though as yet it is only 'ranked eighth in the world by capital investment and job creation overseas' (2011: 4).

The regionalization of trade

While overall FDI figures convey something of the scale of cross-border business transactions, they do not give us a well-defined view of multinational activity. The degree to which MNEs are truly global in terms of their business activities has been investigated by Curran and Zignago (2011). They focus on the degree of integration in each of three regions—the EU, NAFTA, and ASEAN—which together represent 78% of global trade. They conclude that each region has 'relatively high levels of regional integration in terms of trade figures' but that this 'varies over time, by region and by direction of flow' (Curren and Zignago, 2011: 22).

The authors consider a number of factors in reaching their conclusion: flows of imports and exports, types of technology, the purpose of trade, and whether FDI is about asset or resource seeking or about exploitation of markets (Curran and Zignago, 2011: 7). With respect to types of technology, their data show that the EU has high levels of intra-regional trade in both medium-tech and low-tech goods. This is in contrast to ASEAN + 3 (Japan, China, and South Korea), which has high levels of intra-regional trade in predominantly low-tech goods.

Such patterns of trade in relation to levels of technology within each region reflect the prominence of different types of industry and the availability of skilled employees to work in such industries. The low skills environment of ASEAN has also been highlighted by the ILO (2010), including the need to improve productivity, competitiveness, working conditions, and employment prospects. This is especially in relation to China and India, even though labour productivity has surged by 8.7% and 4.0%, respectively. ASEAN also needs to improve its integration by better management of migration (ILO, 2010).

The degree to which MNEs are global or regional has also been examined by Rugman and Verbeke. They acknowledge that a relatively small number of MNEs accounts for the majority of the world's trade and investment, stating that the 'largest 500 MNEs account for 90% of FDI and conduct about half the world's trade' (Rugman, 2000, cited in Rugman and Verbeke, 2004: 3). Yet, according to this research, these MNEs are *not* global, since most of their sales are within their own regions—North America, the EU, or Asia.

Further evidence of the predominantly regional nature of investment comes from FDI reports (2011). Within Asian countries for example Asian investors accounted for 40% of FDI invested in China, much of this through Hong Kong. Countries such as Vietnam and Cambodia are destinations for investment from China, Taiwan, and South Korea. The advantages for investors to Vietnam and Cambodia have been associated with the lack of trade unions, limited legal restrictions, and poor environmental monitoring. The latter was most evident from a visit by the author to Hanoi in the north of Vietnam. She had personal experience of high levels of pollution in the city, plagued with motorbikes, and constant attempts by taxi drivers to obtain excessive fares. She also learned of the rampant corruption reported by those in business (Crawley, 2008; author's personal experience and observations).

Information on FDI flows gives some indication of changes in the location of international business. This is useful for those international HR managers who will need to appreciate the growing demands for expatriates in different parts of the globe and to understand the employment markets and conditions of different localities. At the same time, inflows of FDI are an essential element of a country's ability to grow and an indication of external confidence in their economy. As such, MNEs are typically sought out by governmental departments dedicated to attracting FDI. China, for example, has had Special Economic Zones since 1984, to encourage international investment.

Case Study 2.4 concerns Malaysia, which is a developing country in South-East Asia, with a fast-growing population of about 26 million. It illustrates how Malaysia tries to attract investment.

 Discussion Activity 2.3

Does your country have an institution like MIDA, described in Case Study 2.4 below?
Find out about it and how far it helps encourage inward investment.

Case Study 2.4 Attracting FDI—a developing country's approach

The importance of FDI to developing economies is illustrated by the efforts their governments make to obtain it. In Malaysia, the government has set up an agency, the Malaysian Industrial Development Authority (MIDA) (online at http://www.mida.gov.my), which has responsibility for attracting and facilitating industrial development. MIDA offers assistance with manufacturing licences, tax incentives, expatriate posts, and duty exemptions on raw materials, components, machinery, and equipment.

According to news reports on the MIDA (2010, 2011) website,

> The Ministry of International Trade and Industry (MITI) and its agencies including the Malaysian Investment Development Authority (MIDA) are all geared up to help attain the *overall target* of RM*115 billion in private investments a year, as highlighted in the recently launched 10th Malaysia Plan (2011–2015).

Speaking at the launch of the MITI Report 2009, the Minister said MITI and MIDA were expecting some RM40 billion in direct investments in the *manufacturing sector* this year, after securing RM32.6 billion last year. For the first four months of the year, approved investments in the manufacturing sector amounted to RM7.1 billion. For 2010, manufacturing was expected to continue to register an uptrend, with a number of industries projected to gain significant growth.

The *electrical and electronic* industry was expected to sustain its growth momentum in 2010, supported by the rising demand for semiconductors in Asia, including Japan, the US, and the EU.

Petroleum products, petrochemicals and the plastics industries are projected to expand in line with the economic rebound in Asia in 2010. Other industries doing well include pharmaceuticals. Malaysia attracted FDI of just over $9 billion in 2010, returning to the level of its previous peak in 2007.

Similarly, local governments in Malaysia also promote their own locations as potential investment areas. For example the Penang Development Corporation and the Multimedia Development Corporation are projects designed to attract inward investment especially in the field of e-commerce and electronics (online at http://www.mscmalaysia.my/).

Another organization in Malaysia that has done much for the IT industry and that has encouraged investment in Penang, is the Malaysian Penang Skills Centre, a consortium of 57 international companies providing training in IT and high tech subjects (Gordon, 2000, cited in Sparrow et al., 2004).

*RM = Ringgit Malaysia

The implications of the credit crisis 2008–12

The international credit crunch and the instability of the global financial system arising initially from the sub-prime crisis in the USA in 2008 have created worrying uncertainty over the continued growth of world trade. According to the UN Conference on Trade and Development (UNCTAD) (UNCTAD, 2008) the recent experience of 'contagion and interdependence' has exposed the vulnerability of the global economy and shortcomings in global economic governance (UNCTAD, 2009). As such it provides a compelling reason for a review of public policy and government intervention.

The escalation of the crisis has seen, for example, the EU and its central bank impose harsh demands on countries such as Greece, Italy, Portugal, Ireland, and Spain, requiring them to cut their deficits during 2010–12 (BBC Europe, 2011). These measures have resulted from each nation's excessive domestic overspending in relation to their gross domestic product (GDP). The UK too is faced with considerable deficits, which the coalition government is tackling through a series of austerity policies. In New York the 'Occupy Wall Street' movement and in

Spain the 'Indignados' are manifestations of ordinary people's distrust of financial institutions and their management—as well as their frustrations with the injustices apparently created by the financial sector and the operation of market-based systems (Washington Post, 2011).

In an analysis of the current state of globalization, Quirk (2008) examines such benefits as the expansion of democracy and human rights. Recent uprisings in the Middle East and calls for democratic governments in Algeria, Tunisia, Egypt, Libya, and Bahrain may be the beginning of fundamental changes to dictatorial governments in the predominantly Muslim world. However, there are also instances of government repression and signs of political instability. More pressingly, perhaps, Quirk also identifies the threats of globalization, noting 'the breakdown of international institutions and rise of state control, diplomatic use of energy resources and the abandonment of principles of globalization by the United States' (2008: 342–3). She considers that these changes are for both ideological and pragmatic reasons. On the issue of China, for example, the perception that China manipulates its exchange rate to gain global market share means that Chinese exports will be the main target of anger in the rest of the world. However, the importance of Chinese reserves held in US dollars may limit any escalation of tension by the USA (EIU, 2010).

Another vital issue is the cost of oil and the degree to which oil reserves are disproportionately held by countries without democratic government. Quirk (2008: 349) cites the 're-source nationalism' problems associated with non-democratic, energy-exporting countries such as Russia, Iran, and Venezuela—and the deteriorating relations between them and their customer importers. This adds more uncertainty to world markets, especially in light of the increasing oil requirements of China and India. Other raw materials vulnerable to 'resource nationalism' include iron ore, and 'rare-earths' used in the IT industry. Both are in high demand and have already resulted in disputes between China and Japan.

Finally, since the focus of this chapter is the context of IHRM, we cannot fail to mention how worldwide uncertainties could impact on IHRM. One possibility is a reduced number of expatriate positions. Alternatively, expatriate employees may be asked to accept local conditions of work or be replaced by a local employee. MNEs might also try to use virtual methods of expatriate supervision through online reporting instead of personal overseas visits.

What is more certain is that each organization will need to (a) adjust its HR policies and practices in response to the prevailing market conditions and economic risks; and (b) seek to predict future prospects in times of growing uncertainty. One area of particular significance for IHRM is the demographic changes that are impacting on the IHRM environment, to which we now turn.

Demographic changes, immigration, and economic migration

The past ten years have seen dramatic changes in opportunities for the movement of people between countries for the purposes of employment. As western nations face declining birth rates and ageing populations, they often lack the skilled and less skilled workers they require to support their economies. At the same time the demographics of poorer countries show the opposite trend with younger, growing populations in need of work.

This section provides a brief update on demographic changes in recent years, which have resulted in economic migration. These events affect labour markets and the role of HR professionals as they workforce plan and evaluate the availability of human resources in different countries. Demographic changes in labour markets also imply more **diversity management** issues, as well as the increased administration of work permits, visa requirements, medical insurance, social security, accommodation, and other welfare matters.

The impact of economic migration on local labour markets

During the past ten years movements of labour have increased for a number of reasons, including: population growth in many countries; the extension of the free movement of labour within the larger EU; and the increase in temporary work permits issued for lower skilled workers in developing countries in Asia (Eurofound, 2011).

The USA continues to be the country with the most immigrant and migrant workers in the world. It also has a considerable number of overseas students, with a fair proportion, especially at PhD level, ultimately obtaining employment and permanent residence. With respect to the OECD area, China provided more than one in ten immigrants to the OECD in 2006. Poland, itself an OECD country, contributed one in twenty immigrants to other OECD countries. Immigrants to OECD countries are very much 'essential workers', including those in the healthcare sector: doctors, nurses, care workers, and cleaners. Low-skilled immigrants are evident in a range of industries, notably construction, food processing, household work, catering, and hospitality.

Overall, immigrants tend to earn less than locals, even when their education level is taken into account, and this is particularly the case for migrants from non-OECD countries. In the UK, for example, 'immigration is likely to lead to reduced levels of wages or employment in low skilled jobs' (Somerville and Sumption, 2009: 9). In spite of this characteristic, migrants are attracted by the prospect of working in a richer country. However, such opportunities can lead to illegal as well as legal immigration. For example attempts to get into America illegally from Mexico are relatively common. In the UK one way to become an illegal immigrant is to overstay on a student or visitor's visa. Finally, disparities in wealth levels between the richer parts of Europe and sub-Saharan Africa have resulted in many attempts at illegal immigration. Aboard overcrowded small boats from the coast of West Africa and headed for the Spanish Canary Islands, many would-be immigrants have unfortunately drowned en route (Ferrero-Turrion, 2010).

The realities of employment conditions and the pressures faced by managers to utilize illegal immigrants are aspects that are rarely discussed in IHRM textbooks. They are, however, an important part of Chapter 14 'The dark side of international employment', discussed in the sections *The migrant labour problem* and *Modern-day slavery*, since they may lead to exploitation of desperate migrant workers.

 Stop and Think

Assume that you wish to leave your own country for better employment opportunities. Stop and think about the country (or type of country) to which you would most want to emigrate.

What factors do you consider most important for your choice (e.g. closeness to relatives, standard of living, language, job prospects, climate, and so on)?

Find out what you would need to do (legally) to (a) emigrate from your country; and (b) be allowed to settle in the country of your choice.

Having considered the broader economic context within which organizations operate today, we can now consider more aspects of the internationalization process, which we briefly introduced in Chapter 1, in the section *The internationalization of organizations and IHRM*.

The internationalization process of MNEs

Factors that influence the internationalization process

In response to growing competition, organizations have to make strategic decisions about whether to internationalize. Yip (1989) identifies four main drivers for internationalization:

1. market-oriented drivers, such as a homogenous customer base, the availability of global distribution channels, and transferability of advertising across borders (e.g. drinks, fashion goods, and cars);
2. cost advantages of overseas production and services through efficiencies and logistics;
3. government action in creating a favourable environment for overseas location;
4. the globalization of other firms in the industry, when not to do so would be to remain uncompetitive.

Locating overseas

Two key decisions have to be taken by internationalizing firms: where to locate the business and how to enter a market (Tayeb, 2003). If the key resource to remain competitive in the industry is low-cost labour, as in many low value-added industries, then operations are often moved to Asia, Eastern Europe, or South America. However, if technical expertise is paramount, then the scarcity of this resource overseas may *prevent* the company's internationalization. Transport costs of the final product to market may also determine internationalization decisions, as would restrictions on the import of finished products (as with China's car part import restrictions through tariff imposition, cited above in Case Study 2.1, *China and the WTO*).

Entering the market

The process of internationalization has traditionally followed the need to expand markets for goods when the domestic market is saturated. This Nordic model (Johanson and Wiedersheim-Paul, 1975; Johanson and Vahlne, 1977, cited in Lloyd-Reason, 2004) sees the internationalization process as a steady and deliberate build-up of events over time. This is often described as a sequential learning process, with the firm moving through a number of predictable stages (Johanson and Mattsson, 1993, cited in Lloyd-Reason, 2004). These types of model of internationalization are usually based on the experience of large MNEs and their gradual commitment to a market, as follows:

- first exporting to fill orders;
- then appointing agents to represent the firm;

- next establishing an overseas sales subsidiary;
- finally, setting up a production facility to support sales in that market;
- later developing the inclusion of establishing joint ventures, alliances, or licensing agreements.

Alternative forms of internationalization

However, this gradual development process may not be the one adopted by SMEs or firms driven by the internet, for example. They are just as likely to internationalize as a fully-fledged start-up operation or to develop in a more opportunistic, intermittent way. Sparrow et al. (2004) note how quickly such companies develop their international organizational and HR capability. Understandably, the role of the strategic leader in this internationalization process is key (Lloyd-Reason and Mughan, 2002).

An interesting example of a modern, international SME is O'Bon. This is an eco-friendly stationery firm established in the USA. It has a design arm in California, a unique production process in China, online internet sales to the USA and Canada, and sales and distribution in a dozen countries worldwide, including Malaysia and Australia. It is an example of how a firm can be established with extensive virtual activity, whereby the contributors to design, management, marketing, and production can be based geographically anywhere (O'Bon, 2012).

Manufacturing processes and supply networks

An MNE's supply network is another potential source of competitive advantage. However, the challenges for internationalizing companies are intensified, since their supply chains often serve dispersed markets and hence become more fragmented. As such, they will involve more players: specialized component suppliers, contract manufacturers, and service providers.

However, some companies have found other ways to compete, which depend more on the *configuration* of the supply network than on sophisticated operational processes. Research by the Institute for Manufacturing (IfM)'s Centre for International Manufacturing (CIM) found new models emerging. Essentially, these are designed to support specific business needs while using quite simple management and supply-chain processes, thus requiring only semi-skilled staff (CIM, 2007).

Even so, manufacturing organizations will need to work in tandem with IT providers in order to ensure that adequate support is provided for their processes. To this end software companies continue to develop new products dedicated to supporting manufacturing, supply-chain, and logistics processes. In addition to IT developments, we see cooperative arrangements between manufacturers and their software providers, exemplified by the close collaboration between Caterpillar (2011) and Statsoft (2006). This example illustrates the growing importance of a combination of developments in IT and business cooperation.

The management of supply chains implies that added expertise is required by MNEs. It follows, therefore, that international HR professionals will need to fully understand manufacturing processes, manufacturing alliances, IT and software applications, and business relationships, if they are to successfully contribute to staffing decisions at a strategic level.

Off-shoring

Off-shoring is the movement of production or service centres, and hence jobs, from one country to another. This can occur when companies decide to set up their own facilities abroad or to subcontract some functions to service providers overseas. According to Treacy (2005), off-shoring can help companies become more effective or innovative; it is not just a cost-saving move. For example off-shoring might enable MNEs to make use of the comparative advantage of workforce capabilities in other countries, where specific skills may be superior.

While off-shoring originally affected jobs in manufacturing at the low skills level, it now includes the service sector, incorporating scientific research, clerical jobs, call centre roles, and basic IT maintenance functions. More recently, it has begun to affect professional jobs, including back-office legal activities in India. Off-shoring has been a particularly significant phase of European globalization, being initially dominated by manufacturing and then joined by the service sector, where banking and insurance have been the main industries to operate overseas (Storrie and Ward, 2007).

Opportunities for the rapid expansion of off-shoring have been associated with recent changes in the macroeconomic climate of emerging economies, which have resulted from increased foreign investment, market growth, and demographic pressures. As a consequence, we have seen the spread of production plants to countries with abundant, cheap labour combined with adequate infrastructure and availability of raw materials. China, for example, has long been known for its production of cheap textiles. Hence, in an effort to make use of the expertise available, European companies have increasingly been subcontracting this work to China. This has led to massive changes in the relative competitiveness of both Asian and European clothing manufacturers. More recently, China has also become the dominant destination for foreign investment in plants as well as for subcontracted work in electronic components, computers, and white goods.

Off-shoring has grown in tandem with the development of IT capability and an increased speed of transactions, facilitated by broadband technology and the internet. Countries that have invested in this infrastructure have been able to take advantage of off-shoring possibilities alongside the rapid expansion of **Business Process Outsourcing (BPO)**. Initially this was in the area of call centres and IT help desks, with India and the Philippines being favourite destinations for English-speaking companies (Offshoring Times, 2008). Subsequently, MNEs delivering financial services have taken particular advantage of the large number of graduates in India who speak English, where cities such as Mumbai and Bangalore have become centres for BPO, providing IT services for global corporations such as Novell, CA, BNP Parabis, JP Morgan, and Accenture. We are also noticing that western MNEs are regularly subcontracting IT software development work to firms in India. Hence, as companies are learning to utilize the advantages of off-shoring more effectively, it is a trend that is unlikely to slow down.

Summary

This chapter has discussed the macroeconomic context within which international businesses operate; it has described the role of some of the most important supranational organizations, which support international trade and business; and it has discussed the importance of FDI in countries as a support for business activity. In addition, the human element of globalization has been illustrated through consideration of demographic change and the migration of people across the world seeking to better their economic condition. These macroeconomic and human factors help to form the constantly evolving environment, which is the context in which managers in MNEs work. More specifically, it is the international HR manager who needs to be aware of this environment, in which expatriates among others are required to work.

The impact of off-shoring, supported by developments in ITC, have also been mentioned as contributing to key changes in working systems, providing support while also increasing complexity. Finally, the continuing economic crisis that began in 2008 has been examined, in view of its massive impact in slowing down international investment and adversely affecting global trade.

There are increasing challenges for MNEs as the world adjusts to the growth of developing countries and the relative decline in the economic position of formerly dominant western players. This chapter serves, then, as the foundation for our discussion on IHRM and the topics it comprises.

Review questions

1. Which are the main functions of the WTO? Why does an international HR manager need some knowledge of the work of the WTO?

2. Why is the United Nations important for business? In what ways do the United Nations and its agencies assist the development of human talent?

3. Explain the ways in which the ILO works to improve employment conditions around the world.

4. What are the main activities and functions of the EU for extending employment opportunities for its citizens?

5. Explain the respective roles of the World Bank and IMF, and the current criticisms of their practices.

6. Explain the importance and functions of regional trading blocs such as NAFTA, ASEAN, and MERCOSUR.

7. What risks might deter a potential expatriate from taking up an international assignment?

8. Explain why and how countries seek FDI, and the likely impact upon the work of international HR managers.

9. People are migrating in large numbers, mainly as economic migrants. How does this affect the work of HR managers?

10. What are the advantages and disadvantages of off-shoring for an MNE? In what ways might an international HR manager be involved in this process?

Further reading

FDI Report (2011) Manufacturing makes a comeback, FDI Global Outlook Report, 2011, FDI
Intelligence, *Financial Times*, April/May, online at http://www.fdiIntelligence.com (accessed
1 June 2012).
A useful overview of changes in FDI in different regions and sectors.

OECD (2011) *International Migration Outlook: SOPEMI 2011*, summary in English.
This publication analyses recent developments in migration movements and policies in OECD countries
and some non-member countries, including migration of highly qualified and low-qualified workers,
temporary and permanent, as well as students.

Quirk, J. (2008) Globalization at risk: the changing preferences of states and societies, *Managing
Global Transitions*, 6(4, Winter): 341–71.
This article offers an opportunity to look a little beyond the scope of this text, examining how supranational
institutions are losing power in the face of stronger states and the growing self-interest of nations. This, it
suggests, gives rise to increasing risks to democracy and to principles associated with globalization.

Bibliography

BBC News (2006) Valleys Burberry plant to close,
6 September, online at http://news.bbc.co.uk/2/hi/
uk_news/wales/5319778.stm (accessed 1 June 2012).

— Africa (2012) BBC correspondent's pirate sighting
aboard tanker, 10 March, online at http://www.
bbc.co.uk/news/world-africa-17326672 (accessed
1 June 2012).

— Asia Pacific (2011) Malaysia navy foils ship hijack
attempt, seizes pirates, 22 January, online at http://
www.bbc.co.uk/news/world-asia-pacific-12258442
(accessed 1 June 2012).

— Europe (2011) EU austerity drive country by
country, 21 May, online at http://www.bbc.co.uk/
news/10162176 (accessed 1 June 2012).

— Europe (2012) Spain's unions call general strike over
labour laws, 9 March, online at http://www.bbc.co.uk/
news/world-europe-17315961 (accessed 1 June 2012).

Boddy, D. (2008) *Management, An Introduction*, 4th edn,
Harlow: FT Prentice Hall.

Chambers, M. (2010) *International Piracy and Armed
Robbery at Sea, Hindering Maritime Trade and Water
Transportation around the World*, Special Report,
Bureau of Transport, US Department of Transportation
Research and Innovative Technology Administration
(RITA) Statistics, April, online at http://www.
humansecuritygateway.com/documents/USGOV_
IntlPiracy_ArmedRobberySea.pdf (accessed 1 June 2012).

CIM (2007) Reconfiguring supply chain networks for
competitive advantage, *CIM Briefing* No 2, Institute
for Manufacturing, online at http://www.ifm.eng.
cam.ac.uk/cim/briefings/cim_briefing_supply.pdf
(accessed 1 June 2012).

Computing News (2008) Barclays offshore 1800 roles,
15 July, online at http://www.computing.co.uk/
ctg/news/1834319/barclays-800-it-roles-offshore
(accessed 1 June 2012).

Connect (2008) Barclays moves IT base to Singapore,
2 October, online at http://www.connect.co.uk/news/
news_item/18807860/Barclays+moves+IT+base+to+
Singapore/ (accessed 1 June 2012).

Creer, G. (2004) The international threat to intellectual
property rights through emerging markets, *Wisconsin
International Law Journal*, 22 (1), online at http://
hosted.law.wisc.edu/wilj/issues/22/1/creer.pdf
(accessed 1 June 2012).

Curran, L. and Zignago, S. (2011) Intermediate products
and the regionalization of trade, *Multinational
Business Review*, 19(1): 6–25.

Deresky, H. (2008) *International Management:
Managing Across Borders and Cultures*, 6th edn, Upper
Saddle River, NJ: Pearson Education.

The Economist (2000) 354(8155): 21–22. The world view
of multinationals, cited in Sparrow, P. Brewster, C.
and Harris H. (2004), *Globalizing Human Resource
Management*, Routledge, p. 19.

— (2008) A new kind of eastern promise, 13
September, online at http://www.economist.com/
node/12208572 (accessed 1 June 2012).

— (2011) The WTO and China, hands slapped, a ruling
with ramifications, 7 July, online at http://www.
economist.com/node/18925947 (accessed 1 June 2012).

Economist Intelligence Unit (EIU) (2007) World
investment prospects to 2011: foreign direct
investment and the challenge of political risk, online

at http://graphics.eiu.com/upload/WIP_2007_WEB. pdf (accessed 1 June 2012).

— (2010) World trade growth is boosted by restocking in the OECD, and rise in protectionism has been limited but remains a concern, 15 April, online at http://store.eiu.com/article.aspx?productid=1354289 920&articleid=347070819 (accessed 1 June 2012).

Eurofound (2011) Free movement of workers, European Foundation for the Improvement of Living and Working Conditions, 14 December, online at http:// www.eurofound.europa.eu/areas/industrialrelations/ dictionary/dictionary6.htm (accessed 1 June 2012).

European Union (EU) (2012) Website of the European Union, online at http://europa.eu/index_en.htm Member Countries with map, available at http:// europa.eu/about-eu/countries/index_en.htm (accessed 1 June 2012).

FDI Report (2011) Manufacturing makes a comeback, FDI Global Outlook Report, 2011, April/May, FDI Intelligence: the *Financial Times*, online at http:// www.fdiintelligence.com/content/search?SearchText =FDI+Global+Outlook+Report%2C+2011%2C+April% 2FMay%2C&top-search-submit=Search (accessed 24 December 2012).

Ferrero-Tureon, F. (2010) Migration and migrants in Spain after the bust, in D.G. Papademetriou, M. Sumption, and A. Terrazas, *Migration and Immigrants Two Years after the Financial Collapse, Where Do We Stand?* Washington, DC: Migration Policy Institute.

Fuller, G. (2007) Burberry South Wales factory to close and 300 jobs to go despite high-profile protests, *Personnel Today*, 23 March, 10(4), online at http://www.personneltoday.com/ articles/2007/03/23/39820/burberry-south-wales-factory-to-close-and-300-jobs-to-go-despite-high-profile.html (accessed 1 June 2012).

Hu, Y-S. (1992) Global or stateless corporations are national firms with international operations, *California Management Review*, 34(2): 107–26, in P. Sparrow, C. Brewster, and H. Harris (2004) *Globalizing Human Resource Management*, London: Routledge.

ILO (2010) *Labour and Social Trends in ASEAN2010: Sustaining Recovery and Development through Decent Work*, ILO Regional Office for Asia and the Pacific–Bangkok: vi, 61 p.

International Monetary Fund (IMF) (2012) About the IMF, online at http://www.imf.org/external/about. htm (accessed 1 June 2012).

Internet News Agencies (2007a) Lead in paint, toys from China: Thomas and friends wooden railway trains recalled, ABC News, 13 June, online at http://abcnews. go.com/us/story?id=3275264 (accessed 1 June 2012).

— (2007b) Lead in paint, toys from China: Mattell recalls millions more toys, BBC News, 14 August, online at http://news.bbc.co.uk/2/hi/business/6946425.stm (accessed 1 June 2012).

— (2007c) Lead in paint, toys from China: toys R Us CEO talks toy safety, *MarketWatch*, 17 February 2008, online at http://www.marketwatch.com/story/ toy-fair-notebook-toys-r-us-ceo-talks-toy-safety (accessed 1 June 2012).

— (2008a) Chinese milk powder scandal: Chinese dairy exports in decline, BBC News, 2 December, online at http://www.time.com/time/world/ article/0,8599,1841535,00.html (accessed 1 June 2012).

— (2008b) Chinese milk powder scandal: China's poison milk kills three children, leaves 6000 sick, *Mail Online*, 17 December, online at http://www.dailymail. co.uk/news/worldnews/article-1056151/Chinas-poison-milk-kills-children-leaves-6-000-sick.html (accessed 1 June 2012).

— (2008c) Chinese milk powder scandal: tainted baby-milk scandal in China, *Time*, 16 September, online at http://www.time.com/time/world/ article/0,8599,1841535,00.html (accessed 1 June 2012).

Jen-Siu, M. (2002) New trademark laws may give plaintiffs a fighting chance to stop piracy of intellectual property cracking down on counterfeits, *South China Morning Post*, 22 September, 2002, cited in Creer (2004), p. 19.

Katz, D. and Khan R.L. (1978) *The Social Psychology of Organizations*, New York: John Wiley and Sons.

Lloyd-Reason, L. (2004) *Strategies for Internationalisation within SME's: The Key Role of the Strategic Leader and the Internationalisation Web*, Centre for International Business, (now Centre for Enterprise Development and Research), Lord Ashcroft International Business School, Anglia Ruskin University, Cambridge, UK

— and Mughan, T. (2002) Strategies for internationalisation within SMEs: the key role of the owner-manager, *Journal of Small Business and Enterprise Development*, 9(2): 120–9.

Los Angeles Times (2008) China is faulted in piracy dispute, 10 October, online at http://articles.latimes.com/2008/ oct/10/business/fi-china10 (accessed 1 June 2012).

MIDA (2010) MITI focuses on attracting private investments, *MIDA e News*, 22 June, online at http:// www.mida.gov.my/env3/index.php?mact=News,cntnt 01,print,0&cntnt01articleid=875&cntnt01showtempla te=false&cntnt01returnid=107 (accessed 1 June 2012).

— (2011) Malaysia returns to pre-crisis FDI level for 2010, MIDA Joint Press Release, 26 July, online at http://www.mida.gov.my/env3/uploads/events/ WIR2011/WIR2011JointPressRelease_26July2011.pdf (accessed 1 June 2012).

NBC (2010) *Outsourced*, television comedy series, online at http://www.tv.com/shows/outsourced/ (accessed 1 June 2012).

O'Bon (2012) John Davis, O'Bon International Director in Malaysia, online at http://www.youtube.com/watch?v=o-OtgJTyv9I (accessed 24 December 2012).

Organisation for Economic Cooperation and Development (OECD) (2011) *International Migration Outlook: SOPEMI 2011, Summary in English*, on-line at http://browse.oecdbookshop.org/oecd/pdfs/free/8111121e5.pdf (accessed 1 June 2012).

Offshoring Times (2008) Outsourcing and BPO news, online at http://www.offshoringtimes.com/WhatIsBPO.html (accessed 1 June 2012).

Quirk, J. (2008) Globalization at risk: The changing preferences of states and societies, *Managing Global Transitions*, 6(4, Winter): 341–71.

Reade, C. (2009) Human resource management implications of terrorist threats to firms in the supply chain, *International Journal of Physical Distribution and Logistics Management*, 39(6): 469–85.

Rugman, A. and Verbeke, A. (2004) A perspective on regional and global strategies of multinational enterprises, *Journal of International Business Studies*, 35(1): 3–18.

Somerville, W. and Sumption, M. (2009) *Immigration and the Labour Market, Theory, Evidence and Policy*, London: Migration Policy Institute Equality and Human Rights Commission.

Sparrow, P., Brewster, C., and Harris, H. (2004) *Globalizing Human Resource Management*, London: Routledge.

Statsoft (2006) Predicting quality outcomes through data mining, *Quality Digest*, September, pp. 42–7, online at http://www.statsoft.com/Portals/0/Company/Reviews/Quality_Digest_Quality_Outcomes.pdf (accessed 1 June 2012).

Stein, H. (2004) *The World Bank and the IMF in Africa: Strategy and Routine in the Generation of a Failed Agenda*, Ann Arbor, MI: Center for Afro-American and African Studies (CAAS) and School of Public Health, University of Michigan.

Storrie, D. and Ward, T. (2007) *Restructuring and Employment in the EU: The Impact of Globalisation*, European Restructuring Monitor (ERM) Report for European Foundation for the Improvement of Living and Working Conditions, online at http://www.eurofound.europa.eu/pubdocs/2007/68/en/1/ef0768en.pdf (accessed 1 June 2012).

Tan, C. (2006) *Who's 'Free Riding'? A Critique of the World Bank's Approach to Non-Concessional Borrowing in Low-Income Countries*, Warwick: Centre for the Study of Globalisation and Regionalisation, University of Warwick, Working Paper No. 209/06, June, online

at http://wrap.warwick.ac.uk/1897/1/WRAP_Tan_wp20906.pdf (accessed 1 June 2012).

Tayeb M. (2003) *International Management: Theories and Practices*, Harlow: Financial Times Prentice Hall.

Tiefenbrun, S. (1998) Piracy of intellectual property in China and the former Soviet Union and its effects upon international trade: a comparison, *Buffalo Law Review*, 86(1): 1–69.

Treacy, M. (2005) Ramifications of globalization: Michael Treacy in conversation with Sarah Powell, Editor, Spotlight column, *Human Resource Management International Digest* 13(3): 22–6.

United Nations Conference on Trade and Development (UNCTAD) (2008) *Trade and Development Report*, September.

— (2009) *The Global Economic Crisis: Systemic Failures and Multilateral Remedies*, Report by the UNCTAD Secretariat Task Force on Systemic Issues and Economic Cooperation, UNCTAD/GDS/2009/1.

US Department of State (2010) *Threats from Piracy off Coast of Somalia*, online at http://www.state.gov/t/pm/ppa/piracy/c32661.htm (accessed 1 June 2012).

Washington Post (2011) *PICKET*: Occupy Wall Street protesters post manifesto of 'demands', 3 October, online at http://www.washingtontimes.com/blog/watercooler/2011/oct/3/picket-occupy-wall-street-protesters-post-manifest/ (accessed 1 June 2012).

Workman, D. (2008) China's unfair auto parts tariffs: WTO rules against discriminatory taxes on imported car components, *International Trade @ Suite 101*, 18 February, online at http://daniel-workman.suite101.com/chinas-unfair-auto-parts-tariffs-a45087 (accessed 1 June 2012; no longer accessible).

World Bank (2006) Global development finance 2006: the development potential of surging capital flows (cited in Tan, 2006: 31), online at http://econ.worldbank.org/WBSITE/EXTERNAL/EXTDEC/EXTDECPROSPECTS/0,,contentMDK:23065608~pagePK:64165401~piPK:64165026~theSitePK:476883,00.html (accessed 26 December 2012).

World Trade Organisation (WTO) (2012) Chronological list of disputes cases, online at http://www.wto.org/english/tratop_e/dispu_e/dispu_status_e.htm (accessed 1 June 2012).

Yaw Baah, A. and Jauch, H. (eds) (2009) *Chinese Investments in Africa: A Labour Perspective*, Geneva: African Labour Research Network.

Yip, G. (1989) Global strategy in a world of nations, *Sloan Management Review*, 31: 29–41, cited in Tayeb, M. (2003: 118), *International Management*, Pearson.

 Visit the Online Resource Centre for web links, interactive glossary, and more:
http://www.oxfordtextbooks.co.uk/orc/crawley.

Key academic models, theories, and debates

 Learning Outcomes

After reading this chapter you will be able to:

- understand the main academic concepts used in HRM and IHRM
- appreciate the application of models and theories for the analysis of issues
- explain the key themes and debates included in the study of IHRM.

Introduction

Chapter 1 provides some background into the study of HRM, the meaning of Strategic HRM (SHRM), and the difference between Comparative HRM and International HRM (IHRM). 'Comparative HRM' is the study of how HR practices differ between countries, whereas 'International HRM' is concerned with how businesses manage their international operations. In particular IHRM considers how MNEs utilize their human resources for both local and global competitive advantage. However, these two areas of study are clearly interrelated. An understanding of comparative HRM—and the role of **national business systems** and their institutional and cultural influences—is required to fully appreciate the challenges that may constrain the international organizational activities of MNEs. Cultural factors will be addressed throughout Chapter 4. Institutional factors are explored throughout Chapter 5.

This chapter seeks to provide more detailed coverage of the concepts, perspectives, models, and theories that help us to understand the current debates and challenges within the world of IHRM. It begins with a discussion of two approaches to IHRM: the 'universalistic' and the 'contextual'. This is followed by a review of the historical evolution of the concept of HRM, including an explanation of some early models of HRM. We then consider the internationalization of business, recent theories of HRM, and models more specifically associated with IHRM. Finally, some current themes and debates found in the IHRM literature are addressed.

Studying IHRM: universalistic and contextual/comparative approaches

The discussion of IHRM can be divided into two distinct approaches: the universalist and the contextual or comparative. The universalist approach, which originated in the USA, directs its focus on the organization and suggests that there is 'one best way' to manage that organization. It follows, therefore, that once this way is identified it can be successfully applied universally anywhere in the world, including the company's overseas subsidiaries. By contrast, the contextual approach, also referred to as the comparative approach, considers the study of IHRM as extending beyond the boundaries of the firm. Hence, it regards contextual factors, such as national institutions and culture, as integral to our understanding of HRM and IHRM. It also makes comparisons between the HR policies and practices of different countries, recognizing the influence of culture and institutions at national, regional, and organizational levels.

A comparative or contextual analysis of the activities of MNEs, including not-for-profit, international agencies, suggests that (a) the organization cannot be separated from the influences of its home country origins; and (b) the operation of an overseas organization must also be responsive to its local institutional and cultural environments. By contrast, the universalistic perspective regards these factors as contingencies that are external to the firm and that need to be managed like any other contingent factor.

An additional difference between the universalistic and contextual paradigms is the degree to which there is agreement about the *purpose* of studying IHRM. In the universalistic view, the objective is to improve organizational performance, which is in line with a commonly held definition of SHRM as: 'the pattern of planned human resource deployments and activities intended to enable a firm to achieve its goals' (Wright and McMahan, 1992: 298).

According to Brewster et al. (2007: 66) there is a coherent view in the USA of what constitutes good HRM, which can be summarized within the concept of 'high performance work systems'. This is clarified by (among others) the US Department of Labor as a list of 'best-practice' examples taken from leading US companies. As such it reflects the universalistic paradigm. Consequently, research from this paradigm typically offers advice to practising managers on how to manage more effectively. In this it is criticized for being simply 'prescriptive' and for failing to reflect what is happening in HR in other parts of the world. Moreover, this approach to HRM may recommend practices (such as consultation, reward, and appraisal systems) that may not suit those European environments that are not Anglo-Saxon.

The contextual approach, which is adopted most often by European researchers and writers and sees HRM as operating at levels beyond the firm, is more exploratory in nature, recognizes the different needs and interests of the variety of stakeholders in organizations, and covers more than profit-seeking firms. It also draws upon the comparative approach to IHRM, taking into account, for example, governmental legislation and the impact of trades unions. As a result, research is often more complex. It is certainly less prescriptive, in that it searches for an *explanation* of what is happening—across a wider range of contexts, and not just within the organization. This approach implies, therefore, some overlap with other social science approaches; and its research may be influenced by ideas found in economics, politics, and sociology, as well as business (Brewster, 2007: 67).

Having outlined the two main approaches to the study of IHRM, the following seeks to examine how the study of IHRM has developed.

The evolution of the study of IHRM

In order to appreciate the development of ideas, theories, and debates surrounding IHRM, it helps to be aware of its origins in HRM, which has evolved from the study of organizational behaviour combined with strategic management alongside an increased awareness of the centrality of human behaviour for the success of business in a competitive world. The early management of people or 'Personnel Management' as it was called, was mainly an administrative function that included recruitment, salary administration, and some welfare aspects of employment. Regarding the treatment of people in the workplace, personnel management derived much of its ethos and working methods from both scientific management and the human relations school of ideas. Yet, in spite of this plausible rationale, in practice the function was separated from—and subservient to—the senior and strategic management decision-making strata of the organization.

Interest in the importance of people management developed during the 1980s and by the 1990s the concept of HRM had evolved and was gradually incorporated into a new, more strategic, way of thinking. Seeking to uncover the essential features of HRM, Storey (1992, cited in Beardwell et al., 2004) adopted an 'ideal type' approach that distinguished 'HRM' from 'Personnel Management'. In summary, he offered four defining elements that distinguished HRM from its predecessor, personnel management, as follows:

1. beliefs and assumptions;
2. strategic qualities;
3. the critical role of line managers;
4. key levers.

In turn, these can be explained as:

1. the belief that it is human capability and commitment which distinguishes successful organisations from the rest;
2. HRM is of strategic importance and needs to be considered by senior management in the formulation of the corporate plan and business strategy;
3. HRM has long term implications and is integral to core performance of the organisation. It is therefore the concern of line managers as well as personnel specialists;
4. the key levers which are to be used to seek commitment are integrated management action on recruitment, selection, communication, training, reward, development, restructuring and job design, as well as managing organisational culture. Acting together allows and encourages devolved responsibility and empowerment.

(Storey, 1989, 1992, cited in Beardwell et al., 2004: 22).

Expanding upon this view, Storey (1992) identified no less than twenty-seven differences between the new form of HRM and the more administrative personnel management, distributed between the four headings described above. This provides a way for organizations to see how they have transformed (or not) from a personnel management to an HRM approach (Beardwell et al., 2004: 23).

While most western MNEs would today readily recognize themselves as advocates of HRM, in the 1980s HRM was very much a 'fashionable and controversial concept, with its boundaries overlapping the traditional areas of personnel management, industrial relations, organizational behaviour and strategic and operational management' (Beardwell et al., 2004: 17). However, the steady adoption of the new term can be seen as recognition by practitioners of the centrality of the human resource function in organizations and also the need to raise the standard of HRM, both as a specialist profession and in practice. However, there was no single view of HRM, since of itself it was thought to also incorporate two approaches to the management of people as human resources: **hard and soft HRM**, which are explained below.

Hard and soft HRM

Hard and soft HRM represent contrasting ways of understanding the role of people in the employment relationship. Hard HRM adopts an approach described as 'utilitarian instrumentalism', whereas soft HRM lays its emphasis upon 'developmental humanism'. Thus, supporters of hard HRM consider human resources primarily as costs. This means that the company's headcount needs to be kept under control and expenditure on training is made only if it shows a direct relationship to improving the bottom line. Other examples of hard HRM include employing short-term contract staff rather than permanent employees, managing employee performance through performance-related pay, and individual reward systems.

Critics suggest that such practices might undermine employee commitment, whereas soft HRM:

> focuses on treating employees as valued assets and a source of competitive advantage through their commitment, adaptability and high quality skill and performance. Employees are proactive rather than passive inputs into productive processes, capable of development, worthy of trust and collaboration which is achieved through participation.

Legge (1995: 66–7)

These different versions and understandings of HRM are reflected in the strategy and practice of HRM. They can also be linked to some of the contradictions between what is said and what is done in organizations. This is the gap between **rhetoric and reality**. Most employers might hope to be seen as utilizing a soft approach to HRM. However, its practice is perhaps easier when the firm is successful and not facing significant competition. When times become more difficult, employers tend to revert to a harder version of HRM tactics to save costs. This is illustrated in research by Zhu et al. (2007: 753–4), which evaluates HR policies and practices in several Asian countries before and after the financial crisis of 1997. This illustrates that even though soft approaches are associated with some Asian cultural environments, the impact of the financial crisis was such that many companies changed their policies to incorporate additional harder elements of HRM in order to confront the challenges at that time. A similar set of findings are reported on in Case Study 3.1 below.

 Stop and Think

Stop and think about a place where you have worked or are familiar with.

To what extent do you think your employer was a supporter of hard or soft HRM? Identify some of the practices your employer used and the general treatment of staff, and say whether they support or challenge your view.

Finally, take the opportunity to discuss your ideas with other students. Compare your experiences and decide whether these are influenced by the countries the employers come from.

Case Study **3.1**   Soft and hard HRM: Rhetoric and reality

A study by Gill (1999) on Australian organizations has investigated the gap between what is said by Australian organizations about their HRM approach in their annual reports and the reality of what happens, as indicated in their annual workforce surveys.

The research was carried out to test the view that rhetoric is soft while reality is hard (Truss et al., 1997). This 1997 study had distinguished the soft version of HRM by its focus on employees' commitment generated by training, development, and their control over work. Hard HRM was identified by its emphasis on strategic direction, integration, and performance management techniques, including appraisals.

For soft HRM, Gill's study utilized the constructs of 'developmental humanism', and saw employee commitment being generated through the processes of communication, motivation, and leadership. The focus is on the 'human' of HRM (Legge, 1995). By contrast, hard HRM was based on 'utilitarian instrumentalism', whereby human resources are viewed as passive, to be provided and deployed as skills at the right price. Here the focus is on the 'resource' in HRM (Legge, 1995).

Based on the organizations surveyed, organizational *rhetoric* was 'soft' in the way that it expressed its attitude to people. However, the *reality* reflected a hard approach to HRM. For example training was treated not as an investment in the employee but as an expense, whose primary purpose was to improve organizational performance. Similarly the importance of cost to managements was reflected in quantitative, calculative, strategic aspects of managing headcount, with an emphasis on wages linked to productivity and efficiency.

In summary, the research contains details about the many ways in which the *reality* reflected a model of hard HRM. It concluded, therefore, that the *rhetoric* of soft HRM was not aligned with the hard reality.

Adapted from Gill (1999)

Taking a chronological approach, let us now look at and evaluate the models and debates in strategic and international HRM. These have evolved since the 1980s and it is important to know that the competitive atmosphere at that time resulted from intense competition from Japan, and that this led to a general questioning of western management practices. We first examine two influential models of HRM before going on to explore a number of frameworks that can be applied to develop and support our understanding of international business, and more specifically IHRM.

Models of human resource management

This section will examine the following models:

1. the Michigan matching model of HRM;
2. the Harvard analytical framework.

1 The Michigan matching model of HRM

The way we understand the management of people in organizations was redefined by the work of Fombran et al. (1984, cited in Beardwell et al., 2004: 19). They developed the 'Michigan

Matching Model of HRM', which introduces and underlines the significance of the link be-tween business strategy and human resource strategy. Here people are seen as a resource to be utilized like any other resource of the firm, so that there has to be a tight fit between the HR and business strategies. However, it is clear that it is the business strategy that determines the HR strategy, such as which staff are recruited, how they are deployed and rewarded, and how their performance should be evaluated.

In line with this model, staff 'are to be obtained cheaply, used sparingly and developed and exploited as fully as possible' (Sparrow and Hiltrop, 1994: 7). Unsurprisingly, then, the Michigan framework can be described as a 'hard' model of HRM, since it attaches little importance to the *human* aspect of the employment relationship.

At the same time this model reflects a **unitary** view of HRM. This is a perspective or mind-set that assumes that a conflict of interests does not exist within the business organization, since what is good for the organization is good for employees. Managers and employees are seen, therefore, as working towards the same goal, namely the success of the organization. However, according to Keenoy, 'the needs of business strategy do *not* always coincide with the best interests of the workforce' (Keenoy, 1990, cited in Gill, 1999: 3).

 Discussion Activity 3.1

Taking account of the quotation from Keenoy, to what extent do you agree with the 'unitary' view of HRM?

Can you identify situations between workers and managers when (a) there are shared (common) interests; and (b) where there are conflicting interests?

2 The Harvard analytical framework

The Michigan model was criticized by authors at the Harvard Business School (Beer et al., 1984), who went on to develop a 'multiple stakeholders model'. They argued that employees were one of a number of stakeholders in the employing organization, one of the many play-ers who are integral to the success of the firm, alongside management, government, the local community, trade unions, and shareholders. Neither were employees to be seen as a mere resource, and—since their commitment to the organization was crucial—human resource strategy should be bound up with business strategy and not be subservient to it.

The Harvard analytical framework, also known as the Harvard model (see Figure 3.1), is derived from the human relations approach to organizational analysis and emphasizes the 'soft' aspects of HRM (Beardwell et al., 2004: 20). It also recognizes the influence of situational factors outside the firm, including the labour market, technology, the law, and social factors. Similarly, in addition to the outcomes for the firm, the model includes the long-term conse-quences of business strategy on individuals, the organization, and wider society (Brewster et al., 2004: 8). As such, the model clearly indicates the importance of factors beyond the boundaries of the firm as core to the study of HRM. Consequently, the model is considered as useful for studying comparative HRM (Poole, 1990, cited in Sparrow and Hiltrop, 1994: 13).

Referring to Figure 3.1, the key elements in the Harvard model of HRM can be summarized combining stakeholders' interests with situational factors, which affect and lead to HRM policy choices. These in turn result in HRM outcomes, which finally have long-term consequences for the individual, the organization, and society.

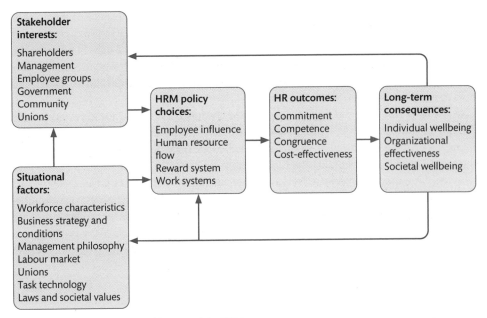

Figure 3.1 The Harvard analytical framework for HRM

Source: Reproduced with the kind permission of the authors, Beer, M, Spector, B, et al. Managing Human Assets. The Free Press, 1985.

During the 1980s, in response to the rapid changes in the environment, practical approaches to the management of people were changing. As a result of greater internationalization, more acquisitions and mergers, new technology, improved products, and increased demands for quality from customers, firms were making productivity improvements through reductions in headcount, while at the same time facing labour market shortages, higher labour turnover, and greater career aspirations from their staff (Sparrow and Hiltrop, 1994: 18). This led to companies seeking to devolve many HR activities to line management and to the introduction for example of more systematic and integrated processes for recruitment, training, and performance management (Sparrow and Hiltrop, 1994: 19).

Meanwhile, international business was developing models, which reflected the challenges of operating overseas. These models impact on IHRM and are still relevant today. Three of them are explained below.

The growth of international business and management

This section will examine the following models, which are used to analyse international business and its management:

3. the 'EPRG' model of mindsets and international strategies (Perlmutter, 1969);

4. the integration–responsiveness grid (Prahalad and Doz, 1987);

5. definitions of international organizations (Bartlett and Ghoshal, 1989).

3 The 'EPRG' model of mindsets and international strategies (Perlmutter, 1969)

The internationalization of business resulted in an interest in the ways large organizations managed their overseas operations, especially the degree of control or independence subsidiaries were allowed by head office or the owning company. However, this theme had already been addressed much earlier by Perlmutter (1969). In his article he charts the specific mindsets of senior managers in the internationalizing firm at various stages in its development. This model has formed the basis for many subsequent models of internationalization and IHRM, and was further developed by Chakravarthy and Perlmutter (1985). As mentioned in Chapter 1, in the section *Organizational orientations and IHRM*, describing the Chakravarthy and Perlmutter 1985, EPRG model), in addition to HRM (referred to its 1969 name of 'Personnel') the model addresses the financial, strategic, marketing, and cultural aspects of the organization's operations. The links between the four mindsets (ethnocentric, polycentric, regional, and global) and these organizational elements are shown in Table 3.1.

Table 3.1 The 'EPRG' model of mind-sets and international strategies (Perlmutter, 1969)

Mindsets	Ethnocentric	Polycentric	Regional	Geocentric
Prevailing organizational culture	Home country	Host country	Regional	Global
Finance	Repatriation of profits to home country	Retention of profits in host country	Redistribution within the region	Redistribution globally
Strategy	Global integration	National responsiveness	Regional integration and national responsiveness	Global integration and national responsiveness
Marketing	Product development determined by needs of home country	Local product development based on local needs	Standardized within region but not between regions	Global products with local variations
Personnel practice	People of home country developed for key positions everywhere in the world	People of local nationality developed for key positions in their own country	Regional people developed for key positions in the region	Best people everywhere developed for key positions everywhere in the world

Source: Adapted from an article by Chakravarthy and Perlmutter (1985) Strategic planning for a global business, *Columbia Journal of World Business*, 20(2, Summer): 3–10. © Elsevier.

The model suggests that within those MNEs characterized by an 'ethnocentric' mindset, control from the head office is tight and overseas subsidiaries have little autonomy. Typically, this control over foreign operations is safeguarded by the appointment to key positions of home country nationals (PCNs). These expatriate managers can then help to impose management control systems and home country HR policies, as well as attempting to propagate the culture of the home organization within the subsidiary. For research on the prevalence and the degree of success of ethnocentric policies, please see articles by Harvey et al., (2001), and Harry and Nakajima (2007).

In stark contrast to the above, a 'polycentric' mindset favours host country ways of operating and allows local employees (HCNs) to occupy key positions, thus indicating less interest in the direct control of the overseas operation by the parent organization, based in the home country. It follows, therefore, that the subsidiary's organizational culture will reflect the local culture. There is no attempt to impose cultural behaviour from the centre.

The 'geocentric' mindset applies global values across the MNE's operations internationally. The organization is supposed to transcend national boundaries, and so it selects the best people from all over the world to fill its jobs. Neither does it try to impose any specific national culture. A similar approach might be said to apply to the 'regiocentric' mindset, but with a focus on a number of nations in an integrated region (rather than globally). It is, therefore, organized on geographic lines, where employees can move within their respective regions, for example Europe, Asia, and America.

While the 'EPRG' model has been incorporated into subsequent models of IHRM, there is no clear evaluation of when, whether, or how organizations ever change their mindsets as they develop. In addition, the practicalities of some of the recruitment and staff appointment preferences, as suggested by the model, may not be possible. This is because the power of nation states may act to restrict the employment of non-nationals. Furthermore, it is debateable whether an ethnocentric mindset can ever be changed.

However, interesting related research has been conducted into the relative power and influence of parent companies with different national origins, comparing this with other influencing factors (Farley et al., 2004). We explore this in Case Study 3.2.

4 The integration–responsiveness grid (Prahalad and Doz, 1987)

International businesses face the difficult task of trying to integrate their activities across their global operations while at the same time being responsive to the local or national needs of their subsidiaries. The degree of difficulty in reconciling these competing aims depends on the type of industry, different consumer demands, and institutional and legal differences between countries.

This model depicts the different strategies and structures that MNEs adopt in assessing the relative importance to them of (a) achieving global and strategic integration; as against (b) responsiveness to local markets. The resulting framework considers these two criteria in terms of whether they are rated as a high or low priority, producing a classification of appropriate forms of organizational structure, which equate to three different types of international organization.

Global organization integration high—local responsiveness low (e.g. consumer electronics company).

Case Study 3.2 Key factors influencing HRM practices in overseas subsidiaries in China

In a study of foreign subsidiary companies operating in China with their headquarters in the USA, Germany, and Japan, respectively, Farley et al. (2004) have investigated the factors that influence HRM practices, and have gone on to question the extent of parent company influence compared with other factors.

The research into 286 subsidiaries found 'significant differences related to financial control from the parent, organizational form (wholly owned, joint venture, or representative office) and time since the entry into the Chinese market' (Farley et al., 2004: 688).

The study also evaluated push-and-pull factors in the context of a contingency framework. With regard to push factors emanating from headquarters, the dominant push factor impacting on HRM practice was *financial control,* particularly over subsidiary investment decisions and joint venture structure (2004: 700). Hence, when financial concerns were dominant there was a push for key HRM policies directed at improving performance. Higher degrees of financial control from the parent went hand in hand with greater implementation of HRM policies closer to '**best practices**' at home (2004: 700).

However, *parent home country nationality* was only a marginal push factor. As the authors state, 'national cultural identity does not significantly affect the management practices' (2004: 700). Also, the effects from the type of industry was negligible, in that different industries did not develop different HRM practices (2004: 701).

Naturally, some pull factors came from local, host country conditions; and the authors suggest that a mix of HRM policies was emerging, thus forming a *hybrid model.* Hence they observed modifications to original MNE practices being made as a result of local environmental and cultural conditions, in order to achieve a better cultural fit.

However, few examples of the transfer of home country social and cultural values to the subsidiaries were found. Indeed, the longer that companies operated in China, the more structured and professional they became in developing HRM policies popular with local managers (2004: 701).

In conclusion, the authors suggest that they expect multinationals in future to adopt more 'best HRM practices' that are not only results-oriented but also fit local cultural and social environments.

Adapted from Farley et al. (2004: 688–701)

Multi-domestic organization integration low–local responsiveness high (e.g. a utilities company).

Transnational organization integration high–local responsiveness high (representing a structure with networks throughout the MNE).

Whereas the existence of global and multi-domestic organizations is very much in evidence, that of the transnational organization is for many academics an ideal that companies can only aspire to reach. According to Bartlett and Ghoshal (2000: 348), this integrated network organization is supposed to have intricate processes of coordination and cooperation in an environment of shared decision making. It is also expected to manage large flows of components, products, resources, people, and information, among interdependent business units. However, its sheer complexity makes its achievement highly problematic. It should not surprise us to learn, therefore, that there is little evidence that the 'transnational' form outperforms either the 'global' or the 'multi-domestic' type of organization (Harzing and Van Ruysseveldt, 2004: 51).

5 Structural forms of international organizations (Bartlett and Ghoshal, 1989)

Bartlett and Ghoshal (1989) have produced an alternative set of descriptors for international organizations by evaluating how their cross-border activities are organized. Their model specifies four types of organization as follows:

Multinational This organization is responsive to local needs and tastes, has little control (of its subsidiaries) from the centre, and is nationally self-sufficient.

Global This centralized organization maintains its knowledge at the centre and implements parent company strategies, while striving to remain responsive to local market needs. According to Jackson (2002: 47), this is typical of very large Japanese organizations such as Matsushita.

International This organization adapts the parent company's expertise worldwide. So while research functions are usually centralized, branding and packaging may be adjusted to suit local tastes. This is evident in the way Proctor and Gamble markets its household cleaning and personal care products.

Transnational According to the authors this is the ideal organization. It is an 'integrated network', whereby it seeks to integrate three forces operating in the international marketplace. These are as follows: the global integration of tastes; local integration to accommodate national legal and protectionist sentiments; and the worldwide integration of innovation, which aims to incorporate research at the centre while appreciating that innovation can also take place locally (Bartlett and Ghoshal, 1989, cited in Jackson, 2002: 47–8).

This model serves to add to the important concepts in international business covered in this section. However, it is constrained by its focus upon product and service markets, rather than on labour markets. For our purposes a more specific study is that by Miah and Bird (2007), which looks at how far Japanese parent company HRM styles are fully or partially utilized in their subsidiaries in various Asian countries. This entails a discussion of the practical barriers faced by a global organization when seeking to impart its centralized HR practices. This is examined further in Chapter 4 in Case Study 4.3, *Culture, HRM styles and firm performance in Japanese companies, subsidiaries, and South Asian companies*. More immediately, we present an overview of some models used to explain the practice of HRM in an international context.

International human resource management (IHRM)

This section considers six further models, which illustrate various ways of examining factors that have an impact on IHRM policy and practice. The models are as follows:

6. integrative framework of strategic IHRM (Schuler et al., 1993);

7. exportive, integrative, and adaptive model (Taylor et al., 1996);

8. product life cycle model (Adler and Ghadar, 1990);

9. organizational life cycle model (Milliman and Von Gillow, 1990);

10. resource dependency theory (Pfeffer and Salancik, 1978);

11. the resource-based view of the firm (Barney, 1991) and Peteraf (1993);

12. a model of global HRM (Brewster et al., 2005).

When assessing the following models, the contingency perspective of IHRM can be used as the basis of analysis. In summary, this way of perceiving the world presumes that: (a) there is no one best way to organize; (b) different ways of organizing are not equally effective; and (c) the best way to organize depends on the environments within which the organization operates (Galbraith, 1973, cited in Farley et al., 2004: 689).

6 The integrative framework of strategic international HRM (Schuler et al., 1993) (See Figure 3.2)

As businesses became more internationalized there was a necessity for a model that combined the MNE's international business strategy with its IHRM. This was the first comprehensive framework to meet this need and it acknowledges the complexity of coordinating the work of various units of the MNE's business, including its head office and its operating units or subsidiaries situated overseas.

This model, which builds on previous models, specifically illustrates the various strategic requirements for achieving both inter-unit integration and local responsiveness. At the same time it recognizes the influence of factors external to the MNE (i.e. exogenous factors), such as its industry and overseas location, as having an equal impact to factors internal to the MNE (i.e. endogenous factors) such as its organizational structure, headquarters' orientation, strategy, and experience in international operations.

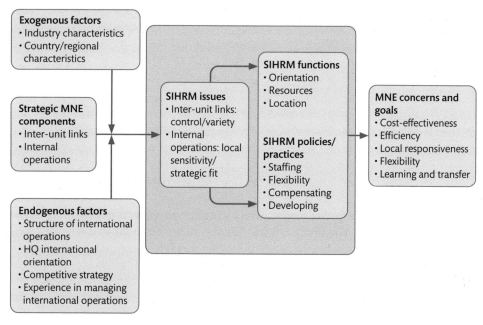

Figure 3.2 Integrative framework of IHRM

Source: Schuler et al. (1993).

Factors both external and internal will affect the way IHRM is conducted in the MNE and the extent to which IHRM contributes to the goals of the MNE, which the framework identifies as including competitiveness, efficiency, local responsiveness, flexibility, learning, and knowledge transfer.

One attraction of this model is the way that it brings together, at the level of the MNE, ideas from business strategy, international management, and strategic IHRM. Also, it is comprehensive and wide-ranging, enabling the framework to be applied to specific MNE contexts. The authors' definition of strategic IHRM is similarly all-encompassing, observing that strategic IRHM is concerned with 'developing a fit between exogenous and endogenous factors and balancing the competing demands of global versus local requirements as well as the needs of coordination, control and autonomy' (Schuler et al., 1993: 451).

7 Exportive, integrative, and adaptive model (Taylor et al.,1996)

Developing from the influential model of Schuler et al. (1993), Taylor et al. (1996) have further explored the specific challenges facing the multinational when seeking to leverage its human resources to effectively contribute to competitive advantage: at national, firm, and subsidiary levels. In so doing it considers how far the MNE's head office HRM policies and practices are adapted, replicated, or integrated in its subsidiaries.

The terminology used and implications of these three approaches are explained as follows.

Exportive HRM The parent company's HR policies are replicated and its HR systems are applied to all staff, both local and expatriate. This approach is ethnocentric, focuses on global integration across the MNE, and implies high control by the parent company.

Integrative HRM The best HR systems from any part of the company are applied across the MNE. This aims to achieve both global integration and local differentiation. This is a geocentric approach. There is also some interdependency between parent and subsidiary, as the MNE can adapt some parts of the system to the local context. However, it is argued that 'resource dependency' will be high only in those areas critical to the MNE's performance.

Adaptive HRM Since the subsidiary's local environment is given recognition, local HRM practices are used and local staff are appointed to senior positions. This approach is polycentric and recognizes the importance of differentiation. Hence, in this scenario there is little control by the head office, and 'resource dependency' by both parent and subsidiary is said to be low (Taylor et al., 1996, cited in Beardwell et al., 2004: 614).

The ideas developed in this model have become the basis for much research into the comparative effectiveness of companies adopting each of the approaches. Large differences have been identified between the way American and European multinationals manage their subsidiaries. The former are more likely to adopt 'exportive' methods compared with the methods of the latter. In addition, the exportive approach is sometimes associated with processes facilitating **convergence** of business systems worldwide, while the adaptive approach would tend to illustrate the process of divergence. (See below in the section *Current themes and debates found in the IHRM literature*, sub-section *The convergence–divergence debate* for a full explanation of these terms.)

An alternative way to analyse the multinational is to consider the stage of its development—and the consequent changes in corporate strategy—as being central to determining its HRM orientation. The next two models take this approach and consider how IHRM practices may change as the organization develops.

8 Product life cycle model (Adler and Ghadar, 1990)

Adler and Ghadar (1990, cited in Beardwell et al., 2004: 616) have approached the study of HRM in the internationalizing organization from the perspective of growth and the corresponding changes of corporate strategy over time. They particularly look at the organization's 'product life cycle' and the consequent cultural adaptation and HR changes required (Jackson, 2002: 48). The product life cycle occurs in conjunction with the organization moving from being a purely domestic organization through phases to become international, multinational, and finally global. The model helps to explain the gradual changes in: control from head office, technology transfer, and training requirements. It also notes changes in the use of expatriates. So, for example, at the global stage both local and expatriate managers are utilized to ensure both integration and local adaptation (Adler and Ghadar, 1990, cited in Jackson, 2002: 48–9).

9 Organizational life cycle model (Milliman and Von Gillow, 1990)

This model (Milliman and Von Gillow, 1990, cited in Beardwell et al., 2004: 619–20) questions the emphasis made by Adler and Ghadar on the 'product life cycle'. Instead it considers changes resulting from the 'organisational life cycle', identifying four phases of internationalization—domestic, international, multinational, and global—and reflecting on renewed interest in the MNEs' management of expatriates.

The model distinguishes four international HRM objectives: timing, cost versus development, integration, and differentiation. It then evaluates what impact these objectives have on the style of HRM, as well as considering the role of expatriates. As expatriates' careers develop, how does their responsibility for the MNE's control systems alter? The model suggests that they become more accountable. The model also suggests that as the MNE becomes more global, head office control is reduced in favour of a more multi-centric approach (Milliman and Von Gillow, 1990, cited in Beardwell et al., 2004: 619–20).

However, empirical research shows that such changes are not so predictable, since companies expand internationally in a number of ways. A company does not necessarily adopt a uniform approach to its expansion into different overseas locations. It may choose instead to vary its path to internationalism. For example in some of its operations internationalism may occur through acquisitions or mergers. As such, MNEs may not go through all of the four phases sequentially. Indeed, research has shown that MNEs that begin with an ethnocentric approach typically retain this, and continue to rely heavily on expatriates to control overseas operations (Mayrhofer and Brewster, 1996).

A further factor that affects the actual practice of IHRM is the national origin of the MNE's parent country. Research by Faulkner et al. (2002) illustrates the degree to which US, Japanese, German, and French HRM practices are adopted in the UK when international mergers and acquisitions take place—and the extent to which parent company practices influence this process. It finds that there are distinct differences, which are influenced by the MNE's national origin. This is explored further in Case Study 3.3.

Case Study 3.3 The adoption of parent company HRM practices in mergers and acquisitions—signs of convergence?

Faulkner et al. (2002) investigated the degree to which US, Japanese, German, and French companies adopted similar HRM practices when they acquired companies in the UK between 1985 and 1994. The article considers the degree to which there were signs of *convergence*, which is often assumed will occur as a result of cross-national acquisitions.

The results of a survey of 201 companies, combined with interviews, showed some convergence in terms of performance-related pay and increased training in their new subsidiaries. However, some distinct differences in HRM practices were still evident, associated with the country of origin of the parent.

The research confirmed that differing HRM policies were adopted by different nationalities, even when they attempted to integrate with and manage their acquired companies. National differences were most evident in recruitment, development, and termination practices. For example Japanese companies' policies were comparatively long term, whereas US companies' policies were short term and results-oriented; these companies were the most likely to hire and fire.

Japanese companies valued seniority as a criterion for promotion, while the French focused on formal qualifications, and the Germans favoured technical expertise. Additional differences were found in terms of career development, with the French placing more emphasis on this than did other nationalities. However, this was tinged with certain 'colonial attitudes', as a result of which a glass ceiling was evident for non-French staff.

The Americans and British tended to see HRM as a 'conscious integration tool', while the Japanese were found to be more 'subtle' in this regard. By contrast, the Germans approached HRM policies in a 'less purposive way' and were perceived to be less effective in their integration efforts as a result.

Finally, the areas of greatest convergence were found to be in compensation policies, particularly performance-related pay, training, team-based product development, and performance appraisal, although none of these was not affected to some degree by company nationality.

Adapted from Faulkner et al. (2002)

Additional research by Gamble (2003) illustrates the difficulties associated with transferring HRM practices from the UK to China in a retail context. It concludes that the strength of local institutional/cultural factors and local firm practices was significant, while the role of expatriates was especially important for transferring the organizational structure and management style.

 Discussion Activity 3.2

The models above often include reference to the use of expatriates as a means of managing and controlling subsidiary organizations. What other methods could MNEs use to help control their subsidiary organizations?

To what extent and how do you think the practice of using expensive expatriate staff is changing?

10 Resource dependency theory (Pfeffer and Salancik, 1978)

Resource dependency theory (Pfeffer and Salancik, 1978) looks at organizations and their dependence on resources such as money, technology, and people's expertise, for achieving their objectives. Any lack of specific resources, therefore, makes organizations dependent on others, whether inside or outside the organization. As a consequence, the theory suggests, organizations will try to reduce their dependence on others and increase the dependence of others on them. As such it can be seen as a theory of power relationships, both internal and external to the firm.

Within the context of international business, the theory illustrates the particular significance of the external environment to the success of the firm. For example a company operating in Malaysia may be dependent on that government's immigration department to provide a professional visa to one of its key overseas directors to enable the company to perform effectively in that country. To obtain this visa takes considerable time (more than twelve months in the author's experience) and incurs significant costs in terms of lost opportunities, monetary fees, and bribes. This gives the immigration department considerable power over the organization (based on the experiences of the author and her partner when setting up a small business in Malaysia in 2008–9).

In such a situation, therefore, the company may even reconsider its investment and involvement in the country. Hence, resource dependency theory offers useful insights when evaluating the environmental factors that can challenge the operation of a business operating overseas.

11 The resource-based view of the firm (Barney, 1991; Peteraf, 1993)

The resource-based view of the firm (Barney, 1991; Peteraf, 1993, cited in Boxall and Purcell, 2008: 86–7) can be used to discuss how to achieve competitive advantage. It sees the firm as a 'bundle of resources', some of which are immobile and which, because of the way they are accumulated over time, are difficult to imitate. It is argued, furthermore, that for these resources to provide competitive advantage they need to be valuable, rare, imperfectly imitable, and non-substitutable.

The resource-based view of the firm is relevant to our understanding of MNEs since it suggests that they will need to transfer and exploit their capabilities worldwide. Hence, this perspective calls into question the idea of keeping expertise at the centre of the organization. It recognizes the expertise of local employees as central to the success of overseas subsidiaries. Thus MNEs need to utilize the expertise of all their staff and enable them to pass on their knowledge and skills across the whole organization. More on issues linked to the transfer of learning can be found in Chapter 9, 'Training, development, and knowledge management', throughout the section *Knowledge management in MNEs*.

12 A model of global HRM (Brewster et al., 2005)

Brewster et al. (2005, cited in Brewster et al., 2007: 225) argue that the field of strategic IHRM (SIHRM) is changing significantly and rapidly. As a result they identified five distinct but interlinked organizational *drivers* of IHRM: efficiency orientation, global service provision, information exchange, core business processes, and localization of decision making. They suggest that these drivers pressure HR specialists and result in three *HR enablers*:

HR affordability A focus on cost efficient, business, and people strategies;

E-enabled knowledge transfer The use of networks and technology to assist organizational learning, such as those described by Brewster et al. (2007: 225): 'The use of centres of excellence; managing systems and advice networks; capitalising on expatriate advice networks;

coordinating international management teams; and developing communities of practice (COPs) or global expertise networks';

Central HR philosophy The need for a common philosophy and coherent practice across countries and workforces.

An example of a company highly aware of the link between its marketing brand and HR philosophy is L'Oreal, which is highly ranked by graduates as one of the most appealing employers. Hence, the phrase *'Because you're worth it'* is not just a marketing slogan but an attitude that is ingrained in the company culture, particularly when it comes to human resources. As a result, the company has been recognized for its human capital initiatives, which are consistent with, and supportive of, the business as a whole. Executive Vice-President of Human Resources, Geoff Skingsley, claims that the company's attractiveness to potential employees is because of the nature of the business, its brands, and its reputation, combined with an HR philosophy of investing in graduates and providing long-term career prospects. It also offers graduates opportunities for early responsibility, an attractive global profit-sharing scheme, a comprehensive ethics charter, and commitment to diversity (Sheppard, 2011).

Having considered a range of models that can be used to evaluate and analyse IHRM, the chapter now introduces some *key themes* that are regularly discussed in IHRM literature.

Current themes and debates found in the IHRM literature

Differentiation and integration in the MNE

This is a theme that is central to SIHRM and that is connected to the 'global versus local' dilemma faced by MNEs. It addresses the problems international firms face when deciding to what extent they should (a) be locally responsive (i.e. to differentiate); and (b) have similar ways of working across the organization (i.e. to integrate). The latter preference might see the corporate centre of the MNE imposing its control through specified procedures and reporting systems.

Some authors suggest, however, that control from the centre is an inappropriate way to manage international organizations as this reduces local innovation and interest (Evans et al., 2002: 30–1, 106–9). Instead, it is argued, international firms need a range of policies and informal mechanisms that promote *coordination*. These would complement centralized control and could include the socialization of new recruits into shared values, incorporating their leadership development and lateral relationships.

The degree of integration or differentiation is to a large extent determined by the strategy and structure of an MNE. These in turn depend on the product, the necessity for operational or strategic coordination, and whether customers are multinational. Thus, for example, a business strategy may result in differentiation because of the market, legislative, and political demands of the countries within which the company operates.

The convergence–divergence debate

The convergence–divergence debate looks at the extent to which management practices are becoming similar across the world and, in the case of HRM, the degree to which the same HR policies and practices are being adopted. Those who support the view that there is convergence suggest that globalization and a common use of technology are driving international managements to adopt single, 'best practices' (Faulkner et al., 2002: 108). There is also a general presumption that these universal practices will have American ancestry. This reflects the original proponents of convergence in the 1960s—Kerr, Dunlop, Harbison, and Myers (see Kerr et al., 1962, cited in Faulkner et al., 2002).

However, recently there has been some debate as to the meaning of convergence. When the term is analysed more deeply it becomes more complex, and in the context of HRM may mean two different things: *directional convergence* or *final convergence* (Brewster et al., 2004: 420–2). 'Directional convergence' can be identified when the proportion of companies using a specific HR practice increases in a number of countries. However, 'final convergence' can be pinpointed when there is change in two or more countries towards a final similar endpoint in an HR practice. Importantly, this may not necessarily see an increase in the use of a practice.

Where no such changes take place there is said to be 'stasis', whereas 'divergence' occurs when there are changes in HR practices that show a move towards difference. For example in one country there may be an increased use of an HR practice compared with its decreased use in another country (Brewster et al., 2004: 421–2).

Applying these concepts into whether convergence or divergence is actually taking place in HR practices, research shows that in Europe there are some signs of directional convergence in relation to trends, but there remain substantial differences in terms of final divergence (Brewster et al., 2004: 434).

Some argue that the convergence of HR systems is made difficult by the existence of national differences through institutions such as legal systems, trade unions, and labour markets. While the common legislation of the EU might be seen as enabling some degree of convergence of HR practices within Europe, this view is countered by those who point to the many cultural differences between nations, as well as the wide variety of business systems and models of capitalism. These aspects, they argue, make convergence less likely (Brewster et al., 2007: 69). The link between the institutional context and convergence is discussed further in Chapter 5, 'Understanding IHRM: the institutional approach', in the section *Legislation as a key institutional factor*, subsection *Employment laws—divergence in human resource practices*.

The MNE as a vehicle for convergence

The MNE is often seen as a vehicle for convergence as it spreads its standardized HR and other management practices across the world. The concept of 'globalization' is also used to explain the increasing commonality of business systems. Its visible effect is graphically illustrated by the term 'McDonaldization' coined by Ritzer (1993). While this concept explains the **societal effects** of McDonaldization, it also makes us aware of the degree of convergence in the area of consumer behaviour, made possible by the work processes adopted in McDonald's outlets to deliver its fast food service. Similar practices have been embraced by retail banks and other service providers. It is suggested, however, that this rational organization of work tasks leads to the dehumanization of labour. This is then combined with the role of consumer as 'unpaid labour', as they operate ATM cash machines and clear their own tables in fast food outlets.

However, the MNE will often find that it is unable to introduce standardized processes across the globe. Instead it has to adapt its product and HR processes to fit the prevailing culture and institutional requirements of the nation state. Thus even where it is desired, complete convergence is not possible. At the same time, the MNE may choose *not* to utilize common HR policies and procedures across all its sites. One reason might be a desire to gain advantage from those very differences. For example less stringent legislation in some countries may make those countries cheaper options for large-scale employment, while high education standards in another location may persuade a company to invest in Research and Development (R&D) activities. From this viewpoint, then, a true convergence of HR policies and conditions worldwide would act against MNEs gaining competitive advantage.

On the other hand, as MNEs seek to take advantage of the differences that do exist between locations, they have been accused of exploitation of labour overseas and **social dumping** at home (Eurofound, 2012). For more on social dumping, please see Chapter 5 under the sub-heading *Employment laws—wages, working hours, and productivity*.

Convergence towards the western or Asian model?

A further consideration in the convergence–divergence debate is the degree to which convergence globally is towards an American (or western) model. This is very much open to question since, for example, the influence of Japanese MNEs has been equally significant in South-East Asian countries. Indeed, recent research has observed a triangular influence between East Asia, Europe, and the USA. It suggests that in East Asia, HRM is moving towards a hybrid people management system (Zhu et al., 2007: 763–5).

Since national institutions and cultures are potential barriers to a convergence of HR systems, we will address this topic again throughout Chapter 4, 'Understanding IHRM: the cultural approach', and throughout Chapter 5, 'Understanding IHRM: the institutional approach'.

 Discussion Activity 3.3

To what extent do you think local companies are adopting HR practices from America, Europe, Japan, or other influential countries?

Based on your answer, do you think that there is any movement towards convergence in the way organizations are being managed in your country?

Two different perspectives on IHRM

The American perspective

There is some difference of opinion regarding the scope of IHRM for academic study between researchers and academics in the USA and those from Europe (Brewster, 2007: 772). In general, however, the study of management and HRM has been heavily influenced by thinking in the USA, resulting from its dominance in the world economy and the ensuing spread of American business practices. Citing many previous authors, Schuler et al. (2002: 41) actually suggest that a consensus has been reached and that broadly 'IHRM is about the world-wide management of human resources'. More specifically, advocates of a consensus view state that the *field of study* of IHRM is about 'understanding, researching, applying and revising all human resource activities in their internal and external contexts as they impact on the processes of managing human resource in organisations throughout the global environment to enhance the experience of multiple stakeholders' (Schuler and Tarique, 2007: 717).

This is tied to the *purpose* of IHRM, which they maintain is 'to enable the firm, the multinational enterprise, to be successful globally' (Schuler and Tarique, 2007: 718).

Notwithstanding these views on a single view of IHRM, many consider that the American approach to IHRM embraces theories that, like scientific research, are mainly *universalistic*. This suggests that 'relationships between the structural characteristics of work organizations and variables or organization context will be stable across societies' (Hickson et al., 1974, cited in Brewster, 2007: 770). The assumption is that there is 'one best way' to manage organizations and that US MNEs will spread this 'best practice' across the globe, thus contributing to a pattern of *convergence*.

Such a dominant perspective can be linked to organizations in the USA having much greater autonomy and much less state interference than those in Europe. The environment in the USA allows management considerably more freedom in their approach to managing people, ranging from decisions on hiring and dismissal to those on salaries and training. In addition the power of trade unions in the USA is very limited and their membership is low. This context can also be associated with the American assumption that the purpose of HRM is essentially strategic: to improve the operation of the organization (Brewster, 2007: 770). Indeed, the definition frequently used for SHRM is: 'the pattern of planned human resource deployments and activities intended to enable a firm to achieve its goals' (Wright and McMahon, 1992: 298, cited in Brewster, 2007: 771).

Finally, much of the research carried out in the USA is deductive, utilizing hypotheses drawn from existing literature and testing these on leading companies and multinationals. A criticism of this approach is that it tends to limit any exploration beyond the firm for explanation or meaning. In a similar way, many published texts on HRM from the USA are prescriptive, offering the practitioner exact recommendations to help deal with practical issues within the organization. As such, they fail to address those broader issues which go beyond the boundaries of the firm.

The European perspective

There is some debate about whether a truly European approach to HRM can be identified, given the diversity of nations that make up the membership of the European Union (EU) in addition to non-member European countries. Sparrow and Hiltrop (1994: 50) identify the significant contextual differences between European countries, by evaluating their institutional factors, competitive advantage, business structure, and national culture. Furthermore, research by Towers Perrin (1992) showed a variety of HRM approaches and practices across Europe.

Even so, Europe also displays certain shared features, which might help explain a European perspective on HRM. The business systems in continental Europe are relatively highly regulated, with greater consultation between government, employers' organizations, and unions. It is a stakeholder economy where confrontation is avoided and the state is a major employer. National business systems are discussed further in Chapter 5, 'Understanding IHRM: the institutional approach', in the sections *National business systems* and *Varieties of capitalism*.

Influenced by these regulatory and stakeholder characteristics, the European study of HRM in Europe is distinguished from its American counterpart. Its perspective recognizes the importance of factors external to the firm, is more exploratory, is more likely to criticize management's strategies, and considers the consequences for the community as well as for the organization (Brewster, 2007: 780). These tie in with HRM being seen as part of the wider environment, including national culture, legislation, and trade union representation.

Individual European countries still operate within their own distinctive national labour markets, which vary in terms of their degrees of employment flexibility, line management HR involvement, employee representation, and consultation. However, there is also commonality, which transcends national boundaries and promotes a more international approach. For example the EU's Works Council Directive has encouraged greater communication within larger organizations (Brewster, 2007: 774, 782). Also, a perceived need for greater commitment from employees has resulted in increased levels of communication that are also more transcontinental. Fundamentally, in conjunction with the European perspective on the study of IHRM, organizations cannot ignore their environmental contexts when deciding their strategic objectives and HR strategy.

Summary

The chapter began with an introduction to HRM and included some definitions of the scope and approaches to IHRM, comparing the universalistic and contextual perspectives. It considered the evolution of our understanding of the concept of HRM before introducing some early models. Key concepts, and the frameworks that organize these ideas, form the basis for understanding the operational aspects of IHRM. They help us to unravel the challenges facing international businesses and to discuss their adaptation to the environment.

The chapter continued with conceptual models that explain IHRM, including its links to strategy and to the process of internationalization. It then considered recent theories that assist our understanding of the challenges facing international managers. Finally, it examined some recent themes and debates, including the concepts of convergence and divergence, as well as an explanation of the key differences in the American and European approaches to IHRM. These differences reflect the business systems and the cultures of the societies in which organizations operate. Similarly, the policies and practices of IHRM reflect the institutions and cultures of the countries in which they are based. At the same time, there is thought to be an increasing cross-fertilization of ideas and an evolution in the ways of working in international companies.

Review questions

1. What is the difference between the universalistic and contextual approaches to HRM? Why is this difference significant for students trying to understand IHRM?

2. What do you consider the main differences between hard and soft HRM? Which of these relates most to your own employment experiences and why?

3. Which model of IHRM most effectively incorporates strategy? Why is this model useful as a basis for understanding organizations?

4. Choose an international organization from a country with which you are familiar and explain its policies in terms of the concepts in the 'EPRG model'.

5. Explain the ways in which MNEs try to integrate their operations in a number of countries and suggest what problems these companies may face.

6. How do expatriates contribute to their MNE's aim to achieve global integration in their HRM policies and practices?

7. In terms of HRM policies, why might differentiation be a more practical approach for companies operating in many countries?

8. Explain the concepts of convergence and divergence. Provide examples, particularly from your own country, of HR practices which (a) are becoming similar across the world; and (b) remain distinctive.

9. Do you think business leaders in your country work according to an American or European view of HRM? Justify your answer with examples of how some companies operate or by reference to their mission statements.

10. In your opinion, which approach to HRM will be adopted in China? Do you think it will be a unique, hybrid, or western approach?

Further reading

Banfield, P. and Kay, R. *Introduction to Human Resource Management*, Oxford: Oxford University Press.
  A useful introductory text, which combines academic content and practical insights into the subject, with Chapter 8 providing a brief introduction to IHRM.

Brewster, C., Mayrhofer, W., and Morley, M. (2004) *Human Resource Management in Europe, Evidence of Convergence?*, Oxford: Butterworth-Heinemann.
  Chapter 1, 'Human Resource Management: a universal concept?', provides an overview of the concept of HRM in the context of Europe and the degree of convergence that exists. Other chapters in this text provide a comparative study of the major European economies, including their labour markets and HR systems.

Brewster, C., Sparrow, P., and Harris, H. (2005) Towards a new model of globalizing HRM, *International Journal of Human Resource Management*, 16(6): 949–70.
  This article explains the 'model of global HRM' and provides a detailed background into how the model was developed.

Chang, Y.Y., Mellahi, K., and Wilkinson, A. (2009) Control of subsidiaries of MNEs from emerging economies in developed countries: the case of Taiwanese MNEs in the UK, *International Journal of Human Resource Management*, 20(1): 75–95.
  An interesting article, which examines why and how headquarters of Taiwanese multinationals exercise control over their subsidiaries in the UK. It finds both output and behavioural control mechanisms are used.

Legewie, J. (2002) Control and co-ordination of Japanese subsidiaries in China: problems of an expatriate-based management system, *International Journal of Human Resource Management*, 13(6): 901–19.
  This article analyses the international management control (IMC) system used by Japanese MNEs in China and the role of Japanese expatriates. It explains reasons for problems with expatriate-focused IMC models and argues that the system prevents a real internationalization of overseas operations in the transnational sense.

Smale, A. (2008) Foreign subsidiary perspectives on the mechanisms of global HRM integration, *Human Resource Management Journal*, 18(2): 135–53.
> This article identifies the key mechanisms of global HRM integration and investigates why they are used. The study is based on interviews with senior management in twenty Finnish-owned subsidiaries in China. Based on the contingency view of organizations, explanations for the mechanisms used are attributed to the internal characteristics of the subsidiaries and to the Chinese institutional environment.

Bibliography

Adler N. and Ghadar F. (1990) Strategic human resource management: a global perspective, in R. Pieper (ed.) *Human Resource Management: An International Comparison*, Berlin: Walter de Gruyter.

Banfield, P. and Kay, R. *Introduction to Human Resource Management*, Oxford: Oxford University Press.

Barney, J. (1991) Firm resources and sustained competitive advantage, *Human Resource Management*, 37(1): 31–46.

Bartlett, C.A. and Ghoshal, S. (1989) *Managing across Borders: The Transnational Solution*, London: Hutchinson.

— and — (2000) *Transnational Management: Text, Cases and Readings in Cross Border Management*, 3rd edn, Boston, MA: Irwin McGraw Hill.

Beardwell, I., Holden, L., and Claydon, T. (2004) *Human Resource Management, A Contemporary Approach*, 4th edition, Harlow: Financial Times Prentice Hall.

Beer, M., Walton, R.E., and Spector, B.A. (1984) The Harvard analytical framework of HRM, in M. Beer, R.E. Walton, and B.A. Spector (eds) *Managing Human Assets*, New York: Free Press, p. 16.

Boxall, P. and Purcell, J. (2008) *Strategy and Human Resource Management*, 2nd edn, Basingstoke: Palgrave Macmillan.

Brewster, C. (2007) Comparative HRM: European views and perspectives, *International Journal of Human Resource Management*, 18(5, May): 769–87.

—, Mayrhofer, W., and Morley, M. (2004) *Human Resource Management in Europe: Evidence of Convergence?*, Oxford: Butterworth-Heinemann.

—, Sparrow, P., and Harris, H. (2005) Towards a new model of globalizing HRM, *International Journal of Human Resource Management*, 16(6): 953–74.

—, —, and Vernon, G. (2007) *International Human Resource Management*, London: CIPD.

Chakravarthy, B.S. and Perlmutter, H.V. (1985) Strategic planning for a global business, *Columbia Journal of World Business*, 3(10, Summer): 5–6.

Chang, Y.Y., Mellahi, K., and Wilkinson, A. (2009) Control of subsidiaries of MNEs from emerging economies in developed countries: the case of Taiwanese MNEs in the UK, *International Journal of Human Resource Management*, 20(1): 75–95.

Eurofound (2012) *Social Dumping, Definition and Discussion*, European Industrial Relations Dictionary, online at: http://www.eurofound.europa.eu/areas/industrialrelations/dictionary/definitions/SOCIALDUMPING.htm (accessed 2 June 2012).

Evans, P., Pucik, V., and Barsoux, J-L. (2002) *The Global Challenge Framework for International Human Resource Management*, New York: McGraw-Hill Irwin.

Farley, J.U., Hoenig, S., and Yang, J.Z. (2004) Key factors influencing HRM practices of overseas subsidiaries in China's transition economy, *International Journal of HRM*, 15(5, August): 688–704.

Faulkner, D., Pilkethly, R., and Child, J. (2002) International mergers and acquisitions in the UK, 1985–94: a comparison of national HRM practices, *International Journal of Human Resource Management*, 13(1, February): 106–22.

Gamble, J. (2003) Transferring human resource practices from the United Kingdom to China: the limits and potential for convergence, *International Journal of Human Resource Management*, 14(4, May): 369–87.

Gill, C. (1999) *Use of Hard and Soft Models of HRM to Illustrate the Gap Between Rhetoric and Reality in Workforce Management*, Working Paper Series, School of Management, RMIT, pp. 1–45, online at http://mams.rmit.edu.au/d4lhtsmk45c.pdf (accessed 2 June 2012).

Harry, W. and Nakajima, C. (2007) Ethnocentric HRM policies in the Asia Pacific region: an explanation of host country resistance, *Management Revue*, 18(4): 454–71.

Harvey, M., Speier, C., and Novicevic, M.M. (2001) Strategic human resource staffing of foreign subsidiaries, *Research and Practice in Human Resource Management*, 9(2): 27–56.

Harzing, A-W. and Van Ruysseveldt, J. (2004) *International Human Resource Management*, 2nd edn, London: Sage.

Jackson, T. (2002) *International HRM: A Cross-cultural Approach*, London: Sage.

Legewie, J. (2002) Control and co-ordination of Japanese subsidiaries in China: problems of an expatriate-based management system, *International Journal of Human Resource Management*, 13(6): 901–19.

Legge, K. (1995) *Human Resource Management: Rhetoric and Realities*, Basingstoke: Macmillan.

Mayrhofer, W. and Brewster, C. (1996) In praise of ethnocentricity: expatriate policies in European multinationals, *International Executive*, 38(6): 749–78.

Miah, K.M. and Bird, A. (2007) The impact of HRM styles and firm performance: evidence from Japanese subsidiaries/joint ventures and South Asian local companies, *International Journal of Human Resource Management*, 15(5, May): 908–23.

Milliman, J. and Von Gillow, M.A. (1990) A life-cycle approach to strategic human resource management in MNCs, *Research in Personnel and Human Resources Management*, supp. 2: 21–35.

Perlmutter, H.V. (1969) The tortuous evolution of the multinational corporation, *Columbia Journal of World Business*, 4: 9–18.

Peteraf, M. (1993) The cornerstones of competitive advantage: a resource-based view, *Strategic Management Journal*, 14: 179–9.

Pfeffer, J. and Salancik, G. (1978) *The External Control of Organizations: A Resource Dependence Perspective*, New York: Harper and Row.

Prahalad, C.K. and Doz, Y. (1987) *The Multinational Mission: Balancing Local Demands and Global Vision*, New York: The Free Press.

Ritzer, G. (1993) *The McDonaldization of Society*, Thousand Oaks, CA: Pine Forge Press.

Schuler, R.S. and Tarique, I. (2007) International human resource management: A North American perspective, a thematic update and suggestions for future research, *International Journal of Human Resource Management*, 18(5, May): 717–44.

—, Dowling, P.J., and de Cieri, H. (1993) An integrative framework of international HRM, *International Journal of Human Resource Management*, 4(4): 717–64.

—, Budhwar, P.S., and Florkowski, G.W. (2002) International human resource management: review and critique, *International Journal of Management Reviews*, 4(1): 41–70.

Sheppard, S. (2011) Inner beauty, HR Management 15, Recruitment and Training, 6 February, online at http://www.hrmreport.com/article/Inner-beauty/ (accessed 3 June 2012).

Smale, A. (2008) Foreign subsidiary perspectives on the mechanisms of global HRM integration, *Human Resource Management Journal*, 18(2): 135–53.

Sparrow, P. and Hiltrop, J-M. (1994) *European HRM in Transition*, Harlow: Pearson Education/Prentice Hall Europe.

Taylor, S., Beechler, S., and Napier, N. (1996) Toward an integrative model of strategic international human resource management, *Academy of Management Review*, 21(4): 959–85.

Towers Perrin (1992) *Priorities for Gaining Competitive Advantage: A Worldwide Human Resource Study*, London: Towers Perrin.

Truss, C., Gratton, L., Hope-Hailey, V., McGovern, P., and Stiles, P. (1997) Soft and hard models of human resource management, *Journal of Management Studies*, 34(1, January).

Wright, P.M. and McMahan, G.C. (1992) Theoretical perspectives for strategic human resource management, *Journal of Management*, 18(2): 295–320.

Zhu, Y., Warner, M., and Rowley, C. (2007) Human resource management with 'Asian' characteristics: a hybrid people management system in East Asia, *International Journal of Human Resource Management*, 18(5, May): 745–68.

 Visit the Online Resource Centre for web links, interactive glossary, and more:
http://www.oxfordtextbooks.co.uk/orc/crawley.

4

Understanding IHRM: the cultural approach

Learning Outcomes

After reading this chapter you will be able to:

- explain the key concepts and theories of national culture
- appreciate the impact of national culture on management behaviour
- understand the reasons for divergent Human Resource Management (HRM) approaches in different cultural contexts
- provide some insights into why culture is often cited as a reason for expatriate difficulties or failure of international assignments.

Introduction

There are generally considered to be two main reasons why operating internationally is problematic for organizations: the culture of the host country, and its institutions. This chapter focuses on the issue of culture and will be followed by a chapter that outlines the challenges associated with institutions.

This chapter concerns the role of culture in multinational organizations or SMEs operating internationally, including not-for-profit organizations. It considers the challenges associated with operating in countries with different national cultures. It also has relevance to domestic organizations that have a multicultural workforce. Since it is understood that the culture within organizations reflects the culture of its country of origin, the chapter considers the challenges that may be faced when these organizations attempt to transfer their organizational cultures and practices to other countries.

National culture is considered important as it is hypothesized to be 'a constraint on management practice and organizational culture' (Gerhart, 2008: 260). However, Gerhart (2008: 260–1) questions the assumptions underlying the study of national culture differences in management research (Gerhart, 2008: 260–1). Further criticism of the type of research conducted by House et al. (2002) in Project GLOBE is given by French (2007: 119), who suggests that the study of national culture often ignores the many sub-cultures that exist in a society; the use of mainly managerial-level employees as the main source of information; the 'culturally-influenced perceptions' of the researchers; 'the conseqent framing of research constructs'; and finally the scope to expand the study to include 'dynamic processes of culture' and synthesis in leadership style, resulting from managers of 'different cultural backgrounds working together' (French, 2007: 119). Such criticisms should be considered when you are reading the discussion of research into national culture in the section entitled *Cultural concepts and the research of key authors*.

The literature on IHRM contains numerous references to the difficulties encountered by managers during their **overseas assignments**, beginning with **culture shock** and sometimes ending in the failure of assignments due to the managers' and their families' inability to adapt. At the same time, companies have to consider whether the policies and practices that are used at home are suitable for application in the new cultural context. In addition, managers today invariably face multicultural workforces, both at home and overseas, and therefore need to appreciate the sensitivities, values, and resulting behaviours of people from various countries, ethnicities, and religions. (See Chapter 10 for discussion of 'Diversity management in an international environment'.)

Finally, the literature contains debate on the degree to which there is convergence of values and behaviours across borders within the business environment as a result of the influence of multinational organizations, indicating the perceived importance of multinationals in unifying the practice of business and organizational behaviour across the world. (Convergence is discussed in Chapter 3, section entitled *The convergence–divergence debate'*.)

The chapter begins with some definitions of organizational and national culture and an overview of the main themes of research from key authors on organizational and national culture. This is followed by some discussion of how these themes are translated into real issues in the workplace. Finally, the relevance of culture to IHRM policies and practices is addressed.

What is culture?

Organizational culture

According to Deal and Kennedy (1982: 4), in the context of organizations culture is: 'the way we do things around here'. This simple definition is a useful starting point for our understanding of culture. Everyone is aware that the way we work together, carry out tasks, and relate to each other varies from office to office, place to place. Their definition is further developed in terms of analysing organizational success, the degree of uncertainty and risk that is incurred in undertaking that company's business, and the speed of feedback from the environment on decision making. However, while this does attempt to explain surface manifestations of culture in terms of employee behaviour in different settings, it does not explain why or how these patterns of behaviour emerge.

In organizations, the basis of its culture is usually contained in its mission statement, which is translated into organizational values and goals. These are cascaded down through the organization by it leaders and through the socialization process, training, performance management, and reward systems. According to Buchanan and Huczynski (2010: 643): '**organizational culture** is the collection of relatively uniform and enduring values, beliefs, traditions and practices that are shared by the organisation's members, learned by new recruits and transmitted from one generation of employees to the next'.

National culture

A further explanation of the culture of a group of people is provided by Hofstede (1984: 51): 'Culture is the collective programming of the human mind that distinguishes the members of one human group from those of another. Culture in this sense is a system of collectively held values.'

Writing on national culture is based on studies in social anthropology, sociology, and psychology. These views have been developed and applied to management by authors such as Schein (1985), Trompenaars and Hampden-Turner (2004), Hofstede (1984, 1991), Hall and Hall (1990), and House et al. (2004), among others.

These authors compare groups of people by considering dimensions of culture, generally dividing groups by nationality or nationality grouping, in terms of: (i) their relationship with and control over nature; (ii) relationships with each other; (iii) the degree to which status or actions are important; (iv) the extent to which people are individualistic; (v) the extent to which they express feelings; (vi) their attitudes to time and space and the way language is used. Finally, with particular reference to Chinese society, Hofstede (1991) has also studied the degree to which people have a long-term orientation and how this affects their behaviour. The importance of some of these concepts for organizational activity will be illustrated in the next section and in terms of specific IHRM activities in subsequent chapters of this book.

While Hofstede (2001) and Trompenaars (1994) have analysed data to identify cultural comparisons and differences at a national level, there are other spheres of culture that also impact on behaviour. These include (a) *regional spheres* within national boundaries; for example in Spain the people of Andalusia have a far more relaxed approach to life compared with people from Madrid; and people from Catalonia and the Basque regions consider themselves different again, reflecting their earlier industrialization and closer links with northern Europe. In the business world we can also discern cultural differences as a result of (b) different *industrial sectors* (Deal and Kennedy, 1982); the *structure* of the organization; (c) *professions*; (e) the role of the *founder* of the organization; (f) the nature of the *product* manufactured and the organization's *stage of development;* but the most significant factor for IHRM is the organization's *country of origin* (Schneider and Barsoux, 2003: 148).

In multicultural societies additional groupings of ethnicity and religion also need to be considered within the corporate culture, especially since these can have a more powerful influence than nationality on the behaviour of employees. Since migration of workers between countries is commonplace today, understanding of this diversity is central to effective management. It is not unusual even in a newly industrialized country such as Malaysia for a factory to employ migrant workers from as many as six different less developed countries in the region. For example in one large factory in Malaysia there may be migrant workers from Bangladesh, Indonesia, Nepal, Myanmar, China, and India, and these employees could be Muslim, Buddhist, Taoist, Hindu, or Christian, while the local workforce comprises three different ethnic and religious groups—Chinese (mainly Buddhist); Malay (Muslim); and Indian (Hindu)—as well as numerous indigenous groups from East Malaysia, i.e. Sabah and Sarawak in Borneo. This implies considerable internal diversity at the shop-floor level and extreme challenges for management. This type of ethnic and religious diversity may occur in many domestic organizations, multinationals, and SMEs in many other countries too, including the UK and USA today.

Why is national culture significant for IHRM?

Before considering the key authors and their work on national culture, it is important to consider why this is important for the subject of IHRM. First, foreign investment decisions may have been made on the basis of cultural distance; that is, how similar the destination country is to the home country. An overview of the various arguments made in this respect is given by Shenkar (2001: 520–2). Cultural considerations also inform staffing decisions and the choice of managers and executives from the parent company country, developing countries, or the host country to work in subsidiaries (Colakoglu et al., 2009: 1293). In the early litera-ture, culture was blamed for most of the problems of expatriate adjustment and resulting assignment failure (Black et al., 1991, cited in Strubler et al., 2011: 1). As a result there has been considerable interest in cross-cultural training as a means to overcome these problems.

Adaptation to the foreign culture is also a concern for accompanying spouses, whose ad-justment can influence the performance of the expatriate. Concerns are also raised about the transfer of HR practices from the home country to the host country and the barriers to this that may exist because of differences in culture.

Culture may also inform decisions regarding reward policies. It has considerable influence on expatriate performance (Claus et al., 2011: 255–6) as well as the concept and application of performance management policies (Harrison and Shaffer, 2005). Culture also affects the transfer of knowledge and understanding of corporate social responsibility and ethics.

Cultural concepts and the research of key authors

Hofstede, Trompenaars and Hampden-Turner, Hall, House et al.

Hofstede, Trompenaars, and subsequently House et al. have carried out complementary work that focuses on the behaviours of people in organizations in different countries. They are mainly concerned with illustrating how values and beliefs translate into action and show significant patterns of behaviour in an organizational context, associated with different societies. Each of these authors and their contribution to the research is discussed in the following sections.

Hofstede

On the basis of his research at IBM on the national culture of 116,000 participants based in 74 countries, Hofstede sought to show the 'collective programming' of people, based on learned behaviours. Hofstede then developed a framework for understanding characteris-tic patterns of workplace behaviour. These four dimensions of culture, which are now used extensively or adapted by other researchers, are: Power Distance (PDI); Individualism (IDV); Masculinity (MAS); and Uncertainty Avoidance (UAI).

Hofstede's research enabled the production of 'maps' to illustrate the relative position of countries in terms of the degree to which they demonstrated these behavioural dimensions. Details of the characteristics of the key countries measured in this research can be found at Geert Hofstede's website (http://geert-hofstede.com/, accessed 25 December 2012) and will be illustrated below with some examples.

Power Distance, according to Hofstede (1994: 2), is the degree to which inequality is ac-cepted in society, as illustrated in terms of hierarchies, positions of status, or power. Societies with relatively high Power Distance, according to Hofstede, include most Asian and South American countries, as well as France and Italy. In contrast, those with relatively low Power Distance include the Scandinavian countries, and Anglo-Saxon countries, including the USA. In terms of business, this implies that hierarchies within companies would be greater in those countries with a high Power Distance; there may be more levels in the hierarchy, less delega-tion, and more power concentrated at the top of the organization.

A combination of high Power Distance and high Uncertainty Avoidance is evident in Arab countries. High Power Distance is generally accepted as part of the culture. Hofstede suggests that, as a result, these countries have limited upward mobility, are highly rule orientated, and have inequalities in wealth and power. These countries are also typified by strong power of the leaders, with laws that reinforce their own leadership and control (Hofstede, 2011).

Individualism and its opposite, **Collectivism**, are the terms Hofstede (1994: 2–3) uses to explain the degree to which people are expected to look after themselves and their immediate families, as opposed to those who have strong ties to their wider family groups in society. American and Anglo-Saxon countries are regarded as high on the 'Individualism' scale. In these societies individual effort is rewarded in the work environment. However, for example in China and Latin American societies, Individualism is low, illustrating their loyalty to the family or clan group. This goes some way to explaining a degree of nepotism in selecting candidates for jobs and a tendency to see the family's needs as more important than rules and regulations.

Uncertainty Avoidance is illustrated by the need for rules and regulations to reduce the level of risk in a society, indicating 'openness to unstructured ideas and situations'. India has a low score on this dimension and fewer rules and regulations to control unknown or unexpected situations. This might reflect the highly religious and fatalistic aspects of this society (Hofstede, 1994: 4–5).

Masculinity is the way in which men's and women's roles are distributed. In a highly masculine society, such as Japan, the male values of assertiveness and competitiveness are dominant; the very weak position of women in the labour market in Japan is evidence of their lack of equality. The high Uncertainty Avoidance of Japan is supported by the traditionally rule-bound society where etiquette is extremely important. The score for individualism is not particularly high, which explains why the concept of teamwork remains strong in Japanese companies. In contrast, the Netherlands has a relatively low score on Masculinity, as females are treated more equally to males in all aspects of the society and it is regarded as an 'openly nurturing one' (see Hofstede, 1994: 3–4, and the Geert Hofstede website http://www.Geert-hofstede.com).

Long- or Short-term Orientation (LTO) This concept was added to Hofstede's research some time after his original research at IBM and is based on a concept also described as Confucian dynamism. It was considered at a time when Asian societies were developing fast and the role of culture in that process was being investigated. LTO deals with 'virtue regardless of truth' and it is considered that those with LTO exhibit values of thrift and perseverance, while the values associated with Short-term Orientation concern respect for tradition, fulfilling social obligations, and protecting one's 'face'. Most Asian countries are said to have high LTO while, for example, the relatively low score of Canada on this dimension is said to reflect a societies' belief in meeting its obligations and an appreciation for cultural traditions. French (2007: 39–40) suggests that this dimension reflects the differences between western countries' tradition of 'analytical' thinking and the more 'holistic' thinking of East Asia.

 Discussion Activity 4.1

Go to the Geert Hofstede website and read about your own country (http://www.geert-hofstede.com). Compare this information with information on a neighbouring country, or a country in which you think you would like to work in future. Discuss how you think any differences identified will be reflected in the work environment.

Case Study 4.1   The application of Hofstede's dimensions to Arab cultures

The Arab countries of Iraq, Kuwait, Lebanon, Libya, Saudi Arabia, and the UAE are evaluated together by Hofstede. According to Hofstede's research, these countries have a very high Power Distance (PDI) score of 80, indicating acceptance of a high level of inequality in society in terms of wealth and power. The Hofstede dimensions also show relatively high Uncertainty Avoidance (UAI) with a score of 68. This reflects a type of caste system that is reflected in very limited upward social mobility, a highly rule-oriented society in which inequalities of power and wealth have been allowed to grow. Leaders have the ultimate power and authority and new political leadership tends to come as a result of military uprisings or revolutionary upheavals (as shown by the Arab Spring 2011), rather than democratic change. The lowest dimension is Individualism (IDV) 38, where the world average is 64. This reflects a collectivist society in which loyalty to the group (family, extended family, or relationships) overrides other societal rules. The Hofstede website states:

> The Masculinity index (MAS), the third highest Hofstede Dimension is 52, only slightly higher than the 50.2 average for all the countries included in the Hofstede MAS Dimension. This would indicate that while women in the Arab World are limited in their rights, it may be due more to Muslim religion rather than a cultural paradigm.

(Adapted from the Geert–Hofstede website (Hofstede, 2011))

Criticism of Hofstede's research

It must be noted that Hofstede's work has been criticized by McSweeney (2002), as well as many others, including Tayeb (1988, 1994, 2001), focusing on methodology issues. McSweeney (2002: 90) argues that Hofstede's research is based on four flawed assumptions. The first assumption is that an organization is a microcosm for a nation as a whole. In other words, that Hofstede's assumption that IBM as an organization, operating in a particular country, will reflect the national culture of that country is not necessarily true. In fact it only represents a portion of that country's working population and ignores the rest. Second is the assumption that respondents were already permanently 'mentally programmed' by three non-interacting cultures—occupational, organizational, and national—assuming that there is only one IBM culture and one worldwide occupational culture. Third is that the main dimensions of national culture can be identified by questionnaire response difference analysis. McSweeney (2002: 102) asks whether the questions were wide-ranging and deep enough. Finally, McSweeney questions the assumption that what is identified in the workplace is location non-specific. In other words, McSweeney questions whether the location and context of the questionnaire affect the results, especially since many of the questions were about the workplace.

Further criticism has been made about the fifth dimension of LTO, or Confucian Dynamism, by Fang (2003), who criticizes the premise on which the dimension is founded as well as some methodological weaknesses, especially in this case, as this element of Hofstede's research is based on a sample of students.

However, despite these views, Hofstede's ideas have stood the test of time and continue to be cited as the basis for much discussion on the influence of culture in management and business activity. Hofstede's results have been supported by subsequent research, and replications of his original work were published in 2001 (Hofstede, 2001). Hofstede's research was intended to show differences between national groups rather than to provide profiles of such groups (Sondergaard, 2010).

Further information on Hofstede, including a critique of his work, can be found at the International Business Centre website. Much of the criticism has been summarized, and the original objectives of Hofstede's research are explained, by Sondergaard (2010) in his article 'In my opinion'.

Trompenaars and Hampden-Turner

Trompenaars and Hampden-Turner (1997, 2004) have conducted research on how cultural differences affect the process of doing business and managing, based on work in thirty companies in fifty countries (French, 2007: 43–4). This research includes some concepts that are similar to those of Hofstede (1991) but also some additional dimensions, including 'neutral versus emotional, diffuse versus specific, achievement versus ascription' and relationships with time. These constructs help us to understand differences in behaviour that are acceptable in various societies.

The category *neutral versus emotional* considers the degree to which people in different countries express emotions or are open about feelings. For example the British and northern Europeans are generally rather reserved, as are the Chinese and Japanese. However, people from Latin backgrounds (Spanish, Italian, Central and South American) tend to be more openly expressive. (Note that the term 'Latin' is derived from a description of those people who speak the 'Romance' languages. It has evolved so that the term 'Latino' is used in North America to describe people who speak Spanish as their first language, regardless of nationality, but does not include people from Spain.)

The concept of *diffuse versus specific* considers how far we separate the task in the work context from the personal relationship—our persona from our work role. To illustrate this, during a training session for senior managers in Spain in a large multinational enterprise (MNE), during a discussion on the value of quality management, the participants turned on the manager of the quality department attacking every aspect of his work and disputing the contribution of his department. For the British trainer this apparently personal attack caused her much distress; she was concerned about the feelings of the manager under attack. However, the whole group happily went to dinner together after the class and remained good friends. There was virtually complete separation of the person's work-based role and the problems this entailed, and the person. The ability of these managers to separate an argument in an office context from their personal friendship was an interesting scenario for the trainer (based on the corporate training experiences of the author in Madrid, 2002).

 ### Discussion Activity 4.2

How far do you separate professional from personal relationships in your culture? If you had been the quality manager in this scenario, would you have been happy to go out for dinner with your colleagues? Would you take professional criticism personally? Discuss this with other students.

This concept of diffuse versus specific is also linked to the extent you are expected to give your personal time to your employer. In a Korean company operating in Malaysia, there is sometimes friction between local employees and the Korean bosses when employees are expected to go out and socialize and drink excessively with their bosses. This problem also arises in Korea, where this type of socializing is perceived as a requirement of the job. This indicates a very diffuse society. It raises the question of whether being obliged to socialize with your employer is part of your understanding of the employment relationship. In this regard there is a large gap between the Malaysian and Korean understanding of employee responsibilities to the boss, and the separation of work roles from social ones (Kim, 2010). This example shows that Malaysian society is generally more specific, compared with the diffuse Korean society.

Achievement versus ascription is concerned with the importance attached to doing a job well (achievement) as opposed to having a focus on status (ascription) or position in society or the organization's hierarchy; that is, a focus on what you have achieved or who you are. While personal achievement is rewarded in Anglo-Saxon societies, in some Asian societies and particularly Japan, the time spent in the organization is respected, while in France, high-status positions are obtained through selection processes that value people who have studied at particularly prestigious educational institutions (Schneider and Barsoux, 2003: 38). According to Gutterman (2010: 2) this concept has some similarity to Hofstede's PDI. Highly ascription-oriented societies place importance on status based on social position, age, gender, wealth, and in organizations according to seniority. They tend to ascribe titles accordingly. In contrast, in achievement-orientated societies, titles are awarded on the basis of competency and achievement in the organization (Gutterman, 2010: 2).

 Discussion Activity 4.3

In your country is respect awarded more because of who you are or what you have achieved? Do some sections of society get 'unfair' opportunities when being selected for jobs, and if so, why? What can be done to enable more equality in this respect?

 Case Study 4.2 Time in Spain

It is common for executives in Spanish companies to be offered English training. However, this is almost always held in the participants' own time. For example training sessions in companies generally started and finished on time, in Madrid often being held before work at 8.00 am, during the long lunch break from 2.00–4.00 pm, or in the evening after 6.00 pm. And while the impression in the UK or overseas is that Spanish people are always relaxed or having a siesta, in reality this is not the case. It is only during three months in the summer when temperatures reach 40°C in Madrid and the south of Spain that some offices close in the afternoons; however, the staff make up for this by working in the evenings. Equally, the long lunch time from 2.00–4.30 pm, is compensated for by returning to work from 4.30–8.00 pm, and it is rare for families to sit down to have dinner before 10.00 pm. Incidentally, there is strong resistance to the idea of moving working hours in Spain so that they are in line with the rest of Europe, i.e. from 9.00 am–6.00 pm, although this has been imposed in a few multinational organizations. It is difficult to change a country's customary eating times (author's personal experience in Madrid, 1999–2002)!

Finally, Hall and Hall (1990) has researched *high- and low-context language*, the differences in the use of language, and the degree to which words alone are sufficient to express meaning. For example in high-context cultures, such as Japan, and sometimes in the UK, words alone may not express all the ideas, but there are assumptions and underlying messages provided by the context or relationships. The style of language used and the degree of eloquence and accent may also provide evidence of class or education in the UK. The USA and Australia are generally regarded as having low-context languages—what you say is what you mean, while China is a high-context society, where networks, relationships, or 'guanxi', have an impact on access to information and communication (Hall and Hall, 1990, cited in Schneider and Barsoux, 2003: 44–5).

Body language, gestures, and rituals

Body language and gestures may also contribute substantially to the communication of a message. In the low-context culture of the USA, the message is spelt out clearly and directly in a functional fashion. In the business context, people from other cultures may feel offended at this directness and lack of ceremony. In Asia, it is customary to have lengthy introductions or acknowledgements of rank and status of participants before the main business meeting. This enables Asian participants to be sure about who should receive the most 'respect' and attention, since hierarchy and status are so significant for them. Similarly, the exchange of business cards and reading these are important preliminary activities at any first encounter, for the same reasons. Even the way to pass the cards and accept them is a two-handed ritual which must be respected.

In addition, the degree to which emotion is expressed is determined by the culture. Feelings, especially negative ones, are rarely expressed openly or directly in the UK or Asia. The tendency would be to avoid the topic. In contrast, it is not unusual for Americans or Spaniards to express their displeasure or disagreement directly and openly, often to the dismay of others present.

House et al. (2004)—Project GLOBE

Project GLOBE by House et al. (2001, 2002, 2004) has further developed the work and dimensions of Hofstede into nine 'culture construct definitions', in order to assess the relationship between national culture, organizational culture, and leadership within organizations (see House et al. (2002) for a summary of the project). Ultimately, it hopes to predict the impact of these factors on the effectiveness of organizational processes (House et al., 2001). In addition to Hofstede's dimensions, the research builds on the work of David McClelland's theories of economic development (1961) and human motivation (1985). The early stages of the House research is largely focused on leadership behaviours, the degree to which they are universally accepted, and how far this depends on cultural contingencies (House et al., 2001: 16). However, the research has received substantial criticism from Fischer (2009: 36), who disputes the mixing of country level, collective cultural constructs, and individual-level data and using collective variables to explain individual behavioural differences.

Second, Fischer (2009: 43) questions what the GLOBE dimensions mean and how they are analysed. Despite these criticisms, early findings on leadership are interesting and seem consistent with perhaps stereotypical, general understanding of the societies they describe, as indicated in the quotation from House et al. on the expectations of leaders:

> Americans appreciate two kinds of leaders. They seek empowerment from leaders who grant autonomy and delegate authority to subordinates. They also respect the bold, forceful, confident, and risk-taking leader, as personified by John Wayne.
>
> The Dutch place emphasis on egalitarianism and are skeptical about the value of leadership. Terms like leader and manager carry a stigma. If a father is employed as a manager, Dutch children will not admit it to their schoolmates.
>
> Arabs worship their leaders—as long as they are in power!
>
> Iranians seek power and strength in their leaders.
>
> Malaysians expect their leaders to behave in a manner that is humble, modest and dignified.
>
> (House et al., 1997: 535–6)

These examples show very different expectations of behaviours and explain why employees from different countries may find it difficult to adapt to leaders from other cultures or expatriate managers, who lead in an unfamiliar manner.

The transfer of culture and resistance to western ideas

There is a considerable amount of discussion in management journals about the degree to which HR and management practices are converging (becoming similar) as a result of economic and industrial development combined with the influence of MNCs all over the world. However, sometimes practices introduced from the West are not appreciated by the Host Country Nationals.

It has been suggested that multinational organizations in developing countries are repeating the work of former colonial bosses by introducing policies from overseas that do not match the host country culture. For example Harry and Nakajima (2007: 459–67) suggest that while in the past, MNCs had utilized ethnocentric policies in their subsidiaries by sending expatriates, they are now imposing their own policies and practices, which is equally ethnocentric. The host country organizations believe that by spreading ideas such as 'diversity' policies from the parent country, the cultural environment and delicate relationships that exist between minority and indigenous groups of people and those traditionally in power are being challenged for the sake of economic dominance. They perceive this as a system of divide and rule, as minority groups gain the support of the parent company and thus disrupt the status quo, threatening the traditional power of the majority. This provides a thought-provoking argument against transferring policies from one society to a completely different cultural environment. The article further explains why Host Country Nationals in the Asia Pacific region are resisting this type of approach.

Stereotyping dangers

While some groups may resist the policies and practices of the West, there are other groups who may be keen to imitate anything and everything that illustrates development and modernity, especially if they belong to a more prosperous socio-economic group.

Individuals in any society may not display the same characteristics or behaviours as the majority, as a result of their socio-economic background, education, and exposure to economic and political events (Fischer, 2009: 27).

In developing countries there are considerable differences between those who have had opportunities for education or exposure to other cultures, and those still largely influenced by local tradition.

For example the young urban middle-class Chinese who are educated in English in Malaysia have, on the surface, more in common with a similar group in Australia or the USA than with their Malay-speaking, Muslim counterparts, who lack their exposure and live in poorer neighbourhoods or villages (author's personal observation). This prosperous, English educated, 'elite' can be observed hanging out in Starbucks, with their state-of-the-art laptops, using the internet. Their UK or Australian degrees are provided by private colleges and their aspirations and lifestyles have little to do with that of their parents or the society depicted in stereotypical cultural generalizations. They watch American television series from Oprah to House and CSI, and are influenced far more by American blockbuster movies than anything local. In developing societies then, we should be wary of the stereotypes presented in cross-cultural literature, which may already be outdated.

Changing location, ethnicity, and culture

While the relative prosperity and education of a group may result in changes in its culture, *the location of an ethnic group* may also influence the way its culture evolves. In addition to the level of economic development, combined with education, which may impact on values, ethnicity is often regarded as offering a way to stereotype values, beliefs, and behaviours. However, ethnicity alone may not indicate common value systems, since these can change as a result of the location of the ethnic group and the socio-economic influences that this implies. Overseas Chinese have been shown to have slightly different value systems than ethnic Chinese in the People's Republic of China, as the following example shows.

In a research paper, Soontiens (2007) has illustrated how the values of the Chinese diaspora people in Singapore, Malaysia, and Hong Kong have diverged slightly from those of mainland China, who have been less exposed to western and other cultures. According to Soontiens:

> The differences and similarities discussed in this paper indicate that there is a significant amount of similarity between especially Singapore, Malaysia and Hong Kong. Although value clusters in mainland China have some similarity there are also clear differences present. Although not conclusive, this suggests that exposure to Western and other cultures outside China has contributed to a minor divergence of Chinese values, especially seen against the more traditional less internationalized regions in China.
>
> (Soontiens, 2007: 333)

One of the advantages of the development of cultural difference by the overseas Chinese is that adaptation by expatriates has been found to be easier in Singapore and Hong Kong than in mainland China. Consequently, it has been suggested that these countries should be used as a preparation location and testing ground to assess adaptation and suitability prior to expatriation to mainland China (Selmer, 2006: 2003). However, adaptation to life in a developed city like Singapore is considerably easier than adaptation to mainland China. In Singapore, business is conducted largely in English and institutions are grounded in British law. There may be some similarities in terms of Chinese Confucian culture and the use of Mandarin by some, but there are major institutional and language differences, as English is not widely spoken in China.

The adaptation of expatriates to different cultures is discussed in Part II of the book and is a major area of concern for multinational organizations. Failure to adapt by the expatriate or his/her family is one reason for early return or assignment failure. Understanding your own and other cultures is an essential first step to adaptation.

Impact of national culture on HR policies of subsidiaries

National culture is assumed to be significant in multinationals when they try to introduce their HR policies and practices overseas. Case study 4.3 discusses the degree to which overseas companies are willing to adopt different practices, introduced by a Japanese multinational, and illustrates how national cultural differences interfered with this process.

 Case Study 4.3 Culture, HRM styles, and firm performance in Japanese companies, subsidiaries, and South Asian companies

This piece of research examined the extent to which Japanese parent company HRM styles are fully or partially utilized in their subsidiaries in various Asian and South Asian countries. The study looked at national and organizational influences among managers of three types of companies: Japanese companies in Japan (JC); South Asian domestic companies (SACO); and Japanese subsidiaries/joint ventures (JV) in South Asia. The study concerned the more elaborate HRM systems of MNCs compared with the traditional, simple, and evolving systems of emerging economies, characterized by a contrast between participative and autocratic approaches to HRM. It confirms the contribution of participative HRM styles to firm performance in developing countries.

The analysis of Japanese company managers 'revealed higher levels of participative management and firm performance' (Miah and Bird, 2007: 919). This is attributed to being a style rooted in the Japanese industrial system. The degree to which this participative style is adopted in subsidiaries and joint ventures depended on the degree to which the manager felt this was context generalizable and applicable. If this was not felt to be the case, significant modifications were made to suit the local environment.

However, the study showed that South Asian HRM is the most autocratic of the three types. 'Subordinate participation in the managerial decision-making process is seldom seen in practice' (Miah and Bird, 2007: 919). Managers use a closed-door policy and put greater emphasis on rules and protocol to maintain their power. In South Asian companies managers prefer an authoritarian style of HRM, are the least participative in HRM practices, and less oriented to employee freedom and participation. The traditional culture results in a lack of delegation and more focus on centralized, paternalistic management. The study concluded that South Asian managers needed extensive training, including working and interacting with Japanese managers, so that they can learn more about participative HRM and best use existing human resources.

The authors' research supports Hofstede's view, suggesting that

'employees resist management initiatives when these clash with their cultural values'.

(Kirkman and Shapiro, 2001, cited in Miah and Bird, 2007: 920)

Adapted from: Miah and Bird (2007)

International student experiences

Culture shock can result in poor performance in the workplace and international students too may take time to settle and adjust to a new environment. The experiences of international students in adjusting to new cultures can also inform us about ourselves and the type of issues that are faced by expatriates and their families. These international students with exposure to other cultures are also potential recruits for international companies who are looking for people who have developed multicultural understanding. For this reason, the opinions of Nigerian students in Malaysia can provide insights into cultural difference that a Western observer might not experience.

Nigeria and Malaysia are two countries at a similar stage of economic development. Both are, according to Hofstede, supposedly countries with high Power Distance. This is usually illustrated in the amount of respect shown to elders, acceptance of hierarchy, and respect accorded to people with titles. According to the students, respect is shown in Nigeria by greeting anyone you know who is older than you. However, one student expressed shock that when he greeted an elderly gentleman in the street in Singapore, the man looked horrified and rushed away! In general, people in Malaysia and Singapore do not greet people they do not know and may not even greet their lecturers anymore. This 'lack of respect' observed by the Nigerians was considered very rude and reflects a different understanding of 'Power Distance' in practice and degree in these two societies.

In Nigeria there is a strong community orientation, which extends to the student community, so that new students to a college would generally be welcomed and helped to integrate. However, students in Malaysia were regarded as unfriendly in this respect. In Nigeria a new student would be encouraged to be part of a group. In Malaysia, foreign students tend to be ignored by the local ones. In addition the Nigerians have the impression that Malaysians in general are frightened of them because they are black. (These ideas are based on the experiences of a group of Nigerian students who were studying in Petaling Jaya, Malaysia, in 2009.)

Some explanation of the problems experienced by foreign students and other nationals derives from the general lack of diversity awareness in Malaysia, so that local people still tend to stare at people from overseas, especially if they are white or black. As a result of the local lack of diversity awareness, Nigerian and other African students have found it very difficult to make friends or have any, even platonic, relationships with the local Chinese and Malay students.

This similar lack of mixing with local students by most Asian students has been a problem discussed frequently by university lecturers in the UK. However, in the view of the author, there was little attempt by British students either to be inclusive or friendly in general to foreign students, regardless of their origin. This resulted in the European and other non-British students becoming good friends with each other; similarly, Chinese students tended to band together, neither group getting the best of the 'British' experience (author's personal experience, Bournemouth, UK, 2003–8).

These examples illustrate how divisions between groups of people can exist, often as a result of prejudice, ignorance, and lack of diversity awareness. It is another factor of which IHR Managers need to be aware, since lack of acceptance and lack of friendship towards the expatriate and family by locals can make an overseas appointment extremely difficult. This explains why support networks in the host country and home country are vitally important for the expatriate and his/her spouse.

These issues are discussed throughout Chapter 10, 'Diversity management in an international environment', in relation to, for example, western expatriates managing a five-star hotel in Nigeria, and Chinese expatriates operating a construction company in Zambia.

National culture and expatriate adjustment

One of the main reasons why national culture is considered important for IHRM is that MNCs often send their employees overseas to supervise or control work in subsidiaries. It is their ability to adjust to the local environment that will determine the success or failure of the assignment. Lack of adjustment to overseas cultures by expatriates can result in failed assignments. This has negative effects on a firm's reputation, relationships with locals, and the psychological health of the expatriates (Strubler et al., 2011).

According to Strubler et al. (2011: 116) we need to recognize that although some expatriates and their families benefit from the experience of expatriation,

> ... the toll that the overseas assignments have on some individuals or families who lack the inherent or learned attitudes, knowledge and skills for the rigors of the long-term cross-cultural experience, is a reasonable concern. Failure can be damaging to individuals, their families, their careers, their companies and even diplomatic relations between countries.
>
> As a result of such problems as well as the financial cost of failed assignments, they suggest that more attention must be paid to issues of selection, training, competency and adjustment of expatriates.
>
> (Strubler et al., 2011)

Culture shock and expatriate adjustment

According to Puck et al. (2008: 2183) expatriate adjustment is the 'degree of psychological adjustment experienced by the individual within a new society or the degree of psychological comfort and familiarity perceived within a new environment'. This adjustment is multifaceted and has three dimensions: general psychological comfort in terms of food, weather, etc; adjustment to the work situation; and adjustment to interacting with host nationals. Despite the efforts of MNEs to try to prepare expatriates for their overseas experience by providing various amounts of cross-cultural training, their research indicates that 'CCT has little if any effect on general interactional or work-setting expatriate adjustment' (Puck et al., 2008: 2182).

Expatriate adjustment depends on national culture of the assignee and the host country, cultural distance between the two cultures, organizational factors, work/role factors, and personality factors. It has been suggested that adjustment is more difficult if the expatriate is placed in a culture that is significantly different/distant from his/her own culture, referred to as the amount of cultural distance (Black and Mendenhall, 1991, cited in Shenkar 2001). However, O'Grady and Lane (1996) and Brewster (1995, cited in Shenkar, 2001) suggest that moving to a culture that is similar is equally difficult, since the differences and difficulties are not expected. Furthermore, more recent research by Selmer et al. (2007: 150) suggests it is not only cultural distance that is significant and implies that this concept is assymetrical. In other words, the difficulties in psychological and sociocultural adjustment experienced by a German national sent to the USA are different from those of an American sent to Germany

(Selmer et al., 2007). (The research showed that the German national adjusted more easily.) The results of this research call into question previous findings regarding the relationship between cultural distance and expatriate adjustment.

The process of adjustment has also been studied extensively. It is suggested that there are a number of phases in the adjustment process, known as the 'U-curve', recognizable by most people who have gone to live overseas. They go through an initial period of fascination and excitement, followed by a period of disillusionment, frustration, or culture shock; ultimately, this is followed by adaptation and mastery. However, some expatriates never recover from the shock or achieve the mastery stage (Oberg, 1960, cited in Friedman et al. (2009: 253). As a result they suffer considerably during the assignment in terms of quality of life, resulting in poor performance or premature withdrawal from the assignment. The so-called 'U-curve' model of adjustment has been criticized by many. According to Freidman et al. (2009: 265):

> Each expatriate may experience culture shock differently, as a function of preparation, assignment type and duration, and differing exposure and vulnerability to culture shocks. A single model of expatriate adjustment may never be adequate to account for the wide range of variables that coalesce to create adjustment.

Friedman (2009), a Canadian expatriate who worked in Hong Kong for three years, examines her own experiences in detail and suggests that culture shock is a discontinuous process and that adaptation is helped to a large degree by acceptance of the host culture and the ability to thrive on uncertainty (Friedman et al., 2009: 264).

What is the difference between adaptation and acceptance? Some expatriates can never accept the underlying values of another country, especially if the values do not match their own strongly held views on the fair treatment of others or tolerance of difference, including religion. If a person is unwilling to accept or ignore cultural differences because of sensitivity to injustice, corruption, or attitudes displayed by men towards women for example, it is unlikely that person will adapt. It is perhaps unrealistic to expect employees to forget or ignore the values that have been instilled in them. The recruitment process then must be able to ascertain whether a person has the flexibility not only to adjust but also to accept a different cultural environment.

Adaptation and adjustment could also be linked to emotional intelligence (EI). According to research by Gabel et al. (2005: 390): 'some dimensions of EI (emotional intelligence) play an important role in explaining the cross-cultural adjustment and thereby success of internationally assigned managers. Intrapersonal and interpersonal abilities and adaptability are predictive indicators of cultural interaction and work adjustment.'

The research concludes that EI is an important skill for international assignees and that it should be used as one of the selection criteria. In addition, this research acknowledges the importance of the spouse and family's adjustment for an international assignees' success (Gabel et al., 2005: 390).

It is not only those sent on the expatriate assignment but the spouses and families who may also go through this experience. It is often the failure to adapt by the spouse or family that can result in the assignment being curtailed. An interesting article by Kupta and Cathro (2007) on the problems of wives of German expatriates explains the frustrations in some detail, in terms of their loss of both social and professional networks. It also explains the failure of German MNEs to address these issues and the potentially negative consequences that arise both for the expatriate's marital relationship and for the assignments.

Stop and Think

Think about a time you went abroad, or even to another area in your own country. Did you experience any form of culture shock? Perhaps people spoke differently (either in terms of language or accent) or you felt out of place, uncomfortable in some way. Try to identify some things that were different or shocking or difficult to get used to. How did you get over this 'culture shock'? Did it take you a long time?

Host language ability and adjustment

In addition it has been suggested that language ability is a more important consideration for competitive advantage in international business and consequently companies should focus more on this in the recruitment process. An interesting overview of the lack of research into the language and communication issues in MNC 'HQ–Subsidiary relationships' is made by Harzing and Feely (2008: 48), in which they 'attempt to provide a more comprehensive and systematic discussion of the effects and implications of the language barrier'.

They discuss the view of Hill (2002, cited in Harzing and Feely, 2008: 52) that language is an essential element of one's social identity and the fact that it is a key way by which we categorize others. They also cite the view of Usunier (1998: 167) who suggests that as cultures homogenize, 'the role of language will remain intact as a key cultural differentiator, while other sources of cultural differentiation will progressively disappear' (Usunier, 1998: 167, cited in Harzing and Feely, 2008: 52).

Their research outlines the main effects of the language barriers in headquarters–subsidiary communication and the resulting problems with achieving a productive, collaborative relationship. Language barriers may ultimately lead to methods of management that avoid communication with local staff, the recruitment of more expatriates, more key decisions being made at headquarters, and strict reporting and control mechanisms being imposed (Harzing and Feely, 2008: 58).

Culture and human resource policies and practices

Culture is a significant element at every stage of the employment of an expatriate employee. As a result this topic will be considered again in later chapters as it discusses those stages.

Table 4.1 summarizes some of the aspects of IHRM that may be affected by the cultural dimensions identified by Hofstede.

Finally, extensive research is currently being conducted into IHRM in the Cranet project, which recognizes the three distinctive trajectories of ongoing research: international, comparative, and cross-cultural (Lazarova et al. 2008). Through the participation of scholars in universities representing forty countries, Cranet conducts a survey every four years on HR's strategic role and a range of policies and practices, as well as organizational performance. The early research papers cover many aspects of these issues, including the impact of institutional factors and cultural influences on HRM practices in MNE subsidiaries; the link between HR practices and organizational performance; the impact of female HR department managers, as well as the strategic integration of HR directors; and the effects of societal, gender egalitarian

Table 4.1 Cultural dimensions and resulting HRM practices

Cultural dimension	Associated IHRM practices and organizational behaviours
High Power Distance	Recruitment to high positions from special colleges/grandes écoles (France)
	Tall hierarchy resulting in slow promotion
	Respect for people in high positions
	Pay reflects position
	Decisions delegated upwards
High Individualism	Pay for individual performance
	Competitive approach to goals set
Lower Individualism	Teamwork recognized and encouraged
	Reward based on group achievement
Collectivism	Recruitment may be associated with family links, 'guanxi', or networks
	Groups are important, and loyalty to groups such as extended families, caste, or ethnic group may influence decisions
	Preference to work in cooperative teams than individually
Uncertainty Avoidance	Rules, defined tasks, and clearly defined roles preferred
	There may be a lack of flexibility or initiative among employees where Uncertainty Avoidance is high
	Decision making is delegated upwards, as people are risk averse if this is high
Masculinity	Hard measurement systems used to define success or failure
	Financial rewards favoured over non-financial
Short-term Orientation	Respect for tradition may result in difficulty in introducing change
	Fulfilling social obligations may put family or friends before rules and regulations
	Protecting one's 'face' may result in difficulty when trying to get to the truth or when giving unpleasant information, as during an appraisal.

Adapted from Hofstede's concepts and ideas in Table 6.1, 'HRM menu: cultural determinants', Schneider and Barsoux (2003: 152–3).

policies. This wide-ranging research is of value for everyone currently studying IHRM and the interplay of societal, institutional, and cultural factors in a globalized environment.

Summary

This chapter looked at the meaning of culture in an organizational and national context and how these concepts overlap. It considered the work of some key authors on culture and the ways they evaluate cultural difference. It then considered some aspects of how culture affects behaviour and the difficulties that can arise in living and working in different cultures because of differences in values and expectations. Culture is also examined briefly as a possible evolving and changing phenomenon as groups of people grow up in or emigrate to rapidly changing societies. Adaptation to the culture is important for the success of expatriates in their assignments.

Failure to adapt can result in a costly, early end to assignments as well as psychological stress to the expatriate and family. Some examples of cultural difference are provided in the short cases to illustrate its importance for day-to-day life, expatriate adjustment, and as a key factor in IHRM policy and practice. Finally, the direct relevance of some of Hofstede's dimensions to IHRM issues is briefly outlined to show how management decisions and local practices are influenced by national culture. While culture is one significant factor that makes managing overseas business challenging, the second factor is the institutional differences between countries, which are discussed in Chapter 5.

Review questions

1. Give a definition of national culture in your own words. Give some examples of typical behaviour in your own culture compared with another.

2. How does national culture affect organizational culture?

3. Explain Hofstede's five dimensions. Describe your own culture using two of these dimensions.

4. Why is time an important aspect of culture? How might this concept affect the behaviour of employees in another culture differently from in your own?

5. Explain how culture is relevant to leadership style. If you were sending an expatriate to lead a team of local employees in India, what style would you advise him/her to use and why?

6. What do you understand by cultural adjustment? Why is this concept important for IHR managers who supervise expatriate employees?

7. What measures do you think should be taken to prepare expatriates and their families for a new overseas assignment? Do you think it is possible for pre-departure training to prevent culture shock?

8. Which HR practices are affected by cultural difference? Give specific country examples to support your answer.

9. Evaluate a country of your choice using ideas from Hofstede and other sources and write a short report on that country for future expatriates.

10. To what extent can culture be blamed for divergence in HR practices between countries?

Further reading

Clissold, T. (2004) *Mr China*, London: Robinson.
> The true story of a Wall Street banker who went to China with US$4m and learned the hard way that China does not play by western rules. This is an entertaining read and a warning to anyone embarking on business with China.

French, R. (2007) *Cross-Cultural Management in Work Organisations*, London: CIPD.
> A book on the intercultural competencies needed by managers of people from diverse cultures, it considers the importance of cross-cultural awareness for communication, leadership, motivation, and HRM.

Schneider, S. and Barsoux, J.L. (2003) *Managing across Cultures*, 2nd edn, Upper Saddle River, NJ: Prentice Hall, esp. ch. 6, 'Culture and HRM'.

> This chapter focuses on the significance of national culture for HRM practices and processes, including training and careers. It includes interesting examples from a range of countries.

Trompenaars, F and Hampden-Turner, C. (1997) *Riding the Waves of Culture: Understanding Diversity in Global Business,* New York: McGraw-Hill.

> A book about cultural difference and its effect on managing and doing business. It is based on the authors' academic and field research and training experiences over many years. (It is easy and entertaining to read—probably available in libraries or on Amazon or in second-hand bookshops.)

Bibliography

Buchanan, D. and Huczynski, A. (2010) *Organisational Behaviour*, 7th edn, Upper Saddle River, NJ: Financial Times Press/Pearson.

Claus, L., Patrasc, A., and Bhattacharjee, S. (2011) The interplay of individual, organizational and societal level variables in predicting expatriate performance, *International Journal of Management*, 28(1): 249–71.

Clissold, T. (2004) *Mr China*, London: Robinson.

Colakoglu, S., Tarique, I., and Caligiuria, P. (2009) Towards a conceptual framework for the relationship between subsidiary staffing strategy and subsidiary performance, *International Journal of Human Resource Management*, 20(6, June): 1291–308.

Deal, T.E. and Kennedy, A.A. (1982) *Corporate Cultures: The Rites and Rituals of Corporate Life*, Harmondsworth: Penguin Books.

Fang, T. (2003) A critique of Hofstede's fifth national culture dimension, *International Journal of Cross-Cultural Management*, 3(3): 347–68.

Fischer, R. (2009) Where is culture in cross cultural research? An outline of a multilevel research process for measuring culture as a shared meaning system, *International Journal of Cross-Cultural Management*, 9(1): 25–49.

French, R. (2007) *Cross-Cultural Management in Work Organisations*, London: CIPD.

Friedman, P-A., Dyke, L.S., and Murphy, S.A. (2009) Expatriate adjustment from the inside out: an autoethnographic account, *International Journal of Human Resource Management*, 20:2: 252–68.

Gabel, R.S., Dolan, S.L., and Cerdin, J.L. (2005) Emotional intelligence as predictor of cultural adjustment for success in global assignments, *Career Development International*, 10(5): 375–95.

Gerhart B. (2008) Cross cultural management research assumptions, evidence, and suggested directions, *International Journal of Cross-Cultural Management*, 8(3): 259–74.

Gutterman, A. (2010) Trompenaars and Hampden-Turner's seven dimensions of culture, *Organizational Management and Administration: A Guide for Managers*, online at http://alangutterman.typepad.com/files/cms---trompenaars-seven-dimensions.pdf (accessed 4 June 2012).

Hall, E.T. and Hall, M.R. (1990) *Understanding Cultural Differences*, Yarmouth, ME: Intercultural Press.

Harrison, D.A. and Shaffer, M.A. (2005) Mapping the criterion space for expatriate success: task and relationship-based performance, effort and adaptation, *International Journal of Human Resource Management*, 16(8, August): 1454–74.

Harry, W. and Nakajima, C. (2007) Ethnocentric HRM policies in the Asia Pacific region: an explanation of host country resistance, *Management Revue*, 18(4): 454–71.

Harzing, A.-W. and Feely, A. (2008) The language barrier and its implications for HQ-subsidiary relationships, *Cross-Cultural Management, An International Journal*, 15(1): 49–61.

Hill, P.M. (2002) Language and national identity, in A.J. Liddicoat and K. Muller (eds) *Perspectives on Europe: Language Issues and Language Planning in Europe*, Melbourne, VIC: Language Australia.

Hofstede, G. (1984) National cultures and corporate cultures, in L.A. Samovar and R.E. Porter (eds) *Communication Between Cultures*, Belmont, CA: Wadsworth.

— (1991) *Cultures and Organizations*, Maidenhead: McGraw-Hill.

— (1994) The business of international business is culture, *International Business Review*, 3(1): 1–14.

— (2001) *Culture's Consequences: Comparing Values, Behaviours, Institutions and Organizations across the Nations*, 2nd edn, Thousand Oaks, CA: Sage.

— (2011) Geert Hofstede website, Saudi Arabia, online at http://geert-hofstede.com/saudi-arabia.html (accessed 5 July 2012).

House, R.J., Wright, N., and Aditya, R.N. (1997) Cross cultural research on organizational leadership: a critical analysis and a proposed theory, in P.C. Earley and M. Erez (eds) *New Perspectives on International Industrial and Organizational Psychology*, San Francisco, CA: New Lexington Press, pp. 535–6.

—, Javidan, M., and Dorfman, P. (2001) The Globe Project, *Applied Psychology: An International Review*, 50(4): 489–505.

—, —, Hanges, P., and Dorfman, P. (2002) Understanding cultures and implicit leadership theories across the globe: an introduction to project GLOBE. *Journal of World Business*, 37: 3–10, online at http://www.thunderbird.edu/wwwfiles/sites/globe/pdf/jwb_globe_intro.pdf (accessed 4 June 2012).

—, Hanges, P.J., Javidan, M., Dorfman, P.W., and Gupta, V. (2004) *Culture, Leadership, and Organizations: the GLOBE Study of 62 Societies* (Global Leadership and Organizational Behavior Effectiveness Research Program), Thousand Oaks, CA: Sage.

Kim, J. (2010) Observations of a University of Derby MBA student from Korea, while at Olympia College, Kuala Lumpur, Malaysia, June, unpublished.

Kupka, B. and Cathro, V. (2007). Desperate housewives—social and professional isolation of German expatriated spouses, *International Journal of Human Resource Management*, 18(6, June): 951–68.

Lazarova, M., Morley, M., and Tyson, S. (2008) International comparative studies in HRM and performance—the Cranet data, *International Journal of Human Resource Management*, 19(11): 1995–2003. (See more papers based on Cranet data in this edition of the journal.)

McClelland, D.C. (1961) *The Achieving Society*, Princeton, NJ: Van Nostrand.

— (1985) *Human Motivation*, Glenview, IL: Scott, Foresman.

McSweeney, B. (2002) Hofstede's model of national cultural differences and their consequences: a triumph of faith—a failure of analysis, online at http://www.uk.sagepub.com/managingandorganizations/downloads/Online%20articles/ch05/4%20-%20McSweeney.pdf (accessed 11 May 2012).

Miah, K. and Bird, A. (2007) The impact of culture on HRM styles and firm performance, *International Journal of Human Resource Management*, 18(5, May): 908–23.

Oberg, K. (1960) Cultural shock: adjustment to new cultural environments, *Practical Anthropology*, 7: 177–82.

Puck, J.F., Kittler, M.G., and Wright, C. (2008) Does it really work? Re-assessing the impact of pre-departure cross-cultural training on expatriate adjustment, *International Journal of Human Resource Management*, 19(12): 2182–97.

Schein, E.H. (1985) *Organisational Culture and Leadership*, San Francisco, CA: Jossey-Bass.

Schneider, S. and Barsoux, J-L. (2003) *Managing across Cultures*, 2nd edn, Harlow, Essex: Pearson Education.

Selmer, J. (2006) Adjustment of business expatriates in Greater China: a strategic perspective. *International Journal of Human Resource Management* 17(12, December): 1994–2008.

—, Chiu, R.K., and Shenkar, O. (2007) Cultural distance asymmetry in expatriate adjustment, *Cross-Cultural Management: An International Journal*, 14(2): 150–60.

Shenkar, O. (2001) Cultural distance revisited: towards a more rigorous conceptualization and measurement of cultural differences, *Journal of International Business Studies*, 32(3): 519–35.

Sondergaard, M. (2010) In my opinion. Mikael Sondergaard on cultural differences, online at http://geert-hofstede.international-business-center.com/Sondergaard.shtml (accessed 5 June 2012).

Soontiens, W. (2007) Chinese ethnicity and values: a country cluster comparison, *Cross-Cultural Management: An International Journal*, 14(4): 321–35.

Strubler, D., Park, S-H., and Agarwal, A. (2011) Revisiting Black, Mendenhall and Oddou (1991) framework for international adjustment model: a prescriptive approach, *Journal of International Business Research*, 10(2), online at http://www.freepatentsonline.com/article/Journal-International-Business-Research/275130697.html (accessed 5 June 2012).

Tayeb, M.H. (1988) *Organisations and National Culture: A Comparative Analysis*, London: Sage.

— (1994) Organisations and national culture: Methodology considered, *Organization Studies* 15: 429–46.

— (2001) Conducting research across cultures: Overcoming drawbacks and obstacles, *International Journal of Cross-Cultural Management*, Vol 1(1): 91–108.

Trompenaars, F. (1994). *Riding the Waves of Culture*, London, Nicholas Brealey Publishing.

— and Hampden-Turner, C. (1997). *Riding the Waves of Culture*, New York, McGraw-Hill.

— and — (2004) *Managing People Across Cultures*, Oxford Capstone Publishing Ltd.

 Visit the Online Resource Centre for web links, interactive glossary, and more:
http://www.oxfordtextbooks.co.uk/orc/crawley

5 Understanding IHRM: the institutional approach

Learning Outcomes

After reading this chapter you will be able to:

- understand how national institutions and their historical development impact on IHRM
- appreciate how political economy and historical context influence today's institutions and the business environment
- explain the institutional and legal issues that influence human resource management (HRM) policies and practices in MNEs
- understand the complexity of diversified MNEs and the variety of institutional and internal influences that impact their operations.

Introduction

In the same way that national culture can provide one way of explaining the differences between the way organizations are structured and managed in different countries, the institutional approach provides a complementary form of explanation. Some authors, such as Redding (2002: 226), consider institutions to evolve 'in relation to the culture of a particular society' and therefore include institutional factors as a subset of culture. However, while cultural differences are the product of social norms and attitudes, institutional analysis considers those differences that are formal, regulated by law, and that can be enforced by sanctions (Tayeb, 2004: 45).

According to Porter and Schwab (2009: 4).

> The institutional environment forms the framework within which individuals, firms, and governments interact to generate income and wealth in the economy ... It plays a central role in the ways in which societies distribute the benefits and bear the costs of development strategies and policies, and it influences investment decisions and the organization of production.

National institutions include government and its ministries, parliament, the legal system and its courts, as well as the police who enforce laws. At a less formal level there are other institutions such as employer or professional organizations. Examples of management organizations from the UK are the Confederation of British Industry, the Chartered Management Institute, and the Chartered Institute of Personnel and Development (CIPD). There are other pressure groups, including trade unions. Together they constitute those players within the national system that influence the way business is conducted.

It has been argued that the strength of institutions is a determinant of investment, education, trade, and so on. At the same time, the quality of institutions is measured in terms of the confidence they give to business organizations. These include the extent of legal protection of private property and how such laws are enforced, the limits placed on political leaders, and the quality of governance, which includes the degree of corruption, political rights, public sector efficiency, and a relative absence of government controls on goods, markets, banking system, and trade (Edison, 2003: 36).

It follows then that multinational organizations will analyse the business environment of countries in which they intend to operate. In so doing they will ascertain the political, economic, and legislative context they face in order to assess the extent of any impediments and restrictions on their business operations. They will also need to appreciate the underlying social, educational, and technological conditions that affect the labour market they are entering.

This chapter looks at various institutional factors that influence national business systems, looking also at their impact upon the employment relationship and human resource issues, which in turn directly affect national and international HRM policies and practices. Thus we might expect to see a clear relationship between the institutions of nation states (notably legislation) and, for example: recruitment and selection methods; employment conditions and contracts; performance management systems; rewards structures; redundancy payments; company pensions; and training and development. Trades unions are another important institution in some countries, and these are discussed throughout Chapter 12. In addition, some of the overarching institutions, which include supranational organizations, are considered in Chapter 2 in the section *Supranational organizations*.

It is against this background that multinationals will need to respond to a host country's institutional factors, which affect the management of their subsidiaries. With this in mind, the chapter begins with a discussion of institutional theory, followed by an evaluation of how a country's political economy and historical context might influence the business environment. This is followed by examples of various legal issues that affect IHRM, and finally provides an illustration of how institutional theory can be applied to the study of MNEs.

Institutional theory

The importance of national institutions for differentiating the way business and labour are managed in different countries has led to significant academic debate relating to institutional theory. The importance of institutions in influencing organizations has been studied extensively and has led to a variety of theories.

'Culture-free' organizations

Early studies of organizations put forward the hypothesis that organizations were 'culture free'. Scholars such as Hickson et al. (1974: 74) put forward their 'culture-free' hypothesis, on the basis of research into manufacturing firms in Britain, the USA, and Canada, where they found that organizations were similarly structured irrespective of national borders. Thus, greater size in organizations would result in greater standardization and greater formalization in any country. Managers would face similar constraints upon their choices, influenced by repeated patterns of relationships between organizational size, dependence, and structure (Pugh and Hickson, 2007: 14).

'Context-free' organizations

Researchers at the Aston school in the UK contended that context made little difference to organizations and that only organizational characteristics, such as size and degree of dependence on other organizations, were significant for the form they take. So they contended that very large organizations, for example, would be associated with employees working in specialized functions, following standardized procedures, and using formalized documentation (Pugh and Hickson, 2007: 14).

'Context-bound' organizations

At the same time, other researchers began to investigate links between institutional theory and economic success, and the impact of institutional factors on particular organizational forms. Institutional contexts are usually defined at the country level of analysis, embracing a number of individual institutions. Thus, institutional contexts are typically viewed as 'systems of somewhat mutually consistent and coherent institutions that have co-evolved' over a period of time (Guillen and Suarez, 2005: 124)

In an attempt to provide a systematic approach to the study of the institutional context of *multinational* activity, Guillen and Suarez (2005: 125) have identified five possible approaches:

Cross-cultural The impact of culture is examined in more detail in Chapter 4, 'Understanding IHRM: the culture approach'—especially in the sections on the work of Hofstede, Trompenaars, and Hampden-Turner and Hall.

Comparative authority and business systems The main argument here is that a country's institutions shape an organization's structure and its actions. The significance of this is discussed below under subsections *The Societal effect* and *National business systems*.

Political economy of foreign investment This argues that the role of MNEs is shaped by the various paths to economic development. Thus investment depends on the country's development strategy (e.g. whether it is based on import substitution or an export-oriented model) combined with whether host government policies towards MNEs are permissive or restrictive. These will result in different HR requirements.

Comparative corporate legal traditions This recognizes how corporate law—and the way it is enacted in different countries—affects an MNE's ownership, governance, and financing.

Political and contractual hazards These institutional factors are perceived by MNEs as hazards, which interact to shape the governance mechanisms of foreign direct investment (FDI). See Guillen and Suarez (2005: 126, Table 7.1), as well as throughout Chapter 2, for more on FDI and political risk.

Institutional effects

Three main schools of thought can be used to evaluate the effects of institutions on MNEs:

- the societal effect;
- national business systems;
- varieties of capitalism.

The societal effect

During the 1980s research by Maurice et al. (1980: 59) into the 'societal effect' investigated links between national institutions, organizational forms, and human resource functions. These authors argue that social institutions influence companies' strategies and organizational practices in a systematic way, so that company structures and processes display typical national patterns.

Initial research into the chemical and mechanical engineering industries in Britain, France, and Germany, indicated that Britain, for example, was more suited to large-batch, mass, and process engineering. This was because of a combination of (a) the weak links between worker and technician careers; and (b) poor communication between shop-floor operations and engineering and planning functions (Maurice et al., 1980; Sorge, 1983; Hartmann et al., 1983, cited in Mueller, 1994: 2).

In contrast, the better education and training structure in Germany is associated with stronger links between managerial and technical competence. This has given German companies, particularly in the mechanical engineering sector, competitive advantage, in spite of facing higher costs, which in part result from German companies' more cooperative relationships with trade unions. German technical ingenuity and managerial expertise have produced 'up-market restructuring', combining technological change and flexible, intelligent forms of work organization (Mueller, 1994: 2).

Mueller concludes that it was this persistent influence of the institutional context that helped create viable firms in Germany. By contrast there was more difficulty modernizing the shop floor in Britain because, the author suggests, 'in an Anglo-American context the **Fordist** inheritance remained much more deeply ingrained and more difficult to overcome' (Mueller, 1994: 2).

In her earlier studies of the industrial orders of Germany, France, and Britain, Lane (1991: 515) contended that even though economies and business organizations are faced with similar opportunities and problems, each society displays distinctive ways of coping with such challenges. This comes about from management, labour, and the state, interacting in nationally distinctive ways. Furthermore, this pattern is likely to continue, since a society's institutional frameworks help to *withstand* pressures towards uniformity, which are exerted by advanced industrialism and the global capitalist economic system. There is also a complementary view, which recognizes that internationalization can strengthen the institutional framework that *transcends* national societies, but sees this as having *different* consequences for different societies (Sorge, 2010).

National business systems

In a similar vein, the 'national business systems' approach emphasizes the influence of national institutions on firms. Whitley (1994: 36) argues that 'business systems are relatively stable and cohesive configurations of hierarchy–market relations that have developed and remain effective in particular and separate institutional contexts, typically within the boundaries of the nation state'. In this approach it is the 'nation state' that is regarded as the obvious starting point for analysis, since it contains so many institutions that impinge on economic activities, including legal, educational, and financial, systems.

Whitley (1999: 33) and Redding (2003: 7–8) subsequently revised the national business systems model, identifying six successful forms of capitalism found in Europe and Asia, which they characterized by differences in ownership, coordination, employment practices, and by distinctive approaches to financial, human, and social capital. These six configurations of capitalism are as follows:

1. **The Anglo-Saxon individualistic form** This is dominant in the USA and UK and has its focus on share-holder value (Redding, 2003: 7).

2. **The European large-scale form** This adopts a communitarian, stakeholder perspective, recognizing the importance of social commitments and obligations, which are reflected in social contracts. This form is predominant in Germany (Redding, 2003: 7-8).

3. **The European industrial district form** This is found in networked enterprises of family-owned firms containing skilled, committed employees. It is found in Scandinavia and northern Italy (Redding, 2003: 8), with Benetton a well-known example of this type.

However, the success of this model is being threatened by competition from low-cost production countries such as China and India. According to Emma Marcegaglia, president of Confindustria, Italy's main business lobby, more than ninety of Italy's 104 officially registered clusters are in difficulty (*The Economist*, 2009a). Benetton's strategy for survival, therefore, is to outsource its manufacturing, while keeping its headquarters and design arm in the clothing cluster of the Veneto region in Italy (*The Economist*, 2009a).

4. **The Japanese form** This emphasizes integration and coordination by means of 'keiretsu' networks. Keiretsu is a Japanese word for a corporate structure in which a number of organizations link together, implying a close business relationship with each other for mutual benefit. Such a form is strongly associated with its prime objective of the stable employment of people (Redding, 2003: 8).

'Horizontal' keiretsu are groups of diverse industry members, communities of equals, with banks at the centre. They host presidents' council meetings and manage the activities of members through lending, equity, and board connections.

'Vertical' keiretsu refers to manufacturing or supply chain groups of 'suppliers, subcontractors, and distributors organized in the vertical division of labor around a large industrial firm such as Matsushita, Nippon Steel, or Toyota' (Lincoln and Shimotani 2009: 7).

However, the recession faced by Japan in recent years has called into question the effectiveness of this system.

5. **The Korean chaebol** This was originally designed to fulfil the national plan for development (Redding, 2003: 8) It was based on the Japanese keiretsu, but did not have the same close links to banks. A chaebol is essentially a family-controlled business conglomerate which, in the past, had close connections with and support from the government. Examples of successful chaebols today include Samsung, Hyundai, LG, and Kia.

6. **The Chinese capitalistic form** This is represented by the family businesses found among Chinese migrants throughout Taiwan, Hong Kong, Singapore, Malaysia, and

Indonesia—and more recently in mainland China itself. It exists to serve the ambitions and wealth of particular families (Evans et al., 2002: 169; Redding, 2003: 8).

The national systems approach has been criticized for ignoring the different levels around which collective action may be organized within and across national boundaries, including 'industries, sectors, districts, regions, production systems, crafts, professions, elites, corporations, kin-networks, religions, parties, ideologies' (Rasanen and Whipp, 1992: 47). These and additional debates will be discussed in the last section of this chapter: *The application of institutional theory to the study of MNEs.*

Katz and Darbishire (2000, cited in Bamber et al., 2004: 83) have further investigated national systems of employment and the extent of convergence or divergence in employment practices. Interestingly, they indicate convergence through cross-national patterns that appear to be challenging national employment systems. They identify these forces for convergence as: low-wage, human resource management, joint team-based, and Japanese-oriented strategies. They relate these changes to a decline in trade unions and growing income inequality.

These findings are based on research into the telecommunications and automobile industries in seven industrialized countries. However, as well as highlighting increasing commonality *across* countries, the authors acknowledge that variations in employment patterns are also increasing *within* countries, notably in relation to wages, work practices, and other employment conditions. It is for this reason that they use the term 'converging divergences' in the title of their work.

Varieties of capitalism

A third way to analyse the effects of institutions is to consider varieties of capitalism as determined by the degree of institutional control that exists in the economy. In this approach, Hall and Soskice (2001: 8) state that nations need not converge to a single Anglo-American model to achieve economic success. Instead, they single out two types of economy for attention: a 'coordinated market economy' (CME) and a 'liberal market economy' (LME), noting that the type of business system that operates in a country, or groups of countries, influences the degree to which HRM is regulated or controlled.

In comparing the two types of economy, it is found that CMEs such as Germany, the Netherlands, Sweden, and Japan, have higher levels of institutional regulation than do LMEs, such as the UK, USA, Ireland, Canada, Australia, and New Zealand (Hall and Soskice, 2001: 8–9; Farndale et al., 2008: 2008). The main difference between them is that in LMEs problems of coordination between the firm, its financiers, employees, customers, and suppliers, are solved mainly through *market* mechanisms. So, for example, wages are subject to, and set by, market forces. However, in CMEs, *formal institutions* play a central role in regulating a firm's relations with its stakeholders. So, for example, we might see employers' associations and trades unions working together to set wages through industry-level collective bargaining. Hence, CMEs tend to focus on integration between legislation, stakeholders, and institutions—with the state playing a more prominent role in the stock market (Farndale, et al., 2008: 2008). In contrast, LMEs exhibit a more short-term outlook, giving greater priority to shareholder returns than to institutional regulation.

The study by Farndale et al. (2008: 2017) focused on a number of HRM practices: participation in pay bargaining, employee voice, corporate information sharing, non-permanent contracts, and spending on training. The researchers found there were significant differences between HRM practices in CMEs and those in LMEs, suggesting that the type of market economy clearly had an impact on these aspects of HRM (Farndale et al., 2008: 2017).

However, the CME and LME distinctions are not designed to simply pigeon-hole and label a country's economy. These terms can also be used to indicate changes and degrees of conformance. The UK for example, because of its membership of the European Union and its being bound by EU legislation, is moving away from an LME model and towards a more regulated, CME model. At the other extreme, Germany is considered to be quite different in its HRM practices from fellow CME countries such as Sweden and the Netherlands (Farndale et al., 2008: 2017).

Brewster and Larsen (1992: 414) had previously suggested, similarly, that there are distinct forms of HRM within Europe, notably in terms of (a) the extent of devolvement of HR practices to line managers; and (b) the degree to which HRM is integrated with business strategy. From their research the authors define four types of HRM and link these with particular countries, as follows:

'Professional mechanics'

This category refers to HR functional specialists, whose role is to ensure the legality of HR processes and to attend to the technicalities of HR management, but who have little involvement with business strategy. Professional mechanics can be found in Germany, the UK, and Italy.

'Guarded strategists'

This role refers to those in HR having strategic influence and strong central control over all HR matters: from recruitment and development to reward and evaluation. This type is located in Norway, France, and Spain.

'Pivotal'

This identifies Sweden and Switzerland as countries with the most devolvement of the HR function to line managers.

'Wild West'

This label is given to countries such as the Netherlands and Denmark, where the researchers found that the HR function had very weak links with business strategy (Brewster and Larsen, 1992: 414).

These and other differences illustrate the wide diversity of approaches to business and HR management within Europe and indicate a continuing *lack of* convergence in some aspects of human resource management practices. However, as this introduction to the institutional approach shows, this remains an area of lively debate between those researchers and writers searching for explanations for the success or failure of different economic systems—and how this may be linked to government policies towards business and their impact on management approaches.

Taking note of work by Redding (2005, cited in Witt and Redding, 2009: 48), we move on to a discussion on key institutional factors that impact on business practices: the political and historical context, the country's stage of economic development, and its legal environment. This will enable some comparisons to be made on the effect of institutions in various countries.

Political economy and historical context

Any organization wishing to do business in another country needs to assess the environment, at least at a basic level, through conducting a PESTLE analysis, as discussed in Chapter 2, section *The organization and its environment*. However, this framework does not adequately consider the historical context. A nation's path to economic development and its policies towards MNEs also need to be considered (Guillen and Suarez, 2005: 133). For example many developing countries have previously been colonies of western nations. So even though they may have been independent for many years, there may still be a legacy of their past, often reflected in the predominant language of business, education, and the legal system. Moreover, this legacy might be remembered with fondness or regarded with distrust. If the latter, the entry of multinationals may be viewed as an attempt at a new form of economic domination by former colonial masters or other rich nations. Put more eloquently, MNEs may be 'depicted as villains that plunder the country's riches, thwarting its economic potential and limiting its national sovereignty' (Guillen and Suarez, 2005: 135.)

The following examples (Case Studies 5.1a, 5.1b) show how a nation's particular responses to a colonial past have influenced governmental policies on language, education, training, and investment. These can present significant issues for MNEs.

 Case Study 5.1a 'Buy British Last' and 'Look East' campaigns in Malaysia

In Malaysia the negative view of British colonial exploitation has resulted in deliberate attempts by the government to encourage business with alternative partners, such as occurred in the 1980s with the 'Buy British Last' and 'Look East' campaigns. Bad feeling between the Malaysian prime minister and Britain arose in 1981 over the 'dawn raids' on the London Stock Exchange to buy a controlling share in, and to effectively nationalize, former British plantations (Kitchen and Ahmad, 2007).

Thereafter, the Malaysian government began to look to other countries for assistance with investment and development, and introduced a 'Look East' policy. This is relevant to MNEs, who will be received according to their home country; and relevant to IHRM because of the educational and training links that were subsequently set up with Japan.

The following extract, which is taken from the Embassy of Japan website (2011), provides an outline of the policy and the reasons for its development.

In July 1981, Prime Minister Dato' Seri Dr Mahathir bin Mohamad became the prime minister of Malaysia. After six months in office, he announced an initiative to learn from the experiences of Japan (and Korea) in the nation-building of Malaysia. He considered that the secret of Japanese success and its remarkable development lay in its labour ethics, morale, and management capability. He felt a programme enabling young Malaysians to learn in Japan would contribute to the economic and social development of Malaysia. For this purpose, Malaysia decided to dispatch their students to Japan, to study not only academic and technical know-how but also to learn labour ethics and the discipline of the Japanese people.

As a result of this policy about 11,000 Malaysians were sent to Japan for academic and technical training between 1982 and 2002. This process was jointly supported by the Malaysian and Japanese governments and went hand-in-hand with significant investment by Japanese companies in Malaysia. This strong relationship between Japan and Malaysia still exists today; and numerous educational scholarship schemes, youth exchange visits, and cultural exchanges, continue.

Discussion Activity 5.1

Consider the links that your own country has with other countries in terms of higher education and training. Which countries, if any, have educational links with your country, through colleges or universities?

Why is this, do you think? For example how far do such links improve the education and skills of the local labour force? Do MNEs and local companies recruit from these colleges or universities?

Consistent with the Malaysian government's animosity towards Britain and its desire to distance the nation from the British, there were further interventions that sought to establish a coherent Malaysian identity. One was to revive Malay by its elevation to being the nationally taught language, in place of English. A second was a policy to favour the indigenous Malay population over the remaining 40 per cent of the population, who were of Chinese and Indian origin. These are discussed in Case Study 5.1b below.

 Discussion Activity 5.2

Which are the main languages used in your country for education and for business? How many, and what, languages do most people speak?

How far is second-language learning encouraged by your government and the education system? To what extent does this have an effect on your country's growth and development?

 Case Study 5.1b   The national language and education policy in Malaysia

An additional negative response to everything associated with the former colonial masters in Malaysia was the National Language policy, which was introduced in the 1960s and reinforced in the 1970s. This ensured that the majority of state schools would provide primary and secondary education in the Malay language in place of English, though a small number of schools were allowed to continue teaching in Mandarin or Tamil. This policy destroyed Malaysia's English language teaching system. As a result, lower levels of English language proficiency meant the loss of a pivotal international business advantage.

At the same time, the government has instituted nationalistic policies, which have sought to give advantage to the country's ethnic Malays through preferential access to state universities and jobs. These have resulted in the majority of ethnic Chinese and Indian students being obliged to continue their education privately, in English-medium colleges, which predominantly provide British and Australian university qualifications. Consequently, these students maintain a degree of fluency in English that the majority of Malay students do not have.

This national language policy has affected the business environment by significantly reducing the number of young people who can speak English fluently. In effect it has diminished the level of employment opportunities available, especially for Malays (Zaaba et al., 2011: 162).

Historical legacy—language and investment

In contrast to the demise of English in Malaysia, the Spanish language (i.e. Castilian) is used by over 329 million people in forty-four countries, notably in the USA and in South and Central America, even though Spain lost the majority of its colonies 200 years ago (Lewis, 2009). This legacy has had a significant impact on MNEs wishing to do business with Spanish-speaking countries. Major European and US multinationals (e.g. BT Global, Software AG, Motorola, Proctor and Gamble, IBM, and Oracle) typically base their headquarters in Spain. Similarly, international law firms are taking advantage of Madrid's new centre for international arbitration for resolving disputes involving parties from Latin America, North Africa, and Europe (Casley Gera, 2007; Pinar Guzman, 2009).

It is clear that a colonial heritage has had a great influence on the language, education, training, and legal system of many countries, which in turn have direct relevance for the labour market conditions encountered by MNEs. As such, a nation's historical legacy can be central to understanding the institutional and cultural environment of the country in which an MNE intends to operate.

Communication—national and corporate languages

Communication problems experienced within MNEs are often a result of commercial decisions on where to invest and the language used in that overseas location. An MNE's first choice of countries is often one with the same language and where there are some cultural ties. However, this will not always be possible, so that expatriates, especially Parent Country Nationals (PCNs), will then need to make some effort to learn another language for their overseas assignments.

However, in an effort to simplify internal communications, some organizations adopt a single corporate language, with IHRM departments offering training in the corporate language or alternative means of enhancing communication, including interpreters. Yet these measures do not guarantee fluency across the organization, nor do they erase all communication problems (Feely, 2003: 225–6).

Stages of economic development

This section will discuss the relationship that exists between a country's history, its economic development and competitiveness, and the link to national skills levels.

Stage of economic development and competitiveness

It seems reasonable to presume that levels of economic development may determine the willingness of companies to invest in countries. However, we can interpret this from two perspectives: the Marxist view, and a theory of stages of economic development (Rostow, 1960, cited in Thirlwall, 2006: 112).

The Marxist view

This suggests that poverty and unequal development are an integral part of the world capitalist system, since development in some parts of the world economic system occurs at the expense of others. As a result, a situation of dependence (e.g. colonial, financial, industrial, technological) of the poorer countries on the wealthier ones arises (Dos Santos, 1970: 231–2). Additionally, Frank (1967) identifies a process called the 'development of underdevelopment', arguing that development itself perpetuates the underdevelopment of others. This is perceived to have started in the economic exploitation of colonial times and is seen to be responsible for the distorted economic structure of the third (now developing) world ever since (Thirlwall, 2006: 20). From this perspective today's multinationals are seen to be the instrument for expropriation of wealth, which is then repatriated to the rich world.

The theory of stages of economic development

This theory was devised by Rostow (1960, cited in Thirlwall, 2006: 112) as an alternative to the Marxist interpretation. It defines a sequence of five, well-ordered stages of development: traditional, transitional, take-off, maturity, and high mass consumption. Rostow's views have been widely criticized because of the difficulty of empirically testing the theory, the lack of quantitative data to differentiate between stages, and because the characteristics of the stages are not specific enough (Kuznets, 1963, cited in Thirlwall, 2006: 113). However, stage theory continues to provide valuable insights into the development process, with some of these ideas used by economists to assess the relative competitiveness of nations.

Porter et al. (2002: 20), for example, advocate the analysis of countries' competitiveness in terms of their stage of economic development. As countries move from resource-based to knowledge-based economies, they face different challenges and priorities, which impact on the nature and extent of government intervention in education, training, and business activity.

The annual Global Competitiveness Report, produced by the World Economic Forum (WEF 2012), analyses the relative competitiveness of nations and the challenges faced by governments in determining growth policies (Martin et al., 2008-9: 3). In its evaluation the report utilizes a variety of factors, which it identifies as the 'Twelve Pillars of Economic Competitiveness'. The first of these is a country's institutions. Other factors include primary and higher levels of education, training, and labour market efficiency.

Hence, vital components for an MNE's analysis of a country with a view to investment will include up-to-date information on its stage of development, the labour market, government incentives or controls on investment, as well as transparency considerations, which indicate the degree of corruption likely to be found. An additional factor is the level of technology available in the country, including internet communication and whether there are government-imposed restrictions on its use. More generally, the availability of technologies has become an essential prerequisite for involvement in a globalized economy (Martin et al., 2008-9: 3–6).

Stage of economic development and the transfer of skills

It has been suggested that MNEs are important vehicles for the transfer of modern human resource practices and skills from more developed economies to less developed environments. However, research indicates that skills transfer does *not* necessarily take place, as multinationals may use less developed environments as suitable places for continuing mass production and **Taylorist management approaches** (Gamble et al., 2004: 407). We can consider these ideas in Case Study 5.2.

Case Study 5.2 Multinationals' HR policies and national skills levels

This case discusses the way MNEs distribute low- or high-skill activities between overseas subsidiaries, and the consequences this has on HR policies.

While Malaysia may be a developing country, it is still being used as a base for the mass production of standardized goods by MNEs from more advanced economies in Asia, such as Japan and Taiwan. Gamble et al. (2004: 405) discuss how this transfer of mass production leads to the continuation of low-trust/low-investment HRM policies in countries where there is poor HRM capability.

In this situation MNE headquarters tends to adopt a policy of tight control over its affiliates. For example in Japanese affiliate companies in China, expatriates closely control operations using 'simple, explicit and fragmented HR practices' (Gamble et al., 2004: 406). In this way these Asian MNEs can retain high-commitment HR policies in their developed, home countries, while they transfer their mass production and de-skilled jobs to China and Malaysia.

Similarly, research has shown that the Japanese consumer electronics sector in Malaysia is characterized by automation and low skills levels, with key components either imported from Singapore or produced in Malaysia by other Japanese companies. The human resource strategy adopted in this case was driven by national differences in skill availability.

In the same way, the work organization found in clothing plants in China owned by MNEs from Japan and Korea reflected a low skills base. In contrast, plants in Japan and Korea employed high-commitment HR policies and practices, focusing on long-term employment, high remuneration, investment in training, and a degree of participation (Gamble et al., 2004: 405).

Adapted from Gamble et al. (2004)

 Discussion Activity 5.3

The research above by Gamble discusses the way MNEs select different countries for production activities, which require either low or high skills, and that this influences the type of HRM practices used.

Does your country have a predominantly low or highly skilled workforce? How does this affect investment there by MNEs?

Economic factors—cost and quality of living

Economic considerations, which influence decisions by MNEs to invest in different countries, will include national policies that promote economic stability and the control of inflation. Both factors affect the cost and the quality of living. The latter are very relevant in either attracting or deterring potential expatriates. Consulting firms conduct regular surveys of these factors. These guide IHRM specialists in working out compensation levels and hardship allowances for senior employees overseas. A review of 420 locations in 2011 identified the following top five cities with the highest *cost* of living: Luanda (Angola), Tokyo, Ndjamena (Chad), Moscow, and Geneva. However, these did not feature in those cities with the highest *quality* of living. These were: Vienna, Zurich, Auckland, Munich, Dusseldorf, and Vancouver (Mercer, 2011a and 2011b).

An additional economic pressure for MNEs has been the recent financial crisis, especially in its effect on currency values and international business. Unsurprisingly, then, multinationals are increasingly looking for ways to cut costs by reducing their reliance upon medium- and long-term expatriate assignments, together with initiatives to base expatriates' compensation on local rates of pay and income (Parakatil, 2009). In 2011 the financial crisis was joined by increased levels of world turmoil, and a resultant focus by MNEs on the personal safety of their expatriates (Parakatil 2011). Chapter 7, 'International reward management', expands on these issues in the section *Expatriate compensation*.

 Stop and Think

Take time to think of cities in your own country and compare them with cities in other countries, ones you have visited or know about. How would you rank these cities in relation to their (a) *cost* of living; and (b) *quality* of living?

Now think of the factors that you personally consider most important for your quality of living. Based on your list, rank the cities that you would personally like to live (and work) in.

Finally, how would you react if you were told your expatriate package was going to be 'localized'?

(For data on the cost and quality of living in different cities, please visit websites such as http://www.numbeo.com and http://www.expatistan.com.)

This section has considered national stages of development as indicated by a country's skills levels, the effect this has on the local labour market, and the country's resulting level of attractiveness for different types of MNE investment. It also identified the importance of the stability of the national economy and its significance for the cost of living and, therefore, for expatriate appointments.

We now move away from economic factors to look at the legal climate of a country. This too can have an impact on the MNE: in terms of the ease of doing business, the labour market, and its management of human resource issues.

National differences in legal systems and employment laws are perhaps the single most important reason for divergence between countries' HRM practices. Hence, IHRM professionals need to be constantly aware when operating in diverse legal jurisdictions and of the need to be up-to-date on legal developments.

Legislation as a key institutional factor

Legislation and ease of doing business

A World Bank report (2010) rates countries according to the ease of doing business. It ranks countries by assessing procedures and regulations associated with starting and conducting a business. These cover obtaining construction permits, employing workers, registering property, getting credit, protecting investors, paying taxes, trading across borders, enforcing contracts, as well as closing a business. The top ten countries include Singapore, Hong Kong, the USA, UK, Ireland, Canada, and Australia. Further down the list are: Malaysia (ranked 21), Germany (27), France (31), Spain (62), and China (91) (World Bank, 2010).

The ranking of China at 91 is indicative of the difficulties that MNEs face there. Legal restrictions, protectionism, and corruption all contribute to difficulties faced by organizations wishing to market their goods and services in China. Naturally, these issues make the work of expatriates in China extremely challenging; and such factors need to be considered by IHRM practitioners, especially when evaluating the performance of their expatriates. We can further explore the situation in China through Case Study 5.3.

Case Study 5.3 Obstacles to doing business in China

A recent article on selling foreign goods in China explains how MNEs continue to face legal obstacles in China (*The Economist*, 2009b). The report indicates that for giant drugs multinationals such as Pfizer, Astra Zeneca, and Bayer, China accounts for fewer than 2 per cent of their sales worldwide. Consumer goods conglomerates fair only a little better. Proctor and Gamble generates only 5 per cent of its sales in China and Unilever sells even less, making its operations barely profitable. AIG, the American insurance corporation, which operates out of Shanghai, is restricted to operating from just eight cities.

While a few foreign firms are doing relatively well, many face 'explicit legal impediments and hidden obstacles', which hamper their access to customers, despite promises made by China on joining the World Trade Organisation in 2001 (*The Economist*, 2009b). Moreover, 'publishing, telecommunications, oil exploration, marketing, pharmaceuticals, banking and insurance all remain either fiercely protected or off-limits to foreigners altogether. Corruption, protectionism and red tape hamper foreigners in all fields' (*The Economist*, 2009b).

Similar issues were again raised a year later in the *New York Times*, as follows: 'Western companies contend that they face a lengthening list of obstacles to doing business in China, including "buy Chinese" government procurement policies, widespread counterfeiting and growing restrictions on foreign investments' (Bradsher and Barboza, 2010).

These inherent problems have been confirmed by groups lobbying on behalf of foreign business. The American and European Chambers of Commerce and the US–China Business Council have reported that complaints concern mainly 'subsidized competition, restricted access, conflicting regulations, a lack of protection for intellectual property and opaque and arbitrary bureaucracy' (*The Economist*, 2009b)

Similarly, as mentioned above, the World Bank (2010) rankings for Ease of Doing Business, place China at number 91.

Finally, while MNEs would like to be able to get more effective legal advice on the situation, they are restricted in this too, since foreign law firms are not permitted to employ local Chinese lawyers (*The Economist*, 2009b).

Adapted from *The Economist* (2009b) and Bradsher and Barboza (2010) in the *New York Times* online.

Legislation and the labour market

Legislation on the marketing of goods by overseas firms is one way in which trade and business is controlled by nation states. Legislation is also used to adjust conditions in the labour market. For example laws on work permits can help to control access to a country in order to balance its need for skilled or unskilled workers. However, MNEs are interested in finding labour at the best price, and are often accused of pushing down wages and salaries in their pursuit of making profits.

Clearly, controlling costs by outsourcing to countries with cheaper labour is one way for employers to achieve their objectives. However, moving production from one country to another is not as simple as it seems, as the following example shows.

In their article on how Chinese companies can improve their performance, Dietz et al. (2008: 3) state that misjudgement of political, labour, and environmental risks can result in MNEs making mistakes in their overseas investments. They go on to suggest that China, as a relatively new player doing business overseas, has failed to assess risk adequately. So, for example, it failed in its attempt to acquire the American oil company Unocal because this was perceived as a threat by the US government to US interests. Also, China's electronics group, TCL Multimedia Technology, misjudged the complexity, cost, and time involved in closing a loss-making part of its newly acquired operation in France. This was because of a lack of awareness of the legal requirements of the redundancy process in France, as well as the prohibitive payments and costs associated with closing a factory there (Dietz et al., 2008: 3).

In light of these deficiencies and the complexities of legal requirements, the authors suggest that Chinese MNEs need to improve their research when considering acquisitions, recommending that they develop a handbook of guidelines and ensuring due diligence for any proposed merger or acquisition. More generally, they also suggest that China needs to upgrade its talent to meet the needs of global business, through training in management, leadership, communication, and cross-cultural skills (Dietz et al., 2008: 4–5).

Employment laws—divergence in human resource practices

The literature on IHRM pays great attention to whether HR policies and practices are converging or diverging across the world and the reasons for this. While culture has often been blamed for hindering any convergence, it is also suggested that national institutions, and significantly the laws associated with employment, are equally responsible for continuing divergence.

An analysis of differences in HR policies and practices across Europe has been based on the Cranet Survey (2008), and a series of related articles suggest that 'differences in HRM practices offerings persist, at least for now, and that differences in institutional environments are important explanatory factors' (Lazarova et al., 2008: 2002). The data collected in the Cranet survey cover six areas of IHRM policy and practice, as follows.

HRM organization and activity covering HR's strategic role and range of policies;

Staff practices such as planning workforce numbers, flexibility policies, diversity, and recruitment practices;

Employee development covering appraisal, training, development, and employee careers;

Compensation and benefits

Employee relations and communication TU membership and recognition, employer associations, and communication channels;

Organization details including data on workforce demographics, and organizational performance.

The following examples provide further insight into the range of working conditions that exist—and why institutional factors, particularly employment legislation, make it difficult for companies to apply human resource policies in the same way in different countries.

Employment laws—wages, working hours, and productivity

Throughout Europe there are collectively agreed statutory regulations on employees' working hours, with limitations set on the maximum hours that can be worked in a week. While these vary considerably between the old and new members of the European Union, the hours worked (including overtime) are much shorter than those found in many developing coun-tries. This applies particularly for factory and domestic workers, and immigrant labour. In addition, in EU countries there are statutory regulations on both annual leave and minimum wage rates.

However, salaries paid and hours worked vary quite considerably between European countries. This means that those in Eastern Europe are especially attractive to organizations wishing to reduce production costs. Less attractive to such MNEs might be Germany and France, where labour costs are higher and restrictions on working hours are stricter. A further consideration for MNEs is the productivity levels of employees. These too differ between countries.

Eurostat (2009) in its section on productivity in the EU, explains:

> Across the Member States there were wide ranging differences in apparent productivity levels and average personnel costs; both these ratios tended to be higher among the EU-15 ... The differences in average personnel costs across the Member States were also consider-able, as an employee working in the non-financial business economy in Belgium cost almost 17 times as much as someone working in Bulgaria.

The extent of national diversity is confirmed by the Eurofound Survey (2007). Thus, for exam-ple, the minimum wage rates paid in countries such as France, Belgium, and Ireland, are four times the rates paid in the Czech Republic, Hungary, and Estonia. Similarly, the actual weekly working hours for full-time employees are highest in Bulgaria, Romania, and the UK, while the lowest are reported in France, Italy, and Denmark—with a four-hour difference between the highest and lowest.

This information illustrates the clear possibility of MNEs being attracted to relocating their manufacturing plants to those European countries with lower pay and longer working hours, assuming productivity levels are comparable. However, when MNEs move operations be-tween countries for this purpose, they have been accused of social dumping. In this respect IHRM practitioners may be faced with difficult ethical decisions, since new jobs in one region result in redundancies in another. Social dumping is a controversial topic within the enlarged European Union, and a discussion on 'social dumping' can be found in the Eurofound Indus-trial Relations Dictionary (2009).

As mentioned above, MNEs are also likely to compare productivity levels between countries. Hence, arguments in favour of moving production to a low labour-cost destination, in Asia for example, may be offset by superior levels of productivity in high-wage, short-hours countries. This may provide a sound economic reason for production to stay in the west. More information on these concepts is available on the OECD website (2010).

Employment laws—annual leave and redundancy pay

According to a Survey on Working Time Developments (EIRO, 2007), annual paid leave varied considerably between member states: 'The average entitlement across the EU27 Member States for which data are available is 25.2 days ... Agreed annual leave entitlement within the EU15 varies considerably, from 33 days in Sweden to 23 days in Greece.'

A further legal difference between countries is the amount paid to employees when they are made redundant. Where this is high, as in France and Spain for example, it tends to lead to a lack of flexibility within the labour market. Employers in Spain have sought to overcome this problem by offering more workers temporary, short-term, and seasonal contracts. The latter are especially important for the tourism and agricultural sectors in Spain (Brewster et al., 2004: 163). In addition, in response to high unemployment and deficit problems in 2012, Spain's new government is seeking significant changes to employment conditions to try to increase flexibility. However, since these changes will reduce employment security they are opposed by the unions (*The Guardian*, 2012).

A particular example of considerable difference in working hours is that which exists between companies based in Europe and Japan. This is considered in Case Study 5.4.

 Case Study 5.4   Death by overwork

In complete contrast to the information on working hours in Europe given above, Japan has a record for expecting exceptionally long working hours as unpaid overtime from its employees. While working hours are stipulated by law for most workers, the legislation excludes managers and supervisors. The regulation states:

> Persons in positions of management or supervision and persons handling confidential administrative work who are closely involved in management are not subject to the regulations on working hours, breaks and days off (with the exception of regulations on night work).
>
> (JETRO, 2010)

As a result of the common practice for executives and managers to work excessive hours, the term *karoshi* has been coined. This means 'death by overwork', but it also encompasses the employee suffering permanent disability caused by this overwork (Iwasaki et al., 2006).

The situation has become so serious that legal claims against employers are increasing, with claimants receiving up to '$20,000 a year from the government and sometimes up to $1m from the company in damages' if their claim of death by overwork is accepted (*The Economist*, 2007). One example is Kenichi Uchino; an employee of Toyota, he was a victim of *karoshi* when he died after putting in more than 80 hours of overtime each month for six months.

Official figures could be misleading, since they indicate that the Japanese work on average 1780 hours a year, slightly less than Americans (1800 hours), though more than Germans (1440). However, these statistics do not count the 60 hours a week of 'free overtime' worked by most middle-aged men.

Cultural factors certainly contribute to this situation. Employees feel obliged to work these long hours. While they do not wish to lose their permanent positions secured through traditional life-long employment, they also put self-sacrifice for the group above the interests of the individual. It is through such sentiments towards extensive unpaid overtime that a company like Toyota is able to achieve its success. According to Hiroko Uchino, widow of Kenichi Uchino, 'It is because so many people work free overtime that Toyota reaps profits. I hope some of those profits can be brought back to help the employees and their families. That would make Toyota a true global leader' (*The Economist*, 2007).

The company promised to prevent *karoshi* in future, but recent press reports and studies indicate that the situation in Japan as a whole is not improving, as 'seven million workers work more than 60 hours a week and could die anytime from overwork' (Koji, 2010). This aspect of working life has been linked to suicide rates. Kondo and Oh (2010: 649) have analysed the potential reasons for the Japan-specific suicide trend over the past twelve years, noting that 'Japan showed the sharpest rise in suicide rate following the (economic) crisis and the rate has hovered at a record high to the present, despite a macroeconomic recovery afterwards.'

Employment laws—gender, age, and diversity

Gender and diversity issues are of growing importance in employment law and management practice, especially in Europe, where recent legislation adds protection given to women in terms of equal pay for equal work. In some countries there is a quota system for their representation at board level. Both France and the Netherlands have legislation pending on compulsory quotas of women on the boards of listed companies (Mercer, 2009).

In the UK a ruling in a landmark case in the Court of Appeal in 2009 prohibits using length of service as a basis for compensation, to ensure women are not discriminated against for time out for maternity leave or caring responsibilities. As the director of legal enforcement at the Equality and Human Rights Commission stated:

> Women should not be disadvantaged in the workforce because they take time out for maternity leave or to meet caring responsibilities. Linking pay to length of service often does them a disservice. Direct discrimination, long hours, and a lack of flexible working options are some of the biggest barriers to achieving gender equality in the workplace.
>
> (Uppal, 2009)

In those countries with ageing populations, employers are being faced with declining availability of an experienced and skilled workforce as the baby-boom generation is beginning to retire. As a consequence, in the UK the new Conservative–Liberal coalition government announced legislation to stop compulsory retirement at sixty-five to allow older workers the option of continuing in work (BBC News, 2010; *The Telegraph*, 2011). In Singapore efforts are being made to ensure that the employment of people over fifty is more attractive to employers, by reducing the contribution that they are required to make into the Central Provident Fund (Mercer, 2009).

The challenges facing Japan are especially visible.

> In 2008, the population of elderly citizens (65 years and over) was 28.22 million, constituting 22.1 per cent of the total population and marking record highs both in terms of number and percentage. The speed of ageing of Japan's population is much faster than in advanced Western European countries or the USA.
>
> (Statistical Handbook of Japan, 2009).

Major changes are required in the Japanese labour market to deal with the challenges of such an ageing population and a growing talent shortage. Perhaps more flexibility and possibilities for women in the workplace will be the outcome.

Diversity and sharia law

Multinational organizations need to pay close attention to local regulations and legal requirements in terms of diversity. They will need to ensure that their own recruitment, selection, promotion, and reward policies are in line with the law for each country in which they operate. International managers responsible for overseas appointments will also need to be alert to local laws.

MNEs may wish to implement their home country policies worldwide for easier internal management. However, managers may find that some of their HR policies do not conform to local legislation. Thus for example 'diversity' and the principles underlying diversity management programmes, which are generally accepted in the West, may prove problematic in Muslim countries. This is especially the case where sharia law is applied, whereby judgements are made on the basis of Islamic religious rules, based on the Koran.

It will be very important for expatriates to be made aware of local sharia laws, which may intrude on their personal lives and relationships and in the working environment. Expatriates need to be informed of what is considered acceptable behaviour inside and outside the workplace, for men and for women, including the acceptability of females working in various sectors, or even working at all. They should also appreciate the strict penalties that exist for disobeying sharia law.

This tension between competing ideas of diversity is discussed throughout Chapter 10, 'Diversity management in an international environment'.

The application of institutional theory to the study of MNEs

Until now we have provided a broad overview of the multiple institutional pressures that impact on the HR practices of MNEs operating in various countries. However, while it is useful to identify the different national and institutional requirements that impact on HRM for comparative purposes, it makes little sense to try to determine the impact of one factor in isolation.

In addition to this, it is evident that each of the factors identified above will impact differently on different MNEs. Much will depend on an MNE's country and sector of operation, its international strategy, and its internal environment. Thus, for any particular MNE we need to know the broader context and the complexity of its IHRM, taking account of its national and international operations, which are affected by multiple laws and employment conditions. It is from this position that we now continue our discussion of institutional theory.

Analysing institutional complexity

Institutional theory has evolved over the past thirty years into one of the leading perspectives in organizational analysis (Mizruchi and Fein, 1999; Palmer and Biggart, 2002, cited in Heugens and Lander, 2009). Its main line of argument is that 'organisations are constrained and supported by institutional forces' (Scott, 1995: 55, cited in Guillen and Suarez, 2005: 123). Quite simply, MNEs are affected by the institutions of their home country, which in turn influence their subsidiaries overseas. At the same time, subsidiaries are also affected by the institutions of the host countries within which they operate.

However, an institutional analysis of an MNE can be highly complex. As MNEs grow they become multidimensional and heterogeneous. Their interests incorporate multiple geographic markets, product lines, and activities. Thus, diversified MNEs have complicated structures and numerous stakeholders, such that MNEs face difficult choices and decisions (Doz and Prahalad, 2005: 21). The complexity of these factors presents a challenge for researchers into institutional theory, as they are faced with unravelling the impact of institutions on MNEs and on their choice of policies and practices. Kostova et al. (2008: 1001) convey the extent of this institutional complexity, suggesting that MNEs 'are embedded in multiple, fragmented, ill-defined, and constantly evolving institutional systems conceptualized at different levels of analysis, each characterized by a distinct institutional process and degree of determinism in shaping organisational behavior'.

As a result MNEs' relationships with institutions are regarded as 'dynamic, discretionary, symbolic, and pro-active' (Kostova et al., 2008: 1001). Moreover, MNEs have not only to *comply* with institutional pressures. They also have an *agency* role, which means they need to 'make sense of and manipulate, negotiate and partially construct their institutional environments' (Kostova et al., 2008: 1001).

This argument, regarding the complexity of the context within which MNEs operate, is the basis of Kostova et al.'s critique of the more simplified approach, which restricts its focus to a relatively narrow type of institution.

One feature of MNE complexity is that they operate within a framework of having to combine global integration with local responsiveness. Thus, managers who set themselves the target of working towards a more transnational MNE form, are faced simultaneously with pressures to localize products and simultaneously benefit from the technical and economic advantages of cross-border coordination and division of labour (Westney, 2005: 59). At the same time they are subject to competing, 'isomorphic' pressures to achieve consistency. On the one hand there are 'isomorphic pulls' that act as 'pressures for consistency within the MNE'. On the other hand there are 'pressures for isomorphism within the local environment' (Rosenzweig and Singh, 1991, cited in Westney, 2005: 60).

Isomorphic pressures

According to neo-institutionalist theory, organizations also face pressure to imitate *each other*. This can be in one of three ways: **coercive**, **mimetic**, and **normative**. This version of homogenization or **isomorphism** is a 'process that forces organisations that face the same set of environmental conditions, to use similar practices' (DiMaggio and Powell, 1983, cited in Muratbekova-Touron, 2009: 611).

These pressures are said to be 'coercive' when practices are political, being imposed by a more powerful authority, which could be the organization on which the MNE depends or the institutions and cultural expectations of the society within which it functions. An MNE's 'mimetic' response to uncertainty is when it adopts a standard solution or strategy already successfully used by others, including competitors. Finally, an MNE's actions can be described as 'normative' when the practices adopted are considered the norm or are regarded as 'professional' in that environment. Hence, neo-institutional theory suggests that organizations become increasingly isomorphic over time as they collectively incorporate templates for organizing from their institutional environments, in search of legitimacy (Heugens and Lander 2009: 61 and 68).

Agency theory

However, those who advocate **agency theory** disagree and suggest that organizations can respond to institutional pressures in different ways. By way of example, this approach seeks to explain different responses by MNEs to institutional pressures and internal conflicts, as when an MNE faces internal conflicts between the interests and preferences of its headquarters (the *principal*) and those of its subsidiary (the *agent*). Muratbekova-Touron (2009: 609) explains that 'The principal assumes that the agent will behave opportunistically in pursuit of his/her personal interests, which are in conflict with those of the principal.' However, the principal has imperfect information regarding the behaviour and performance of the agent, leading to increased **agency costs**, which arise when the interests of the principal conflict with those of its subsidiaries. The cultural and geographical distance between principal and agency further increase information asymmetry and hence agency costs (Muratbekova-Touron, 2009: 610). See Chaper 13 for further discussion of agency theory, in the section *Headquarters subsidiary distance*.

Managing international HRM

It is evident from research on institutional theory that there are multiple drivers, including complex institutional factors, which combine to determine the behaviour of MNEs in global markets and more especially their choice of global and national HRM policies and practices (Farndale and Paauwe, 2007: 355).

MNEs have to manage conflicting external environments, not only their home country institutional influences, but also those facing their various subsidiaries. In addition, according to Kostova et al. (2008: 997), MNEs also have to deal with 'complex internal environments, with spatial, cultural, and organisational distance; language barriers; inter-unit power struggles; and possible inconsistencies and conflict among the interests, values, practices, and routines used in the various parts of the organisation'.

Farndale and Paauwe (2007) focus on the different ways MNEs react to institutional and competitive pressures when selecting their approach to IHRM. They suggest that organizations face external global competitive pressures, national institutional pressures, and the simultaneous internal processes of strategic choice and competitive differentiation. As a result, MNEs may choose different patterns of *adoption*, *adaptation*, or *innovation* of IHRM practices.

These authors investigated fourteen financially successful MNEs operating in seventeen countries, to find out what HR policies they used to achieve their impressive level of performance (Farndale and Paauwe, 2007: 357, and 361–2). Their research illustrates how organizations need to handle potentially conflicting theoretical perspectives, such as neo-institutional theory, the resource-based view, strategic balance theory, human agency, and strategic choice. It also indicates that *similarities* amongst MNEs at the global level were driven by external competitive factors such as the adoption of best practices. Similarities at the national level were the result of external institutional sources such as legislation, national traditions, and expectations. However, by contrast, the authors conclude that '*Differences* in approach between MNEs at both the global and national levels seem to be predominantly led by *internal competitive processes*, such as the corporate strategy, structure or culture' (Farndale and Paauwe, 2007: 371).

The impact of institutional influences

The most effective way to investigate the impact of institutional influences is to examine the behaviour of individual MNEs and the pressures they face when adopting IHRM policies and practices. Ideally such policies and practices will help tackle inherent conflicts by coordinating and regulating behaviours across the organization.

Case Study 5.5 considers a particular approach: an MNE's adoption of a competency-based leadership model. It also deals with a complex range of institutional factors, which come into play because it involves an acquisition.

Case Study 5.5   Why a multinational company introduces a competency-based leadership model: a two-theory approach

This case is based on research into the reasons why a French MNE adopted a competency-based leadership model, following its acquisition of an Anglo-Saxon MNE, which led to the company doubling in size and geographical spread. The case illustrates the multiple pressures and factors surrounding the choice of this leadership model.

The research uses both (a) neo-institutional theory; and (b) agency theory to provide insights into (i) the driving forces; and (ii) the rationale for the MNE's decision to introduce a competency-based leadership model. The neo-institutional view emphasizes the pressures on the MNE from its institutional environments, pointing to a need to adjust structures and behaviours if the NME is to gain legitimacy and improve its chances of survival. The agency view stresses the initiative taken by the MNE's decision makers, so that their strategy-based competency approach is cited as a reason for the choice. The analysis also reveals how both institutional and cultural concepts can become blurred when explaining HR policy choices.

The competency-based leadership model was chosen to resolve some of the agency cost factors, resulting from problems associated with conflicts between the principal and its subsidiaries. In this case these agency cost factors probably arose due to the relationship between the principal (French) with its multiple (Anglo-Saxon) subsidiaries (agents). To manage the global integration–local adaptation, the company had to choose between (a) Anglo-Saxon formalized processes; and (b) socialization, favoured by European countries. The leadership model was chosen to help build a common, formalized language regarding leadership requirements, and to develop leaders who shared organizational values. Both institutional and cultural differences (values) were cited, with the model being chosen to resolve potential conflicts and to introduce consistency in leadership development and evaluation.

The concept of 'mimetic isomorphism' is also used to explain the choice of model, as the model is a currently popular practice, used successfully by other multinationals.

In adopting this competency-based model the company hoped to gain both internal and external organizational legitimacy, and a mechanism of cultural control, to develop trustworthy agents, and to reduce agency costs.

This case provides an excellent overview of institutional theory combined with agency theory, and their application to an HR policy decision in a multinational. It shows that national institutional pressures are not sufficient to explain policy decisions in MNEs, and that both internal and external pressures on MNEs need consideration.

Adapted from: Muratbekova-Touron (2009)

Summary

This chapter has discussed the impact of national institutions on IHRM and has introduced different approaches to its study. It then examined a number of institutional factors that impact on the management of human resources, and that need to be considered by organizations operating overseas. This will include the historical context within which business operates. This was explored through national policies on language and education. The relevance of the stage of development was also evaluated, including the political, economic, and legal climate within which business operates. More specifically, this was considered through the ease of doing business, the cost and quality of living, and the impact of legislation on labour markets and on IHRM. Diversity in HRM practices in terms of wages, hours, leave, and redundancy, were briefly considered, as were some of the contemporary pressures in the social environment, such as gender issues, ageing populations, and diversity in the context of sharia law.

This enabled us to appreciate that whilst national institutions and legislation may result in divergence of HR practices, regional policies and legislation such as that in the European Union is leading to some degree of convergence. Although for the most part such institutional effects seem easier to identify than cultural effects, we can best understand the way business is done and how employees are managed by considering both of these factors together.

Finally, a review of recent debates on the value of institutional theory indicated that in large MNEs, cultural, institutional, and numerous internal pressures, determine the IHRM policies and practices chosen and the strategies they adopt. However, the complexity of applying institutional theory across a diversified MNE suggests that it may be very difficult to unravel the national institutional pressures and differentiate them from other influences. In determining IHRM policy choices it would seem unwise to make sweeping statements regarding the strength of institutional pressures alone.

Review questions

1. Identify and outline the main approaches to analysing institutions.

2. Why is the historical context an important element to consider when evaluating a country as a destination for an international business?

3. Compare the business systems of two countries. In what ways do they differ and what effect does this have on their labour markets and human resource management?

4. Why is it important for an IHR manager to understand a country's stage of development?

5. Why does an IHR manager in charge of expatriate appointments need to know about the cost and quality of living of a country? Which HR policies will enable these aspects to be managed?

6. Why is the 'ease of doing business' in a country a significant factor when considering the performance of an expatriate? Support your answer with specific examples.

7. Explain some of the key differences that exist within Europe in terms of employment conditions. What effect might these have on MNEs and their expansion plans?

8. In your opinion which diversity issues are most pressing in your country and why?

9. To what extent can institutional theory be used to evaluate the HR policy decisions of MNEs?

10. International mergers and acquisitions provide particular difficulties for HR managers. Given the range of ideas presented in this chapter, which HR practices might be most influenced by institutional differences? To answer this question, consider two countries you know well.

Further reading

Farndale, E. and Paauwe, J. (2007) Uncovering competitive and institutional drivers of HRM practices in multinational corporations, *Human Resource Management Journal*, 17(4): 355–75.
This article attempts to explain firms' different reactions to institutional and competitive demands and the ways they select their approach to IHRM. Based upon extensive case-study research, it identifies how MNEs adopt, adapt, or innovate, in the face of internal processes and external global/national pressures.

Kostova T., Roth, K., and Dacin, M.T. (2008) Institutional theory in the study of multinational corporations: a critique and new directions, *Academy of Management Review*, 33(4): 994–1006.
This is an excellent critique of recent literature on the institutional perspective, which challenges the validity of the traditional approach to this research.

McGuire, J. and Dow, S. (2009) Japanese keiretsu: past, present, future, *Asia Pacific Journal of Management*, 26(June): 333–51.
This provides an insight into the continued role of keiretsu in the Japanese economy, in the light of the post-1992 decline, with a discussion of the persistence and benefits of these groupings today.

Warner, M. (ed.) (2003) *Culture and Management in Asia*, London: RoutledgeCurzon.
This book provides insights into the history, economy, culture, and management of thirteen Asian countries.

Bibliography

Bamber, G.J., Lansbury, R.D., and Wailes, N. (eds) (2004) *International Comparative Employment Relations, Globalisation and the Developed Market Economies*, 4th edn, London: Sage.

BBC News (2010) Fixed retirement age to be axed, 29 July, online at http://www.bbc.co.uk/news/business-10796718 (accessed 4 May 2012).

Bradsher, K. and Barboza, D. (2010) Google is not alone in discontent, but its threat to leave stands out, *New York Times*, Global Business, 13 January, online at http://query.nytimes.com/gst/fullpage.html?res=9505E3DE1F3AF937A25752C0A9669D8B63&pagewanted=all (accessed 10 June 2012).

Brewster, C. and Larsen, H. (1992) Human resource management in Europe: evidence from 10 countries, *International Journal of Human Resource Management*, 3: 409–34.

—, Mayrhofer, W., and Morley, M. (eds) (2004) *HRM in Europe, Evidence of Convergence*, Oxford: Butterworth Heinemann.

Casley Gera, R. (2007) International arbitration: Spanish ambition, *Chambers* Magazine, 22, online at http://www.chambersmagazine.co.uk/Article/International-Arbitration-SPANISH-AMBITION (accessed 4 May 2012).

Cranet Survey (2008) Articles using the Cranet Survey data, *International Journal of Human Resource Management*, November Vol. 19, No. 11.

Dietz, M.C., Orr, G., and Xing, J. (2008) How Chinese companies can succeed abroad, *McKinsey Quarterly*, May: 1–8.

Dos Santos, T. (1970) The structure of dependence, Papers and Proceedings of the 82nd Annual Meeting of the American Economic Association, *American Economic Review*, May: 231–6, online at http://pics3441.upmf-grenoble.fr/articles/inde/The%20Structure%20of%20Dependence.pdf (accessed 10 June 2012).

Doz, Y.L. and Prahalad, C.K. (2005) 'Managing MNCs: a search for a new Paradigm, in S. Ghoshal and E. D. Westney (eds) *Organization Theory and the Multinational Corporation*, 2nd edn, Basingstoke: Palgrave Macmillan, pp. 20–44.

The Economist (2007) Death by overwork in Japan, jobs for life, 19 December, online at http://www.economist.com/node/10329261 (accessed 10 June 2012).

— (2009a) Italy's business clusters sinking together, Italian manufacturing hubs have not withstood the recession as hoped, 15 October, online at http://rss.economist.com/node/14667830 (accessed 10 June 2012).

— (2009b) Selling foreign goods in China, impenetrable, 15 October, online at http://www.economist.com/node/14660438 (accessed 10 June 2012).

Edison, H. (2003) How strong are the links between institutional quality and economic performance? *Finance and Development* [quarterly magazine of the IMF], 40(2, June): 35–7., online at http://www.imf.org/external/pubs/ft/fandd/2003/06/index.htm (accessed 24 October 2012).

Embassy of Japan (2011) The Malaysian look east policy, Culture and Education, Japan Information Service, Embassy of Japan, Malaysia, online at http://www.my.emb-japan.go.jp/English/JIS/education/LEP.htm (accessed 4 May 2012).

Eurofound (2007) European Foundation for the Improvement of Living and Working Conditions, EIRO, Working time developments—2007, Annual leave, online at http://www.eurofound.europa.eu/eiro/studies/tn0804029s/tn0804029s.htm (accessed 4 May 2012).

Eurofound (2009) European Industrial Relations Dictionary, 'Social dumping', online at: http://www.eurofound.europa.eu/areas/industrialrelations/dictionary/definitions/socialdumping.htm (accessed 4 May 2012).

Eurostat (2009) Statistics explained, European business, facts and figures, section 1.5 productivity, online at http://epp.eurostat.ec.europa.eu/statistics_explained/index.php/Business_economy_-_expenditure,_productivity_and_profitability (accessed 27 July 2012).

Evans, P., Pucik, V., and Barsoux, J.-L. (2002) *The Global Challenge, Frameworks for International Human Resource Management*, Boston, MA and London: McGraw-Hill.

Farndale, E. and Paauwe, J. (2007) Uncovering competitive and institutional drivers of HRM practices in multinational corporations, *Human Resource Management Journal*, 17(4) 355–75.

—, Brewster, C., and Poutsmac, E. (2008) Coordinated vs liberal market HRM: the impact of institutionalization on multinational firms, *International Journal of Human Resource Management*, 19(11, November): 2004–23.

Feely, A. (2003) Communication across language boundaries, in M. Tayeb (ed.) *International Management, Theories and Practice*, Upper Saddle River, NJ: Prentice Hall, pp. 225–6.

Frank, A.G. (1967) The underdevelopment of development, February 1991 revision, online at http://www.druckversion.studien-von-zeitfragen.net/The%20Underdevelopment%20of%20Development.htm (accessed 10 June 2012).

Gamble, J., Morris, J., and Wilkinson, B. (2004) Mass production is alive and well: the future of work and

organisation in East Asia, *International Journal of Human Resource Management*, 15(2): 1–13.

The Guardian (2012) Austerity: the pain in Spain, 29 March, online at http://www.guardian.co.uk/commentisfree/2012/mar/29/austerity-pain-in-spain (accessed 10 June 2012).

Guillen, M.F. and Suarez, S.L. (2005) The institutional context of multinational activity, in S. Ghoshal and D.E. Westney (eds) *Organization Theory and the Multinational Corporation*, 2nd edn, Basingstoke: Palgrave Macmillan, pp.123–45.

Hall, P. and Soskice, D.W. (2001) *Varieties of Capitalism: The Institutional Foundations of Comparative Advantage*, Oxford: Oxford University Press.

Heugens, P.P. and Lander, M.W. (2009) Structure! Agency! (and other quarrels): a meta-analysis of institutional theories of organization, *Academy of Management Journal*, 52(1): 61–85.

Hickson, D.J., Hinings, C.R., McMillan, C.J., and Schwitter, J.P. (1974) The culture-free context of organization structure: a tri-national comparison, *Sociology*, 8(January): 159–80.

Iwasaku, K., Takahshi, M., and Nakata, A. (2006) Health problems due to long working hours in Japan: working hours, workers' compensation (*karoshi*), and preventive measures, *Country Report, Industrial Health*, 44: 537–40.

JETRO (2010) Investing in Japan, Section 4.5 Laws and regulations on setting up a business in Japan, Legislation on working hours, breaks and days off, online at http://www.jetro.go.jp/en/invest/setting_up/ (accessed 4 May 2012).

Katz, H. and Darbishire, O. (2000) *Converging Divergences: Worldwide Changes in Employment Systems*, Ithaca, NY: Cornell University Press.

Kitchen, P.J. and Ahmad, S.Z. (2007) Outward investments by developing country firms: the case of emerging Malaysian corporations, *International Journal of Business and Management*, 2(4, August): 122–35.

Koji, M. (2010) Seven million Japanese could possibly die from overwork, *Japan Press Weekly*, 14 July, online at http://www.japan-press.co.jp/modules/news/index.php?id=1453 (accessed 4 May 2012).

Kondo, N. and Oh, J. (2010) Suicide and *karoshi* (death from overwork) during the recent economic crises in Japan: the impacts, mechanisms and political responses, *Journal of Epidemiological Community Health*, 64: 649–50.

Kostova, T., Roth, K., and Dacin, M.T. (2008) Institutional theory in the study of multinational corporations: a critique and new directions, *Academy of Management Review*, 33(4): 994–1006.

Kuznets, S. (1963) Notes on take-off, in W. W. Rostow (ed.) *The Economics of Take-Off into Sustained Growth*, London: Macmillan, ch. 2.

Lane, C. (1991) Industrial reorganization in Europe: patterns of convergence and divergence in Germany, France and Britain, *Work Employment & Society*, 5(4, December): 515–39.

Lazarova, M., Morley, M., and Tyson, S. (2008) Introduction: international comparative studies in HRM and performance—the Cranet data, *International Journal of Human Resource Management*, 19(11, November): 1995–2003.

Lewis, M.P. (ed.) (2009) *Ethnologue: Languages of the World*, 16th edn, Dallas, TX: SIL International, online at http://www.ethnologue.com/ethno_docs/distribution.asp?by=size (accessed 10 June 2012).

Lincoln, J.R. and Shimotani, M. (2009) *Whither the Keiretsu, Japan's Business Networks? How Were They Structured? What Did They Do? Why Are They Gone?*, Institute for Research on Labor and Employment, Working Paper Series, Berkeley, CA: University of California Press, Paper iirwps 188–09, online at http://www.irle.berkeley.edu/workingpapers/188-09.pdf (accessed 4 May 2012).

McGuire, J. and Dow, S. (2009) Japanese keiretsu: past, present, future, *Asia Pacific Journal of Management*, 26(June): 333–51.

Martin, X.S.I., Blanke, J., Handuz, M.D., Geiger, T., Mia, I., and Paua, F. (2008–9) *Global Competitiveness Report*, World Economic Forum, chapter 1.1.

Maurice, M., Sorge, A., and Warner, M. (1980) Societal differences in organizing manufacturing units: a comparison of France, West Germany, and Great Britain, *Organization Studies*, 1(1, January): 59–86.

Mercer (2009) *Mercer International Headlines*, France and the Netherlands announce proposals to implement quotas for women on boards. Singapore incentive of reduced CPF contribution for over 50s to remain in place to encourage them to stay at work, 4 November.

— (2011a) Quality of living, worldwide city rankings 2011, online at http://www.mercer.com/press-releases/quality-of-living-report-2011 (accessed 4 May 2012).

— (2011b) Mercer worldwide cost of living survey 2011, city rankings, online at http://www.mercer.com/press-releases/1311145) (accessed 4 May 2012).

Mueller, F. (1994) Societal effect, organizational effect and globalization—special issue on cross-national organization culture, *Organization Studies*, Summer, online at http://findarticles.com/p/articles/mi_m4339/is_n3_v15/ai_15687867/?tag=content;col1 (accessed 10 June 2012).

Muratbekova-Touron, M. (2009) Why a multinational company introduces a competency-based leadership model: a two-theory approach, *International Journal of Human Resource Management*, 20(3, March): 606–32.

Organisation for Economic Cooperation and Development (OECD) (2010) International comparisons of labour productivity levels—estimates for 2004, September 2005, online at http://www.oecd.org/dataoecd/31/7/29880166.pdf (accessed 10 June 2012).

Parakatil, S. (2009) Quality of living global city rankings, 28 April, in *Global HR News*, online at http://www.globalhrnews.com/story.asp?sid=642 (accessed 4 May 2012).

— (2011) Mercer's 2011 Quality of living ranking highlights—global (including a short video report), online at http://www.mercer.com/articles/quality-of-living-survey-report-2011 (accessed 4 May 2012).

Pinar Guzman, B. (2009) The Court of Arbitration of Madrid launches new arbitration rules, *Lexology*, 25 February, online at http://www.lexology.com/library/detail.aspx?g=71f4c31e-31ee-4fd0-a49f-20030c5e1a25 (accessed 4 May 2012).

Porter, M.E. and Hickson, D. (2007) *Great Writers on Organizations*, Aldershot: Ashgate.

— and Schwab, K. (2009) *2008-9 Global Competitiveness Report*, Harvard University & World Economic Forum, ch. 1.1, p. 4, online at https://members.weforum.org/pdf/GCR08/GCR08.pdf (accessed 27 July 2012).

— Sachs, J.D., and McArther, J.W. (2002) *2001–2 Summary, Global Competitiveness Report: Stages of Economic Development*, Geneva: World Economic Forum.

Rasanen, K. and Whipp, R. (1992) National business recipes: a sector perspective, in R. Whitley (ed.) *European Business Systems: Firms and Markets in their National Contexts*, London: Sage, pp. 46–60.

Redding, G. (2002) The capitalist business system of China and its rationale, *Asia Pacific Journal of Management*, 19: 221–49.

— (2003) *The Evolution of Business Systems, Euro-Asia Centre Report No 72*, INSEAD, Fontainbleau and Singapore, online at http://www.insead.edu/facultyresearch/research/doc.cfm?did=1287 (accessed 9 June 2012).

— (2005) The thick description and comparison of societal systems of capitalism, *Journal of International Business Studies*, 36(March): 123–55.

Rostow, W.W. (1960) *The Stages of Economic Growth*, Cambridge: Cambridge University Press.

Sorge, A. (2010) *Internationalisation and Organisation, Conceptual Approach*, Berlin: Research Unit, Social Science Research Centre, online at http://www.wzb.eu/gwd/into/default.en.htm (accessed 10 April 2011).

Statistical Handbook of Japan (2009) *Declining Birth Rate and Ageing Population Statistics Bureau*, ch. 2, Japan: Ministry of Information and Communication, online at http://www.stat.go.jp/english/data/handbook (accessed 4 May 2012).

Tayeb, M. (2004) *International Human Resource Management*, Oxford: Oxford University Press.

The Telegraph (2011) Government scraps default retirement age, 13 January, online at http://www.telegraph.co.uk/finance/personalfinance/pensions/8256828/Government-scraps-default-retirement-age.html (accessed 4 May 2012).

Thirlwall, A.P. (2006) *Growth and Development, with Special Reference to Developing Economies*, 8th edn, Basingstoke: Palgrave Macmillan.

Uppal, S. (2009) Statement by Susie Uppal, Director of Legal Enforcement at the Commission, The Equality and Human Rights Commission, on 20 October, online at http://www.equalityhumanrights.com/news/2009/october/women-in-some-jobs-who-have-time-off-to-raise-children-get-pay-equality-boost-after-landmark-ruling/ (accessed 27 July 2012).

Warner, M. (ed.) (2003) *Culture and Management in Asia*, London: RoutledgeCurzon.

Westney, D.E. (2005) Institutional theory and the multinational corporation, in S. Ghoshal and D. E. Westney (eds) *Organization Theory and the Multinational Corporation*, 2nd edn, Basingstoke: Palgrave Macmillan, pp. 47–67.

Whitley, R. (1994) *European Business Systems: Firms and Markets in their National Contexts*, London: Sage.

— (1999) *Divergent Capitalisms: The Social Structuring and Change of Business Systems*, Oxford: Oxford University Press.

Witt, M. and Redding, G. (2009) Culture, meaning, and institutions: executive rationale in Germany and Japan, *Journal of International Business Studies*, 40(5): 859–85, online at http://www.insead.edu/facultyresearch/faculty/personal/mwitt/research/documents/Witt_Redding_JIBS_2009.pdf (accessed 10 June 2012).

World Bank (2010) Doing business, economy rankings, online at http://www.doingbusiness.org/rankings (accessed 10 June 2012).

World Economic Forum (WEF) (2012) *Global Competitiveness Report 2011–2012*, online at http://www.weforum.org/reports (accessed 26 December 2012).

Zaaba, Z., Ramadan, F.I., Niane, I., Anning, A., Gunggu, H., and Umemoto, K. (2011) Language-in-education policy: a study of policy adjustment strategy in Malaysia, *International Journal of Education and Technologies*, 2(5), online at https://dspace.jaist.ac.jp/dspace/bitstream/10119/9488/1/509.pdf (accessed 10 June 2012).

 Visit the Online Resource Centre for web links, interactive glossary, and more: http://www.oxfordtextbooks.co.uk/orc/crawley.

Part II

The challenges of HRM in MNEs

6

Global staffing

 Learning Outcomes

After reading this chapter you will be able to:

- explain how different approaches to international staffing have evolved
- explain and discuss why different approaches are found in different countries
- identify issues relating to the international use of different selection methods
- understand resourcing strategies and practices in MNCs.

Introduction

Selection, resourcing, and staffing are all used to describe the processes through which organizations attract, select, and align people into jobs. Collings et al. (2009) defined global staffing in the context of multinational companies (MNCs) as filling key positions in head-quarters and subsidiaries—but a broader definition is adopted here to embrace staffing across a wider range of jobs. International human resource management (IHRM) captures two distinct aspects of staffing: understanding how selection decisions are made in different countries; and the selection of people for international assignments. Getting staffing decisions right, whether at local or global level, is important because poor staffing decisions have big downsides: the cost of lost opportunities (what could have been achieved with 'better' people); the costs of re-recruiting if people leave soon after being appointed; and the costs of managing poor performers. But what differences do international operations make to the way people are recruited and selected? Six reasons have been identified to explain why global staffing has become a critical and distinctive area for IHRM (Collings and Scullion, 2006).

1. There is increasing recognition that organizational success is linked to having the right people in key posts.
2. Global staffing is more complex than staffing solely at a domestic level.
3. Expatriate performance can be problematic.
4. There is a shortage of international management talent, which means that organizations need to look harder to find it.
5. International staffing is important to more organizations as they internationalize their operations.
6. New strategies such as inpatriation (foreigners relocated to the parent country for education and training) reflect greater emphasis on developing the international manager.

Staffing is central to acquiring and developing human capital, and the unique social relationships that arise among groups of employees contributes to the unique resources that underpin competitive advantage. As organizations recognize the potential impact of strategic human resource management (HRM) on organizational performance, staffing is arguably the human resource practice that has the most impact overall. Other practices, such as reward and training, can be redesigned to fit strategic priorities, as can selection; but the legacy of past selection decisions, and the time to harvest impact from new appointments, emphasize the criticality of getting staffing decisions right. This chapter begins by noting how international staffing has recently been evolving, before looking at the contextual factors that help to explain why approaches to staffing differ on an international scale. Cross-cultural and biasing effects on the main selection methods are then considered.

Broad approaches to staffing

Corporate approaches

The classic approach to staffing in MNCs used Parent Country Nationals (PCNs) (expatriates) to manage and oversee the employment of local labour (Briscoe et al., 2009). It is now much more complicated. Contemporary organizational structures (joint ventures, mergers, acquisitions, alliances) call for a more mobile cadre of managers from the parent country and elsewhere. There is also more concern for the exercise of social responsibility in relation to terms and conditions of employment for local labour in developing countries, where employee protection through the law may be minimal. Social responsibility considerations also negate the classic model of gearing around expatriate PCNs as it was always imperialistic in nature and ignored the availability of local talent. Four general approaches can now be identified (Shen and Edwards, 2004):

1. traditional strategy of filling key positions with Parent Country Nationals (an ethnocentric approach);
2. filling key positions in host countries with Host Country Nationals (polycentric);
3. ignoring nationality and filling key posts with the best people (geocentric);
4. dividing the organization into regional operations (for example Africa, Europe) and staffing from within the region (regiocentric).

(See Chapter 3, 'Key academic models, theories, and debates', Perlmutter's EPRG model of international strategies, in the section entitled *The growth of international business and management*.)

The choice of approach is an outcome of a range of factors such as organizational strategy, local economic and political conditions, stage of organizational development, and subsidiary performance. Ethnocentric approaches might be favoured if an MNC needs to manage a new venture, turn around a struggling subsidiary, or expand into new territories where there is little local knowledge of technologies or markets. Political commitment to employing locals, as is currently found in the Gulf States through policies of Omanization and Saudization, for example, supports a polycentric approach.

Ethnocentric approaches describe the classic staffing approach and give tight control over subsidiary operations. They are, however, harder to justify, given the much wider availability of talent on an international level compared to the 1960s and 1970s, when IHRM was an emerging discipline. Host country policies may also clash with ethnocentric staffing if it is deemed to be against national interests. Polycentric approaches leverage local knowledge of language and culture and circumvent the need for expatriate reward packages. The downside can be one of 'distance' between the parent company and local managers in terms of management approaches and objectives. Geocentric approaches require high investment in **learning and development (L&D)** for global managers and high relocation costs. Regiocentric approaches are a sub-set of geocentric approaches but have the advantage of limiting managers to geographic regions where cultural and ethnic differences are smaller (Shen and Edwards, 2004).

One implication of the complex situation that now exists is the role of planning in relation to staffing the global enterprise. This is about planning to put people into key positions and planning to ensure the right skills are available and in place. Staffing, therefore, interconnects with management development, career planning, and the new theme of global talent management (discussed throughout Chapter 13, 'Global talent management'). A lack of data about the labour market in some countries may impede planning. Labour markets differ in terms of the number of people available for work, age structures of the workforce, education levels, participation of women, wage levels, and attitudes to work, among other variables. These local differences have to be considered when making staffing decisions. However, labour markets are only one of a set of local, contextual factors that influence the shape of recruitment and selection strategies.

Local factors

In addition to an MNC's preferences for how it wants to place people in different countries, five local factors influence staffing decisions.

1. **Legal frameworks and legislative cultures** In the USA, for instance, employers and employee representatives are sensitive to the principle that decisions based on selection methods are valid and as such there needs to be evidence that performance in a particular method relates to performance in a job. Weak evidence for a link means that employers will have little or no faith in the test and there have been several lawsuits in the USA challenging an employer's use of tests on the basis of insufficient evidence that the decisions arising from them are valid predictors of future performance. As such, the legislative culture in a country affects the ways in which new appointments and promotions are made.

2. **The level of concern and commitment to equality and fair and equal treatment** Cultures that are dominated by the value of networks and relationships are more likely to use simple, unstructured selection methods because simpler methods can more easily be used to justify selection decisions. Highly structured methods and processes would generate evidence that makes justifying the appointment of 'preferred' candidates much harder.

3. **Attitudes towards applicant privacy** Where a local culture values personal privacy, then selection methods are less likely to use group selection methods such as assessment

centres, in which group selection exercises are common. Hence the choice of process is influenced by the level of social interaction deemed acceptable.

4.   **Perceived relevance of different methods in relation to different jobs** While a wide range of selection methods is available to use, opinion will differ on which methods are best matched to a particular job. Selection for high-level, high-impact jobs typically involves a series of data collection stages and decision points such that a shortlist of potentially appointable candidates is produced. Personality assessment may be used for senior management posts, but not for junior appointments. Lower-level jobs are less likely to use intensive selection methods.

5.   **The labour market** The state of the market in terms of levels of unemployment, competition for jobs, demographic characteristics, and the competences sought by employers influence selection options, and this is discussed in more detail in the following section, *Labour markets*.

Labour markets

The conditions that exist in a labour market help to explain why different organizations adopt different HRM practices at any point in time. Depending on the skills needed, an MNC may be recruiting locally, for example, for low-skilled operatives, or recruiting globally for senior managers. Labour markets vary widely on a range of dimensions that include:

1. the availability of skills to employers—this is not simply a feature of market size, as skill shortages can occur in a large labour market with full employment;

2. local education systems that have considerable influence on the skills sets that are available to recruiters;

3. wage levels and contemporary trends in wage rises. Wage levels in developing sectors such as telecommunications and banking may outstrip wages in other sectors. This has been seen in China during a period of fast economic development and there have also been large wage differentials between state-owned and privately owned organizations (SEPI, 2002);

4. population age profiles that change slowly but do change. Surpluses of young, cheap labour can diminish over time, along with corresponding changes to the number of older people whose expectations in terms of wages and living standards may increase. The youth of China that migrated to factory regions like Guangdong is no longer simply a source of cheap labour, but now has rising expectations of its own in relation to consumer spending power (*The Economist*, 2010).

Even in generally healthy labour markets, specific local skills shortages can exist and can constrain organizational development. Shortages make it difficult for firms to recruit people with particular skills and to keep them. Multinational enterprises may move into an area to take advantage of labour supply, but within a few years become a victim of their successes as the supply of skilled and technically competent employees diminishes. Firms in some regions of China responded to skills shortages by developing their own training and development facilities and working more closely with vocational education and training providers to develop transferable skills (Li and Sheldon, 2010). Poaching of employees from other employers is, of course, an option, although it may start a wages spiral if other firms engage in a poaching war.

Discussion Activity 6.1

> Think about a labour market that you are familiar with. What are the main features of the market and how are they changing?

Labour markets change at different speeds. In Latin America, for instance, they have not changed much in recent decades and several factors explain this high level of inertia (Schneider and Karcher, 2010).

- There are large, informal sectors characterized by micro-businesses and self-employment.
- There is low skills availability deriving from low general education levels. Adults in Latin America receive on average about six years of schooling and provision of vocational education is poor.
- Unions are politicized yet weak, with little shop floor presence and collective bargaining power. Union participation is generally low at around 10–20 per cent of the workforce.
- Extensive regulation such as a reliance on high severance costs is at the expense of weak unemployment and social insurance provision by the state.
- Short job tenure averages about three years, which is lower than in most other regions.

These features can be seen as an outcome of the different ways that capitalism takes shape around the world (Hall and Soskice, 2001). (See Chapter 5, 'Understanding IHRM: the institutional approach', in the section *Varieties of capitalism*.) While not all Latin American countries are exactly the same, they do form a distinctive cluster on a world stage in terms of labour market characteristics compared to other regions. In contrast, labour markets elsewhere, such as Vietnam, China, and South Africa, have changed much more rapidly in the past twenty years as a result of democratic and liberal reforms. Having seen how contextual factors can differ from country to country, the chapter now explores selection processes in more detail.

Recruitment and selection strategy

A conventional recruitment and selection strategy is shown in Figure 6.1. The whole process is shaped by organizational decisions about staffing that set the way recruitment and selection are handled. They cover decisions about the jobs and competences that are needed and the rigour of the processes used. Attracting applicants takes in a range of approaches and issues. Apart from choices about where to advertise jobs, other strategies include social networking, headhunting, building the attractiveness of corporate websites and documentation, and the management of the overall employer brand, which has a major influence on organizational attractiveness (Edwards, 2010).

Following some sort of job analysis, which may be very loose or highly structured, descriptions of jobs and specifications of the knowledge, skills, and attributes needed are produced. In weak systems these may only exist as different mental models carried by managers but in more structured systems they will be formal documents used to assist staffing decisions. Applicants are sifted against these job descriptions. This is often a manual process of comparing

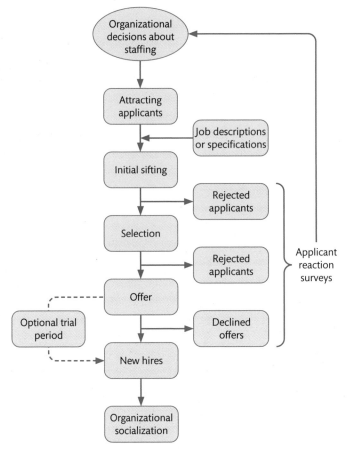

Figure 6.1 Flow chart of organizational staffing strategy

application papers against person specifications but can include online testing of general abilities such as numeracy and literacy.

After an initial sifting, surviving applicants go deeper into the selection process, and this ranges from a simple interview to a series of staged assessments where multiple traits of applicants are tested with multiple methods. Selection can simulate the future work environments, for example with realistic exercises, job previews, and briefings on political and cultural situations if international assignments are intended.

Candidates surviving the full selection process receive an offer that captures the **employee value proposition** (Moroko and Uncles, 2008). New hires then start a socialization process in the organization, which needs to match early experience in a job with expectations developed during selection. Throughout the selection process some applicants will be rejected at various stages, and organizations are giving increasing attention to understanding how applicants react to rejection (Schmitt and Chan, 1999). Selection should not be seen as a one-way process, although it often is, as unsuccessful candidates may be able to offer very useful advice to organizations that can lead to improving the employer brand or selection procedures.

Case Study 6.1. Selection of high-flyers at Alcatel

Alcatel is a 'very French' company. Operating in the telecommunications sector, it is one of France's largest employers and has strong links to government. Alcatel has hundreds of subsidiaries in France and abroad. Its selection methods for high-potential senior staff are characterized by three dynamics.

The competitive examination model

This driver of selection decisions emphasizes previous attendance at one of a few elite French schools of engineering or public management. Time spent working with the national government is also highly valued and is seen as a right of passage to the highest management levels.

The feudal model

Despite extensive international operations, being French is a characteristic of those who reach the highest positions, although there have been a few exceptions. The feudal model is so-called because it captures the importance of a person's social ties over and above their position in a hierarchy. Climbing up the organization requires interpretation and leverage of the power structures that are in play.

The professional model

Alcatel Belgium, in contrast, takes a more formal and structured approach to selection. The future potential of employees is assessed via appraisals. Employees who are rated as high potential receive career guidance and benefit from development and assessment centre interventions. This model emphasizes the competences of senior executives rather than the elitism of a person's former university.

Across Alcatel's worldwide operations, versions of these models exist in different countries yet the dominant Competitive Examination model reflects the dominant French national culture and makes the organization 'a theatre of hidden power struggles'.

Source: Adapted from Falcoz and Rousillon (2007)

While many organizations can point to a logical–rational selection strategy, there is often a strong political overlay to the fine details of how strategies work. This is illustrated in Case Study 6.1 on selecting high-flyers at Alcatel.

Core concepts

Two key concepts underpin research and practice in employee selection—reliability and validity. Reliability is about obtaining consistent scores, measurements, or agreements about a person's potential. For example if five interviewers who each rate a set of candidates broadly agree on their assessments, then the process shows good reliability. Little agreement between the interviewers on the candidates' potential indicates low reliability of assessment. But good reliability doesn't mean that what assessors agree on is a valid predictor of performance in the job; they may all have shown poor judgment.

This brings us to the second key concept of validity, which is concerned with how accurate the selection decision is—that is, how accurately selection decisions predict future

Validity

	Low	High
High	Good agreement between assessors but poor connection to actual job performance.	Good agreement between assessors. Good connection between predicted and actual job performance.
Low	Little if any agreement between assessors. No ability to predict future job performance.	Low reliability and high validity cannot co-exist.

Reliability

Figure 6.2 Reliability and validity in employee selection

performance. The reliability/validity relationship is shown in Figure 6.2. If reliability is low then validity has to be low—in this scenario there is no ability to predict future performance. High reliability can, however, associate with low validity which could manifest, for example, as assessors agreeing that a candidate is good when they are weak or agreeing they are weak when in practice they would be good. The desired position to achieve in selection processes is high reliability and high validity, which manifests as good agreement between assessors and translates into accurate predictions of job performance. (High validity cannot occur if the reliability of processes is poor.)

Different selection methods vary in their *reliability and validity*. Assessment centres show relatively high reliability and good predictive validity. Interviews show moderate reliability, but their effectiveness is increased when they are combined with other selection methods. The main point to note is that different methods have different validities and that validity is highest when methods are bundled together in a selection process, for example interviewing, work sampling, and testing of cognitive ability (Robertson and Smith, 2001).

 Stop and Think

Think about the last interview or selection process you went through as a candidate for a job. To what degree do you think that the process was 'reliable and valid'? If you did not get the job, did you blame (at least partially) the interviewers and/or selection process?

Selection methods in global staffing

Staffing on an international scale brings the threat of discrimination on the basis of race, sex, or religion into sharp focus. Organizations need to know to what extent their practices are discriminating, albeit unintentionally, against people drawn from a range of cultures, education systems, and races. International selection brings out the question of 'adverse impact'; that is, whether organizational practices are adversely impacting one group by virtue of some characteristics irrelevant to performance in the job (Ployhart and Holtz, 2008). The main methods used are summarized in Table 6.1, together with issues arising from their use on an international scale.

Table 6.1 Cross-cultural issues relating to selection methods

Selection method	Strengths	Cross-cultural issues
Application forms and CVs	They should represent a definitive record of the applicant's qualifications and experience.	In some countries, applications and CVs may be all that is used. Giving false information or omitting relevant information could be treated differently according to prevailing legal frameworks.
Interviews	Structuring interviews around pre-set questions and scales that rate candidates' responses raises validity.	Structured, panel interviews could disadvantage applicants who are not used to them. Different cultures value different behaviour; question–response behaviour normal in one culture could be seen as inappropriate in another.
Assessment centres	The actual behaviour of candidates in relation to realistic job situations is observed.	US design of AC exercises may favour women and whites over Hispanics or Blacks (Dean et al., 2008).
Psychometric testing	Gives additional insight into personality and intelligence of individuals. Can assess traits such as openness to experience and ability to handle others, which could predict success in international assignments (Jordan and Cartwright, 1998).	Design of tests can be culturally biased. Most are developed in the USA or Europe and translation into other languages can lead to lower scores (Goodwin and Mottram, 2004; Mottram, 2004; Matheson et al., 2008).
Biodata	Biodata works on the identification of the biographic details that characterize people who are successful in jobs, such as levels of qualifications achieved, social networks, and examples of extraverted behaviour. These characteristics are then looked for in applicants.	Taking the characteristics of successful people in one country, e.g. USA, and looking for the same characteristics in people from different social, religious, and educational systems is problematic.
Realistic job previews	RJPs give candidates an insight into what a job is really like, e.g. by shadowing or video clip. They are good for screening applicants out of a process and help to align successful candidates' expectations with the eventual realities of a job.	RJP and realistic living conditions previews are good at enabling better informed decisions about the reality of future international assignments (Caligiuri and Phillips, 2003; Richardson et al., 2008).

Issues in global staffing

Selecting expatriates

Traditional approaches to international resourcing focused on putting expatriates, i.e. PCNs, and to a lesser extent Third Country Nationals, into foreign subsidiaries (Sparrow, 2007). Expatriate careers can simply span one international assignment or may embrace several different consecutive assignments. The success of expatriate selection has often been considered low, with a high percentage of assignments ending prematurely; lack of employee preparation for international assignments receives a fair share of the blame (Grainger and Nankervis, 2001). Expatriates face up to a new set of cross-cultural obstacles and challenges that traditional selection methods were not taking into account; far greater testing of cross-cultural 'skills' along with greater attention given to the feelings of accompanying family were needed (Mendenhall et al., 1987). Alongside the need to review selection for individual postings there is a need to synchronize local recruitment and selection methods with corporate philosophies, policies, and practices. This does not mean imposing a uniform system across the board—rather, it means adapting local practices to fit with a corporate view of principles and methods.

The issues surrounding the traditional expatriate can be seen in terms of an expatriate cycle of selection, preparation, reward management, performance management, and re-entry to the parent company when the assignment is completed. Typical selection considerations include cross-cultural compatibility, technical ability, and impact on the expatriate's family. While increasing MNC activity should promote parent country expatriation it has an increasingly imperialist feel about it and, while still an important strategy, it has been challenged by events and changes in the macro-environment. These include:

- concerns about its cost-effectiveness in an increasingly cost-driven competitive environment;
- better education systems in host countries, which raise the chance of finding skilled local staff,
- information and communication technology, which enables new ways of controlling and organizing on a global scale and of monitoring subsidiary performance and thus reducing the need for an expatriate presence;
- attitudinal change away from thinking that only PCNs have the requisite skills and more openness to finding skills locally.

Cross-border movement and residence are now far easier, and McKenna and Richardson (2007) make the point that new models of managing international assignments have emerged. They point to growing numbers of people who are not organizationally sponsored, as parent country expatriates are, but who see working in a portfolio of countries as a career strategy. Given that expatriates are often highly qualified—about half the expatriates in the USA, New Zealand, Japan, and Australia have a university education, although in other countries the levels are much lower (Dumont and Lemaitre, 2005)—organizations selecting for international assignments no longer have to think only in terms of a parent country expatriate strategy but can think more in terms of an external labour market as well. Benefits of tapping into the internationally mobile talent pool include (Banai and Harry, 2004):

- lower costs deriving from employee acceptance of reward packages that fit with local benchmarks, not parent country benchmarks. Typical expatriate benefits such as return flights and costs of children's education can be saved;

- reduced need to manage the career of the employee; no re-entry career management is needed, for example;

- accessing the external pool raises choice and flexibility in relation to the strategic aim of the assignment;

- appointments can be up and running more quickly; the employee–organization relationship can be more transactional in the sense that there are not necessarily any expectations of continuing employment once the international assignment is completed.

Following a rational–strategic approach and the time available to manage in this way, Figure 6.3 summarizes the choices open to organizations. Starting from a consideration of strategic needs (how does the assignment fit with the strategic thrust of the organization?), the purpose and scope of the assignment would be set out. Decisions arising from purpose and scope could hinge, for example, on the extent of control over local managers that the organization is looking for. If high control is needed, then an expatriate strategy could be favoured. If control systems are already in place and the focus is more about knowledge transfer or developing workforce skills, then selecting from the internationally mobile pool could be better suited. (See discussion throughout Chapter 9, 'Training, development, and knowledge management'.)This triggers a choice between classic internal labour market selection approaches and the expatriate management cycle that goes with it, or a 'lighter touch' approach using the external labour market. Although socially responsible organizations will need to consider the appointee's situation and compatibility with the requirements of the post and think about their training and development and perhaps their family's education and safety, the primary focus can be on managing contribution and performance.

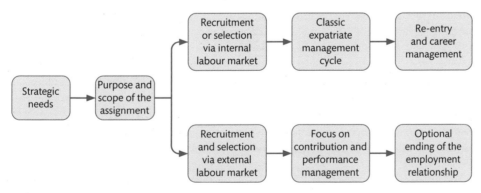

Figure 6.3 Selecting for international assignments

Case Study 6.2   Expatriate staffing a London health authority

The National Health Service (NHS) is the largest employer in the UK with over one million employees in a wide range of clinical, managerial, and administrative positions. There is high demand for doctors and nurses and this is met to a significant extent by recruitment from overseas. Expatriate nurses, for example, typically come from the Philippines, South Africa, Australia/New Zealand, Nigeria, and Ghana. The NHS set out an ethical position that covered the use of fair and equitable recruitment and selection processes that would not do harm to the health services in the countries from which it is recruiting. Websites were used to set out the conditions based upon the vocational and professional body interests. Assessment of English language proficiency was central as it is essential to ensuring a correct understanding of clinical and administrative procedures and ultimately the safety of patients.

The international resourcing strategy had three dimensions:

1. targeting specific skill sets and sources (countries) for the skills and setting-up infrastructures to recruit and select;

2. responding to 'passive' recruitment opportunities, e.g. where applicants took the initiative in seeking employment;

3. a long-term view of recruitment and selection in international markets.

Some key issues arose from the substantial intake of expatriate labour in the NHS:

- figuring out which agencies and bodies could help locate the skills and expertise needed;

- assessing technical competence in potential recruits, i.e. what mix of assessment methods is appropriate;

- ensuring the ethical content of campaigns;

- coping with increased workforce diversity that resulted from employment of large numbers of expatriates;

- ensuring that the reputation of units receiving international labour is enhanced (at least not diminished) to bolster future campaigns and reassure service users.

Source: Adapted from Sparrow (2007)

International management skills

When organizations want to select people for international assignments, what additional competences are sought? What makes international management different from management on a domestic level? As well as leading change, motivating others, and strategic awareness (among others), which are now fairly generic, international management calls for additional competences. Jordan and Cartwright (1998) suggest four additional competences as a minimum set.

Relational abilities strong social skills enabling interaction with Host Country Nationals (HCNs) and other expatriates, managing first impressions, maintaining regard for others, and active listening.

Cultural sensitivity this involves understanding, empathy, adaptability, and the ability to understand the cross-border nature of a business and the linkages and risks that this creates.

Linguistic ability over and above the obvious advantages of aiding communication, culture and language are linked and acquisition of, or at least an understanding of, another language can help broaden intercultural competences.

Managing stress international assignments are often stressful events and the ability to handle stress has a bearing on success.

In addition, Hurn (2006) identifies the following competences of the international manager:

- ability to work with and manage people who hold very different ethical and cultural views, which may result in very different attitudes to work and organizing;
- ability to work in and lead multinational and often dispersed (virtual) teams;
- ability to manage personal situations such as schooling for children and the work–life choices of a spouse or partner.

 Case Study 6.3   Expatriate selection in Chinese MNEs

A study of expatriate selection in ten Chinese multinational enterprises found distinctive approaches different from those found in the West. Managers would discuss possible candidates and evaluate them in terms of track record, technical skills, attitudes, language skills, compliance with company procedures, good relations with managers, and willingness to work outside China. No formal testing or assessment centres were used. Selection decisions were effectively made before candidates were interviewed and interviews were largely there to discuss the details of assignments, not to make selection decisions.

Cultural fit and domestic situations were not taken into account in selecting people for foreign assignments. To be selected as a representative of the organization in a foreign land was a great honour, which would not normally be refused, and domestic circumstances had to adjust to make it work out. Family issues were seen as something that the chosen employee had to deal with.

The expatriate failure rate was relatively low at 4 per cent. This was attributed to the motivation to complete the assignments which, if not completed, would lead to loss of face. Other success factors were relatively short assignment periods and the use of objective performance appraisal criteria that focused on hard targets, rather than subjective criteria such as cultural and moral adjustment. Repatriation was handled rather coldly. There was little forward career planning or commitment to job security for those who had worked abroad. International experience was not generally seen as being of much relevance to domestic operations. Gaunxi (connections and networks) was used to try to leverage favourable appointments on return, but prolonged absence from base had weakened the 'pull' that returning employees had. There was little connection between a posting abroad and future career development. Weak repatriation strategies led to former expatriates leaving the company. The study found a strong preference to select Chinese nationals for foreign assignments, and this is grounded in greater trust and security in those sharing the same culture and language. Using HCNs, for example, would unsettle the trust/control relationships that management had with their subordinates abroad.

The general finding of the study was that recruitment and selection was more ad hoc and took place in the absence of the more formal and systematic procedures that take a wider view of employees and family and have become more accepted in the West.

Source: Based on Shen and Edwards (2004)

Cultural differences and their influence on practice

Selection and assessment practices are often based on a long tradition of Anglo-American research in occupational psychology. These methods are used widely in other cultural contexts but what differ internationally are not so much the methods used but the attitudes towards them and how and when they should be used.

In Europe, Levy-Leboyer (1994) points out that practice in Britain has closely followed American practices because British psychologists and managers can easily evaluate the steady stream of research in the same language. There are arguably shared assumptions about approaches to selection in Britain and the USA because of cultural and institutional similarities. For HR managers and psychologists in many other countries there is a language barrier. Furthermore, in Eastern Europe under communist regimes, philosophical and political ideologies led to highly distinctive approaches to selection. Position and influence in political parties had considerable influence on appointments and promotions to management roles. In summarizing studies of selection methods in Western Europe, Levy-Leboyer (1994) found that:

- personal references were widely used, but less so in France;
- interviews were widely used;
- assessment centres or situational testing was ahead in the UK, Germany, and the Netherlands;
- methods used varied with the nature of the job and the size of the organization.

The survey also revealed that 'very few' organizations collected any information on the predictive validity of the methods that they were using. There is no evidence that this situation has got any better.

Huo et al. (2002) found evidence for convergence of selection practices while retaining national cultural values. They found that technical ability is widely tested and a personal interview is very common. They found similarities between the USA, Canada, and Australia, and between Japan and Taiwan, reflecting shared cultural roots. Practices in China stood out from other countries. In Japan, selection emphasized a person's ability to fit in a workplace reflecting Japan's historic emphasis on lifetime employment; this translates into finding people with perceived high person–organization fit, on the grounds that technical skills can be learned. There is good logic in this view; developing a person's technical skills is probably easier than developing the social skills needed to fit into a particular management style and work culture.

 Discussion Activity 6.2

'Hire for attitude, train for skill'. To what extent do you agree with this staffing principle and how might it be influenced by local, cultural norms?

From a rational point of view, employers should be concerned about the predictive validity of the tests they use and this has become very important in the USA. However, Schuler (1993) introduced the idea of 'social validity'—the notion that different methods have different levels of acceptance in different societies. This is an interesting concept that helps to explain cross-national differences. Social validity is emphasized in some examples of selection practice given below.

Outside countries where selection is geared around the objective assessment of merit and potential, there is more emphasis placed on the assessment of *who* a person is, their standing in society, and their connections. This different perspective has implications for the use of empirical, data-generating assessment methods (Brewster et al., 2007). In China, for instance, the interview is widely used but in different ways from those of the UK or USA, because the influence of a person's political affiliations, their moral convictions and networks are substantive considerations in a selection decision (Overman, 2001) and these factors will have been assessed before an interview occurs. Internal recruitment therefore becomes more likely as these factors will be clearer for internal candidates. There is a wonderful story about a selection process in a large Chinese enterprise that, after a recruitment exercise, spent a day interviewing people to find the best candidate. After everyone had been seen, the cleaner was given the job because he was a known quantity who always showed good behaviour. Whether the story is true cannot be verified—but it makes a point. Japanese staffing practices also emphasize the importance of moral character more than professional knowledge, which helps to explain their traditional preference for the employment of graduates, long organizational tenure, and extensive training and development (Jackson, 2002).

Selection in Nigeria uses a combination of universal and local practices but is shaped by a strong emphasis on further testing after interview (Anakwe, 2002; Azolukwam and Perkins, 2009). High Power Distance means that top management will dominate staffing decisions, and this involvement will not be questioned. While Nigeria is a collective society, the value of networking in career strategies is 'muddled with nepotism, bribery and corruption' (Anakwe, 2002: 1054).

In the larger Greek organizations and MNC subsidiaries, selection processes are often guided by HR specialists and consultants and can be relatively sophisticated. However, the more traditional family-owned Greek enterprises are strongly influenced by family members with whom decision making is concentrated. This translates into a preference for people who are known to the decision makers as there will be doubts about the reliability and trustworthiness of less well-known candidates. Personal recommendation plays a large role in identifying new staff in the smaller organization (Papalexandris, 1992).

Small behavioural differences can have a big influence on how a person is perceived. Tayeb (2003), for example, points out that eye contact between interviewer and interviewee, which is usually seen as a normal, reassuring behaviour in westernized settings, can be interpreted as a sign of untrustworthiness elsewhere. In Korean culture, a pause before answering a question is seen as respecting the seriousness of the question; deeper questions call for longer pauses. In western cultures, pausing before answering could be seen as a sign of the candidate's uncertainty and unfamiliarity with the topic (Brewster et al., 2007).

Using dimensions taken from Hofstede's (1980) conceptualization of national culture and from the GLOBE study, which has extended and updated Hofstede (House et al., 2004), some theoretical links between aspects of national culture and staffing practices are shown in Table 6.2.

Table 6.2 Cultural dimensions and theoretical relationships to selection practice

Culture dimension	Low	High
Power Distance	Staffing decisions devolved to lower levels	Top management dominance of procedures and decisions
Uncertainty Avoidance	More relaxed approach to the factors opposite	Greater emphasis on seeking fit with existing work culture
		High emphasis on moral behaviour
		Greater selection from within
		Greater use of recruitment consultants
		Extensive collection of biographic information
Individualism–Collectivism	In collective cultures:	High concern for individual performance and impact
	More emphasis given to 'soft' criteria	
	Greater concern for integration into existing social systems, e.g. work groups	High use of competitive, data-generating selection processes
	Greater use of referral to identify candidates	
Performance Orientation	Reduced focus on objective methods	High use of multi-phase, data-generating, and objective assessment procedures
	Emphasis on selection from among known candidates	Comfortable with selecting previously unknown candidates

(See further discussion throughout Chapter 4, 'Understanding IHRM: the cultural approach'.)

Perceived fairness

Perceived fairness in all human resource management practices is important and staffing is no exception. In selecting new starters, existing employees want to see new hires being appointed using fair and valid methods. Employees who see new colleagues appointed using weak procedures or procedures that compromise standards can be expected to react adversely. If, for example, employees see that lower standards are being applied to appointments from outside than for internal appointments and promotions, then the conditions for feelings of favouritism and discrimination to develop are present. No-one wants to think that people are being appointed to higher posts on the basis of unequal criteria. As well as internal consistency, it is also necessary to consider the effects on unsuccessful applicants, who usually outnumber successful applicants. Selection is a filtering process, with people being rejected stage by stage. Organizations need to design systems that are seen as fair and that do not lead to unfavourable reactions when people are rejected, possibly after considerable emotional investment in undergoing interviews and other testing.

Gilliland (1993) proposed a model of selection with special reference to perceived fairness. The key point of the model is that applicants need to see that procedures and methods

Case Study 6.4   Selection in Mexico

Trade between the USA and Mexico has increased recently and Rao (2009) identifies a range of issues facing US multinationals operating there. Applying national cultural frameworks such as GLOBE to Mexico helps to explain why practice is like it is.

The high Power Distance feature of Mexican society means that people are promoted because they are known and trusted and to a lesser extent through any rational assessments of knowledge and skills. High Power Distance leads to managers wanting to be involved in staffing decisions (it underlines their authority). Staffing decisions are a domain of the higher manager—lower managers are usually excluded. Processes such as panel interviews where different levels interact are less likely. Internal appointments are favoured.

High Uncertainty Avoidance leads to rules and procedures that aim to reduce unpredictable events. Extensive biodata are sought, such as height, weight, personal appearance (photographs), family structure, and personal economic circumstances as a 'comfort blanket' to reassure decision makers. This information is seen as irrelevant to job performance in many countries to the extent that basing selection decisions on personal demographic factors could be unlawful. In Mexico, however, personal information is seen as an indicator of suitability and future success.

High in-group Collectivism manifests in strong social networks around the family or other in-groups such as the Church. Recruitment of people with in-group connections often by word-of-mouth is a natural outcome. Selection has a strong social exchange aspect to it relating to personal contacts, which mitigates against 'rational' processes and internet recruitment. Internet recruitment in Mexico is also compromised because internet usage in Mexico is much lower than in the USA.

Gender Egalitarianism—the machismo culture shapes selection and impedes the progress of women into higher management. There is more open discrimination against women on the basis of physical attractiveness and social contacts. Gender equality is not promoted.

Performance Orientation—a moderate Performance Orientation works against the use of rational and impersonal processes such as job analysis, person specifications, and the use of external agencies to select the potentially highest performers.

Rao traces the prevailing attitudes in Mexico to the distant past. Pre-conquest Mexico was dominated by civilizations that were intensely hierarchical and in which unquestioning loyalty was expected. The Conquest introduced Catholicism, which perpetuated the authority of the Church and loyalty to it. Modern politics has been dominated by a single party with complete authority and calling for unswerving loyalty. In Mexico, a 'glass ceiling' exists for all people without social connections. Male leaders dominated the religious and institutional landscape for centuries and the 'exaggerated display of masculinity' (machismo) has become the norm. The situation in Mexico calls into question the extent to which MNCs can micromanage local practices, for example imposing their ideas of equality onto a system that routinely specifies age and gender of applicants.

Source: Rao, 2009

are related to jobs, that applicants are given the opportunity to showcase their knowledge and skills, and that interpersonal relationships with the recruiters are respectful. If, for example, applicants are asked to undergo selection methods that they cannot relate to performance in the job, they may feel unfairly treated. High importance is given to the idea of face validity; that is the idea that a selection method does, on the face of it, relate to predicting performance in the job. While fairness is a universal concept, what constitutes fairness varies across cultures. What is unfair in one context may be seen as fair in another (Scroggins et al., 2008).

Steiner and Gilliland (1996) compared fairness reactions to selection tests among young people poised to enter the job market in the USA and France. They found similar results overall but noted that Americans, more than the French, felt that resumés, interviews, and biographical information were fairer methods to use. The French felt that graphology and personality tests were fairer than did Americans. No differences were found in attitudes to work samples, written ability tests, or personal references. Americans put a stronger emphasis than did the French on scientific evidence and logic behind the use of methods. The implication is that using the same logic as is used in the USA to justify the use of selection

---

 Case Study 6.5   The rhetoric and reality of selection

This case describes a situation that was occurring recently in a large company in the Gulf. Skills shortages are a problem in the labour market. Expatriate labour is available but nationalization policies limit the number of expatriates that can be employed and the organization is reluctant to put non-nationals in customer-facing positions.

Selection starts with advertisements in Arabic and English placed internally and externally. The HR department collates CVs and does an initial sorting. Panel interviews are organized with the HR managers and the head and deputy head of the department with the vacancy. Candidates performing best at interview are asked to do written tests. Final decisions are then made. So far so good you might think—but what is going on at a deeper level?

Several hundred applications can be received for some posts; the HR department does little initial sifting and does not keep a tally of who has applied. Heads of departments do not want to read hundreds of applications so they distribute them among their staff to review. Perhaps through feelings of self-preservation, staff hide the CVs from the applicants they perceive as good, perhaps as threatening, and put forward 'average' CVs for consideration. Others are picked at random as the employee has no idea what the department is looking for. Selected CVs are returned to HR to arrange interviews, at which point staff in the HR department add some CVs of their friends and relatives.

By this time, most good CVs have been removed. When interviews take place, high ratings are given to people with connections to the interviewers. A written exam, set by HR non-finance specialists, covers basic mathematics, but not a knowledge of finance. Exam papers are marked by HR and are not seen by the interviewers. Finally, the HR department selects candidates who have strong connections to them, overriding departmental preferences. As a consequence, departments are refreshed with new recruits often unfamiliar with financial systems and procedures, and with poor English language ability.

Appraisal is also compromised. Each year, managers rate their staff on a range of factors such as attitudes, skills and knowledge, teamwork, and relations with clients. Managers send completed appraisals to HR, who then send them to top management, who make judgements about bonuses, increments, and promotion. The head of department's rating is final and is influenced by office politics and personal liking. Employees without good relations with their manager never get high scores. Appraisal outcomes are not discussed with employees, hence employees cannot use them to improve their own performance. If employees move between departments and get a new appraiser, then ratings may fall simply because different personal relationships are operating. Top management does not follow up on why a series of high ratings for a person suddenly comes to an end.

This short case shows how HR practices are easily influenced by local cultural practices and raises some good discussion questions.

(See discussions throughout Chapter 8, 'Performance management', for more on performance appraisals.)

methods will lead to different outcomes. The French are perhaps attuned to more elegant explanations of a person's potential than to psychometric data. (Compare this to Case Sudy 6.1, and Case Study 13.5, Managing talent: UK and French perspectives, in Chapter 13, 'Global talent management).

 Discussion Activity 6.3

Following on from Case Study 6.5,

1. What changes would you make to the selection and appraisal procedures in the organization? Why?

2. Now think about your ideas for change. How culturally embedded is current practice and what else has to change if your changes are to have any chance of working?

3. Whose interests would be served if your changes were successful? Exactly who would be better off?

Equality of opportunity

Employers do not want to be accused of unfair practices, and in some countries can be taken to tribunals to resolve accusations of discrimination. While organizations are free to set their own selection criteria it is important not to set criteria that impede equality of opportunity. While this may sound obvious, it is not as easy as it sounds, since it is easy for non-essential criteria to creep in to selection because of weak job analysis or simple bias. Indeed, Huo et al. (2002) suggested that, perhaps without exception, selection criteria are not set following a democratic process. Rather, they reflect past trial and error, prevailing assumptions about the competences needed, and the views of dominant managers involved in selection situations.

Other practices can be considered to compromise equality. It is quite common for organizations to encourage people to apply for a particular job and, while this is very reasonable and pragmatic behaviour, it can give people an unfair advantage, as it is inevitable that those who were encouraged to apply start as a preferred candidate. Building social networks has a big influence on career growth, which means that candidates are often known to the recruiter. It is also easy to leverage (some might say abuse) positions of managerial power with a little social engineering. Some occupational sectors are small worlds such that recruiters have a good idea of who they want to attract. It is easy to write a person specification and design selection exercises that fit around a preferred candidate's experience to give them a better chance. If the organization knows that a person they want has experience of X, then experience of X becomes an essential criterion to the disadvantage of other applicants. It is easy to decide on questions for an interview that, although they will be asked of everyone, clearly favour a preferred candidate.

Selection can be seen as a psychological problem, i.e. how to measure potential, as well as a decision problem, i.e. whom to pick and whom to reject (Newell, 2006). But success in a job is not just down to the individual. A very competent internal candidate can be undermined by lack of support or by a devious colleague who dislikes them or sees them as a threat. People of limited competence can do very well with strong support and training.

Discussion Activity 6.4

To what extent do you agree with the proposition that use of social networking to find and encourage people to apply for posts compromises equality of opportunity?

Women executives

Literature on expatriate selection is largely about the experiences of men rather than women. This is perhaps because of the relative scarcity of women in international assignments, which can be attributed to different social networks from those as are 'enjoyed' by men, such as mentoring, sponsorship, personal recommendation, and lack of role models (Linehan and Scullion, 2001; Linehan and Walsh, 1999). In addition, pools of international managers that are predominantly men perpetuate the selection of men—a situation influenced by perceived clashes of styles, i.e. beliefs that male management styles are more suited to overseas opera-tions. As well as internal organizational barriers, we also suggest that in some regions where societies are male dominated, being female could make becoming accepted into a manage-rial elite very difficult. Linehan and Scullion (2001) propose several strategies for improving opportunities for women in international operations.

- Organizations should specifically target women for international careers.
- Management development programmes should cater for the specific needs of women executives, such as tailoring to dual-career couples and the issues facing the partner.
- MNCs should use more inpatriation of women, i.e. transferring HCNs to the parent country.

Summary

Global staffing has to take into account influencing factors at national level such as legal frameworks, local factors such as labour market conditions, and organizational factors such as size, strategy, and structure. When staffing occurs across an MNC operating in several regions the complexities of selection are magnified. Rational–logical and impersonal approaches to selection that emanate from the Anglo-American model to find the highest performer and that are based on empirical data taken during the selection process do not necessarily travel very well. Organizational and national cultures interact to produce distinctive approaches to staffing. Indeed, there are good grounds for thinking that selection is the one HRM practice that varies the most between countries. However, caution is needed before criticizing staff-ing systems that deviate from the empirically based, performance-chasing models. Ideas of performance vary from place to place and staffing practices that aim to implement a universal set of social processes into another culture are questionable. If imposed they may compromise the wider social systems that underpin levels of organizational performance. Deciding to offer someone a job is a starting point, not an end point, and should be seen as a first step in integrating a new personality into an organization. Staffing needs to align with other HR architecture if benefits are to be fully realized.

Review questions

1. What could employers learn from feedback from applicants who have been rejected at some stage of a selection process?

2. How culturally sensitive is the idea of obtaining applicant feedback on selection processes?

3. How might different local cultures shape the ways in which feedback is obtained?

4. Think of a job-related selection process that you have experienced. How could the fairness and validity of selection processes be improved?

5. What factors should an employer consider before sending employees on expatriate assignments?

6. What responsibilities do employers have when employees return from expatriate assignments to their home countries?

7. What are the forces for and against the increasing adoption of Anglo-American selection methods and principles being adopted in other countries?

8. How might employees react if they think that selection processes in their organization are unfair? How might these reactions vary between countries?

9. Think of the job-related selection processes that you have experienced. Do any aspects of the process discriminate against the selection or promotion of women?

10. How does national culture affect the selection process? Give some examples of the different selection processes that are used in a few countries and try to explain why these differences occur.

Further reading

Briscoe, D., Schuler, R., and Claus, L. (2009) *International Human Resource Management—Policies and Practices for Multinational Companies*, 3rd edn, London: Prentice Hall.
> To understand more about how staffing can be forecast at an international level, selecting people for international assignments, and the causes of assignment failure, see Chapter 5, Global talent management and staffing.

Harris, H., Brewster, C., and Sparrow, P. (eds) (2003) *International Human Resource Management*, London: CIPD.
> To understand more about international influences on selection methods, see Chapter 6, Comparative HRM: resourcing and rewarding.

Scullion, H. and Collings, D. (2006) *Global Staffing*, Abingdon: Routledge.
> This book has a comprehensive focus on international aspects of recruitment and selection.

Stahl, G. and Bjorkman, I. (eds) (2006) *Handbook of Research in International Resource Management*, Cheltenham: Edward Elgar.
> For a consideration of staffing issues in subsidiaries and the use of expatriates and inpatriates, see Part 8, Global Staffing, by H. Scullion and D. Collings.

Tayeb, M. (ed.) (2005) *International Human Resource Management*, Oxford: Oxford University Press.
> To understand more about the role of expatriates in MNCs and subsidiaries, see Chapter 9, Foreign assignment.

Bibliography

Anakwe, U.P. (2002) Human resource management practices in Nigeria: challenges and insights, *International Journal of Human Resource Management*, 13(7): 1042–59.

Azolukwam, V. and Perkins, S.J. (2009) Managerial perspectives on HRM in Nigeria: evolving hybridization? *Cross Cultural Management: An International Journal*, 16(1): 62–82.

Banai, M. and Harry, W. (2004) Boundaryless global careers, *International Studies in Management and Organization*, 34(3): 96–120.

Brewster, C., Sparrow, P., and Vernon, G. (2007) *International Human Resource Management*, London: CIPD.

Briscoe, D.R., Schuler, R.S., and Claus, L. (2009) *International Human Resource Management*, 3rd edn, London: Routledge.

Caligiuri, P.M. and Phillips, J.M. (2003) An application of self-assessment realistic job previews to expatriate assignments, *International Journal of Human Resource Management*, 14(7): 1102–16.

Collings, D.G. and Scullion, H. (2006) Global staffing, in G.K. Stahl and I. Bjorkman (eds) *Handbook of International Human Resource Management*, Cheltenham: Edward Elgar, pp. 141–57.

—, —, and Dowling, P.J. (2009) Global staffing: a review and thematic research agenda, *International Journal of Human Resource Management*, 20(6): 1253–72.

Dean, M.A., Roth, P.A., and Bobko, P. (2008) Ethnic and gender subgroup differences in assessment center ratings: a meta-analysis, *Journal of Applied Psychology*, 93(3): 685–91.

Dumont, J-C. and Lemaitre, G. (2005) *Country Livings and Expatriates in OECD Countries; A New Perspective*, Social, Employment and Migration Working Paper, Paris: OECD.

The Economist (2010) The next China, *The Economist*, 29 July.

Edwards, M.R. (2010) An integrative review of employer branding and OB theory, *Personnel Review*, 39(1): 5–23.

Falcoz, C. and Rousillon, S. (2007) Career management of high fliers at Alcatel, in M.E. Mendenhall, G.R. Oddou, and G.K. Stahl (eds) *Readings and Cases in International Human Resource Management*, 3rd edn, London: Routledge, pp. 138–56.

Gilliland, S.W. (1993) The perceived fairness of selection systems: an organizational justice perspective, *Academy of Management Review*, 18: 694–734.

Goodwin, N. and Mottram, R. (2004) How well do psychometric tests travel?, *Selection & Development Review*, 20(4): 31.

Grainger, R.J. and Nankervis, A.R. (2001) Expatriation practices in the global environment, *Research and Practice in Human Resource Management*, 9(2): 77–92.

Hall, P.A. and Soskice, D. (2001) An introduction to varieties of capitalism, in P.A. Hall and D. Soskice (eds) *Varieties of Capitalism*, New York: Oxford University Press, pp. 1–68.

Harris, H., Brewster, C., and Sparrow, P. (eds) (2003) *International Human Resource Management*, London: CIPD.

Hofstede, G. (1980) *Culture's Consequences: International Differences in Work-related Values*, London: Sage.

House, R., Hanges, P.J., Javian, M., Dorfman, P.W., and Gupta, V. (2004) *Culture, Leadership and Organizations: The GLOBE Study of 62 Societies*, Thousand Oaks, CA: Sage.

Huo, Y.P., Huang, H., and Napier, N. (2002) Divergence or convergence: a cross-national comparison of personnel selection practices, *Human Resource Management*, 41(1): 31–44.

Hurn, B. (2006) The selection of international business managers: part 1, *Industrial and Commercial Training*, 38(6): 279–86.

Jackson, T. (2002) *International Human Resource Management: A Cross-cultural Approach*, London: Sage.

Jordan, J. and Cartwright, S. (1998) Selecting expatriate managers: key traits and competences, *Leadership & Organization Development Journal*, 19(2): 89–96.

Levy-Leboyer, C. (1994) Selection and assessment in Europe, in H.C. Triandis, M.D. Dunnette, and L.M. Hough (eds) *Handbook of Industrial and Organizational Psychology*, Palo Alto, CA: Consulting Psychologists Press, pp. 173–90.

Li, Y. and Sheldon, P. (2010) HRM lives inside and outside the firm: employers, skills shortages and the local labour market in China, *International Journal of Human Resource Management*, 21(12): 2173–93.

Linehan, M. and Scullion, H. (2001) Selection, training and development for female international executives, *Career Development International*, 6(6): 318–23.

— and Walsh, J.S. (1999) Recruiting and developing female managers for international assignments, *Journal of Management Development*, 18(6): 521–30.

McKenna, S. and Richardson, J. (2007) The increasing complexity of the internationally mobile professional,

Cross-Cultural Management: An International Journal, 14(4): 307–20.

Matheson, I., Sykes, J., and Welford, C. (2008) Assessment in the international arena: it's not as straightforward as it might seem, *Selection & Development Review*, 24(4): 6–9.

Mendenhall, M.E., Dunbar, E., and Oddou, G. (1987) Expatriate selection, training and career-pathing: a review and critique, *Human Resource Management*, 26(3): 331–45.

Moroko, L. and Uncles, M.D. (2008) Characteristics of successful employer brands, *Journal of Brand Management*, 16(3): 160–75.

Mottram, R. (2004) The challenges of cross-cultural testing: a reply, *Selection & Development Review*, 20(6): 19–20.

Newell, S. (2006) Selection and assessment, in T. Redman and A. Wilkinson (eds) *Contemporary Human Resource Management—Text and Cases*, 2nd edn, London: FT Prentice Hall, pp. 65–98.

Overman, S. (2001) Recruiting in China, *HR Magazine*, 46(3, March): 86–93.

Papalexandris, N. (1992) Human resource management in Greece, *Employee Relations*, 14(4): 38–52.

Ployhart, R. and Holtz, B. (2008) The diversity–validity dilemma: strategies for reducing racio-ethnic and sex subgroup differences and adverse impact in selection, *Personnel Psychology*, 61: 153–72.

Rao, P. (2009) The role of national culture on Mexican staffing practices, *Employee Relations*, 31(3): 295–311.

Richardson, J., McBey, K., and McKenna, S. (2008) Integrating realistic job previews and realistic living conditions previews, *Personnel Review*, 37(5): 490–508.

Robertson, I.T. and Smith, M. (2001) Personnel selection, *Journal of Occupational and Organizational Psychology*, 74: 441–72.

Schmitt, N. and Chan, D. (1999) The status of research on applicant reactions to selection tests and its

implications for managers, *International Journal of Management Reviews*, 1(1): 45–62.

Schneider, B.R. and Karcher, S. (2010) Complementarities and continuities in the political economy of the labour markets of Latin America, *Socio-Economic Review*, 8(4): 623–51.

Schuler, H. (1993) Social validity of selection situations: a concept and some empirical results, in J. Schuler, L. Farr, and M. Smith (eds) *Personnel Selection and Assessment: Individual and Organizational Perspectives*, Hillsdale, NJ: Erlbaum, pp. 11–26.

Scroggins, W.A., Benson, P., Cross, C., and Gilbreath, B. (2008) Reactions to selection methods: an international comparison, *International Journal of Management*, 25(2): 203–15.

Scullion, H. and Collings, D. (2006) *Global Staffing*, Abingdon: Routledge.

Shen, J. and Edwards, V. (2004) Recruitment and selection in Chinese MNEs, *International Journal of Human Resource Management*, 15(4): 814–35.

Social and Economic Policy Institute (SEPI) (2002) *Overview of Current Labour Market Conditions in China*, Hong Kong: SEPI.

Sparrow, P. (2007) Globalization of HR at function level: four UK-based case studies of the international recruitment process, *International Journal of Human Resource Management*, 18(5): 845–67.

Stahl, G. and Bjorkman, I. (eds) (2006) *Handbook of Research in International Resource Management*, Cheltenham: Edward Elgar.

Steiner, D.D. and Gilliland, S.W. (1996) Fairness reactions to personnel selection techniques in France and the United States, *Journal of Applied Psychology*, 81(2): 134–41.

Tayeb, M.H. (2003) *International Management. Theories and Practices*, London: Prentice Hall.

— (ed.) (2005) *International Human Resource Management*, Oxford: Oxford University Press.

 Visit the Online Resource Centre for web links, interactive glossary, and more:
http://www.oxfordtextbooks.co.uk/orc/crawley

7 International reward management

 Learning Outcomes

After reading this chapter you will be able to:

- understand the concepts of labour markets, reward philosophy, and strategy
- explain and compare the main ways of rewarding employees
- explain influences on reward strategies in MNEs
- analyse the connections between national culture and reward practices
- explain the importance of satisfaction with pay and reward.

Introduction

Human resource management is built upon the smooth operation and integration of several distinct practices including selection, development, performance management, and reward. Indeed, Fombrun et al. (1984) saw staffing, developing, appraising, and rewarding as the 'big four' HRM practices which, if optimized, give the best chance of linking HRM to business strategy. Each practice needs to be internally coherent and needs to fit with and reinforce other practices; for example an excellent reward strategy should not be compromised by poor selection.

Before the strategic role of HRM was recognized, reward (also termed compensation or remuneration) was seen largely in terms of wages and pay. Modern reward management extends far beyond pay because it recognizes a much wider range of financial and non-financial rewards that, when combined, produce a total reward package for employees. A good skills development programme, for example, has a value to employees since it can raise their employability and career prospects. Reward is made up of tangible and intangible components as captured in the following definition: 'Reward refers to all the monetary, non-monetary and psychological payments that an organization provides for its employees in exchange for the work they perform' (Bratton and Gold, 2007: 360).

Increasing multinational business activity raises questions about how far pay and reward systems in subsidiaries need to adapt and reflect local conditions. Interest has also developed in understanding the range of factors that cause international variations in reward strategies and why they occur. This chapter begins by looking at the costs of employment and at how labour markets have changed. The main components of reward management are summarized before the effects of international and cross-cultural contexts on reward management are discussed. Factors affecting employee satisfaction with pay are then reviewed.

Employment costs and labour markets

Employment costs

The contribution of employment costs (i.e. wages, salaries, and benefits) to an organization's overall operating costs varies widely. In service sectors, for example, the costs of employing people can reach 60–70 per cent of total expenditure. In labour-intensive industries (e.g. clothing) labour costs also take a high share of spending. In more technologically advanced, capital-intensive sectors, employment costs can fall to around 10–30 per cent of total outlay.

Wages and salaries in developed countries are typically around 75 per cent of total employment costs; and in Europe, the lowest percentages are found in France, Belgium, and Sweden at around 67 per cent. Germany and the UK are around 77 per cent and the highest share is 85 per cent for Denmark (Eurostat, 2009). Wage costs also comprise about 78–80 per cent of total labour costs in Japan and the USA. The remaining share of total labour costs is made up largely of employers' social security contributions, vocational training costs, and redundancy costs. Actual wage and salary levels vary, of course, and Figure 7.1 shows annual average earnings in a range of European Union (EU) countries. Average earnings are highest in Denmark and other northern European countries, where they can be ten to twenty times higher than in the former Eastern Bloc countries recently admitted to the EU.

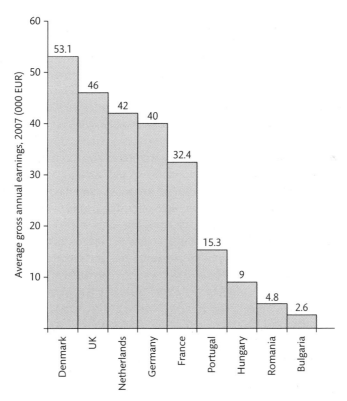

Figure 7.1 Annual gross earnings 2007 (€000) (organizations with fewer than ten employees excluded)
Source: EUROSTAT (2009).

Pay inequalities

Wage levels, however, do not reveal anything about income inequality or how income is distributed among wage earners. Income inequality is expressed using the **Gini coefficient** (which ranges from 0 to1), where low coefficients reflect lower inequality. In the mid-2000s, Sweden, Denmark, and Austria showed the least inequality (Gini coefficients around 0.24), the UK was about 0.34, the USA relatively high at about 0.45, and China about 0.47. South American countries are generally high in wage inequality (0.5–0.6) and African countries rank among the highest in terms of wage inequality (0.6–0.7). In general, wage inequality has been rising for the past twenty years (OECD, 2009).

Another measure of wage inequality is the gender wage gap. This is expressed as the difference between the median or mean earnings of men and women expressed as a percentage of male earnings. The gap in median earnings of full-time employees across OECD countries is about 17–18 per cent. It is highest, by some distance, in South Korea and Japan at about 35 per cent (i.e. median earnings of women are about 65 per cent those of men). It is about 22 per cent in Germany and 18–20 per cent in the UK and the USA. The gap is lowest in Belgium (8 per cent) and is also low in New Zealand, Denmark, and Poland. In the past thirty years, and despite equal pay legislation in many countries, gender wage gaps have usually either reduced slightly or stayed the same (OECD, 2009).

These headline figures, however, mask some large differences by occupation, age, level of earnings, and level of educational attainment. Younger women tend to earn more, expressed as a percentage of male earnings, than do older women, i.e. the gap for younger women is lower. Gender pay gaps are usually accentuated at the top of the earnings distribution among higher paid people. In South Korea, for example, the gap among high earners climbed to over 40 per cent in 2006, although it was lower elsewhere. This higher gap among high earners is not found in all countries; Canada and Germany are exceptions. However, Vieito and Khan (2012) found that the gender pay gap in executive compensation is reducing, particularly since 2000, and this is seen as an indication of better labour market operation.

Higher pay gaps among higher earners can be interpreted through the barriers that hinder women in reaching senior management positions. Relative powerlessness is one explanation and relates to the often patriarchal nature of societies where the high-earning jobs are found in finance, marketing, and production; areas often dominated by men (Morgan, 1997). A survey of women in the boardroom shows that across Europe there are slow increases in the proportion of women in top jobs, but the overall level remains low. Scandinavian countries have the highest rates of boardroom participation; the UK, Netherlands, and Ireland are average. Germany and France are below average, whereas Italy and Portugal lag well behind. Despite progress into the boardroom in some countries, very few women have reached the top CEO position (EPWN, 2008).

(For more on women and diversity, see this discussed throughout Chapter 10, 'Diversity management in an international environment'.)

In the UK, the overall pay gap has fallen over the past ten years (Daniels, 2008), but the gap increases with age and is highest for women over 40 years of age. By occupation, the median gap is lowest for professional employees (presumably reflecting returns on investment in education) and is highest among managers and senior officials and in skilled trades. The gap is lower for younger women in low-skilled work, and this is explained by the impact of the minimum wage policies that are found in many countries, except the Middle East, and which are usually set at around 40 per cent of average wages (ILO, 2009).

 Discussion Activity 7.1

How concerned are different nations and cultures about the existence of a gender wage gap? What explains the differing levels of concern?

Internal labour markets

In common with other HRM practices, reward management continues to be a focus of review and change as organizations reconfigure internal systems to match top managers' interpretations of changes in their external environments. Until the late 1970s and early 1980s, reward management had a largely internal focus geared around **internal labour markets** (Dulebohn and Werling, 2007), which represented the 'jobs for life' ethos that a good proportion of employees experienced for the bulk of the twentieth century. An internal labour market exists in a whole organization, or part of one, in which wages, benefits, and other rewards are determined by organizational policies and procedures. An internal market functions through systems for grading different jobs, different rewards allocated to different jobs, grades and systems for pay, and reward progression such as links to qualifications, tenure, or seniority. As employees increase their job-specific and organization-specific knowledge, then progression through the reward system follows (Dulebohn and Werling, 2007), although employability outside the organization can diminish as organization-specific knowledge increases.

The classic internal labour market was a workforce of almost all full-time staff on permanent contracts where the organization preferred to recruit at the bottom and promote from within and where there was a high proportion of long-serving employees. Seltzer and Sammartino (2009) show that the classic features of internal markets that underpinned reward theory and practice in the USA until the 1970s were also present in large Australian employers as early as the late nineteenth century.

Internal labour markets started to dismantle as a result of changes in thinking triggered by, or at least coincident with, economic shifts in the 1980s and 1990s. Recession, downsizing, and the accompanying rapid shift in global manufacturing locations led to new ways of thinking about the employment relationship and reward was no exception. A key outcome of the new thinking was a stronger focus on external market forces and a weakened ability among some employers to offer the security and promotion deal that had existed before.

However, it is important to recognize that internal labour markets still prevail in many organizations, although there does seem to have been a shift in attitudes and HRM practices (Grimshaw et al., 2001), reflecting both external pressures and opportunities. Japanese employers known for the concept of job security, training, and promotion in return for loyalty have questioned their intensely strong internal markets given the country's weak economic performance over the past twenty years. Internal labour markets were affected by the introduction of performance-related pay and by greater use of part-time and temporary staff. However, the substantive features of the market (lifetime employment and wages linked to tenure and seniority) remain and provide continuity with past arrangements. It is still hard to join a Japanese company, except when young (Keizer, 2009).

It is important, however, not to see internal market changes as simply a result of rational responses by employers to economic conditions beyond their control. These conditions can explain some of the problems inherent in HRM (Thompson, 2011) and employers may be responding to and taking advantage of a political economy that they see as conducive to their interests. The current political economy of the UK is influenced by the financial crisis and has produced a rhetoric that emphasizes that employers cannot afford to employ as many people as before, that they cannot afford wage rises or the same pension rights any longer. At the same time, there is a narrative that managerial elites still need to be handsomely rewarded, otherwise society will not benefit from their rare skills and the economy will be worse off.

The political economies of the former Soviet states still exert an influence on HRM practices in those countries (Horowitz, 2011). A marked change in political economy occurred in the UK when the Labour government of the late 1970s was replaced by several terms of Conservative government. Changes to employment law substantially altered the role of trades unions in employee relations, for example. The upshot is that changes in the political economy can give employers the 'excuses' they need to push through HRM changes that they have wanted to make for some time. Management practices that were not possible before, or that at least would have been very risky, become acceptable because a new political will is operating.

Reward philosophy and strategy

Changes in labour markets led to changes in the ways that employers thought about reward and ways of paying people—their philosophies and strategies. Reward philosophies are shaped by organizational choices around management style, which is shaped by organizational history, current predicament, size, and location. A unitary style is one that attempts to get all employees committed to organizational goals and working together towards the goals as a team. A pluralist style recognizes that the harmony implicit in the unitary approach is unlikely to occur and so accepts that different interest groups exist and that conflict will, at times, exist between employers and employees (Gennard and Judge, 2005). Purcell and Sisson (1983) expanded on this binary concept to propose five styles.

Authoritarian typical in small, owner-dominated organizations where employee relations are not seen as important.

Paternalistic common in small, owner-dominated situations but where there is much more concern for employee involvement. Reward is seen as a key factor influencing employee relations.

Constitutional this assumes that trades unions are present, but here the management style is more adversarial than it is consultative.

Consultative encourages union participation in management decision making.

Opportunist management style is transient and changes to respond to local conditions.

As organizational contexts change, it becomes important for managers to be aware of the style that is predominating in their workplace and to adapt style if necessary. Of course, this is extremely difficult to do and could lead to disputes, for example following attempts to re-verse union recognition. Against this background, a **reward philosophy** sets out the broad beliefs and principles that the organization has about how employees should be rewarded and so summarizes how decisions about rewarding employees fit with the organization's vision and mission. These beliefs shape much of the detail of actual reward practices and shape decisions, for example about how executives should be rewarded, to what extent individual performance should be related to reward, and combinations of base and variable pay. For instance a profit-seeking multinational with an emphasis on growing shareholder value is likely to articulate a different philosophy from a government organization that has a completely different set of stakeholders and, because of political control, fewer degrees of freedom open to it when deciding how to reward people.

Reward philosophies and the finer details of actual reward practices, including levels of pay and other benefits, are often determined by a remuneration committee or similar group. This provides some degree of independence from the top management which, in turn, enables organizations to defend and justify decisions about reward practices to employees and other stakeholders, such as shareholders and the media. Once the overarching philosophy is in place, then a more detailed **reward strategy** can be developed.

Reward strategies are forward-looking statements that link where the organization is now to where it wants to be in relation to how people are rewarded. They articulate how reward will contribute to achieving corporate strategy, for example by showing how important workforce changes needed to hit strategic targets will be rewarded. As such, reward strategy has to align with other HRM policy areas, such as career management, and take into account the views of both employers and employees. Employers need to provide a fair and motivational system to foster the knowledge, skills, and characteristics that they need. Strategies also have to be affordable and controllable given that employment costs can be very high. Reward strategies give employers an opportunity to signal the kinds of skills and behaviour that the organization needs and to show how they will be rewarded. Despite the conflicts of interests that could arise (e.g. with unions) more organizations have developed reward strategies because they are increasingly conscious of the impact that human capital strategies have on performance (Gross and Friedman, 2004). Strategy deals with aligning reward programmes to what the organization wants to achieve and shows how the philosophy is put into practice.

Reward strategies

Total reward

The idea of **total reward** is to recognize that, over and above pay, many other aspects of a reward package have a strong monetary equivalence or attraction (Kaplan, 2005). Total reward recognizes this and is more attuned to individual employee preferences, e.g. unique profiles of financial and psychological rewards, and as such creates a more attractive employee value proposition. Organizations are increasingly allowing employees to 'pick and mix' tangible rewards up to a value for their grade. The balance of money and psychological rewards is set out in Figure 7.2, recognizing that these factors could map differently for different jobs. Base pay, bonuses, and performance-related pay usually represent the highest money value rewards. Share purchase options, pension contributions, and type of pension scheme may

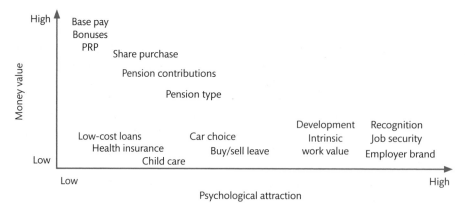

Figure 7.2 Financial and psychological components of reward

also be substantial. Low-cost finance (i.e. cheap loans) or health insurance have relatively lower money values.

Psychological factors operate with a range of benefits, and factors with a high psychological component include the intrinsic nature of the work itself, the **employer brand,** and the learning and development opportunities that come from being associated with a particular employer. Five years' service with a market-leading multinational may have a higher present and future value to an individual than five years' experience with a market follower, for instance. These factors can have a strong reward value if the individual employee believes that they can leverage them to obtain promotion or a retention package.

Pay strategies

Several strategies are open to employers when deciding how to organize the pay component of reward. Underpinning choices of pay strategy is a process of job evaluation that decides how much a particular job is worth. Organizations need mechanisms for comparing and rating jobs across different areas, such as engineering and marketing, so that employees get equal pay for work of equal value; these methods have been increasing (Watson Wyatt, 2004). Factors used to compare jobs depend on the nature of the work and the strategic priorities (Heneman, 2003), although they typically include:

- technical knowledge;
- level of responsibility for income, expenditure, or resources;
- working conditions (e.g. safety hazards, unsocial hours);
- level of responsibility for people (leadership and change);
- level of intellectual content and innovation/creativity needed.

The extent to which each factor applies to a particular job is then assessed and the outcome is a ranking of different jobs based on the level of knowledge, skills, and responsibility present in the job. When the relative values of jobs have been determined each job is linked to actual levels of pay and a pay structure or grading system. Market rates and external benchmarking are influential in setting actual pay levels.

Narrow banding

A classic approach to structuring basic pay that is still widely used uses narrow-banded grading systems in which the difference between the top and bottom of a grade (the band width) is relatively small. **Narrow banding** gives management tight control over wages but can be frustrating for employees, who rely on promotion to increase their salaries, but even after several grade promotions may not be earning much more. Because of its rigidities some employers have concluded that narrow banding is not flexible enough to match employee expectations about reward growth and have switched to broadbanding.

Broadbanding

Broadbanding was a response to the market conditions of the 1990s and the accompanying organizational rhetoric of flatter structures and faster responsiveness. It tackles the limitations of narrow banding by condensing several narrow bands into fewer broad bands with a bigger salary range. This gives greater freedom to locate employees in a more flexible system and the freedom to increase rewards without the need to promote people in order to give them a pay rise.

In the UK and the USA some organizations have moved from narrow to broadbanding, although the trend has not been extensive (Giancola, 2009). However, it is widely distributed in multinational subsidiaries in the Far East (Brock and Siscovick, 2007). Armstrong and Brown (2005) describe a broadbanding arrangement in Glaxo Smith Kline, which is based on five bands; two for top managers, one each for directors and managers, one for professionals, technicians, and one for administrators. Each band is divided into pay zones and is accompanied by a different entitlement to benefits. Professional jobs, for example, would be clustered into the various zones in the band depending on overall job content.

Performance-related pay

Performance-related pay (PRP) is based on the premise that an additional reward component will raise individual performance. It is widely used among senior managers, where the performance-related component of a reward package can be up to several times the base salary. A key requirement is to measure performance fairly and reliably and there are two main approaches to this; PRP linked to the achievement of quantifiable targets such as profit targets or share price; or PRP linked to the outcomes of a performance review process (for more on performance management and the appraisal process see discussions throughout Chapter 8, 'Performance management').

The effectiveness of PRP is dependent on the context of a particular organization and this contextual overlay explains why it is much more widely found in some sectors and cultures than others. For instance PRP in the French civil service was found to 'undermine the public service motivations that drive civil servants' (Forest, 2008). In a review of PRP schemes in the US public sector Perry et al. (2009) drew the following conclusions.

1. PRP failed to change employee thinking and motivation. Often the basic components of expectancy theory were not present; employees could not see the links between performance and pay or did not believe that the extra pay would materialize, incentives were too small to be motivational, and employees perceived that it could be divisive.

2. Contextual factors including the type of public service, trust levels in the workplace, and good performance management moderated how well PRP worked.

3. PRP works at low levels as well as at high levels. This was explained through ability to measure job performance at both levels and improved goal setting.

4. Implementation of PRP schemes is fraught with difficulties. In the public sector these can be linked to heightened sensitivity to issues such as transparency, scheme management, fairness of outcomes, and acceptability of related practices such as appraisal style.

5. Public organizations introducing PRP schemes should not feel coerced into mimicking existing schemes used elsewhere but should design tailored systems to suit them.

Forms of performance-related pay

Team-based pay

Team-based pay is used with a clearly identifiable work group such as a project team or management team. It tends to be used with managers and professionals but is not very widely found. An extensive pilot study in UK hospitals (Reilly et al., 2005) gave mixed results. Where improvements were found it was difficult to determine whether they were because of team-based pay or whether they were caused by better managers and management systems. There were also difficulties in defining team composition, which caused some resentment among people outside the teams. Target setting was also difficult; hospital managers found it much easier to measure inputs, rather than outcomes. Where targets were externally imposed it was easy for teams to argue why they were inappropriate or unachievable.

Skills-based pay

This approach links pay to learning and is more focused on the person than on the job. A core assumption is that higher learning will, in time, impact upon personal development and job performance. This is supported by empirical evidence that skills-based pay does associate with employees maintaining and acquiring skills (Dierdorff and Surface, 2008). In a manufacturing setting it has also been associated with reducing labour costs, improved quality, and greater productivity (Murray and Gerhart, 1998). Perhaps because of its indirect focus on outcomes and performance, skills-based pay is not widely used and may be declining further (Giancola, 2011). Organization type also appears to have an influence; skills-based pay is more likely to work in manufacturing than service environments and where technical innovation is needed (Shaw et al., 2005).

Competency-based pay

Competence is closely linked to skills but is a little different. Competences can be thought of as the outcomes of a bundle of knowledge, skills, and attributes that a person has, which might link to, for example, their ability to influence others, lead change, or create networks. They are highly behavioural and can be closely related to specific work contexts. To underpin competence-based pay, organizations need to identify the critical competences that link to their strategies, and these are often published in organizational competence frameworks. Difficulties arise when it comes to assessing and measuring the extent to which a person displays particular competences.

Case Study 7.1 Linking compensation to performance

E.On

E.On is a worldwide power and gas company with about 93,000 employees in 2008 in over thirty countries. Compensation is based on the principles of supporting the company's need to attract and retain 'performance-oriented people'. Most employees are compensated in accordance with collective wage agreements made with trades unions; 88 per cent in Central Europe and 99 per cent in Nordic countries. However, many employees have a PRP component in the reward package. Investment plans allow employees to acquire shares 'under especially favourable conditions'. In 2008 in Germany, about 60 per cent of employees acquired on average about 50 shares each. Additional benefits include access to a pension plan and access to training at the E.On Academy (a corporate university), on-line learning modules, and collaboration with business schools.

Johnson and Johnson

Johnson and Johnson is a world leading manufacturer of health-care products. Net sales were over $63 billion in 2008 from over 250 companies in fifty-seven countries. It is committed to offering 'fair and adequate' compensation, which needs to 'support the movement of talent' across the company's global operations. The reward strategy is designed to underpin a high-performance culture and includes reward components linked to 'individual performance and business results'. The benefits package is flexible and varies across the group's companies in an effort to match rewards to what individuals want, rather than impose the same across all employees. Employees are able to mix cash bonuses with share options in tailored packages. Other components of reward include recognition for leadership at individual, business, and company levels, each of which is accompanied by a financial payment. Employees are also able to nominate colleagues for 'Encore Awards' in recognition of 'exceptional performance and enthusiastic commitment to success'. There are five levels of this award reflecting performance 'above and beyond normal expectations'.

Henkel

Henkel, headquartered in Germany, has over 50,000 employees worldwide in homecare, cosmetics, toiletries, and adhesives businesses. Their reward strategies aim to 'attract, motivate and retain highly skilled, talented and best performing employees all over the world'. Strategy is built upon:

- fixed base salary determined by local market conditions, individual skills, and performance;
- short-term incentives—an annual incentive plan open to managers;
- long-term incentives—open to the 'core management team' to reward long-term value creation.

A conventional cascade approach is used in which ambitious and quantifiable targets for the company are filtered down to individual level. PRP is also extended to about 65 per cent of non-managerial employees worldwide.

- Employees in China receive annual bonuses based on team targets, individual targets, and work attitude, such as initiative and customer orientation.
- In South America, targets for each business unit cascade to team and personal targets.
- In Luxembourg, quarterly bonus payments are linked to the rate of utilization of production machinery.
- In Italy, a PRP component is 'determined in consultation' every four years with unions and a works council.

Employees worldwide have access to an employee share purchase scheme allowing them to invest up to 4 per cent of their salary (up to a maximum of €5000) each year.

Source: corporate websites

Discussion Activity 7.2

> Why are team-based and skills-based pay not more widely used? What particular problems would arise for multinational companies that wanted to use team and skills-based pay?

International influences on reward strategy

Pay determination

Across international business operations, many factors influence decisions about pay and reward. Firms in the USA, for instance, tend to use more equity in their reward strategies than firms outside the USA and this can be partly explained by national legal structures; the more shareholders are protected by law, then generally the more equity features in reward (Bryan et al., 2011). Reward was also affected by relations between owners and managers and between types of shareholders, depending on how much control and influence they have.

A model of pay determination developed by Werner and Ward (2004) includes the following key factors illustrated in Figure 7.3. Determinants of pay can be grouped as follows:

- national environmental factors, such as minimum wage agreements, wage-setting practices, legislation, inflation, and levels of unemployment. These environmental factors influence the degrees of freedom that employers have over how pay is determined, pay levels, and as such influence organization practices. Sayim (2011), for example, found that Turkish companies were 'pulling' advances in reward practices from the USA as a result of the permissive (i.e. relatively unregulated) ways that business can operate in Turkey;

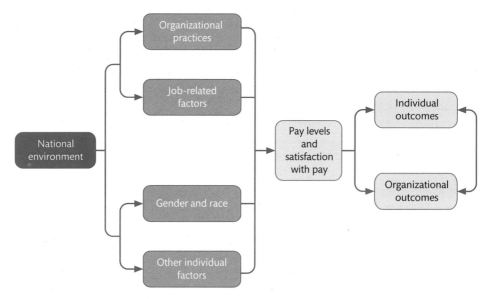

Figure 7.3 Determinants and outcomes of reward

Source: Based on Werner and Ward (2004).

- organization practices, including union recognition, efforts to implement **high performance work systems**, outsourcing, the extent of the organization's focus on external labour markets and pay relativities, internal decision processes, and actual pay strategies. These influence job-related factors;

- job-related factors, including the type of work, shifts and other conditions, seniority, job design, and the extent of teamwork. Job-related factors are not simply a consequence of organization practices, however, as the nature of the work will influence organizational decisions;

- gender and race issues, including levels of education, access to power networks, occupational choices (e.g. women preferring part-time work; or Third Country national (TNC) gravitating towards certain types of job), and tenure (women may have shorter tenure due to decisions about parenting). TNCs are, for example, Indian workers for an American company in Saudi Arabia and are distinguished, in this example, from Host Country Nationals (HCNs) (Saudis) or parent company nationals (PCNs) (Americans);

- other individual factors, such as social skills, workplace behaviour, career management, education, and family structure. These influence individual ability and motivation in relation to the levels of reward sought and the hunger for higher levels of reward.

Purcell (1989) provides a useful model of how employee relations decisions are taken. If, say, a German engineering company acquires a subsidiary in France, that can be seen as a first-order strategic decision. Second-order decisions are then made about how far the French company's operations should be integrated into, or kept apart from, mainstream operations. Third-order decisions are then needed about the detail of different HRM strategies. Local managerial competences and headquarters' decision preferences interact to shape eventual third-order outcomes.

The determinants listed above interact to produce a specific pay system and level of satisfaction with pay that can be positioned as an antecedent of individual attitudinal and behavioural outcomes and of organizational outcomes. Individual work-related outcomes that are linked to pay satisfaction include engagement, performance, job search decisions, absenteeism, and citizenship behavior. Outcomes at the organizational level include employment costs, how well the employer brand is perceived, and staff retention which, among others, impact upon overall organizational performance. Work-related and organizational outcomes are interrelated. For example poor organizational performance may influence the attitudes and motivation of employees.

Expatriate compensation

Multinational companies face the problem of designing reward policies and practices for expatriates. The expatriate balance sheet is one common approach where the basic idea is that, compared to other home country employees, expatriates should not lose or gain financially, and that different international assignments should be equally attractive (Reynolds, 1997). Reward is adjusted to allow for increased costs of living, for example, or for very different living conditions. A problem with the balance sheet, however, is that it could lead to inequities

Case Study 7.2 Global oversight of total remuneration programmes

Towers Perrin's 2008 survey of 150 major global companies found increasing senior management involvement in reward programmes due to rising corporate spending on pay and budgets, growing volatility, and risk attached to benefits such as pension costs, which have long-term obligations for organizations, and the increasing need to present a global brand that attracts customers and top talent. Areas for improvement to reward strategies identified through the survey were:

- Only about 50 per cent of companies had a documented total reward philosophy.
- Policies were often only 'loosely integrated with key business goals'.
- Fewer than half had a senior committee to set remuneration policy. Governance of policy remains fragmented despite a tendency towards decentralization.
- Fewer than half the companies surveyed use metrics or benchmarks to monitor the performance of reward policies.
- Comprehensive reward programmes were more likely to cover management groups; workers at lower levels were more likely covered by local practices 'loosely connected with overall goals'.

Despite changes to the way reward strategies are controlled, in particular increasing regional influence, less than half the companies surveyed regularly monitor how well remuneration policies are working. The most common metrics and benchmarks used were employee turnover, the ratio of fixed to variable costs, employee satisfaction, pension asset performance, and total employment costs per employee.

Source: Towers Perrin white paper, Effective global governance and oversight of total remuneration programs: an elusive business imperative, February 2009.

between what expatriates receive relative to locals (Bonache et al., 2011; Leung et al., 2009), and between expatriates working out of different countries, which can cause problems based on perceptions of inequity and injustice.

Despite being a fairly simple concept, executing a **balance sheet approach** is complex. In compiling the balance sheet, a wide range of economic and social factors is involved, which vary from country to country and can change in the short term through inflation or exchange rate changes. Large numbers of expatriates in an organization can make the scheme expensive and difficult to administer. In a study of Finnish expatriates, the most difficult issues they faced were with tax rates, lack of local information about living costs, risks of currency movements along with social security and pension concerns; but common satisfiers were higher net incomes locally and allowances (Suutari and Tornikoski, 2001). One tactic used to offset currency movement problems is 'split pay', where an expatriate's pay is split and paid in different currencies (Shelton, 2008).

 Stop and Think

How could locals react to perceptions of 'overpaid' expatriates? How might their reactions vary in different countries/regions? How would *you* react if an expatriate were employed in your organization to do a very similar job to your own, but with a much higher salary or expatriate package than you currently receive?

National cultural influences

Institutional differences govern differences in the way pay and rewards are set, yet differences in national and local culture would also be expected to have some influence. Geert Hofstede's work on national cultures, which offered a way of assessing and quantifying culture and thus of connecting it to other management practices, has been highly influential in cross-cultural research. However, after around thirty years of culture-driven explanations of differences in management practice doubt is growing about how much national culture, in reality, is now influencing reward practices (e.g. see Sparrow, 2000; Kirkman et al., 2006; Wei and Rowley, 2009). (See discussions throughout Chapter 4, 'Understanding IHRM: the cultural approach', for more on this topic.)

In theory, culture makes a difference because of its influence on the way people think rewards should be distributed, i.e. rewards–allocation preferences, which link to the idea of **distributive justice**. Three general approaches to allocating rewards are found (Leventhal, 1976).

- The equity norm requires that rewards are distributed in proportion to inputs and contributions. Classic PRP systems that match bonuses to performance fit the equity norm.
- The equality norm sees rewards divided among people equally.
- The need norm sees rewards distributed to people according to need.

The equity norm is widely seen in western situations and increasingly elsewhere. Indeed, it is so widespread that it underpins western models of workplace productivity. However, while one of the three norms may dominate thinking in an organization or country, they are not mutually exclusive; all of the norms may also have some influence on rewards system design. Table 7.1 shows the theoretical associations that we would expect to exist in relation to Hofstede's cultural schema.

The GLOBE study proposed nine dimensions of national culture, which overlap considerably with Hofstede's five dimensions. Of particular interest to reward, however, are GLOBE's additional dimensions of Gender Egalitarianism and Achievement/Performance Orientation (House et al., 2002). Gender Egalitarianism is the 'extent to which an organization or a society minimizes gender role differences and gender discrimination' and Performance Orientation is the extent to which an organization or society rewards performance improvement and excellence. On most GLOBE dimensions there are large differences between countries. Northern and western European countries are mostly high on Performance Orientation, Collectivism, and Uncertainty Avoidance. Southern and eastern European countries score more highly on assertiveness, Power Distance, and Collectivism (Koopman et al., 1999). Theoretical assumptions that integrate culture, leadership, and organizational behaviour include the following:

- Cultures affect what the leaders of organizations do and therefore what organizations do.
- Organization cultures are strong enough to influence the behaviour of new leaders.
- 'Strategic organizational contingencies' such as the number of employees, type of technology used, and competitive conditions influence organizational decisions, but these decisions will be moderated by cultural forces (House et al., 2002).

Tosi and Greckhamer (2004) found that the way CEO reward is structured in an organization within a particular culture has a 'symbolic meaning within the organization'. Reward

Table 7.1 Culture and reward—theoretical predictions

Cultural characteristic	Example	Expected reward practices
Collectivist, feminine	Scandinavian countries	Group and team-based rewards, the equality norm, greater generosity to out-group members, access to personal and family welfare benefits, greater union involvement in wage determination, relatively low pay differentials
Individualist	USA	Strong emphasis on PRP, variable pay, incentives, bonuses and commission, the equity norm, recognition schemes (e.g. employee of the month), employee share ownership plans, high pay differentials
High Power Distance	Mexico	Seniority-based, higher subjective influence of individual managers in determining employees' pay awards and levels, low use of PRP, less likelihood of employee ownership plans, e.g. stock options, High Power Distance suggests high reward differentials
High Uncertainty Avoidance	Japan	Qualification-based, seniority-based pay and skills-based pay, avoidance of variable pay and PRP due to the risks of not getting it (high UA = high risk avoidance)
High Masculinity	Hong Kong	Emphasis on PRP and material rewards, rewards used to emphasize achievement and success, less use of personal and family benefits

Sources: Based on Aycan (2005); Chiang and Birtch (2006); Gerhart (2008); Hofstede (2001); Kirkman et al. (2006); Schuler and Rogowsky (1998); Tosi and Greckhamer (2004)

structures also express 'deeper social values' such that the expression differs from one culture to another. This shows that reward practices are not culturally neutral—a particular practice is interpreted in different ways in different local cultures.

Cultures with a high achievement and Performance Orientation would be expected to favour PRP systems. By definition, nations high on Gender Egalitarianism would be expected to have anti-discrimination legislation in place and to have workplace systems for bringing about equal pay for equal work. Schuler and Rogowsky (1998) tested a range of theoretical culture/reward propositions across twenty-four countries and found partial support for their predictions. Their results support the idea that multinational companies shape reward systems around cultural types and that they should continue to do so. However, the research took no account of factors such as industry type or organization size, which could explain some or all of the associations found. Furthermore, Gerhart (2008) brings into question cross-cultural research that relies upon scoring cultural dimensions in questionnaires based on Hofstede and similar theoretical models, and relating them to differences in such HRM practices as reward. In particular, he questions the core assumptions that underpin research in this area.

1. First, if national culture is to shape and constrain management practices then differences between countries need to be larger than differences within countries. For example differences in Power Distance scores between China and France need to be greater than the variation across Power Distance scores within China and France. If, for instance, a region of

China exhibits Power Distance scores equal to those found across France, then the assumption is broken, as an organization in that region breaks the pattern for China. Gerhart shows that the differences between countries are not as large as is often assumed by simply comparing the scores obtained through Hofstede-type culture questionnaires.

2. A second assumption is that differences in national culture outweigh variations in organizational culture. Research shows, however, that organization cultures often do not fit national culture profiles. In the USA, Brazil, and India, Nelson and Gopalan (2003) found clusters of organizations with cultures that matched the national culture (isomorphism) and clusters of organizations that did not match the national culture (rejective). They suggested that rather than discuss the extent of convergence and divergence in management practices, it would be better to focus on how forces for convergence interact with forces for divergence in the local setting. A study of international alliances found that differences in professional cultures had the most disruptive effect on outcomes, followed by organizational culture, which was more disruptive than differences in national cultures (Sirmon and Lane, 2004). Professional cultures exist in groups of people in similar occupations and develop through systems of education and training, how knowledge is generated, and the ways competence is demonstrated—consider, for instance, differences in medicine, engineering, and law. In sum, differences in national culture do not explain much of the variation that we see in organization culture and yet it is distinctive organization cultures that shape the detail of reward practices.

3. Third, it is often assumed that a mismatch between cultural types and management practice will be detrimental to performance; for example not using PRP in an individualistic context, or using PRP in a highly collective setting. Research, however, shows only small effects of national culture on reward practices related to PRP (Gerhart, 2008). A comparison of reward in Finland and Hong Kong, two countries that map quite differently in terms of cultural dimensions, found no clear differences. This suggests that micro- and macro-variables, such as state welfare systems, levels of taxation, organizational priorities, and sector norms explain much of the variation seen.

These finding suggest that the links between national culture and reward practices are not as strong as are sometimes assumed.

Influences on pay satisfaction

Pay satisfaction

Job satisfaction is an important variable in explaining how people behave at work and is a multidimensional construct including satisfaction with colleagues, supervision, promotion, the work itself, and with pay (Kinicki et al., 2002). Pay satisfaction according to Heneman and Schwab (1985) can be further split into satisfaction with the level of pay (i.e. direct wages), with raises, with benefits, and with the way it is administered, e.g. the pay given to different jobs (Garcia et al., 2009).

Studies generally confirm that individual pay dissatisfaction is related to a range of outcomes, such as looking for a new job and absenteeism (Currall et al., 2005). But to what extent do employee attitudes when aggregated across a workforce impact on organizational performance? Currall and colleagues found that 'shared attitudes can influence organizational outcomes' (Currall et al., 2005: 632) and, more specifically, Schneider and colleagues (2003)

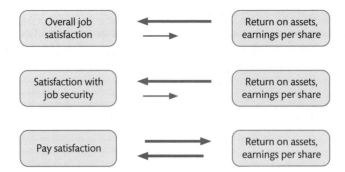

Figure 7.4 Relationships between organizational performance and aggregate workforce satisfaction
Source: Based on Schneider et al. (2003).

found in a sample of US profit-seeking companies that organizational performance was more of a cause rather than a consequence of overall job satisfaction and satisfaction with job security. When it came to satisfaction with pay, however, they found evidence of a much more reciprocal relationship over time, as illustrated in Figure 7.4, in which the larger arrows indicate the bigger causal influence.

Unravelling relationships among the variables that impact on pay satisfaction is highly complex and Williams et al. (2006) give a useful summary. Based on equity theory (Adams, 1965) and discrepancy theory (Lawler, 1973), at the heart of pay satisfaction lies the discrepancy between what people think they should be paid and what they are paid. Perceptions of what a person thinks they should be paid are influenced by three things. First, personal factors such as age; older people may think they deserve more pay than younger people. Higher levels of education could also associate with expectations of higher pay. Second, perceptions of the job, such as responsibility or its impact on the organization, could raise pay expectations. Indeed, increasing responsibility could be linked to decreasing pay satisfaction if the employee's expectations of pay are unmet. Third, employees compare themselves to others and look at the inputs and outputs that others give in the workplace. Looking around and seeing someone doing less and getting paid more is likely to lead to pay dissatisfaction. If others are seen as doing more but also as getting higher rewards then that is less likely to lead to pay dissatisfaction.

Perceptions of the pay (reward) received are related to the actual reward given. It is interesting to note, however, that research consistently finds little positive relation between the amount of reward and satisfaction with that reward (Williams et al., 2006). Highly paid people can be just as dissatisfied with their pay as low paid people.

 Discussion Activity 7.3

Both high and low earners can be dissatisfied with their pay. What are the reasons for pay dissatisfaction and are they any different for high and low earners?

Organizational justice

Pay satisfaction is assumed to correlate with both distributive and procedural justice (see Folger and Konovsky, 1989). Distributive justice (a person's assessment of whether they have been treated fairly) covers a wide range of organizational actions, not just pay and reward, and concerns the fairness with which outcomes, like pay, promotions, and development opportunities are distributed. Procedural justice concerns how well employees see the reward processes operating, i.e. how fair are the procedures by which pay and rewards are set.

Tremblay and colleagues (2000) found, in a French-Canadian cultural context, that employees distinguished clearly between satisfaction with pay and satisfaction with benefits. They also found that distributive justice was a better predictor of pay satisfaction than distributive justice, whereas procedural justice was a better predictor of benefits satisfaction than distributive justice. The implications are that employers need to be aware of employee sensitivity to justice in the implementation of reward strategies. Workforce expectations about justice and their responses to actions by employers, however, are to some extent determined by national cultural influences such as the Confucian doctrine found in South Korea (Mueller et al., 1999).

Equity sensitivity

Equity theory (Adams, 1965) is a powerful theoretical force in reward management and a refinement of the theory relating to equity sensitivity is worth noting. Central to equity theory is the comparison that individuals make of their own inputs and outcomes in relation to the inputs and outcomes of others. Inputs might be in terms of effort or initiative and outcomes are rewards given by the organization, which may be monetary or in terms of status. Where an individual sees, for example, a colleague getting higher reward for what they see as the same inputs, then a state of perceived inequity exists. Equity theory is perhaps most useful in explaining what happens when people feel they are under-rewarded. Actions to restore equity then follow and these include lowering inputs (giving less effort), redefining what the comparator contributes, or finding another comparator.

Stemming from this is the question of whether people react in broadly similar ways or whether we differ in our sensitivity to inequitable situations. Huseman et al. (1987) propose three groups of people; equity sensitives, entitleds, and benevolents. Equity sensitives are the most likely to react if they feel under-rewarded in relation to a comparator. They are mindful of their equity balance or equilibrium and when it is disturbed they will act to restore it, acquiring peace of mind when they feel the input/outcome ratio is in harmony. Entitleds have more interest in seeing themselves as over-rewarded in relation to others. They think that whatever they get they deserve. If they give to a social situation they will want something in return. Benevolents are those who will give without necessarily wanting reciprocation in money or in kind. They are more resistant to inequity and as such are less likely to react to under-reward. They experience feelings of guilt if they feel they are being over-rewarded.

Equity sensitivity theory predicts the following relations between job satisfaction and equity perceptions (Huseman et al., 1987: 229).

1. For the entitled, job satisfaction will steadily increase as they move from feeling under-rewarded, through to feeling equitably rewarded, and then over-rewarded.

2. For benevolents, job satisfaction will decrease as they move from feeling under-rewarded to over-rewarded.

3. For equity sensitives, job satisfaction will rise as they move from feeling under-reward to equitably rewarded and then fall if they move from feeling equitably rewarded to feeling over-rewarded.

Of interest to international managers is whether there are cross-national and cross-cultural differences in equity sensitivity. Much more research is needed in this area, and studies so far do point to some differences—for example Allen et al. (2005) found that Japanese employees had an entitled orientation and were more likely to react to inequity compared to American employees.

Summary

Employment costs represent a big slice of corporate spending and reward strategies influence the achievement of business objectives. Reward, however, is arguably the most difficult human resource management practice to optimize and in multinational companies it becomes even more difficult. A wide range of institutional, cultural, organizational, and job-related factors influences the detailed design of reward programmes. Employee satisfaction with reward is influenced by a range of personal factors. Although there is evidence that increasing multinational activity is spreading the use of different reward practices, there is also evidence that the adoption of reward practices is relatively immune to cultural differences.

Review questions

1. What are the advantages to MNCs of developing and publicizing a reward philosophy?

2. In equity sensitivity theory, how would equity sensitives, benevolents, and entitleds react differently if management asked them to raise their performance but do not offer any additional rewards?

3. Why does the gender wage gap exist and what measures can multinational organizations take to reduce the gap?

4. Assuming that a workforce contains a balance of the three equity sensitive types, can an employer ever expect to have a workforce satisfied with its reward strategy?

5. From question 4, what features of a reward strategy would help to minimize pay dissatisfaction?

6. In relation to a workplace with which you are familiar, what do you think is the dominant reward-allocation rule; equality, equity, or need?

7. If MNC activity continues to increase, are reward strategies and practices likely to converge on a global scale? What are the barriers to convergence?

8. Reward is often portrayed as an HRM practice that is relatively immune to cultural influences. Why is this?

9. In light of the recent international financial crisis and public concerns about executive pay, discuss the proposition that the pay and bonuses of bankers and other senior executives needs to be much more closely controlled.

10. Why might large organizations be attracted to broadbanding?

Further reading

Briscoe, D.R., Schuler, R.S., and Claus, L. (eds) (2009) *International Human Resource Management—Policies and Practices for Multinational Companies*, 3rd edn, Abingdon: Routledge.

For more information on compensation and benefits including more detail on the balance sheet approach, see Chapter 7, Global compensation, benefits and taxes, pp. 236–85.

Dillon, K. (2009) The coming battle over executive pay, *Harvard Business Review*, 87(9): 96–103.

See this article for an account of overhauled reward strategies at MNC Reckitt Benckiser linking it more closely to executive performance.

Sims, R.H. and Schraeder, M. (2005) Expatriate compensation: an exploratory review of salient contextual factors and common practices, *Career Development International*, 10(2): 98–108.

This article provides a summary of factors affecting expatriate compensation and approaches used.

Stahl, G.K. and Bjorkman, I. (eds) (2006) *Handbook of International Human Resource Management*, Cheltenham: Edward Elgar, pp. 158–75, 2006.

For a detailed review of expatriate compensation, see J. Bonache, Chapter 9, The compensation of expatriates: a review and future research agenda, pp. 158–75.

Bibliography

Adams, J. (1965) Inequity in social exchange, in L. Derkowitz (ed.) *Advances in Experimental Social Psychology*, New York: Academic Press, pp. 267–99.

Allen, R.S., Takeda, M., and White, C.S. (2005) Cross-cultural equity sensitivity: a test of differences between the United States and Japan, *Journal of Managerial Psychology*, 20(8): 641–62.

Armstrong, M. and Brown, D. (2005) Reward strategies and trends in the United Kingdom: the land of pragmatic dreams, *Compensation and Benefits Review*, 37(4): 41–53.

Aycan, Z. (2005) The interplay between cultural and institutional/structural contingencies in human resource management practices, *International Journal of Human Resource Management*, 16(7): 1083–119.

Bonache, J., Sanchez, J., and Zarraga-Oberty, C. (2011) The interaction of expatriate pay differential and expatriate inputs on host country nationals' pay unfairness, *International Journal of Human Resource Management*, 20(10): 2135–49.

Bratton, J. and Gold, J. (2007) *Human Resource Management: Theory and Practice*, 4th edn, London: Palgrave.

Briscoe, D.R., Schuler, R.S., and Claus, L. (2009) *International Human Resource Management—Policies and Practices for Multinational Companies*, 3rd edn, Abingdon: Routledge.

Brock, D.M. and Siscovick, I.C. (2007) Global integration and local responsiveness in multinational subsidiaries: some strategy, structure and human resource contingencies, *Asia Pacific Journal of World Business*, 45(3): 353–73.

Bryan, S., Nash, R., and Patel, A. (2011) Law and executive compensation: a cross-country study, *Journal of Applied Corporate Finance*, 23(1): 84–91.

Chiang, F. and Birtch, T. (2006) An empirical examination of reward preferences within and across national settings, *Management International Review*, 46(5): 573–96.

Currall, S.C., Towler, A.J., Judge, T.A., and Kohn, L. (2005) Pay satisfaction and organizational outcomes, *Personnel Psychology*, 58(3): 613–40.

Daniels, H. (2008) Patterns of pay: results of the annual survey of hours and earnings 1997-2007, *Economic and Labour Market Review*, 2(2): 23–31.

Dierdorff, E. and Surface, E. (2008) If you pay for skills, will they learn? Skill change and maintenance under a skill-based pay system, *Journal of Management*, 34(4): 721–43.

Dillon, K. (2009) The coming battle over executive pay, *Harvard Business Review*, 87(9): 96–103.

Dulebohn, J.H. and Werling, S.E. (2007) Compensation research past, present and future, *Human Resource Management Review*, 17(2): 191–207.

European Professional Women's Network (EPWN) (2008) *European PWN Boardroom Monitor 2008*, online at http://www.europeanpwn.net (accessed November 2009).

Eurostat (2009) Total Wages and Salaries, Eurostat Database, online at http://epp.eurostat.ec.europa.eu/portal/page/portal/labour_market/earnings/main_tables (accessed 19 December 2012).

Folger, R. and Konovsky, M.A. (1989) Effects of procedural and distributive justice on reactions to pay raise decisions, *Academy of Management Journal*, 32(1): 115–30.

Fombrun, C., Tichy, N., and Devanna, M. (1984) *Strategic Human Resource Management*, New York: Wiley.

Forest, V. (2008) Performance-related pay and work motivation: theoretical and empirical perspectives for the French civil service, *International Review of Administrative Sciences*, 74(2): 325–39.

Garcia, M.F., Posthuma, R.A., Mumford, T., and Quinones, M. (2009) The five dimensions of pay satisfaction in the Maquiladora plant in Mexico, *Applied Psychology*, 58(4): 509–19.

Gennard, J. and Judge, G. (2005) *Employee Relations*, 4th edn, London: CIPD.

Gerhart, B. (2008) Cross cultural management research: assumptions, evidence and suggested directions, *International Journal of Cross-Cultural Management*, 8(3): 259–74.

Giancola, F. (2009) A framework for understanding new concepts in compensation management, *Benefits and Compensation Digest*, 46(9): 13–16.

— (2011) Skills-based pay: fad or classic, *Compensation & Benefits Review*, 43(4): 220–26.

Grimshaw, D., Ward, K.G., Rubery, J., and Beynon, H. (2001) Organizations and the transformation of the internal labour market, *Work, Employment and Society*, 15(1): 25–54.

Gross, S.E. and Friedman, H.M. (2004) Creating an effective total reward strategy, *Benefits Quarterly*, Third Quarter: 7–12.

Heneman, H.G. and Schwab, D.P. (1985) Pay satisfaction: its multidimensional nature and measurement, *International Journal of Psychology*, 20(2): 129–42.

Heneman, R.L. (2003) Job and work evaluation: a literature review, *Public Personnel Management*, 32(21): 47–72.

Hofstede, G. (2001) *Culture's Consequences: Comparing Values, Behaviors, Institutions and Organizations across Nations*, 2nd edn, Thousand Oaks, CA: Sage.

Horowitz, F. (2011) Future HRM challenges to multinational firms in Eastern and Central Europe, *Human Resource Management Journal*, 21(4): 432–43.

House, R., Javidan, M., Hanges, P., and Dorfman, P. (2002) Understanding cultures and implicit leadership theories across the globe: an introduction to project GLOBE, *Journal of World Business*, 37(1): 3–10.

Huseman, R.C., Hatfield, J.D., and Miles, E.W. (1987) A new perspective on equity theory: the equity sensitivity construct, *Academy of Management Review*, 12(2): 222–34.

International Labour Organization (ILO) (2009) *Global Wage Report Update* 2009, Geneva: ILO.

Kaplan, S. (2005) Total rewards in action: developing a total rewards strategy, *Benefits and Compensation Digest*, August: 32–7.

Keizer, A. (2009) Transformation in and outside the internal labour market: institutional change and continuity in Japanese employment practices, *International Journal of Human Resource Management*, 20(7): 1521.

Kinicki, A.J., McKee-Ryan, F.M., Schriesheim, C.A., and Carson, K.P. (2002) Assessing the construct validity of the job descriptive index: a review and meta-analysis, *Journal of Applied Psychology*, 87(1): 14–32.

Kirkman, B., Lowe, K., and Gibson, C. (2006) A quarter century of culture's consequences: a review of empirical research incorporating Hofstede's cultural values framework, *Journal of International Business Studies*, 37: 285–320.

Koopman, R., den Hartog, D.N., and Konrad, E. (1999) National culture and leadership profiles in Europe: some results from the GLOBE study, *European Journal of Work and Organizational Psychology*, 8(4): 503–20.

Lawler, E.E. (1973) *Motivation in Work Organizations*, Monterrey, CA: Brooks Cole.

Leung, K., Zhu, Y., and Ge, C. (2009) Compensation disparity between locals and expatriates: moderating the effects of perceived injustice in foreign multinationals in China, *Journal of World Business*, 44(1): 85–93.

Leventhal, G.S. (1976) Fairness in social relationships, in J. W. Thibaut, J. Spence and R. Carsa (eds) *Contemporary Topics in Social Psychology*, Morristown, NJ: General Learning Press, pp. 211–39.

Morgan, G. (1997) *Images of Organizations*, London: Sage.

Mueller, C.W., Iverson, R.D., and , Jo, D-G. (1999) Distributive justice evaluations in two cultural contexts: a comparison of US and South Korean teachers, *Human Relations*, 52(7): 869–93.

Murray, B. and Gerhart, B. (1998) An empirical analysis of a skill-based pay program and plant performance outcomes, *Academy of Management Journal*, 41(1): 68–78.

Nelson, R.E. and Gopalan, S. (2003) Do organizational cultures replicate national cultures? Isomorphic, rejective and reciprocal opposition in the corporate values of three countries, *Organization Studies*, 24(7): 1115–51.

Organisation for Economic Cooperation and Development (OECD) (2009) *Society at a Glance 2009*, Paris: OECD.

Perry, J.L., Engbers, T.A., and Jun, S.Y. (2009) Back to the future? Performance-related pay, empirical research and the perils of resistance, *Public Administration Review*, 69(1): 39–51.

Purcell, J. (1989) The impact of corporate strategy on human resource management, in J. Storey (ed.) *New Perspectives of Human Resource Management*, London: Routledge, pp. 67–91.

— and Sisson, K. (1983) Strategies and practice in the management of industrial relations, in G.S. Bain (ed.) *Industrial Relations in Britain*, Oxford: Oxford University Press.

Reilly, P., Phillipson, J., and Smith, P. (2005) Team-based pay in the United Kingdom, *Compensation and Benefits Review*, 37(4): 54–60.

Reynolds, C. (1997) Expatriate compensation in historical perspective, *Journal of World Business*, 32(2): 118–32.

Sayim, K.Z. (2011) Pushed or pulled? Transfer of reward management policies in MNCs, *International Journal of Human Resource Management*, 21(4): 2631–58.

Schneider, B., Hanges, P.J., Smith, D.B., and Salvaggion, N. (2003) Which comes first: employee attitudes or organizational and market performance?, *Journal of Applied Psychology*, 88: 836–51.

Schuler, R. and Rogowsky, N. (1998) Understanding compensation practice variations across firms: the impact of national culture, *Journal of International Business*, 29(1): 296–308.

Seltzer, A. and Sammartino, A. (2009) Internal labour markets: evidence from two large Australian employers, *Australian Economic History Review*, 49(2): 107–37.

Shaw, J., Gupta, N., Mitra, A., and Ledford, G. (2005) Success and survival of skill-based pay plans, *Journal of Management*, 31(1): 28–49.

Shelton, T. (2008) Global compensation strategies: managing and administering split pay for an expatriate workforce, *Compensation & Benefits Review*, 40(1): 56–60.

Sims, R.H. and Schraeder, M. (2005) Expatriate compensation: an exploratory review of salient contextual factors and common practices, *Career Development International*, 10(2): 98–108.

Sirmon, D.G. and Lane, P.J. (2004) A model of cultural differences and international alliance performance, *Journal of International Business Studies*, 35: 306–19.

Sparrow, P. (2000) International reward management, in G. White and J. Druker (eds) *Reward Management—a Critical Text*, London: Routledge, pp. 193–214.

Stahl, G.K. and Bjorkman, I. (eds) *Handbook of International Human Resource Management*, Cheltenham: Edward Elgar.

Suutari, V. and Tornikoski, C. (2001) The challenge of expatriate compensation: the sources of satisfaction and dissatisfaction among employees, *International Journal of Human Resource Management*, 12(3): 389–404.

Thompson, P. (2011) The trouble with HRM, *Human Resource Management Journal*, 21(4): 355–67.

Tosi, H.L. and Greckhamer, T. (2004) Culture and CEO compensation, *Organization Science*, 15(6): 657–70.

Towers Perrin (2009) Effective global governance and oversight of total remuneration programs: an elusive business imperative, White paper, February.

Tremblay, M., Sire, B., and Balkin, D. (2000) The role of organizational justice in pay and employee benefit satisfaction, and its effects on work attitudes, *Group and Organization Management*, 25(3): 269–90.

Vieito, J.P. and Khan, W.A. (2012) Executive compensation and gender: S&P 1500 listed firms, *Journal of Economics and Finance*, 36(2): 371–99.

Watson Wyatt (2004) Global compensation practices, Watson Wyatt Worldwide, online at http://www.worldatwork.org/pub/globalsurvey04 (accessed 12 March 2012).

Wei, Q. and Rowley, C. (2009) Changing patterns of reward in Asia: a literature review, *Asia Pacific Business Review*, 15(4): 489–506.

Werner, S.G. and Ward, S. (2004) Recent compensation research: an eclectic review, *Human Resource Management Review*, 14(2): 201–28.

Williams, M.L., McDaniel, M.A., and Nguyen, N.T. (2006) A meta-analysis of the antecedents and consequences of pay level satisfaction, *Journal of Applied Psychology*, 91(2): 392–413.

Visit the Online Resource Centre for web links, interactive glossary, and more:
http://www.oxfordtextbooks.co.uk/orc/crawley

Performance management

 Learning Outcomes

After reading this chapter you will be able to:

- understand the purpose and elements of performance management
- appreciate the challenges faced by MNEs, SMEs, and other international organizations managing performance in an international context
- illustrate some of the critical differences that national culture implies in performance management of expatriates
- explain the challenges MNEs face in trying to standardize performance management systems across the organization
- understand the issues involved in managing expatriate performance management.

Introduction

Performance management is a process used by HR professionals to improve corporate performance. This is achieved by using corporate strategic objectives as the basis for developing work goals for departments and for individuals. It is believed that through improved individual performance, overall corporate performance can be enhanced.

Performance management has evolved from concepts found in management by objectives (MBO). This term was coined by Alfred Sloan in the 1950s and popularized by Peter Drucker (1954) in his book, *The Practice of Management*. Performance management is also based on some fundamental theories about human motivation and behaviour in the workplace.

The performance management process involves several elements. These include, identifying the specific tasks in a role; setting work expectations, goals, and objectives; evaluating and measuring the achievement of these objectives; carrying out a regular appraisal interview or review; planning training and development; and recommending promotion and reward, based on the review of performance.

Some aspects of performance management, particularly the performance appraisal or review, training needs evaluation, and promotion recommendation are administered by the HR Management department but it is the line managers who are the key facilitators and owners of the process.

The appraisal, a core element of the performance management process, is given most attention in management literature mainly because of the many questions it raises related to fairness.

Performance management in an international organization is more complex because of the distance between head office HR departments and the expatriates being managed overseas. There is the added difficulty of the diverse roles international executives perform, the more complicated lines of reporting, the situational environment, and local culture. These issues will be developed later in this chapter.

In the following section, some theoretical background is provided on performance management, before considering the topic specifically in relation to MNEs.

How performance management is linked to theory

The theoretical and conceptual bases of performance management include Expectancy Theory (Vroom, 1964), Goal Setting (Locke and Latham, 1990), and the AMO (ability, motivation, and opportunity) framework (Boxall and Purcell, 2008: 173). Other concepts that also have relevance to performance management are the Psychological Contract (Rousseau, 1995) and Attribution Theory (Heider, 1958). While many of these concepts originated many years ago, they still have relevance to the performance management process today.

Expectancy Theory suggests that people are motivated to work towards goals that they believe are achievable and when they value the rewards that are offered. Rewards may be extrinsic—for example money or status—or intrinsic, such as a sense of challenge or interest, which leads to satisfaction or pride at personal achievement.

Goal Setting theory maintains that people are motivated by having difficult but achievable goals. Knowledge of results is an important aspect of this. Leonard et al. (1999: 984–92) assert that motivation is also linked to our sense of self, our traits, competencies, values, and beliefs.

The AMO framework sees performance as a function of ability, motivation, and opportunity. This means that for effective performance to occur, a person must have ability, adequate knowledge, and skills, for the task. In addition the person must be motivated to perform, with interest in and adequate incentives to carry out the task, and a choice about the level of effort and degree of persistence that will be brought to the task. Finally, the framework also acknowledges that there must be the *opportunity* to perform well. The social context, work structure, technology, and tools must be available to enable performance (Boxall and Purcell, 2008: 5–7, 173).

The Psychological Contract (Rousseau, 1995), is 'an individual's belief about the terms of their relationship with the organisation'. According to Schein (1978: 48) it is: 'a set of unwritten reciprocal expectations between an individual employee and the organisation'. The psychological contract is formed when an employee is recruited into an organization and is given expectations about the organization and role. The degree to which an employer meets the expectations of the employee, in terms of work conditions, praise, rewards, and promotion, determines the extent of the employee's motivation to perform well. This is very relevant to the expatriate employee who may find differences between the expectations of his or her headquarters managers and those of the subsidiary superiors. If pre-assignment preparation is not adequate, there may be poor interpretation or understanding of the assignment realities, resulting in a breach of the psychological contract.

Finally, Attribution Theory (Heider, 1958), considers how far we consider ourselves to be responsible for events and to what extent we attribute causes to the situation itself or to external events. In an international context, there are significant differences between national cultures in this respect. Employees from different countries attribute causes of their performance at work differently (Chiang and Birtch, 2007: 243–4). In more individualistic societies, such as the USA or the UK, performance at work is largely attributed to the employee's own actions, not to actions of others or external factors. However, in more collectivist cultures—in Asia for example—good performance may be attributed to external factors or even luck, fate, or destiny, rather than to individual intrinsic characteristics (Chiang and Birch, 2007: 243–4). Performance management in other cultures, therefore, may be more complex, and requires local understanding by those conducting performance appraisals.

The above theories and concepts can help to inform our understanding of why performance may be above or below expectations. (For more information on academic theories linked to IHRM see throughout Chapter 3, 'Key academic models, theories, and debates'.)

What is performance management?

This section outlines the main features of performance management and the key elements in the process. These key elements are equally relevant to the international context.

Performance management is also just one aspect of the whole employment relationship. (The employment relationship is discussed in more detail throughout Chapter 12, 'Managing the employment relationship in international organizations'). For Armstrong (2006: 3–4), performance management is a comprehensive process, which incorporates setting, monitoring, and evaluating the achievement of developmental goals. It encompasses agreeing expectations, responsibilities, skills, and behaviours. Performance management is a joint process involving dialogue between line managers and subordinates. It implies a continuous review of performance with formal review meetings, which focus on values, behaviours, and objectives.

The performance management process and the line manager

The performance management process has received criticism for the wide range of people management activities it tries to encompass. Goal-setting methods, fairness of measurement systems, and the ability and motivation of those who have to implement the process, are all controversial issues.

An overview of the wide range of elements contained within the performance management process and the knowledge, skills, and abilities required by line managers who implement it is illustrated in Table 8.1 below. This range of activities comes above and beyond the other day-to-day line management responsibilities. Since many expatriates also have line management responsibilities while overseas, this topic also has relevance to their work and also to their own appraisals. They may have the added difficulty of appraising staff from a different culture.

The range of skills required, especially for the interview aspects (2, 4, and 5 in Table 8.1) cannot be underestimated. This is because, despite the range of computerized/electronic performance management systems in use today, which often incorporate 'tick box' results of achievement of KPIs (key performance indicators) and grading systems, it is the individual's personal relationship and experience with the line manager, on a day-to-day basis, as well as during the appraisal interview, which conveys most personal meaning to the employee being appraised.

This role of the line manager is highly demanding as it includes review of past performance, considers potential, and recommends rewards. Some authors consider these three

Table 8.1 **Performance appraisal** elements linked to the knowledge and skills required by **line managers**

	Performance appraisal element	Knowledge and skills required by line managers when conducting appraisals
1	Planning of individual goals and objectives	Awareness of corporate business plans and departmental goals and ability to translate these into individual goals, in collaboration with the individual.
2	Discussion of the plan with the employee	Communication and negotiation skills in order to get agreement with or to renegotiate the details of the plan.
3	Objective monitoring and measurement of achievement of objectives	Awareness and use of a range of performance measurement techniques and instruments. Ability to conduct a fair evaluation in relation to agreed standards and the performance of other similar staff.
4	Appraisal interview or review meeting	Ability to explain results of the evaluation and the performance instruments used; ability to listen to views, counsel or reprimand, and motivate staff. (Coaching and mentoring skills are essential for all line managers with appraisal responsibilities.)
5	Training needs discussion and plans for the future	Knowledge of training opportunities available, relevant to employee. Sensitivity in recommending appropriate training and development activities in line with realistic predictions of their value for the employee's career opportunities within the organization and budget restrictions.
6	Recommendation of reward and promotion. Career planning discussions	Knowledge of reward and promotion possibilities. Realistic and honest discussion of opportunities given wider organizational constraints. Career planning discussion.
7	Documentation completion for HR department	Ability to complete a written/electronic document accurately to provide a fair assessment and record for the HR department. Concise but persuasive writing style to enable senior management to make decisions on pay and promotion.
8	Negotiation of employee ranking and reward	Communication skills to sell the relative ability of staff, to promote their interests in ranking and reward discussions (where forced ranking is used across departmental boundaries). Ability to persuade others.

aspects of an appraisal may be incompatible, as the **evaluator** has conflicting roles to play as **rater** or judge and mentor or coach (Murphy and DeNisi, 2008: 86–7), and the nature of the relationship between rater and ratee can be affected in the long term, by the role taken primarily. (See throughout Chapter 7, 'International Reward Management', for a discussion of performance and reward.)

These wide-ranging expectations of performance management have led to criticism that performance management is trying to do too many things at once. Armstrong and

Ward (2005: 5) in their Work Foundation study, considered seven elements that organizations need to get right to maximize the effectiveness of performance management (see Case Study 8.1, below). Their conclusion suggests there is confusion about what performance management is used for; a reward mechanism, a learning and development experience, or an exercise in control. The research showed that motivation appeared to be less of a priority. The report suggests that most organizations have forgotten that performance management should aim to enhance performance by motivating staff (Armstrong and Ward, 2005: 15–17).

Case Study 8.1 provides more information from The Work Foundation study, particularly on the activities of line managers.

 Case Study 8.1   Performance management abilities of managers

This example summarizes some of the key findings from case study research carried out by the Work Foundation and published in 2005. The findings were derived from studies of six organizations in banking, the environment, health, pharmaceuticals, and consultancy services in the UK. The objective of the research was to identify critical elements that organizations must address to ensure that performance management makes a contribution to wider business goals. The seven elements of performance management that were evaluated are, the process, people management capability, motivation, measurement and reward, the role of HR, learning organizations, and role of culture and clarity of purpose.

This extract will focus on people management capability: the skills, attitude, behaviours, and knowledge that line managers need in order to raise the performance standards of those around them, and also some aspects of measurement and reward. These issues are raised frequently in international management literature.

The case studies indicated that the issue of management capability was critical and that organizations struggled to develop their managers' capacity to manage performance. The delivery of feedback by line managers in a constructive way and having 'difficult' conversations with poor performers were identified as skills gaps. The training in organizations tended to focus on the process of performance management, rather than the people management skills.

The case studies also revealed that some managers were misusing the rating system to avoid confronting poor performers. Others used the pay–performance process to compensate staff they regarded as being poorly paid or to reward those who were at most risk of leaving. At the same time there are many aspects of measurement and rating that lack transparency, allow management inconsistency, and cause confusion between rating and ranking. Debates about these issues reduce focus on the more important valuable aspects of performance management, feedback, motivation, and performance improvement.

The report considers that performance management reflects the organizational culture and that if it is not working effectively, this could indicate deeper issues such as lack of organizational agreement about clarity of purpose, priorities, or standards, or a mismatch between espoused values and actual behaviours.

Finally the report asserts: 'What we need is a revolution in thinking and a determination to deal with the difficult issues and the root causes, rather than continually tweaking and applying 'elegant bureaucracy' (Armstrong and Ward, 2005: 28).

Adapted from: Armstrong and Ward (2005)

Discussion Activity 8.1

Discuss the individual experiences you have had of the process and effectiveness of the performance appraisal and management systems in companies where you have worked.

How far did you consider the process to be evaluative, judgemental, or developmental?

How far was your last appraisal experience a motivating one?

International research by Towers Perrin (Jesuthasan, 2007a), encompasses views of 637 HR and compensation managers in twenty-one countries. The results indicate that when it came to performance management, most firms put too much emphasis on technological advances, such as automating processes and online self-service systems. These cannot take the place of human interaction between manager and employee (Jesuthasan, 2007b).

While the discussion above has focused on performance management in general, *all* the issues raised have equal relevance to the international context and the management of international employees.

We now consider performance management in an international context.

Performance management challenges in an MNE

As mentioned in earlier chapters, the cultural and institutional context of the MNE informs the policies it can adopt in relation to HRM. In addition, the orientation of the MNE (Chakravarthy and Perlmutter, 1985) determines how much control of performance management lies at the parent/home office or local level of the organization (see Chapter 1, in the section *Organizational orientations and IHRM* and Chapter 3, in the section *The 'EPRG' model of mindsets and international strategies (Perlmutter, 1969)* for more discussion of MNE orientation). This affects whether the parent company imposes its HR practices and procedures on the subsidiary, to have conformity of systems across the organization, or whether it accepts the necessity for adaptation of these practices to the local environment. The stage of development of the organization and degree of independence in HRM at local level also depend on the parent country of the MNE and its national culture. Additionally, the level in the organization of the expatriate and the job role also dictates who takes charge of the individual's performance management and appraisal.

The challenge facing MNEs is to ensure that there is vertical and horizontal integration in the HRM and performance management policies and practices of its headquarters and subsidiaries. This is achieved when there is 'fit', and human resources are used to help achieve organizational goals. In other words, there is alignment of HR policies with the strategic objectives of the firm. There must be both vertical fit between HR policies and practices, including performance management, with the strategic management processes of the whole organization, and horizontal fit or congruence of all HR practices across the organization. Thus all HR practices also need to be coordinated effectively (Wei, 2006: 49–57).

According to Shen (2005: 70) in multinational enterprises 'international performance appraisal (IPA) is a strategic HRM process that enables it (the MNC) to evaluate and improve continuously individual, subsidiary unit, and corporate performance against clearly defined, preset objectives'. It exists so that international employees and subsidiaries act in the interests of the home company. It is complex because of 'information asymmetry' and 'goal incongruence' between the parent and subsidiaries.

These differences between parent and subsidiary are described by Vance (2006: 37) as 'dynamic tensions of duality and competing forces of convergence and divergence in global business management' between headquarters 'upstream' and local country 'downstream' processes, which need to work in sync to build synergies and implement company strategy. The upstream processes and activities of global performance management, which Vance considers, include 'strategic performance management integration and coordination, workforce internal alignment, knowledge management, and organizational learning', while 'downstream considerations include responsiveness to local conditions, sensitivity to cross cultural differences, establishment of the performance management relationship, and comprehensive training efforts'.

Vance (2006: 50–1) also notes that the conflicting requirements of headquarters and local needs often require management by the international assignee. The chapter now goes on to consider some of the specific factors that impact on the operation of performance management in MNEs, beginning with national culture.

National culture and performance management

Organizations and their subsidiaries operate within a national context and as a result their management and operating systems are influenced by national institutional and cultural factors (Whitley, 1994, 1999; Child et al., 2003). This is evident in their management of overseas subsidiaries. Many examples of attempts by MNEs to transfer their HRM practices to other countries are found in the literature. The problems encountered when trying to do this often illustrate the power of local national culture in preventing full adoption. The strength of local national culture in this respect is analysed by Miah and Bird (2007: 908) in three types of companies, Japanese parent companies, Japanese subsidiaries/joint ventures, and South Asian local companies. Japanese parent company culture tends to have less influence in shaping the HRM styles and practices in Japanese subsidiaries and joint ventures operating in South Asia. This suggests that South Asian firms still tend to maintain their national culture and traditional ways in the operating systems of their organizations (this is discussed further in Case Study 4.3, Chapter 4, 'Understanding IHRM: the cultural approach').

In contrast, an article by Ying et al. (2007) suggests that in East Asia, HRM is a reforming process towards a hybrid people management system. However, this reforming process is not one-way only. A triangle-influence between East Asia, Europe and the USA is the reality. Multiple factors are shaping the outcome of reforming people management systems in East Asia, identified as foreign influence, the state's influence, the stage of social and economic development, and national and organizational historical path.

Case Study 8.2 illustrates the limitations that exist in India to the effective implementation of performance management, largely caused by the effects of tradition and the high Power Distance culture in the society.

Finally, different countries have different degrees of acceptance of performance management even within Europe. The IBM/Towers Perrin survey in 2000 found differences in the percentage of organizations that considered performance appraisal to be a top or priority item. The results were: France 78 per cent, the UK 57 per cent, Germany 55 per cent, and

Case Study 8.2 Performance evaluation in India

The following example, from Dr A. Srinivasa Rao, showed the problems associated with implementing an effective performance management process in India in 2007. It summarizes the results of a study of performance management systems in ten Indian companies across eight major Indian industries: Textiles; Staple Fibres; Chemicals; Cement; Insulators; Aluminium; Mining, and Service sectors.

The Indian socio-economic context is an influential factor. Work organizations have been shaped by the traditional caste system, British colonization, and post-independence socialism. These have evolved into a stratified, hierarchical socio-economic class system. The British colonization resulted in administrative bureaucratization and polarization of manager and non-manager groups.

Post independence development goals with socialistic ideology strongly influenced the business community. Summarizing views of other authors, Rao suggests that the antagonist nature of trade unions makes it very difficult to make them work as a team and that the scene is further aggravated by the pro-labour stance of most labour legislation.

The study tested and confirmed four hypotheses.

1. Performance factors, such as system awareness, performance planning, feedback mechanisms, and support systems are responsible for the effectiveness of the performance management systems.

2. Linkages of the performance management system with other HR sub-systems such as career planning, reward mechanisms, and support systems influence appraisers and appraisees in its implementation.

The researcher found a lack of full involvement by seniors and management. Most employees felt that the performance management system was not seen as an organizational/business tool.

3. Although there was awareness about the performance management system, it was mostly used as an annual exercise for administrative decisions, not as a developmental tool.

4. Finally, the research findings indicated that managers having good academic backgrounds were effective implementers of the system. System discipline, exposure, and team working were the essential qualities/competencies required.

The study concluded that in view of globalization, Indian organizations' performance will witness unparalleled pressures. The performance management systems currently used in India may not be adequate for the future. The systems need to be completely revamped.

The researcher recommended high involvement of the CEO and all levels of management in the communication of company objectives and the alignment of these to functional, departmental, and individual goals. Managers should have exposure to the performance management system and feedback/coaching sessions, to strengthen team working and interpersonal relationships.

Adapted from: Srinivasa Rao (2007)

Italy 49 per cent. Statistics on the actual take up of performance management systems and comparisons between these systems are not well documented. Surprisingly, despite the importance of performance management to IHRM, a survey of large MNEs with foreign subsidiaries report that most (83 per cent) did not use performance management to measure the success of their international assignees (Arthur Andersen, 2000, cited in Briscoe and Claus, 2008: 23).

The role of performance management within the wider context of the international organization is now considered by looking at various ways in which performance management is used.

Performance management as a control mechanism

According to Evans et al. (2002: 110–11, 128) from the perspective of the globalizing organization, performance management is a tool that can 'facilitate (or hinder) global integration through local subordination of local business results to global objectives and standards'. The parent company aligns decision making to ensure local decisions reflect a global perspective, through the activities of expatriates and the management of their performance; it may standardize processes to achieve efficiencies and uniform behaviour, using formalized control. In addition through the socialization of key individuals in central expatriate leadership positions, it exercises normative control and attempts to ensure global orientation.

Other authors (Fenwick et al., 1999; Kopp, 1994; Ferner et al., 2004) have also acknowledged that HRM policies and processes, including performance management, are vehicles for control or standardization within international organizations. Kopp (1994) found that US firms were more likely than Japanese or European MNCs to have performance evaluation measures that were standardized across all international operations. The study by Ferner et al. (2004: 4) includes empirical evidence of the centralized policies, including performance management systems, being disseminated globally by US subsidiaries in European countries.

The performance management process

A performance management model in an MNE

According to Varma et al. (2008: 18), in 'A model of employee performance management in an MNE', the performance management process takes place within a global context. It is influenced by the structure and institutional elements and culture of the country in which it takes place, as well as the language used. Performance management also occurs within an organizational context, so that it is influenced by the organizational culture, the degree of importance attached to performance management, the international and HR strategy, organizational design or structure, and global staffing policy. This performance management model (Varma et al., 2008: 18) has three key components, Performance Management Process Choices, Moderators, and Outcomes.

While this model provides a useful overview of the performance management process within the organization, the model does recognize the contextual factors but perhaps does not emphasize sufficiently their impact or the complexity of an international assignee's role. It may not be suitable for evaluating the international assignee's contribution to the organization fairly. The impact of contextual factors on the international assignee's performance is understated here. Cultural and national institutional factors plus organizational factors may act as further moderators on performance. (Further coverage of such issues is found in the following sections of this chapter.)

Having considered the Varma model briefly, the chapter now continues with discussion of more factors that impact on performance management, beginning with the various roles that are played by expatriates.

The expatriate's role and performance management

Expatriates are sent to subsidiaries of MNEs to perform a variety of roles and this occurs in a similar way to international assignees in SMEs or other organizations with international offices. There are many types of expatriate executives and managers, or international assignees, who fulfil a variety of functions. When considering performance it is therefore essential to consider the position in the organizational hierarchy, the reporting relationships, and the objectives associated with the role.

Pucik (1992) has suggested that we can divide international appointments into two types: demand driven or learning driven. A demand-driven appointment would facilitate control and knowledge transfer in the long term or fix a problem in the short term. However a learning driven appointment would facilitate individual or organizational learning by facilitating competency development and global integration or by providing short-term career enhancement opportunities for high-potential professionals.

Traditionally, expatriate roles were perceived as long term—three years or more—and fulfilled a 'corporate agency' role, incorporating control or knowledge transfer. Short-term roles, used often today, are typically start-up or problem-solving roles, which last only as long as the task takes (Evans et al., 2002: 119).

According to Caligiuri and Colakoglu (2007: 403) their research into twenty-seven mature MNEs indicated that management strategy is one of the factors determining the use of expatriates. Firms with a global management strategy made greater use of developmental expatriates and recognized the importance of these assignments to increase global competence.

International assignees are most commonly defined by their country of origin as follows:

Parent Country Nationals (PCNs) those from the same country as the head office;

Third Country Nationals (TCNs) those from a country other than the parent country and host country;

Host Country Nationals (HCNs) those from the country where the subsidiary is based. They may be sent on assignment to head office, when they are referred to as **inpatriates**.

According to Colakoglu et al. (2009), the choice of PCN, HCN, or TCN is significant for subsidiary performance in their host markets and within the MNE network. Their model suggests that 'different national categories of subsidiary managers have unique knowledge bases that provide differential value under different conditions', (Colakoglu et al., 2009: 1302). This could be the tacit knowledge of HCNs, MNE-specific knowledge and the social capital of PCNs, or the knowledge integration and resulting innovation that is created out of diversity, when a variety of nationalities are employed. PCNs may pass knowledge of political and power issues at headquarters to subsidiaries. The research concludes that staffing decisions need to be made in the light of each subsidiary's internal and external contingencies and their specific strategic, competitive, cultural, and institutional environments (Colakoglu et al., 2009: 1303–4). (For further discussion of knowledge management, see throughout Chapter 9, 'Training, development, and knowledge management'.)

Tahvanainen (2007: 175) uses the nature of the job in her study of expatriate performance in Nokia, while Caligiuri (2006: 235) identifies four types of international assignments: technical, developmental, strategic, or functional. In each of these types of assignment, the goals, objectives, and reporting relationships are different and the performance evaluation of the expatriate may take place locally or by a head office manager or both. She recognizes the challenges of performance management in the context of diverse cultural backgrounds and acknowledges that the culture of the evaluator is significant (Caligiuri, 2006: 234).

Earlier investigation by Harzing (2001: 13–19) included an analysis of expatriates from a coordination and control perspective, and utilized the analogy of 'bears, spiders and bumblebees' to indicate the type of coordination or control the expatriate's role implied, whether direct expatriate control, control through socialization and shared values, or an informal communication role. This research also considers the relative value of expatriates in these roles in different types of subsidiaries. Harzing's work also considers the role of international assignees as knowledge agents. (This role is considered further in Chapter 9, 'Training, development, and knowledge management', in the section *The complexity of knowledge sharing and knowledge transfer*.)

More detailed discussion of the motives for various types of international assignments are provided by Reiche and Harzing (2009). Other terms that are used to describe international employees include: non-standard short-term, commuter, and virtual employees. Generally, less attention is paid to these types of employees in the international HRM literature, despite the fact that they are becoming increasingly important. Each of these types of employee is evaluated using different performance management systems, depending on the type of organization and its country of origin. Regardless of the role of the international assignee, a key person in the performance management process is the rater or evaluator.

The next section considers the issues that need to be considered when assigning the role of performance evaluator to a line manager.

The evaluators' ability and the performance of expatriates

While the wide range of roles of international employees can make managing performance more complex, a further aspect of the process is the ability of the person who carries out the performance evaluation.

As discussed earlier in the chapter, the knowledge and skills of the evaluator are critical for an effective performance evaluation. The most common form of performance evaluation used in international companies is an appraisal by the local line manager and/or the head office manager based in the home country (Gregersen et al., 1996, cited in Briscoe and Schuler, 2004: 366). In a study of expatriate evaluation by Suutari and Tahvanainen (2002, cited in Tahvanainen and Suutari, 2005: 95) the most typical evaluator found was the supervisor in the host country (54 per cent) and in a third of cases it was the supervisor in the home country. The choice of evaluator depended on the role of the expatriate being appraised. The Brookfield Global Relocation Trends Survey (2010) provides some detailed statistics on performance review methods. The ranking of these puts performance review in the host country top, followed by performance review in both the host and home country, and third, performance review in the home country (Brookfield, 2010).

There are a great many differences between organizations in how performance management processes are managed. There is no generic expatriate performance appraisal system. According to Evans et al. (2002: 129): 'Some keep expatriate managers in the parent company pool for appraisal purposes, some treat expatriates as they would a local employee in the same job, while others add specific criteria reflecting the nature of the expatriate's job.'

This is significant for the career opportunities of expatriates who may be forgotten and miss promotion opportunities. If an expatriate is treated as a local employee for appraisal purposes, the specific difficulties of being employed overseas are not considered and the evaluation may be incomplete. Recognition will not be given to the learning and personal development resulting from working overseas.

The quality and reliability of a performance appraisal or evaluation depend to a large extent on the skills of the evaluator. According to Tahvanainen and Suutari (2005: 97) the person selected to do the performance evaluation should be qualified for the job. The evaluator should be aware of the goals of the employee's job and tasks and have regular contact with the employee. They must be capable of determining performance level and be persons whose opinions are valued by the organization. They should be trained to re-cord and report their findings to the employee's manager or to the employee him/herself. (See also Table 8.1, Performance management elements linked to the knowledge and skills required by line managers.)

In an international context, a number of factors may affect the ability of the evaluator to provide a fair evaluation of the employee. The local line manager will be influenced by his or her own cultural frame of reference (Oddou and Mendenhall, 2007: 209; Caligiuri 2006: 234). A line manager who is close to the employee may be reluctant to reprimand or correct the behaviour for fear of losing friendship, goodwill, or cooperation.

It may not be in the interests of the subsidiary manager to reveal problems that could imply weaknesses in his or her management. Thus an appraisal may omit problems and not be entirely truthful, particularly in Asia, where conflict avoidance and 'harmony' are culturally very impor-tant. A good relationship between the head office manager and expatriate, plus regular reports on challenges being encountered, are essential to ensure a full picture. (For more on the impact of cultural difference, see throughout Chapter 4, 'Understanding IHRM: the cultural approach'.)

The head office manager may write the performance evaluation report based on informa-tion from the subsidiary manager. Many home managers responsible for expatriates have no international experience and cannot visualize the constraints under which they work. If the home manager has limited communication with the expatriate, he/she cannot evaluate the expatriate appropriately (Oddou and Mendenhall, 2007: 211).

Difficulties may arise when the expectations of the local subsidiary manager of the expatriate differ from those held by the head office management. For example in Asian, au-tocratic environments, the local manager may try to exercise a greater degree of control over the expatriate than he/she is used to. For example in the People's Republic of China, superiors have absolute authority to evaluate subordinates and there may be little room for discussion or participation in decision making (Huo and Von Glinow, 1995, cited in Jackson, 2002: 179). This is also the author's experience of working in a school in China, where the headmaster, or 'leader', was all-powerful, controlling staff activities both during and after school hours.

Finally, research by Guthridge et al., 2006 indicates that line managers are often unwill-ing to have hard conversations. In research with fifty CEOs, business unit leaders, and HR professionals around the world, fifty per cent observed that 'line managers were unwilling to categorize their people as top, average, or underperforming, and forty-five per cent failed to deal with chronic underperformance by employees'. One interviewee noted that 'we recognize underperformance, but the challenge is what to do about it. We find it difficult to have the "hard" conversations.' (Guthridge et al., 2006: 6).

 Discussion Activity 8.2

1. Discuss the advantages and disadvantages of a local line manager being responsible for the performance management of an expatriate employee.

2. Why is the involvement of the parent company head office an important aspect of the performance management process?

3. How can the parent company head office management maintain better understanding of the challenges faced by expatriates and thus evaluate performance more fairly?

Further aspects of performance management that receive critical treatment in the literature include goal-setting and measurement issues. These issues are equally problematic in both the domestic and international scenario and will be dealt with in more detail later in the chapter. The next section considers how adjustment issues affect expatriate performance.

Expatriate adjustment issues

As well as considering process-specific problems associated with evaluating expatriate performance, we need to understand the factors that affect the ability of the expatriate to work effectively in a new country and role. This aspect of expatriate performance management is closely linked to the AMO framework (ability, motivation, and opportunity), described at the beginning of the chapter, since it illustrates situations that may limit the opportunity to perform well. One of these situations is the ability of the expatriate to adjust to the new job and overseas environment.

Brewster et al. (2007: 250–1) suggest that adjustment can be determined by four factors, summarized as:

1. individual factors: self-efficacy, interpersonal skills and self-confidence, language ability, cultural empathy, and emotional stability;

2. non-work factors: spouse adjustment, family, cultural difference;

3. organizational factors: novelty, social support, and logistical help;

4. job factors: role novelty, role conflict, role ambiguity, and role discretion.

These adjustment factors are borne out in previous research by Hechanova et al. (2003), based on empirical studies covering over 5000 expatriates.

There are also external factors that contribute to difficulties with adjustment and ability to perform, as shown in Table 8.2.

Farh et al. (2010: 434) suggest that one further key factor in adjustment is having a support network in the new location. They develop a process model to illustrate how expatriates form 'adjustment facilitation support ties in a culturally unfamiliar context', which provides both informational and emotional support. The model examines the factors that influence the types of relationships expatriates form and attempts to enrich our understanding of the role of networks as a critical mechanism for adjustment and successful assignments (Fahr et al., 2010: 451).

Table 8.2 Factors that impact on expatriate adjustment

Factor	Explanation of potential impact
Host country environment	The degree of difference in level of economic development, culture, language, climate, and living conditions contribute to the expatriate's feelings of personal security, comfort, and adaptation.
Host organizational environment	The role of the expatriate, level of acceptance, and support given by host country employees affect ability to perform well.
Head office support for the expatriate	The amount of practical support from head office, including pre-departure training, and ease of contact with head office, contribute to the expatriate's adjustment.
Stage of development of the subsidiary organization	An organization in the early stages of development may need more guidance, training, and control from the head office. This will affect the parameters of the job role and difficulty in achievement of objectives.
Relationship between head office and subsidiary	The degree of understanding between the head office and subsidiary managers, which assists in the acceptance of and support for the expatriate employee.
Philosophy of the organization (Perlmutter, 1985)	The degree to which the organization is ethnocentric, geocentric, or polycentric will affect the acceptance level of the expatriate and the degree to which head office policies will be applied (see Chapter 3, Table 3.1, Perlmutter's EPRG model of international strategies).
External environmental factors	The prevailing political, economic, social, and legal environment may impact on the expatriate's ability to adjust to the country and perform the role assigned. For example an expatriate posted to a country that is corrupt and that lacks a fair legal system may find acceptance of the society difficult. Similarly, constraints placed on activities by cultural or religious requirements may restrict optimum performance.
Spouse and family adjustment	Adaptation of the spouse and family to the new cultural environment are key to the success of the assignment, as this provides support for the expatriate in his/her role.

(Adapted from Stone, 2008: chapters 21, 22)

In conclusion, there are societal, organizational, personality and family factors, as well as task factors, which impact on the ability of the expatriate to perform his/her role. If employers are genuinely concerned about the success of their expatriates, then support must be provided in the form of pre-departure training, on-site support or mentoring, on-going training, and practical help to assist with cultural adjustment and other practical issues, including employment search for the spouse if required, to facilitate expatriate, spouse and family adjustment. (For further discussion of knowledge management, see throughout Chapter 9, 'Training, development, and knowledge management'.)

The following case study considers some aspects of *adjustment* of expatriates to working in the area known as 'Greater China'.

Case Study 8.3 Expatriate adjustment to Greater China

This case discusses an article that evaluates the relative adjustment of expatriates to life and work when sent to Hong Kong, Singapore, Taiwan, and mainland China, this area being labelled 'Greater China' (cf. Brick, 1992 and Harding, 1993, cited Selmer, 2006).

Data were collected from 251 business expatriates in Hong Kong, mainland China, Singapore, and Taiwan. The largest nationality group in the sample was British (11 per cent), followed by Hong Kong and the USA with a similar number of respondents. Other respondents came from Germany, Australia, and Japan. The majority (82 per cent) came from outside Greater China.

The article looks at both how far expatriates are well integrated into daily life and work in the host location (socio-cultural adjustment) and how quickly an acceptable level of performance at work has been achieved.

It suggests that the *experience* of business expatriates could be of strategic importance for the expansion path of their firms, many of which begin their expansion into mainland China through having offices in Hong Kong or Singapore. However, mainland China offers a very different business environment and the differences may increase uncertainties for the expatriates and decrease economic performance. Firms may differ in their ability to overcome such difficulties, depending on their previous experience gained at other locations in Greater China.

Factors such as level of economic development, modernity of office facilities, and language contribute to adjustment. Business expatriates in mainland China tend to see *language* differences as a fundamental obstacle to interaction adjustment (Zimmermann et al., 2003, cited in Selmer, 2006). The language barrier is substantial in mainland China and in Taiwan, where English is not widely spoken. Even though English is one of the official languages of Hong Kong, the general level of proficiency is not high. However, both Singapore and Hong Kong are large, modern cosmopolitan cities with significant international business communities in a relatively small geographic area.

Results show that expatriates assigned to Singapore had a higher degree of general adjustment and interaction adjustment than their counterparts elsewhere in Greater China, while expatriates both in Hong Kong and Singapore were more quickly adjusted to work than those in mainland China. Finally, the research indicated that familiarity with the business environment in Singapore did not necessarily imply easy adjustment to life in other parts of Greater China.[1]

Adapted from: Selmer (2006)

 Stop and Think

1. Consider how far being isolated from other people from your own country might affect your ability to perform in your work role.

2. What can companies do to help expatriates adjust to working in a place with few other expatriates nearby?

3. What you would do in such a situation? How far would the internet assist you?

[1] Author's note: Adjustment in mainland China depends very much on the exact location, an urban or rural area, as stated in the article, as well as distance from major cities where there is an international community. In addition, the presence of international companies in the area and therefore a network of other expatriates can facilitate adjustment. Having lived in Kuala Lumpur, Malaysia, for twenty years, the author imagined adjustment to living in China in 2002 would not be difficult. However, language was a key barrier to adjustment, as was being sent to an area, Jiaxing, Zhejiang province, with limited international investment and no substantial expatriate network. The scenario for expatriates in cosmopolitan cities such as Shanghai and Beijing is entirely different.

Goal-setting and performance measurement issues

A major area for discussion in the literature on performance management is goal setting and the measurement of performance. Issues that may cause problems are: who sets the goals; whether the goals are subjective or objective; how far the achievement of goals can be fairly measured; what rating systems are being used and how suitable they are; documentation and reward issues.

In domestic performance management, goals are typically agreed between the individual and their line manager or immediate supervisor. However expatriates may agree their goals with their host country manager, home country manager, or a third country manager. The following issues regarding goal setting and evaluation have been identified by Oddou and Mendenhall (2007: 215–17), Tahvanainen and Suutari (2005: 94–6), Evans et al. (2002: 313–4, 331–3) and Schuler et al. (2004: 138–9).

Goals may be set by host country manager or home country or third country manager. Where goals are set by managers in the home country or a third country, there may be lack of familiarity with the difficulties in the host country and consequently lack of validity in the performance evaluation process.

Goals of the head office and subsidiary manager may not be aligned: broader global goals may not be fully compatible with the immediate goals of the subsidiary. If one of the objectives is to have a loyal head office employee on site to oversee or control local activities, the host manager may perceive the expatriate as having more loyalty to the head office than to the local operation. This may result in tension and negative evaluation by the local manager.

Goals set by head office may not reflect the expatriate's need to develop cultural competencies and, as a result, this may not be recognized within the evaluation process. Similarly, goals of the individual and organization may not be aligned. For example the expatriate may be looking for new experience to enhance career prospects but may find that the role is a functional or problem-solving one, which does not provide this opportunity.

External (institutional) factors may prevent the achievement of goals. Local bureaucratic processes may delay or interfere with the achievement of goals. Further, local management interference may prevent the expatriate's achievement of goals set by head office. These factors may not be appreciated by the head office management.

In terms of measurement, goals may be ambiguous or difficult to measure. 'Hard' goals (objectives that are quantifiable) may not fully reflect expatriate achievements and may not adequately reflect the complexity of the role of the expatriate. 'Soft' goals are subjective and hard to measure. These include behaviours or personality or character traits such as initiative, cooperation, loyalty, and attitude. These may also be culture bound. For example initiative may not be appreciated in Asian societies where humility and respect for seniority may be valued more highly. Finally, Rose (2000: 44–5) suggests that short-term, preset targets may be constraining and may not reflect the rapidly changing requirements of a role.

A further issue, which results in some lack of validity of expatriate performance evaluation, is the documentation. Standard evaluation forms produced for domestic use are commonly used for expatriates. Cultural adjustment issues, which are essential for success overseas, are not included. As a result, the expatriate may not receive the recognition deserved for performance, behavioural adaptation, and learning (Gregersen et al., 1996, cited in Briscoe and Schuler, 2004: 366).

Performance measurement

Measurement of performance can be done through the use of a variety of instruments including: self-assessment, ranking employees against each other; **forced ranking**, allocating a certain percentage of employees to categories such as excellent, good, poor etc.; rating employees on a scale; **360-degree feedback**, using subordinates, peers, and even customers as well as supervisors, to evaluate employees; and upward appraisal, evaluating superiors. Each of the measurement processes involves some degree of simplification of achievement into crude numerical values. (Further information on these concepts can be found on the Chartered Institute of Personnel and Development (CIPD) website and in specialized HRM texts.)

A technique increasingly being used by large organizations is 360-degree feedback, or some form of **multi-source feedback** system. These systems are designed to offer a fairer assessment of an employee's contribution to the organization by allowing evaluation from different perspectives. However, it is costly and time consuming to use and results in a lot of bureaucratic paperwork. Discussion of 360-degree feedback and the problems faced in its use in Fortune 500 organizations is provided by Ghorpade (2000: 142–5). The article shows that it has serious problems related to privacy, validity, and effectiveness. It looks at five paradoxes of these programmes.

Employee Development Paradox while the main objective of 360-degree feedback is to develop the employee, in practice it is confused with appraisal, creating confusion and loss of utility as a developmental tool.

Multiple Constituents Paradox using more evaluators increases the range of information obtained, but this might not provide better feedback.

Anonymous Ratings Paradox anonymous ratings are more honest than signed ratings. However, honest ratings may not necessarily be more valid.

Structured Feedback Paradox quantitative and structured feedback based on generic behaviors is easy to acquire, score, and disseminate. However, this might not be relevant to the role or workplace.

Appointing the 360-Degree Administrator a key issue is who should gather, process, and have custody of the feedback data (Ghorpade, 2000: 145)

Despite these paradoxes, the author concludes that the system can be beneficial to organizations. He suggests that there is a need for an atmosphere of trust, openness, and sharing and that feedback can be meaningful when both sides want an honest exchange of perceptions.

Further UK research by Armstrong and Ward (2006), in a study of six organizations, similarly indicated that the organizations studied used:

> various techniques including 360-degree feedback to produce vast amounts of quantitative data. Often, this data is synthesized into a single rating that is intended to represent an individual's net contribution and determine their remuneration. This frequently describes an individual's performance as 'satisfactory' or 'average' which the authors suggest is not a particularly motivating message.
>
> (Armstrong and Ward, 2005: 17)

Performance management in different cultural contexts

Case Study 8.4 considers the system and its relative success when used in different cultural contexts, in six different countries.

As Case Study 8.4 illustrates, the effective implementation of the performance management process by managers or supervisors is one of the stumbling blocks in its use. An earlier study by Entrekin and Chung (2001: 980) examined the attitudes of three groups of managers in Hong Kong, towards different forms of performance evaluation. Overall, the findings indicate that the traditional Chinese values favour supervisory appraisal. The study points out the importance of the compatibility of norms and beliefs regarding management practice, such

 Case Study 8.4 The use of 360-degree evaluation systems in six countries

This study investigated the use of multi-source feedback systems (MSFS) in six countries using interview data from HR managers and consultants from Argentina, Australia, China, Slovakia, Spain and the UK and demonstrated that MSFS are being implemented, in slightly different ways, in each country. The main challenges in the application of MSFS are the communication efforts necessary before and after implementation, and the difficulty in giving and receiving feedback.

The literature review revealed that over a quarter of organizations are using some form of MSFS in the USA and it is still gaining popularity. The study investigates the culture on MSFS and suggests that the process of using evaluators, other than the supervisor, runs counter to the power structure of influence within organizations. It is speculated that cultural dimensions, such as Power Distance, for example, may be related to a resistance to this. Furthermore, objective, individual feedback from others—a central feature of MSFS—is rooted in western, individualistic thinking. The manner by which individuals give and receive feedback in organizations varies around the world and is likely to be influenced by cultural factors.

The first objective of the paper was to examine how MSFS is adapted to different cultural contexts. Second, it tried to depict the challenges associated with the international application of MSFS. Finally, the study looked to future prospects for the countries being studied.

The challenges associated with MSFS included resistance to evaluating others; in Argentina partly due to the paternalistic culture and in China because of the importance of both hierarchy and maintaining harmony. In Australia, poor feedback-giving skills were mentioned, while in Slovakia there was general reluctance at the idea of evaluating peers and some suspicion of management. In Spain, the social cost of evaluating peers and supervisors as well as lack of faith in confidentiality of data were perceived as challenges. However, the MSFS was well accepted in the UK, having been introduced twenty years ago.

The report concluded that despite the numerous challenges encountered in implementing MSFS, respondents were, in general, very positive regarding the future outlook for this practice. Most MSFS users expected the practice to increase or at least remain stable in the future, though some respondents made the point that the use of MSFS will be dependent on wider economic circumstances. Also, the precise nature of the MSFS applications is likely to evolve with time.

Brutus et al. (2006: 1895–903)

as performance appraisal, with the local national cultures for the acceptance and transferability of that practice across countries.

Similarly, the importance of national culture on the choice of performance appraisal systems has also been investigated by Fried et al. (2012: 25–8) from the Society for Human Resource Management (SHRM) Foundation (http://www.SHRM.org. This investigation of 5991 organizations in twenty-one countries, showed the importance of choosing an appropriate system to match the national culture. Individual-based merit performance appraisal practices were found to have a positive impact on organizational outcomes in the USA. Societies with a high Power Distance are less likely to benefit from 360-degree appraisal systems. They report that 360-degree systems had a positive impact in terms of absenteeism, innovation and productivity in lower Power Distance societies. Societies with high Uncertainty Avoidance have productive results when they use formal appraisal systems. The research concludes that organizations should understand the cultural values of where they operate, so that they can choose the type of performance appraisal that is most appropriate and effective. (See throughout Chapter 4, 'Understnding IHRM: the cultural approach' for more on this topic.)

 Discussion Activity 8.3

1. Discuss the advantages and disadvantages of 360-degree appraisal processes.

2. How far would such a format assist an expatriate to obtain a fairer appraisal?

Performance management outcomes

One of the results of the performance management process is the allocation of additional pay in the form of bonuses or promotion. However, given the difficulties associated with measuring performance, there is often dissatisfaction following performance evaluation. This can arise from lack of transparency in the links between achievement of goals and rewards. Furthermore, poor financial results over the whole company may result in failure to pay promised rewards, even though that particular employee has achieved the objectives set. (For more information on this topic, see throughout Chapter 7, 'International reward management'.)

According to Evans et al. (2002: 129–30), there is another critical tension that impacts the performance criteria—the difference in time horizon of expatriates and locals—short-term success in the job versus the long-term performance of the business unit. Expatriates who work in one position for less than a couple of years may not show interest in the long-term results of the subsidiary, but may focus more on obtaining visible short-term results, which will be reflected in their performance evaluation. Short-term focus is one of the most frequent criticisms of expatriate managers by local subordinates. Expatriates are perceived to care about results only within the time frame of their appointment (Evans et al., 2002: 129–30). Similarly, expatriates who work for short periods of time, such as under a year, in a variety of locations, to gain international experience, rarely see the long-term effects of their activities.

The timing of the appraisal itself might affect the outcomes of the performance evaluation. Appraisals are usually conducted annually, but evaluation and advice are given on an ongoing basis, within this time frame. If an appraisal is held only once a year, this could result in an appraisal being too late to detect, intervene in, and solve problems. On the other hand, one year may not be enough time for an expatriate to achieve goals, as a period of adjustment to the new position and international environment may be required. Japanese MNEs recognize this problem and generally send their expatriates on longer international assignments, understanding the time it takes for their employees to adapt (Scullion and Collings, 2006: 61).

Recent academic discussion includes the view that expatriate return on investment (ROI) should be measured in order to illustrate the contribution of the long-term expatriate to the organization, especially given the high cost of this type of appointment (McNulty et al., 2009: 1310). However, the research suggests that there are cultural, operational, and strategic barriers to such an approach and that global managers sometimes consider expatriates to be a cost of doing business, which does not need to be measured. Surprisingly, the research on 51 global firms indicates that 'many firms do not have formal procedures in place to measure expatriate ROI and instead rely heavily on informal practices which are seldom aligned to a global strategy' (McNulty et al., 2009: 1309). The article concludes by stating the importance of greater understanding of how global firms evaluate the effective management of international assignments and expatriate careers. It acknowledges that expatriate ROI may only be part of this complex whole (McNulty et al., 2009: 1323).

Repatriation issues

When the expatriate's position comes to an end, ideally a repatriation plan will already have been agreed, with the appointment to a position that utilizes the experience gained. This is also included in the career planning discussions that should take place before the overseas assignment and during performance appraisal discussions, so that a suitable appointment can be made on completion of the assignment. Unfortunately, research indicates that these appointments are not well managed, as the following information indicates. This poor career management often results in attrition and loss of valuable talent.

The Brookfield Global Relocation Trends Survey (2010) also covered the issue of repatriation. Repatriation discussions were held less than six months before assignment completion in 38 per cent of cases and only 25 per cent took place before departure. Companies were reluctant to commit to post-assignment expatriate duties and this commitment was made in only 12 per cent of cases. The authors blame the uncertain economic situation for this, but maintain that repatriation discussions should be held twelve months before completion of the assignment and commitments made to those employees they wish to retain (Brookfield, 2010).

Ninety-five per cent of companies helped repatriating employees identify new jobs within the company. In 24 per cent of cases, employees had to rely on formal job postings and 23 per cent on informal networking. Mandatory assistance by transferring departments was offered at only 31 per cent of companies. In terms of expatriate attrition, 20 per cent of respondents to the survey cited an increase in expatriate attrition, with more expatriates leaving within the first year after repatriation, 38 per cent in this report (2010), while only 22 per cent left after two years. The report suggests that this low figure is because employees realize there are fewer opportunities outside their companies and choose to remain (Brookfield, 2010).

Performance management and international teams

Most discussion of performance management in the literature refers to the individual employee. However, increasingly both domestically and internationally, employees are being deployed as part of a team to complete projects. It is the ability of the individual to work in a team context that contributes significantly to the successful completion of the project. However, the evaluation of performance is invariably more complex, especially as multiple stakeholders may be involved. International projects conducted in teams occur in outsourcing arrangements in the service sector when cross-functional teams are required. Team-based assignments are also used in new foreign operations, expansion, acquisitions, or to ensure integration or to respond to crises (O'Sullivan and O'Sullivan, 2008: 1000).

A study of performance management of international teams in the aerospace industry by O'Sullivan and O'Sullivan (2008) discusses the experiences of an international project with multiple teams drawn from different national providers. The article concludes with a discussion of the IHRM implications of the many challenges experienced. These include:

Performance evaluation The necessity for multi-stakeholder evaluation. In this case, expatriate team peers would serve as an important source of feedback about individual on-site performance.

Human resource planning and selection The significance of team selection and the importance of cross-organizational competencies to manage competing expectations *leading up to assignment of the expatriate team*. The parent organizations, by adequate staffing, can facilitate better on-the-job adaptation (O'Sullivan and O'Sullivan, 2008: 1014–15).

Finally the chapter considers an aspect of performance management not often included in texts on IHRM. This concerns the management by parent companies of their subsidiary managers. These managers, who are local employees (HCNs), often report to the parent company, or to regional managers overseas, from a different national culture and at a distance. The following section looks at some of the problems that can emerge.

Host country managers' appraisals in subsidiary companies

Host country managers (HCMs) in subsidiaries of MNEs play a major role in implementing head office policies and ensuring the performance of the subsidiary. Their performance is also critical to the effective management of the subsidiaries. These HCMs are managed at a distance. This results in lack of understanding of local issues, includes problems of cross-cultural misunderstanding and lack of face-to-face contact. The following case study explains this issue in more detail.

Case Study 8.5 Host country managers' appraisals in the health care industry, Australia

Research by Maley and Kramar (2007) has investigated the extent, nature, and limitations of performance appraisals for HCMs in medium-sized subsidiaries in a sector of the health-care industry in Australia. The multinationals were from the USA, UK, Denmark, France, Sweden, Norway, and Germany. Since HCMs of subsidiaries are key to their success, an effective performance appraisal can help to ensure that the HCM and the subsidiaries are acting in accordance with the parent MNC's interests.

The research into the experiences of the eighteen HCMs indicated that they were isolated from the supervisor as they reported directly overseas. They met their supervisors infrequently—on average twice a year—and even then they did not spend much time with the supervisor. The quality of the relationship was also affected by the willingness of the superior to understand Australian conditions and the role of the HCM. Judgements were also affected by superiors' own similar task experience.

Eighty per cent of the appraisals were perceived by the HCMs to be ineffective. This was often because of the focus on the bottom line, the relationship with the supervisor, and the effect of the parent company strategy, structure, and nationality. Nearly half the appraisals were conducted over the phone and there was considerable dissatisfaction with feedback and follow-up. The HCMs believed that they were not important to the MNC and only a third felt the appraisal was beneficial to them. While the appraisals were used to make bonus decisions in 85 per cent of the companies, less than a quarter used them to make training and development decisions.

The parent company strategy and structure impacted on the effectiveness of the appraisal, so that a company having a global or transnational strategy combined with a geocentric or regiocentric structure resulted in the likelihood of the appraisal being assessed as effective by the HCMs. In contrast, HCMs in companies with an international strategy and ethnocentric structure were dissatisfied with their performance appraisals.

The analysis of the research includes a discussion of the relevance of agency theory and motivation theory to the scenario and the importance of improving the performance appraisal process for developing an appropriate talent pool for the MNC in the future.

Maley and Kramar (2007)

 Discussion Activity 8.4

1. What can MNEs do to improve the performance management of HCNs within their subsidiaries?

2. Could this be perceived as unfair treatment of HCNs and a diversity issue?

3. To what extent is this problem the responsibility of the headquarters or the subsidiary management?

Summary

The chapter introduces the topic of performance management and its purpose and goes on to explain its links to theory. The complex role of the line manager in the appraisal process is then discussed.

It explains that performance management is a process of planning, goal setting, and evaluation of individual performance, ideally linked to specific strategic organizational objectives.

It may also include recommendations for training, career development plans, and links to performance-related pay or promotion. The chapter suggests that the performance management process should include regular assessment of individual performance based on role-specific goals and behaviours. Goal agreement, measurement criteria and the effectiveness of the evaluation process make performance management problematic even in the domestic scenario.

In the context of IHRM, the chapter explains that there are difficulties of standardization of performance management in different national contexts. The complex nature of an international assignment makes the management of expatriate performance more difficult and there are concerns about who is best suited to do the evaluation. There may be different views of the purpose of the assignment held by the headquarters management and local managers. The local manager may also have reasons for withholding local information from the headquarters. Appraisal may also be influenced by relationship issues with the local manager. Headquarters managers though, may not fully understand the complexity of overseas assignments and the challenges of cultural difference. Spouse and family concerns also complicate the adjustment scenario and may prevent successful assignment completion. However, some responsibility may also lie with the headquarters for failure to provide adequate cross-cultural training before or during the assignment.

The existence of a pre-arranged repatriation appointment can affect the decision of the expatriate to stay with the organization, since failure to appreciate the experience gained may result in the decision to leave. The chapter argues that such plans should be made in the interests of both the expatriate and the organization.

The performance management of expatriates then needs considerable planning and effective management, because failure in these areas can result in talent loss.

Finally, it is argued that more attention should be paid to the needs of HCMs, especially those who are managed from a distance. These are key employees who need to receive appropriate care from headquarters or regional superiors. Adequate time needs to be spent on appreciating their contribution and the challenges they face.

Review questions

1. Which theoretical concepts used to explain the importance of performance management have most relevance to international assignees and why?

2. What is the purpose of performance management? Why is the topic controversial?

3. What factors make the standardization of performance management across MNEs problematic?

4. What factors make international performance management more complex than domestic performance management?

5. Why is the role of the expatriate significant for his/her performance management?

6. Why might reports from subsidiary line managers not accurately reflect a true picture of subsidiary and expatriate performance?

7. What are the main adjustment problems that may impact on expatriate performance?

8. What are the advantages and disadvantages of using 360-degree evaluation for expatriates?

9. What types of information and support might be provided by the MNE to the expatriate and his/her spouse to facilitate a successful assignment?

10. To what extent are headquarters of HR departments responsible for the performance management of HCMs? Why is their management problematic?

Further reading

Armstrong, K. and Ward, A. (2006) *What Makes for Effective Performance Management?* London: The Work Foundation.

This reports on the study of six UK organizations in banking, the environment, health, pharmaceuticals, and consultancy services. It identifies critical elements that organizations must address to ensure performance management makes a contribution to wider business goals. See Case Study 8.1 for further information on this research. Also available online at http://www.theworkfoundation.com/Reports/163/What-makes-for-effective-performance-management (accessed 5 May 2012).

Chiang, F.F.T. and Birtch, T.A. (2007) Examining the perceived causes of successful employee performance: an East–West comparison, *International Journal of Human Resource Management*, 18(2): 232–48.

This study considers the factors that are perceived to influence employee performance in four countries: Canada, China (Hong Kong), Finland, and the UK. Differences were found in how individuals consider internal or external factors to influence their performance. Emphasis was placed on internal factors in the West, while in Hong Kong respondents believed both internal and external factors were significant. These are important considerations for the design of performance management systems to be used across borders and for future research.

Claus, L., Patrasc Lungu, A., and Bhattacharjee, S. (2011) The effects of individual, organizational, and societal variables on the job performance of expatriate managers, *International Journal of Management*, 28(1, Part 2): 249–71.

This research considers predictors of expatriate job performance, at individual, organizational, and societal levels. It also considers six different theoretical explanations, including personality, cultural adjustment, the environment, institutional factors, and social networks for adjustment and work performance. This article illustrates the complexity of managing expatriate performance.

Kupka, B. and Cathro, V. (2007) Desperate housewives—social and professional isolation of German expatriated wives, *International Journal of Human Resource Management*, 18(6): 951–68.

This article provides an overview of the difficulties faced by expatriate wives, especially when they are professionals, who are unable to work in the host location. It illustrates the importance of managing their needs in order to maintain their identity and notes the lack of support provided by German corporations for them in their search for work.

Shih, H.-A., Chiang, Y.-H., Kim, I.-S. (2005) Expatriate performance management from MNEs of different national origins, *International Journal of Manpower*, 26(2): 157–76.

This study considers how expatriate performance is conducted in five European and Asian MNE subsidiaries in the IT industry. The findings show the lack of on-the-job training for expatriates and the use of standardized performance forms, not tailored to local needs. It illustrates the significance of parent company culture on divergent performance management practices.

Bibliography

Armstrong, K. and Ward, A. (2005) *What Makes for Effective Performance Management?* London: The Work Foundation, online at http://www.theworkfoundation.com/Reports/163/What-makes-for-effective-performance-management (accessed 5 May 2012).

Armstrong, M. (2006) *Performance Management*, 3rd edn, London: Kogan Page.

Boxall, P. and Purcell, J. (2008) *Strategy and Human Resource Management*, Basingstoke: Palgrave Macmillan.

Brewster, C., Sparrow, P., and Vernon, G. (2007) *International Human Resource Management*, 2nd edn, London: CIPD.

Brick, A. (1992) *The Emergence of Greater China*, Washington, DC: The Heritage Foundation.

Briscoe, D.R. and Claus, L.M. (2008) Employee performance management: policies and practices in multinational enterprises, in A. Varma, P. S. Budhwar, and A. DeNisi (eds) *Performance Management Systems, A Global Perspective*, London: Routledge, pp. 15–39, ch. 2.

— and Schuler, R.S. (2004) *International Human Resource Management*, 2nd edn, London: Routledge.

Brookfield (2010) *Global Relocation Trends Survey, 2010*, Brookfield Global Relocation Services, online at http://www.brookfieldgrs.com/knowledge/grts_research/ (accessed 5 May 2012).

Brutus, S., Derayeh, M., Fletcher, C., Bailey, C., Velazquez, P., Kan Shi, K. et al. (2006) Internationalization of multi-source feedback systems: a six-country exploratory analysis of 360-degree feedback, *International Journal of Human Resource Management*, 17(11, November): 1888–906.

Caligiuri P.M. (2006) *Performance Measurement in a Cross-national Context.* Working Paper Series in Human Resource Management, Center for HR Strategy, Rutgers, NJ: Rutgers University, online at http://chrs.rutgers.edu/pub_documents/PerformanceMeasureinCrossNationalContext2.pdf (accessed 5 May 2012).

— and Colakoglu, S. (2007) A strategic contingency approach to expatriate assignment management, *Human Resource Management Journal*, 17(4): 393, online at http://chrs.rutgers.edu/publications/ (accessed 26 December 2012).

Chakravarthy, B.S. and Perlmutter, H.V. (1985) Strategic planning for a global business, *Columbia Journal of World Business*, Summer: 3–10.

Chiang, F.F.T. and Birtch, T.A. (2007) Examining the perceived causes of successful employee performance: an East–West comparison, *International Journal of Human Resource Management*, 18(2): 232–48.

Child, J., Faulkner, D., and Pikethly, R. (2003) *The Management of International Acquisitions*, Oxford: Oxford University Press.

Claus, L., Patrasc Lungu, A., and Bhattacharjee, S. (2011) The effects of individual, organizational and societal variables on the job performance of expatriate managers, *International Journal of Management*, 28(1, Part 2): 249–71.

Colakoglu, S., Tarique, I., and Caligiuri, P. (2009) Towards a conceptual framework for the relationship between subsidiary staffing strategy and subsidiary performance, *International Journal of Human Resource Management*, 20(6): 1291–308.

Drucker, P. (1954) *The Practice of Management*, New York: HarperCollins.

Entrekin, L and Chung, L.W.(2001) Attitudes towards different sources of executive appraisal: a comparison of Hong Kong Chinese and American managers in Hong Kong, *International Journal of Human Resource Management*, 12(6, September): 965–87.

Evans, P., Pucik, V., and Barsoux, J-L. (2002) *The Global Challenge: Frameworks for International Human Resource Management*, New York: McGraw Hill Irwin.

Farh, C.I.C., Bartol, K.M., Shapiro, D.L., and Shin, J. (2010) Networking abroad: a process model of how expatriates form support ties to facilitate adjustment, *Academy of Management Review*, 35(3): 434–54.

Fenwick, M.S., de Cieri, H.L., and Welch, D.E. (1999) Cultural and bureaucratic control in MNEs: the role of expatriate performance management, *Management International Review*, 39(Spec. issue, October): 107–24.

Ferner, A.M., Almond, P., Clark, I., Colling, T., Edwards, T., Holden, L. et al. (2004) Central control and subsidiary autonomy in US MNCs, *Organisation Studies*, 25(3): 363–91, online at https://www.dora.dmu.ac.uk/handle/2086/1631 (accessed 8 May 2012).

Fried, Y., Peretz, H., and Kaminka, S. (2012) *The Link Between Performance Appraisal and Culture: An Examination across 21 Countries*, SHRM Foundation, online at http://www.shrm.org/about/foundation/research/Documents/Fried%20Final%20Report%20508.pdf (accessed 5 May 2012).

Ghorpade, J. (2000) Managing five paradoxes of 360-degree feedback, *Academy of Management Executive*, 14(1): 140–50, online at http://www.

zigonperf.com/resources/pmnews/paradox_360.html (accessed 9 May 2012).

Gregersen, H.B., Hite, J.M., and Black, J.S. (1996) Expatriate performance appraisal in US multinational firms, *Journal of International Business Studies,* fourth quarter: 711–38.

Guthridge, M., Komm, A.B., and Lawson, E. (2006) The people problem in talent management, *McKinsey Quarterly,* 2(May),online at https://www.mckinseyquarterly.com/The_people_problem_in_talent_management_1755 (accessed 1 November 2012).

Harding, H. (1993) 'The concept of "Greater China": themes, variations, and reservations', *China Quarterly,* 136: 660–86.

Harzing, A-W. (2001) Of bears, bumble-bees and spiders, the role of expatriates in controlling foreign subsidiaries, online at http://www.harzing.com/download/spiders.pdf (accessed 8 May 2012).

Hechanova, R., Beehr, T.A., and Christiansen, N.D. (2003) Antecedents and consequences of employees' adjustment: a meta-analytical review, *Applied Psychology: An International Review,* 52(2): 213–36.

Heider, F. (1958) *The Psychology of Interpersonal Relations,* New York: Erlbaum.

Huo, Y.P. and Von Glinow, M.A. (1995) On transplanting human resource practices to China: a culture driven approach, *International Journal of Manpower,* 16(9): 3–15.

Jackson, T. (2002) *International Human Resource Management,* London: Sage.

Jesuthasan. R. (2007a) *Rewards Challenges and Changes,* Survey Report, Towers Perrin, online at http://www.towersperrin.com/tp/getwebcachedoc?webc=HRS/USA/2007/200712/RCC_Survey_Report_Dec_2007.pdf (accessed 7 May 2012). [Towers Perrin is now Towers Watson.]

—— (2007b) *Rewards Challenges and Changes,* Survey Report, Towers Perrin, in N. Paton Timid tinkering no way to address the talent crisis, online at http://www.management-issues.com/2007/9/7/research/timid-tinkering-no-way-to-address-the-talent-crisis.asp?section=research&id=4473&is_authenticated=0&reference=&specifier=&mode=print (accessed 5 May 2012). [Towers Perrin is now Towers Watson.]

Kopp, R. (1994) International human resource policies and practices in Japanese, European, and United States multinationals abroad: comparative and prospective views, *Labour and Society,* 4(1): 1–25.

Kupka, B. and Cathro, V. (2007) Desperate housewives—social and professional isolation of German expatriated wives, *International Journal of Human Resource Management,* 18(6): 951–68.

Leonard, N.H., Beauvois, L.L., and Scholl, R.W. (1999) Work motivation: the incorporation of self-concept-based processes, *Human Relations,* 52: 969–98, online at http://www.uri.edu/research/lrc/scholl/research/papers/Leonard_Beauvais_Scholl-1999.pdf (accessed 9 May 2012).

Locke, E. and Latham, G. (1990) *A Theory of Goal Setting and Task Performance,* Englewood Cliffs, NJ: Prentice Hall.

McNulty, Y, de Cieri, H., and Hutchings, K. (2009) Do global firms measure expatriate return on investment? An empirical examination of measures, barriers and variables influencing global staffing practices, *International Journal of Human Resource Management,* 20(6): 1309–26.

Maley, J. and Kramar, R. (2007) International performance appraisal: policies, practices and processes in Australian subsidiaries of healthcare MNCs, *Research and Practice in Human Resource Management,* 15(2): 21–40.

Mendenhall, M., Oddou, G., and Stahl, G.K. (2007) *Readings and Cases in International Human Resource Management,* 4th edn, London: Routledge.

Miah, M.K. and Bird, A. (2007) The impact of culture on HRM styles and firm performance: evidence from Japanese parents, Japanese subsidiaries/joint ventures and South Asian local companies, *International Journal of Human Resource Management,* 18(5, May): 908–23.

Murphy, K.R. and DeNisi, A. (2008) A model of the appraisal process, in A. Varma, P. S. Budhwar, and A. DeNisi (eds) *Performance Management Systems, A Global Perspective,* London: Routledge, ch. 6.

Oddou, G.R. and Mendenhall, M.E. (2007) Expatriate performance appraisal: problems and solutions, in G.R. Oddou, M.E. Mendenhall, and G.K. Stahl (eds) *Readings and Cases in International Human Resource Management,* 4th edn, London: Routledge, rdg 3.3.

O'Sullivan, A. and O'Sullivan, S.L. (2008) The performance challenges of expatriate supplier teams: a multi-firm case study, *International Journal of Human Resource Management,* 19(6): 999–1017.

Pucik, V. (1992) Globalization and human resource management, in V. Pucik, N. Tichy, and C. Barnett (eds) *Globalising Management: Creating and Leading the Competitive Organisation,* New York: Wiley.

Reiche, S. and Harzing A.-W. (2009) International assignments, in A.-W. Harzing and A. Pinnington (eds) (2010) *International Human Resource Management,* London: Sage, online at http://www.harzing.com/papers.htm#ihrmchapter (accessed 8 may 2012).

Rose, M. (2000) Target practice, *People Management,* 23 November, 44–5.

Rousseau, D. (1995) *Psychological Contracts in Organizations*, Thousand Oaks, CA: Sage.

Schein, E. (1978) *Career Dynamics: Matching Individual and Organisational Needs*, Reading, MA: Addison Wesley.

Schuler, R.S., Jackson, S.E., and Luo, Y. (2004) *Managing Human Resources in Cross-border Alliances*, London: Routledge.

Scullion, H. and Collings, D.G. (eds) (2006) *Global Staffing*, London: Routledge.

Selmer, J. (2006) Adjustment of business expatriates in Greater China: a strategic perspective, *International Journal of Human Resource Management*, 17(12, December): 1994–2008.

Shen, J. (2005) Effective international performance appraisals: easily said, hard to do, *Compensation Benefits Review*, 37(4): 70–9.

Shih, H.-A., Chiang, Y.-H., and Kim, I-S. (2005) Expatriate performance management from MNEs of different national origins, *International Journal of Manpower*, 26(2): 157–76.

Srinivasa Rao, A. (2007) Effectiveness of performance management systems: an empirical study in Indian companies, *International Journal of Human Resource Management*, 18(10, October): 1812–40.

Stone, R.J. (2008) *Human Resource Management*, 6th edn, Milton, QLD: John Wiley & Sons.

Suutari, V. and Tahvanianen, M. (2002) The antecedents of performance management amongst Finnish expatriates, *International Journal of Human Resource Management*, 13(1): 1–21.

Tahvanainen, M. (2007) Expatriate performance: the case of Nokia Telecommunications,

in M. Mendenhall, G. Oddou, and G.K. Stahl (eds) *Readings and Cases in International Human Resource Management*, 4th edn, London: Routledge, pp. 174–84, ch. 3.1, case study.

— and Suutari, V. (2005) Expatriate performance management in MNCs, in H. Scullion and M. Lineham (eds) *International Human Resource Management: A Critical Text*, Basingstoke: Palgrave Macmillan, pp. 91–113, ch. 5.

Vance, C.M. (2006) Strategic upstream and downstream considerations for effective global performance management, *International Journal of Cross Cultural Management*, 6(April): 137–56.

Varma, A., Budhwar, P.S., and DeNisi, A. (eds) (2008) *Performance Management Systems, A Global Perspective*, London: Routledge.

Vroom, V. (1964) *Work and Motivation*. Chichester: John Wiley.

Wei, L. (2006) Strategic human resource management: determinants of fit, *Research and Practice in Human Resource Management*, 14(2): 49–60, online at http://rphrm.curtin.edu.au/2006/issue2/strategic.html (accessed 7 May 2012).

Whitley, R. (1994) *European Business Systems: Firms and Markets in their National Contexts*, London: Sage.

— (1999) *Divergent Capitalisms: The Social Structuring and Change of Business Systems*, Oxford: Oxford University Press.

Ying, Z., Warner, M., and Rowley, C. (2007) Human resource management with 'Asian' characteristics: a hybrid people management system in East Asia, *International Journal of Human Resource Management*, 18(5, May): 745–68.

 Visit the Online Resource Centre for web links, interactive glossary, and more:
http://www.oxfordtextbooks.co.uk/orc/crawley

Training, development, and knowledge management

 Learning Outcomes

After reading this chapter you will be able to:

- appreciate the issues associated with the training and development of expatriates and potential global managers in an MNE context
- understand the importance of training and development for the success of all types of expatriate assignments and their adjustment to overseas environments
- explain the role of the expatriate in the knowledge transfer process
- outline the factors that contribute to or prevent knowledge transfer within MNEs.

Introduction

Following a brief theoretical discussion, this chapter has two main parts; the first discusses training and development within the context of expatriation, and the second addresses knowledge management in the context of international business. These topics are closely connected as the expatriate is often seen as a vehicle for knowledge transfer and also a repository for extensive **tacit knowledge** obtained during international assignments. For this reason, an expatriate or international assignee has considerable value for the organization and is an asset whose career should be carefully managed so that he/she will wish to stay with the organization.

The chapter will begin with a brief overview of theoretical concepts linked to the impact of national training systems, culture, and organizational factors on training and development as well as an outline of theories of individual learning, which are a critical factor in the effectiveness of organizational learning practices.

The next section on training and development will look at the type of international assignments that exist and the type of training that is most frequently provided. The importance of cross-cultural awareness for expatriates is discussed. The training of potential 'global' managers who are groomed by large multinationals for their international careers is evaluated. Here the international assignment is a training ground in itself, often used to develop the manager. Global managers may be recruited from across the world and are an important element in the development of truly transnational organizations.

Finally the support of the expatriate in his/her role as an international assignee, as well as his/her family, is a further element in the process of ensuring a successful international assignment.

In this respect, career plans for the assignee and potential opportunities for the future need to be borne in mind by the HR team managing the assignee. Some attention will also be given to the impact of training and development on career development, especially with respect to women and the reasons why they are under-represented in international management.

The second part of the chapter will consider knowledge management (KM) and the role of the expatriate in knowledge transfer. The significance of KM for MNEs and the processes involved in knowledge transfer from headquarters to subsidiaries and across the organization are important. A discussion of the challenges of managing knowledge, types of knowledge, and factors that assist in knowledge transfer or prevent it, including the role of expatriates and the influence of culture, will be discussed. The incentives to pass on knowledge to locals by expatriate managers and reasons for their reluctance to participate in this practice will be considered. A discussion of factors that facilitate knowledge transfer will be included.

Theoretical considerations: training and development context

The discussion of training and development within MNEs cannot be adequately discussed without an understanding of the wider social, economic, and cultural context within which it takes place, the impact of national education and training systems on management training, and the technical development of employees in the national context (Ashton, 2002; Garavan and Carbury, 2012). Today, Human Resource Development (HRD) is more than training and development and includes links to corporate strategy, individual learning, team learning, career development, organizational learning, knowledge management, and nurturing intellectual capital (Easterby-Smith and Cunliffe, 2004; Walton, 2006, cited in Metcalfe and Rees, 2005: 450). It has evolved as an academic concept from foundations in psychology, education, economics, and management, and incorporates issues of culture, leadership, and organizational learning to become a multidisciplinary area of study and research (Metcalfe and Rees, 2005: 450).

International HRM and International Human Resource Development (IHRD) are both strongly influenced by contextual factors. The importance of national education and training programmes is illustrated in reports and recommendations of the International Labour Office (ILO, 2004) and United Nations Development Programme (UNDP), which recognize the significance of supra-governmental and national involvement in the development of human capital, across the globe (UNDP, 2006). Organizations such as the WTO and World Bank have also recommended state intervention in human capacity building and worked in an advisory capacity with countries in Asia and Africa for their skills development in the 1980s and 1990s. These institutions recognize the role of the state as a catalyst in social and economic development. For example the WTO 'trade-related technical assistance (TRTA) activities and programmes are geared towards sustainable trade capacity-building in beneficiary countries' (WTO, 2010). Similarly the OECD and the ILO provide support for national governments in developing policies and institutions for national education and vocational training in order to make their VET (vocational education and training) more responsive to their labour market needs (OECD, 2012). (Please refer to the ORC for more links to the websites of the organizations mentioned.)

Dodgson (2009: 589) suggests that the 'growth of technology-based industries has been a critically important element of Asian industrial development and has required extensive institutional support for the diffusion of innovation and technological learning'. Based on research on Taiwan and Korea, Dodgson (2009: 589) considers the role of *national innovation systems* and technological collaboration and recognizes the influence of 'cultural legacies', but emphasizes the importance of 'social and economic institutional adaptation'. The research concludes that in Taiwan, new institutional forms are emerging, perhaps as a result of the 'large number of US-trained and work experienced scientists and engineers returning to Taiwan and the strong political and social leanings of many... towards the US'. However, Korea's attempts to 'encourage entrepreneurship are hampered by a lack of corresponding social institutional change and its continued dominance of the chaebol' (Dodgson 2009: 605). (See Chapter 5 'Understanding IHRM: the institutional approach', in the section *National business systems*, for more on this topic.)

Human capital theory

Human capital theory suggests that 'investments made in educating and developing a workforce and developing their skills will pay dividends to a country that is seeking to improve its economic viability and industrial development' (Metcalfe and Rees, 2005: 454–5).

An example of the role of the state in education, training, and skills formation can be seen clearly in Malaysia's New Economic Policy and its five-year plans (now numbering ten), its establishment of a national HRD fund, produced by a levy on companies of 1 per cent of payroll (recently reduced to 0.5 per cent of payroll), similar to that implemented in Singapore, used to provide apprenticeship schemes and training programmes for employees (HRDF, 2012). These types of schemes are examples of human capital theory in action.

An example of the close relationship between the UN, the Malaysian government, and a Japanese multinational in developing national skills is illustrated in Case Study 9.1.

 Case Study 9.1 The Honda Dreams Fund

The Malaysian government has made an appeal to the private sector to assist in the country's national development. It has identified 'challenges such as the widening economic and social disparities between the rich and the poor, as well as between the urban and rural populations' (HDF, 2011).

As a result, an interesting development is the joint activities taking place between a Japanese multinational, Honda, and the UNDP in support of the Malaysian government. The UNDP has embarked on a collaboration scheme with Honda in Malaysia to provide scholarships to deserving students. According to a press release, Honda Malaysia Sdn Bhd in partnership with the UNDP Malaysia, renewed their pledge to aid underprivileged but meritorious students in Malaysia ... through the Honda Dreams Fund (HDF, 2011).

'The Honda–UNDP CSR (corporate social responsibility) initiative aims to provide full and nonbinding scholarships to twenty underprivileged, but determined students annually to pursue higher education or skills training' (HDF, 2011).

The Honda Dreams Fund provided full scholarships to twenty promising youths from underprivileged backgrounds. They focused on less fortunate youths and empowered them with education and knowledge so that they might achieve their dreams and aspirations. The scheme ended in December 2011 after five years (HDF, 2012).

(UNDP, 2010)

The above example illustrates the complexity of the study of international HRD as it combines a variety of stakeholders, including global, supranational agencies such as the UN, national governments, multinational organizations such as Honda in this case, and individuals. From an academic point of view the study of IHRD is multidisciplinary and may focus on economic and social development, education, national training systems, organizational behaviour, and HRM. There are also links into contemporary studies of the learning organization, lifelong learning, knowledge management, and learning communities at organizational or international levels.

Terminology in training and development in an international context

In line with definitions of IHRM, comparative HRM and cross-cultural approaches to HRM used by the Cranet survey in 2008, authors such as Metcalfe and Rees (2005: 456) suggest that we may consider the study of IHRD in three streams: *Global HRD*, largely tied to the study of multinationals; **Comparative HRD**, which focuses on comparing different countries' HRD systems, educational and vocational systems, institutional and cultural analysis; and *National HRD*, which considers government skill formation policy, institutions, and partnerships with international agencies as well as NGOs, which contribute to societal development. The focus of the rest of this chapter, using these definitions, is global HRD, or training and development in multinationals.

Harrison notes that 'Learning and Development is replacing what used to be called HRD' (Harrison, 2004, cited in Lucas et al., 2006: 149)

 Discussion Activity 9.1

Discuss how your country's government cooperates with or obtains support from international agencies or other countries to develop the training and development opportunities available in your country. To what extent do you think this helps people to build their skills, knowledge, and opportunities for employment?

Theoretical considerations: training and development of the individual

This topic cannot be understood without some background understanding of learning theory. Bass and Vaughan (1966, cited in Reid et al., 2004: 49) have described learning as 'a relatively permanent change in behaviour that occurs as a result of practice or experience'. Other writers have added that in an organizational context it includes the development of the required knowledge, skills, and attitudes to carry out tasks which contribute to the achievement of the organization's strategic objectives. Early writers on learning such as Skinner (1965, cited in Reid et al., 2004: 51) focused on the behavioural aspects of learning, and how learning shaped behaviour through conditioning, positive reinforcement, and reward. Such ideas have been translated into management in such practices as merit rewards and the general belief that employees need to receive feedback and have knowledge or results as part of the process of learning. However, human learning is a far more complex process than this.

Learning is both a cognitive and behavioural process, and it can take place in a planned, intentionally arranged situation or spontaneously, as a result of experience. This learning is known as *experiential learning*, described by Kolb (1974, 1995, cited in Reid et al., 2004: 56–7) as 'The Learning Cycle', a cyclical process involving four stages: (i) the concrete experience; (ii) observations and reflections; (iii) formation of abstract concepts and generalizations; (iv) testing the implications of concepts in new situations. However, not everyone is able to utilize these four stages fully because of previously learned abilities and learning preferences. Honey and Mumford (1986, 1992, cited in Reid et al., 2004: 57) have identified four learning styles, which correspond to Kolb's learning cycle: activists, reflectors, theorists, and pragmatists. These styles reflect the dominant way in which different learners think and respond to experiences, and the ways different people learn. In the same way, this concept has significance for trainers, who need to understand the individual training needs of participants and to adapt their training methods to provide opportunities for the satisfaction of all types of learners.

In an international context, trainers and expatriate managers must be able to appreciate that learning has a different meaning in each culture. Teaching and training in Asia is predominantly didactic, with the teacher, trainer, or leader having an authoritative role. As a result, managers or executives from this background find participative learning processes difficult to adapt to. In addition, Asian participants may avoid participation because of the predominant fear of losing face by saying or doing something 'wrong'. In contrast to this, in the author's experience, managers in Spain are very willing to speak up and openly criticize every aspect of what is being learned as well as how it is being taught, even more so than might occur in the UK.

Experiential learning may not take place if managers have not learned how to learn and how to reflect on experience. Today, managers, and particularly international expatriate managers, need to utilize both single- and double-loop learning. While during single-loop learning there may be reflection on techniques and making these more efficient, goals, values, frameworks, and strategies are taken for granted. However, in double-loop learning the reflection is more fundamental, focused on 'questioning the role of the framing and learning systems which underlie actual goals and strategies'; the basic assumptions behind ideas or policies are confronted and hypotheses are publicly tested (Argyris, 1982: 103–4). Thus double-loop learning occurs when errors can be 'detected and corrected in ways that involve modification of an organisation's norms, policies and objectives' (Argyris and Schön, 1978: 2–3). Managers may need to learn how to do this, but may have particular difficulty, especially if these managers come from a cultural context that is high in Power Distance and Uncertainty Avoidance (Hofstede, 1991). Questioning authority or existing corporate behaviours may be difficult if not impossible for them to visualize, let alone do. It has been suggested, therefore, that recent discussions of learning and development including learning styles and the concept of the Learning Organization (Senge, 1992, cited in Lucas et al., 2006: 155) reflect ethnocentric, Anglo-American assumptions and that learning and development is a 'cultural' phenomenon (Lucas et al., 2006: 155). As a result, the transfer of knowledge, learning styles and approaches to training across borders may be constrained by cultural barriers.

Further, the Learning Organization (Senge, 1992, cited in Lucas, 2006: 153) includes the concept of learning collectively, which can result in improved performance. It emphasizes the need to facilitate learning in teams. Thus employees in organizations need to develop skills of 'participation': 'the capabilities of individuals to work and learn together in a particular context' (Lucas et al., 2006: 149). The Learning Organization also includes the use of information technologies to enable higher-level learning and ways to transfer learning from experience into the organizational memory (Lucas et al., 2006: 154).

Finally, learning and development today includes acquiring and utilizing two types of knowledge; explicit (that which can be captured or codified in manuals, information systems, and handbooks) and tacit knowledge, which resides in individuals' minds (Lucas, 2006: 259–60). As will be discussed later in the chapter, it is this tacit knowledge that is more difficult to transfer and that is seen used in communities of practice (see Case Study 9.5, Hewlett Packard's learning communities).

Training and development issues in MNEs

The importance of training and development for MNEs

Training and development, sometimes also referred to as talent development today, is an issue which, it is suggested, is key to competitive advantage. A McKinsey Global Survey on Building Organizational Capabilities (Gryger et al., 2010) found that, despite this view, 'only 33 per cent of companies actually focus their training programs on building the capability that adds the most value to their companies' business performance' (Gryger et al., 2010: 1). This is because building organizational capacity is seen as an essential part of their culture. However, the survey found that it was only when senior managers were involved in setting the agenda and companies focused on 'certain capabilities for competitive reasons', that they 'gain(ed) a stronger competitive advantage' (Gryger et al., 2010: 7). The topic of identifying and managing talent is discussed throughout Chapter 13, 'Global talent management'.

Training and development in multinational organizations cannot be entirely separated from its national context. The location of decisions about training and development depend on the strategy of the multinational. Training and development in international organizations should be closely aligned with their business strategy. Because organizations may have offices dispersed across the globe, the location and control of developmental, expatriate training will be influenced by the degree of centralization, decentralization, global integration, or local responsiveness (Caligiuri and Colakoglu, 2007: 394).

Colakoglu et al. (2009: 1291) propose a model of three multinational staffing strategies (using PCNs, TCNs or HCNs), and the associated transfer of knowledge, and assess the relationship with subsidiary performance. These different national categories of subsidiary managers have 'unique knowledge bases, that provide differential value under different conditions' (Colakoglu et al., 2009: 1302). In global organizations an ethnocentric strategy facilitates the transfer of culture, technology, and processes or corporate way of doing things through expatriate Parent Country Nationals (PCNs). In regionally centred organizations a Third Country National (TCN) may be used to ensure that the company is making the best of local market information and best international practices. In a transnational, training and development is synergistic and collaborative, utilizing the subsidiary's unique contribution to the whole. The authors, however, argue that 'the relationship between subsidiary staffing strategy and their associated knowledge flows' and subsidiary performance depend on each subsidiary's environmental contingencies (Colakoglu et al., 2009: 1298).

In some subsidiaries, in which there is a move towards localization, Host Country Nationals (HCNs) may receive training by the incumbent expatriate or at the parent country headquarters. Known as inpatriates, they are groomed to replace expatriates in subsidiaries. (Training of local employees by the expatriate is discussed in Chapter 11, Case Study 11.3, Expatriates and localization policies.) Harvey et al. (2001) also provide an overview of the options and challenges associated with developing a candidate pool of local managers to become *global managers*, through an inpatriate programme. Much of the discussion concerns the cultural adaptation of the inpatriate to the home country/head office culture and the acceptance of the inpatriates by head office employees, which is a critical element in their development (Harvey et al., 2001: 911).

It is generally assumed that the training and development of all other employees is left within the control of the local employing organization, and is not discussed within the IHRM literature except in a comparative context.

The next section discusses the perception and expectations of leadership behaviour in different cultures. This affects training expectations of employees from different countries and needs consideration when training HCNs and when PCNs are being prepared for operating across the globe.

The impact of culture on leadership styles

National attitudes to management training and understanding of the role of managers can be evaluated through a national cultural lens, as both the behavioural expectations and skills requirements of managers vary between cultures (Evans et al., 2002: 364).

Differences in management expectations and leadership styles of managers from different cultural backgrounds have been extensively researched (Evans, 2007; Kowske and Anthony, 2007). While Evans (2007) focused on difficulties of leading multicultural teams in Franco-British collaborative ventures, Kowske and Anthony (2007), in their research into leadership competencies in twelve countries, concluded that leadership competence is conceptualized differently depending on the country. They warn against having expectations of similarities in leadership style and behaviour within the same regions, and found countries to have unique profiles. Some extracts from the findings are, for example:

> US managers are expected to be direct in their leadership style, but to be sensitive and humane as well...
>
> French managers are expected to be less sensitive and more directive than other countries' managers. In fact, sensitive, self-sacrificing, and self-effacing managers commonly are viewed negatively in French culture...
>
> In China managers are expected to work effectively through others and utilize relationships to carry out orders. They have a greater focus on work results because their primary driver is responding to orders deriving from higher organizational levels...
>
> Singaporean managers are likely to plan but take fewer risks and to rely on authority structures...
>
> Italian managers are expected to be experts and have to be able to make and execute plans for the future.
>
> (Kowske and Anthony, 2007: 35–6)

Leadership training in each country would necessarily reflect these cultural traits and might influence the perceptions of potential global managers with regard to their own future leadership roles and behaviours.

Additional ideas on the qualities required in leaders in different countries, developed by House et al. (2002) in the early stages of Project Globe, were mentioned in Chapter 4, in the section *House et al., 2004—Project GLOBE*. Similarly, the competencies required to carry out the role of international manager are perceived differently and are reflected in models produced by each country's management associations (for example the American Management Association Competence Model, the UK Management Charter Initiative). (For more on Project GLOBE, see Chapter 4, in the section *House et al., 2004—Project GLOBE*.)

 Stop and Think

Can you identify the common behaviours or leadership style adopted by managers in your country? Which leadership competencies would employers look for in potential executive employees in your country? Which leadership competencies do you think *you* have?

The chapter now goes on to focus on the aspect of management most frequently discussed in IHRM literature; that is, the expatriate, the role, and associated training issues.

Expatriate roles and training issues

While most textbooks on IHRM focus on the traditional long-term expatriate, who is recruited from headquarters for a fairly senior role, there are increasingly many other types of 'non-standard international assignments' including short-term commuter, contractual, rotational, and virtual assignments (Brewster et al., 2001; Mayrhofer et al., 2004; Welch et al., 2003, cited in Welch et al., 2007). This is due to cost constraints and difficulties in finding people willing to take on traditional assignments, often because couples face dual career issues. A study by Welch et al. (2007: 179) focuses on the international business traveller (IBT) who, despite playing a major role, receives little support for all the pressures he/she faces. In addition IBTs gain knowledge, information, and skills as well as networks, and could become valuable agents for knowledge transfer, but this role is hardly recognized by the IBTs or their organizations as part of their job descriptions (Welch et al., 2007: 180).

Another group is the self-initiated expatriate, who take on total responsibility for their own careers and self-development (Jokinen et al., 2008). It is suggested that the self-initiated expatriate may learn more about cultures and people than assigned expatriates, who are buffered by organization support and the secure environment of the organization that is also familiar. The self-initiated expatriate has to learn about both the organization and the culture on his/her own (Jokinen et al., 2008: 990).

McKenna and Richardson (2007: 311–12) also discuss the wide range of 'independent internationally mobile professionals' (IIMPs) available around the globe and some of the issues involved in recruiting these professionals from the external labour market. They suggest that this offers the benefit of not having to prepare the professional for the assignment. However, they also express concern that many international assignees are ill-prepared for the situations they face; situations often change rapidly and in those circumstances 'learning by doing' may be dominant (Baruch, 2002, cited in McKenna and Richardson, 2007: 312). They suggest that more research is needed on this form of learning and how organizations can manage this knowledge.

All these less traditional types of expatriates are generally very poorly looked after in terms of support and training for international assignments by multinational organizations, for a variety of reasons, but will need more attention as the traditional expatriate role becomes too expensive and the range of types of assignments increases.

Research tends to focus on the training given to the longer-term expatriates. The Brookfield Global Relocation Trends Survey (Brookfield, 2010: 16) defines the different types of assignment according to assignment objectives. In 2009 the most common assignment objective was:

- filling a managerial skills gap (22 per cent);
- filling a technical skills gap (21 per cent);
- building management expertise (17 per cent);
- technology transfer (16 per cent); and
- launching new endeavours (13 per cent).

These assignment objectives illustrate the importance of expatriate assignments for knowledge and skills transfer, as well as their importance for developmental purposes (building management expertise).

Ideally, each type of assignment should involve a distinct type of training and preparation. Various models or processes that can be used for deciding on the most appropriate form of expatriate training have been suggested, such as one by Caligiuri et al. (2005b, cited in Scullion and Lineham, 2005: 83) as follows:

'Systematic process of designing effective cross-cultural training process':

- Phase 1: Identifying the type of global assignment for which CCT is needed;
- Phase 2: Determining specific CCT needs;
- Phase 3: Establishing goals and measures;
- Phase 4: Developing and delivering the CCT;
- Phase 5: Evaluating the effectiveness of the CCT.

The details, format, type of instructional method, and length of the training depend on the requirements of the particular assignment, the organizational conditions, and the person assigned to it.

Research indicates, however, that since most expatriate assignments are filled in an emergent fashion, in a less than organized and coherent manner, the preparation of most assignees is poor (Bonache et al., 2001: 9). At the same time, suitability and selection for expatriate postings is usually based on technical expertise and former success in the home country environment. Unfortunately, success in the home country may not provide the best indicator for success overseas (Rubens, 1989, cited in Graf, 2004: 1142). Following research on intercultural competence Graf concluded that past successes in the home country should not be used as the basis for selection for international assignments. This is because the behaviours required for success abroad, such as soft skills, sensitivity, and empathy, are quite distinct from those exhibited by successful employees in the home environment, such as being ambitious, task-oriented, and an aggressive problem solver (Graf, 2004: 1142).

Training provided for expatriates and international assignees may include pre-departure training, cross-cultural awareness/adjustment training and language training. Training is generally provided to help with adjustment, to assist the expatriate adapt to the new cultural environment and ultimately to complete the assignment successfully. However, the training might take many forms. Today, programmes are available both using electronic resources and traditional presentation. Expatriates may be assigned mentors in addition to training programmes, and today even professional coaching is added to the list of ways they can be supported (Abbot et al., 2006). Programmes may include ongoing support when the expatriate is overseas. However, there are wide variations in the extent and quality of the training provided. Organizations sometimes provide preparation for the spouses of expatriates too.

Cross-cultural training

Who should have cross-cultural training?

While training in *cross-cultural awareness* is often reserved for managers going on longer expatriate assignments, according to Irving (2010: 4) all potential leaders and members of virtual multinational teams require intercultural competence. Further, an understanding of cross-cultural differences would result in setting realistic training expectations for potential global managers and leaders selected from around the globe, in addition to those from the parent company home country.

It is often assumed that technical assignees require less training on cross-cultural issues since the work that they are assigned to do is largely technical and similar to the job done at home.

 Case Study 9.2 A 'technical' assignment with cross-cultural challenges combined with language difficulties, Mexico and Malaysia

It is sometimes assumed that most cross-cultural training (CCT) comes from a developed western society into a less developed culture. This case study illustrates the fact that training can come across the world between two developing countries, with very distinctive cultures, in this case from Mexico to Malaysia.

A factory manufacturing metal fastenings for clothes, such as press-studs, was sold by a company in Mexico recently and re-established in Malacca, Malaysia. The machines were set up in Malacca just as they had been used previously in Mexico. Technical support was provided by three technical staff sent from Mexico, to train the local Malaysian staff to operate the machines for one month and ensure that the machines were working properly. Training in the correct use of the machines had to be interpreted from Spanish to English (for the supervisors) but since many operators had minimal understanding of English they required further explanation by their supervisors in the Malay language. The motivation to work among the Malaysian staff was low and little respect was given to the Mexican technicians by the local Chinese management. As a result the Mexicans felt they did not have the full management support and could not provide adequate training to the staff.

A major constraint on learning was that the local Malaysian staff did not wish to 'lose face' by asking questions or admitting that they did not understand fully how to carry out the processes. This resulted in considerable tension between the Mexican technicians, who had not been given any training for this different cultural environment, and the Malaysian employees. The technicians used a direct approach in pointing out faults or mistakes made by the Malaysian staff. This would have been appropriate in their culture in Mexico, but was not in an Asian one, where it caused discomfort for the local staff (experiences of Manuel Sanchez-Canovas as an interpreter in Malaysia, 2010).

The case above illustrates that some of the problems the Mexican trainers encountered could perhaps have been prevented had they been given minimal cultural awareness training and warned of the different cultural traits to expect on their assignment. They might then have been able to adapt the way that they dealt with the local employees and have had a less stressful experience.

However, technical assignments overseas often involve interacting with other local 'technical' people, not just the machines. In reality there is often a degree of contact with host employees, who will perhaps continue to use or maintain technical equipment after the departure of the overseas technical assignees. As a result, the ability to communicate effectively with host nationals and to understand cultural difference is very important. The following example illustrates this.

Cross-cultural training for international assignments

Within the context of training for international assignments, it is CCT that still predominates. It is assumed that assignees have the technical skills required for their overseas jobs but the common belief is that cultural differences will cause difficulties. Early research frequently referred to high rates of 'expatriate failure', which was often blamed on cultural adjustment difficulties. As a result, interest in the value of pre-departure training on cross-cultural differences and adjustment developed (see Harzing, 1995; Harzing and Christensen, 2004, for a discussion of expatriate failure).

Various writers have suggested that CCT is of use to all types of assignees, long- or short-term or those in global teams who need to work effectively overseas. It is suggested that CCT can help individuals to:

- learn appropriate cultural behaviours and suitable ways of performing necessary job tasks in another country (Black and Mendenhall, 1990; Kealey and Protheroe, 1996);
- develop coping methods to manage unforeseen events in the new culture, and to reduce conflict due to unexpected situations (Earley, 1997);
- form realistic expectations with respect to living and working in the new country (Black et al., 1991, cited in Caligiuri et al. 2005a: 77).

Caligiuri et al. (2001) suggest that if the pre-departure and CCT is relevant and tailored to the expatriates' needs, their expectations of the assignment are more likely to be met. Accurate expectations as well as the language spoken in the host environment assist in adjustment. This research explains the importance of having realistic expectations, provided through appropriate pre-departure training, which in turn will affect cross-cultural adjustment.

Despite these beliefs, CCT is regularly criticized as being ineffective, too short, and held at the wrong time. More cross-cultural support is required during the assignment, not just before it begins, since adjustment takes time.

Cross-cultural training is the most common form of training offered to potential expatriates, but the length, type of training, and timing vary. This is because, according to Bonache et al. (2001) cited in McKenna and Richardson (2007: 309) 'organizations manage international assignments and the expatriate cycle in an emergent way, depending upon the resources they have at their disposal to fill a vacancy at any particular time. The role of HRM in these processes is often negligible.'

Citing Bonache et al. (2001) the article later states: 'The reality of IA [intellectual asset] management, however, is far from being strategic and is often haphazard, disorganized, incoherent, and chaotic' (McKenna and Richardson, 2007: 309).

Thus as most expatriate assignees are appointed in an ad hoc fashion, CCT is often an afterthought.

The literature further highlights the continuing lack of adequate international training and suggests that there is a 'considerable gap between academic theories and multinational enterprises' practices' and that this 'ineffective international training and management development' is detrimental to the multinational enterprises (Jie Shen, 2005: 656).

While much of the literature addresses the failure of western multinational corporations to adequately prepare their expatriates, some recent research reveals the limitations in training Chinese expatriates too, which appear to be making similar mistakes. Jie Shen and Darby (2006: 342), following in-depth interviews with thirty Chinese managers and executives found that 'Chinese MNEs provide only limited training to expatriates and other nationals, and lack a systematic international management development system. They adopt usually an ethnocentric approach to international training and development.'

However, some positive results are found for CCT when it is carried out. Waxin and Panaccio (2005) evaluated the effectiveness of different types of CCT for the adaptation of managers from four countries—France, Germany, Korea, and Scandinavia—expatriated to India. While they concluded that CCT is effective, they also highlighted the impact of cultural distance and previous international experience on the effectiveness of the training.

Tarique and Caligiuri (2009: 148) similarly evaluated the effectiveness of CCT if the training was spread over time, both before and after departure and the impact of previously accumulated knowledge on the absorption of further cultural information. This research concluded that 'in-country cross-cultural training, like pre-departure cross-cultural training, is also a viable intervention for knowledge acquisition'. However, while Selmer (2010) reiterates the need for more CCT for expatriates going to China, his research suggests that this should preferably take place a few weeks before departure. The participants in this research, however, were experienced expatriates in China who viewed CCT positively, saying that it 'improved core managerial activities' and 'could have helped them become better managers in China' (Selmer, 2010: 41).

Case Study 9.3 supports the view that more preparation and support were needed by expatriates from Australia, especially when being sent to a country such as China.

In addition to CCT, multinational organizations sometimes provide diversity training, language training, management training, coaching, and mentoring on cultural experiences, immersion cultural experiences, cross-border global team experiences with debriefing, global meeting skills, and international assignment rotations and debriefing, or coaching (Caligiuri et al., 2005a).

The training methods used and their effectiveness vary. While some training is *didactic* and aimed to provide general or specific information about culture, through lectures, videos, briefings, and case studies, *experiential* methods include exposure to a different culture, role-playing, interaction with individuals from that culture, visits, and language training. Today, a considerable amount of training is provided through electronic methods, online and also by using specialist training organizations (Caligiuri et al., 2005a).

One final comment on how training is carried out needs to be made in terms of how people learn, the teaching style of the instructor, culture, and training effectiveness. Learning style and cross-cultural differences are considered in research by Lee and Li (2008: 600) in the context of expatriate training programmes. The research evaluates 'the moderating effects of learning–teaching fit and cross-cultural differences on the relationships between expatriate training and training effectiveness' (Lee and Li, 2008: 602). The research, carried out among expatriates in Taiwan and China concluded that their results 'implied that expatriates who perceived higher levels of fit between their learning styles and instructor teaching method,

Case Study 9.3 Australian expatriates in China

The experience of Australian expatriates in China has also been studied by Hutchings (2005). Her interviews of expatriates in China revealed that while the importance of prior experience and knowledge of China for expatriate adaptation was recognized, organizational support for expatriates and their spouses was weak.

Notice of the assignment varied but frequently was too short to allow time for any pre-departure training. For example the report states:

> the majority of expatriates complained that they had not had enough time to organize themselves for the move or prepare themselves emotionally, much less to have received adequate training to allow them to cope socially and in a business setting in their new posting. As one expatriate commented, 'I was just asked if I was willing to live in China for two years and then sent on a one-day language course. I came to China two weeks later.
>
> (Hutchings, 2005: 561)

The research concludes:

> This research affirms previous research suggesting that organizations still need to develop strategic expatriation processes, including correct selection, comprehensive pre-departure and post-arrival training and in situ support for expatriates and their families. This expatriate cohort advocates that the major areas that need to be conveyed during cultural training for China relate to the importance of relationship building, the value of family, hierarchy and authority, the giving and preserving of face, trust, reciprocity and payback, and negotiating and bargaining.
>
> (Hutchings, 2005: 563).

The expatriates also mentioned the need for support while in China to deal with problems arising from skills and education levels of the workforce, telecommunications inadequacies, poor transport infrastructure, and issues arising out of the Communist bureaucracy (Hutchings, 2005: 563).

While this research is based on a relatively small sample, the findings are in line with other research into preparation for assignments in China. They represent a mixed sample of companies, 70 per cent of which were multinationals and 30 per cent of which were private companies or individuals working on their own. The larger companies generally provided more support to their assignees (Hutchings, 2005).

perceived lower cross-cultural differences and those who perceived that they had a higher demand for training tended to achieve higher training effectiveness' (Lee and Li, 2008: 600).

 Discussion Activity 9.2

The examples above have mainly considered difficulties faced by people from developed countries going to less developed countries such as China. Discuss which countries you feel are most culturally different from your own and the type of training you would like to receive before going there. Is it equally difficult for a person from a developing country to adapt to a developed one?

Experiential learning during international assignments

In terms of the process of learning, modern learning theory informs us of the factors that need to be present for effective adult learning to take place (Kolb et al., 1995; Evans et al., 2002; Sparrow and Hiltrop, 1994; Tayeb, 2004). The value of experiential learning is recognized by companies that utilize expatriate assignments as a part of the learning programme for potential global managers. Similarly, most reputable MBA programmes include some first-hand work-based learning and reflection in their courses. Hocking et al. (2007), in their study of how expatriates contribute to the transnational firm's strategic objectives, also confirm the importance of experiential learning for corporate assignments.

Evans et al. (2002) had previously suggested that challenging assignments and hardship experiences are necessary for real development and resilience to be built up, but that this needs to be accompanied by some risk management, which implies 'coaching, mentoring, feedback, assessment, and expectation setting' during the process (Evans et al., 2002: 352).

The lack of cross-cultural training provision for spouses

While it is agreed that the happiness of an accompanying spouse and family will do much to ensure the success of an international assignee, there is substantial criticism in the literature of the failure of multinationals to ensure that they too are prepared for the cultural differences of the host country. The problem of 'trailing' spouses is even more problematic when they too are professionals who may have to give up careers to accompany their partners. Some of the difficulties experienced by the wives of German expatriates are explained by Kupka and Cathro (2007), who discuss the social and professional isolation of German expatriated spouses. The article explains the importance of meeting some of the professional needs of the spouses, maintaining their sense of identity through continuing their careers, and the creation of support networks, to enable them to positively influence the expatriate.

The Brookfield Global Relocation Trends Survey (Brookfield, 2010) indicates that despite the belief that CCT is helpful there has, surprisingly, been a drop in the amount of provision:

> While 80 per cent of responding companies provided formal cross-cultural preparation, the percentage that provided it on all assignments dropped by 8 per cent (from 35 per cent in the 2009 report to the current 27 per cent)... At the same time, fewer companies mandated cultural preparation—only 17 per cent in this report compared to 22 per cent in the 2009 report.
>
> As alternatives to face to face cross-cultural training, 35 per cent of respondents provided media-based or web-based cross-cultural training—an all-time high.
>
> (Brookfield, 2010: 11)

The training of expatriates for assignments overseas is varied in both amount and quality. This lack of training provision may result in poor performance of employees in their assignment. At the same time it gives a poor message to the assignees concerning their welfare. If expatriates do not do well, their future career opportunities are put in jeopardy, yet this may not be their fault in the first place. The literature suggests that more attention needs to be paid to the whole process of planning and preparation for overseas assignments, on-site support and career progression, which utilizes these overseas experiences and enables expatriates to share their knowledge and experience with other potential expatriates on their return.

Expatriate learning and careers

Transfer of expatriate learning

According to Guthridge and Komm (2008) of McKinsey & Company, organizations are still having difficulties managing their talent and are not getting the benefit of knowledge gained by expatriates, which is dissipated or lost on their return. The survey identified ten factors in talent management that are linked to better financial performance. The top three factors were:

1. ensuring global consistency in management practices;
2. achieving cultural diversity in global settings;
3. developing and managing global leaders (Guthridge and Komm, 2008: 3).

The report stressed the importance of rotating talent to create more cultural awareness and diversity. It encourages global mobility programmes so that talent is shared between units and countries. However, the report noted that international career moves were feared as something that could damage career prospects and that many companies were still struggling to overcome barriers to international mobility (Guthridge and Komm, 2008: 1). This finding highlights the importance of establishing a link between the international assignment and the career of the expatriate, which is discussed in the next section.

The link between training, development, and career planning

One issue that concerns international assignees and expatriates is the development of their career following the international assignment. This is one factor that may prevent some potential international assignees taking up such an opportunity. The experience and development opportunities provided by an overseas assignment are often not fully appreciated by the head office, and this experience leaves the assignees out of the loop for opportunities at home. The time overseas, if not well managed, may result in the feeling of having wasted time and of not being valued by the organization. In addition the perception of career support from the home organization can positively affect the assignment and the expatriate's decision to stay with the company (Feldman and Thomas, 1992; Rhoades and Eisenberger, 2002, cited in van der Heijden et al., 2009: 832). In a review of recent expatriate research it was found that when expatriates perceive little career support, they start to seek employment elsewhere (McCaughey and Bruning, 2005, cited in van der Heijden et al., 2009: 833).

On returning home the international assignee may experience reverse culture shock as he/she adapts to the home country and organization and perceives it with a new mindset. It is suggested that returnees may need support during this readjustment period. If the experience gained while overseas is not appreciated by the company, and the next appointment does not take this valuable knowledge and development into account, it is likely that the returnee will begin to look elsewhere for better opportunities (Vidal et al., 2007: 1397).

The international assignment cannot be seen in isolation, but must be seen as an integral part of a whole career plan. The expatriate cycle does not stop with returning home, but unfortunately in many cases, no plan has been made for a suitable appointment and the returnee is put in a stop-gap position until something turns up. This is the time when the returnee will start looking for better opportunities elsewhere.

The next section considers a different group of employees, those who are specially selected and groomed for international careers.

Training potential global managers

In some large multinationals, specific employees are selected to be part of a management development programme that prepares them for an international career. As part of this process, the employees are sent overseas to work on one or more international assignments. In some cases the assignment is purely developmental, designed purely for the expatriate to learn. They may be sent on various overseas postings over as many as three to six years, in order to develop their knowledge and skills and to provide them with challenging experiences across many sectors and functional areas of the organization (Caligiuri et al., 2005a). The participants are closely monitored by senior managers and, based on their evaluation, they are coached and mentored for future management roles. This is an expensive investment. These global leadership development programmes are generally confined to the very large multinational organizations with significant numbers of overseas subsidiaries. For example, GlaxoSmith-Kline (GSK) runs their 'Esprit GSK Global MBA Development Programme', a four-year programme designed to groom future leaders who already have an MBA and some experience, for a senior international role, which could be anywhere from 'Africa to Australia, Chile to China, Europe to US' (GSK, 2010).

Despite the positive results that can arise from developing global managers, recent research into global talent management in 260 multinational enterprises (McDonnell et al., 2010: 150) indicated that less than half had both 'global succession planning and formal management development programs for their high-potentials', and that many adopted an ad hoc or haphazard approach. The authors conclude that there is still a long way to go for universal appreciation of the need to manage key employees strategically. The research showed that larger MNEs were more likely to undertake global talent management. Surprisingly, MNEs operating in low-tech/low cost sectors were more likely to have formal global systems to identify and develop high-potentials (McDonnell et al., 2010: 150).

Finally, one group of employees that is often overlooked when international opportunities arise is female employees. The next section looks briefly at why they are under-represented in training and development for international assignments.

Women in international management

Research shows that women are under-represented in international management positions (Lineham, 2005: 181). This is not surprising given that they represented only 20 per cent of senior management positions globally in 2011, down from 24 per cent in 2009 (Grant Thornton IBR, 2011). The research also indicated that the percentage of privately held businesses without any women in their senior management has increased to 38 per cent, compared to 35 per cent in 2009. If women are not being considered for senior management positions within the company at home, they are even less likely to be considered for senior positions abroad.

One of the main reasons for their under-representation in international management positions is that they are often not considered as potential expatriates and are not offered the same developmental training opportunities as their male counterparts. Organizational culture often favours the male corporate career development model, which is not appropriate for all women's careers, so that women miss out on career development opportunities. Women still have to break down the barriers of prejudice and misconceptions about both their ability and interest in being expatriates, among their predominantly male superiors, before they can even be considered. Selectors for international assignments are predominantly male and their stereotypical attitudes may prevent women being selected. Women lack other female mentors to promote their interests and are excluded from male networks where opportunities may be informally advertised or discussed and where recommendations for potential candidates may be made (Lineham, 2005: 181–2, 185).

Despite the fact that women are probably better suited to men in many expatriate positions, because of their better communication skills and ability to show empathy to others, they are still assumed to be 'at risk' in international positions. Recent research on Host Country National attitudes to expatriates, so critical to their adjustment and development in their role, indicates that in India, for example, female expatriates from the USA have an advantage over males. According to Varma et al. (2006: 28):

> In contrast to the US, India is a highly collectivistic society, where traits such as nurturance, group orientation, and harmonious relationship building are emphasized. Indeed, these are the very characteristics that are often attributed to females, and it is thus possible that Indian HCNs prefer female expatriates as they see them as representing these values.

Tung (2004) had previously suggested that perhaps females might well be the 'model' global manager. Her research of both male and female expatriates from North America showed that 'women are indeed willing to undertake international assignments; and women are equally as successful as men in culturally tough environments'. Further, an 'argument is made that women appear to possess certain attributes that may render them particularly suited to succeed in international assignments' (Tung, 2004: 243).

In 2009, Harvey et al., proposed that a new form of mentoring (reciprocal mentoring) may assist women by creating an effective support system for global female managers and that it could become a strategic tool in organizational knowledge creation and transfer. In this form, mentoring occurs when information is exchanged dynamically on a regular basis between mentor and protégé (Harvey et al., 2009: 1345–7). This takes place within the context of mentoring networks and may be cross-organizational or intra-organizational because of the constant changes in people's jobs and positions. They suggest that this may be essential today in hypercompetitive and aggressive global markets.

The topic of women in international HRM is also discussed throughout Chapter 10, 'Diversity management in an international environment'.

 Discussion Activity 9.3

Discuss the factors that prevent women receiving equal opportunities for training, development, and promotion in your country. Why are women selected less frequently for international assignments in your industry/sector and country? How far might diversity management programmes, as discussed in Chapter 10, improve the opportunities for women in international management?

Having considered a range of factors that impact on the training and development of expatriates and international assignees, the chapter now continues with the theme of knowledge management.

Knowledge management in MNEs

The subject of knowledge management is too large to discuss comprehensively in half a chapter. For this reason the topic will be discussed only in so far as it is connected to the training and development of expatriate employees and its relevance to multinational enterprises.

The importance of knowledge for the competitive advantage of the firm is expressed in the theory of the knowledge-based view of the firm (Grant, 1996, cited in Curado, 2006). This considers knowledge to be the most strategic resource and therefore an extension of the resource-based view of the firm. Knowledge resources are difficult to imitate and are seen as the 'foundation for sustainable differentiation' (Wiklund and Shepherd, 2003, cited in Curado, 2006: 5).

Knowledge management and knowledge transfer are important for multinational enterprises as they grow. The spread of knowledge, information, control systems, management techniques, and practices has in the past been assumed to be a natural process in the development of subsidiary organizations, which are expected to adopt these from the headquarters or parent organization. It used to be assumed that convergence of such processes and practices was bound to occur, especially as best practices would be imitated in an effort to produce more efficient and effective operations. The convergence argument has been criticized, however, as it has become evident that there are many factors, particularly institutional and cultural ones, which prevent total convergence.

The role of the expatriate assignee was, in the past, associated with overseeing the adoption of head office prescribed ways of working. Expatriates were used to bring the 'superior' knowledge and expertise with them and today continue to be expected to be the conduits of technical skills as well as organizational processes, practices, and culture. In mainly ethnocentric organizations, this expectation continues. This is illustrated in the predominance of expatriates (PCNs) sent from the home country of the organization to the subsidiary. A study by Harzing (2001) showed that of 250 MNCs, a PCN was appointed to the managing director position in just over 40 per cent of foreign subsidiaries. However, this figure varied depending on the home country, host country cluster, and industry (Harzing, 2001, cited in Harzing and van Ruysseveldt, 2004: 253). Today however, there is more emphasis on the spread of knowledge and information across organizations, in more than one direction, as it is acknowledged that good ideas, innovation, and research may occur on more than one site. In the multinational with a geocentric orientation, global managers, international teams, and informal management networks are expected to distribute information from various centres of excellence across the organization. Knowledge management has become an important element in the pursuit of competitive advantage.

The development of potential global managers, selected from anywhere in the multinational organization, is also linked to the geocentric approach of knowledge management and transfer. The future role of global managers will include maintaining networks of relationships with other global managers. According to Evans et al. (2002), they will be distinguished from others by their 'global mindset', and will have developed their experiential learning on international assignments, where they will have assimilated information about local markets and cultures. Such people would have a 'dualistic perspective', having been immersed in local culture while retaining a 'cross-border orientation' developed through learning-driven expatriation, cross-border projects, experiential, and action learning (Evans et al., 2002: 392–3).

While some may assume that knowledge is acquired and applied automatically, the process is far more complex. A study of learning and knowledge application has shown that the ideal situations for these to take place are different. Hocking et al. (2007: 513) suggest that knowledge application and expatriate learning occur in distinctive ways. 'Expatriate knowledge applications result from frequent knowledge access and communication with the corporate headquarters and other global units of the firm', while in contrast, 'their experiential learning derives from frequent access to host country (local) knowledge that subsequently is adapted to the global corporate context' (Hocking et al., 2007: 513). This would imply that the expatriate needs to maintain close ties with the corporate headquarters, as well as time in host country locations, to link the knowledge gained in each place. Since knowledge is acquired through social interaction, the concept of **social capital** is used to describe 'the sum of actual or potential resources embedded within, available through, and derived from the network of relationships possessed by an individual or social unit' (Nahapiet and Ghoshal, 1998: 243, cited in Reiche et al., 2008: 6).

However, according to Bonache and Zárraga-Oberty (2008) there could be multiple factors that affect the successful transfer of knowledge by international assignees within a multinational organization. In drawing up a model to depict this, the type of factors at a micro-level, which the research suggests should be considered, includes the individual employees involved in the process as the primary variable. Factors to be measured include the abilities and motivation of local staff, high commitment work practices and knowledge characteristics, and the relationship between the local (transferor) and international staff (recipients of the knowledge). The article includes details of many HR factors at an individual level, which will determine the interest of the international assignee in this aspect of his/her role. It also considers the nature of the tacit knowledge being transferred and whether it might require a team approach to transfer. This article pays attention to a wide range of micro factors, which could influence knowledge transfer and is a useful way to consider the realities of how transfer happens, successfully or not (Bonache and Zárraga-Oberty, 2008: 9).

We now look at some more recent research, which illustrates the complexity of knowledge sharing and transfer.

The complexity of knowledge sharing and knowledge transfer

Recent research has shown that the dispersal of knowledge and information is very complex and not so easy to ensure (Kale, 2010: 223). **Explicit knowledge** can be easily transferred in documents and policies, though the implementation is another matter and may need regular supervision for full compliance to occur. Tacit knowledge, which resides in people's minds and experiences, may be something they are not even aware of. The transfer of this type of knowledge is more complex. Even the transfer of explicit knowledge may be prevented by any number of factors, including the fact that it is context specific; there is cultural distance (Lucas, 2006: 271); or institutional difference (Saka-Helmhout, 2007: 272); or people who simply do not wish to learn; or poor organizational support for learning processes to take place, etc.

There are many reasons why the transfer of expatriates may not result in shared knowledge. Husted and Michailova (2002) suggest six reasons for expatriates' hostility towards sharing knowledge:

1. potential loss of value, bargaining power, and protection of individual competitive advantage due to a strong feeling of personal ownership of the accumulated, 'hard won' knowledge;

2. reluctance to spend time on knowledge sharing—knowledge senders may not be interested in knowledge sharing, since the time and resources spent on it could be invested in activities that are more productive for the individual;

3. fear of hosting 'knowledge parasites'—knowledge senders may be reluctant to share their knowledge with someone who has invested less or no effort in his/her own development;

4. avoidance of exposure—by not sharing knowledge, individuals protect themselves against external assessment of the quality of their knowledge;

5. strategy against uncertainty—due to the uncertainty regarding how the knowledge receiver will perceive and interpret shared knowledge, knowledge senders may be highly cautious about revealing the relevant knowledge;

6. high respect for hierarchy and formal power—knowledge senders may be reluctant to share crucial knowledge for fear of losing a position of privilege and superiority (Husted and Michailova, 2002, cited in Minbaeva and Michailova, 2004: 668).

One aspect of knowledge transfer is the *willingness* of expatriates to be part of this process. This is studied by Minbaeva and Michailova (2004) in their analysis of ninety-two subsidiaries of Danish multinationals located in eleven countries. This investigated the extent to which disseminative capacity (i.e. the degree of knowledge transfer) depends on the ability and willingness of organizational actors (i.e. expatriates) to transfer knowledge where it is needed in the organization. This is discussed further in Case Study 9.4.

 Case Study 9.4 Ability and willingness of expatriates to transfer knowledge

The willingness of expatriates to transfer knowledge is key to successful dispersal of both explicit and tacit information. Research by Minbaeva and Michailova (2004: 665) examines 'how different types of expatriate assignments influence knowledge sharing behavior of expatriates and thereby the degree of knowledge transfer to subsidiaries'. It suggests that 'expatriates' *willingness* to transfer knowledge can be enhanced by the employment of long-term expatriation assignments, while expatriates' *ability* to transfer knowledge may be increased through their involvement in temporary assignments, such as short-term assignments, frequent flyer arrangements and international commuting' (Minbaeva and Michailova 2004: 675).

This is explained by their finding that expatriates' 'ability to transfer knowledge is positively associated with the use of temporary expatriate assignments ... these alternative forms of expatriation are tools of expatriate development. By moving between several countries, expatriates deepen their knowledge, acquire globally applicable skills, and become better teachers, for example' (Minbaeva and Michailova, 2004: 676).

However, their willingness to transfer knowledge is acquired though long-term assignments that 'positively influence expatriates' willingness to transfer knowledge across MNC subsidiaries. When permanently stationed at a foreign subsidiary, expatriates experience greater autonomy and responsibility for employees' performance and exhibit greater commitment and willingness to perform better.'

Minbaeva and Michailova (2004: 676)

See Chapter 1, Case Study 1.2, Managing knowledge transfer between Parent Country Nationals (Australia) and Host Country Nationals (Asian countries) (Massingham, 2010) for another example of knowledge transfer issues.

Following this research on the motivation, ability, and willingness of expatriates in their role in knowledge transfer, Reiche et al. (2008: 4) have suggested too that the mere movement of staff does not guarantee knowledge transfer across units. Their research considers 'intellectual capital', which is defined as the 'knowledge that can be shared through interpersonal exchanges'. They consider the role of international assignees as both *knowledge brokers* and *knowledge transmitters*, both to the host unit and also in reverse, from the host unit and back to the home unit. The article argues that home unit and host unit *power of the assignee* affect the assignee's ability to develop inter-unit social capital, and that the employment relationship of the assignee, as well as the stability of the network of relationships, contribute to the process of knowledge transfer. The conceptual framework presented by Reiche et al. (2008: 20) indicates that knowledge flow processes across MNCs are complex, ongoing, and require multiple levels of analysis.

 Discussion Activity 9.4

Discuss the main factors that enable knowledge transfer in multinational organizations and the main factors that prevent it happening. Consider situations in which you or your colleagues may withhold information from others and explain why this might happen within your own organization.

Culture and knowledge transfer

Lucas (2006: 272) argues that the proximity of cultures can assist in the process of knowledge transfer. In viewing multinationals as networks of resources, Lucas considers the transfer of knowledge not only from head office to subsidiary but also between subsidiaries. Using Hofstede's four dimensions, Lucas concludes that knowledge transfer is easier to achieve when each subsidiary is located in a similar cultural context, but the relationships between head office and subsidiaries and between subsidiaries will also determine the success of knowledge transfer, regardless of the cultural dimensions.

In the case of India, attitudes by HCNs to US expatriates and vice-versa and especially the acceptance of female expatriates by HCNs were examined by Varma et al. (2006). Since acceptance by HCNs would facilitate expatriate adjustment and subsequently any knowledge transfer, this research contains important findings for MNEs in both countries. Earlier myths suggested that female expatriates always face prejudice, wherever they go, but not in all countries in Asia (Adler, 1984; 1987, cited in Lineham, 2005: 183). However, this needs to be examined as each country has its own culture and prejudices. As a result the research concludes that female expatriates in future might 'have a distinct advantage over their male counterparts' in India (Varma et al. 2006: 118).

Organization structure and knowledge transfer

Organizational structure and culture may also impede individual, team, and organizational learning in international strategic alliances (ISAs). Research into sixty-five high-tech manufacturing companies in the Malaysian electronics sector, engaged in ISAs, indicated that flexible organization structures as well as a level of shared trust between partners were needed to enhance learning (Hashim and Abu Bakar, 2007).

Impediments to knowledge transfer included a lack of qualified employees, cultural differences that distorted collaboration and the perceived lack of trust when partners were 'reluctant to provide details on problems when asked, new and challenging tasks were not assigned to locals, new skills and technologies are not introduced to the locals, and some critical knowledge was reserved in the home country' (Hashim and Abu Bakar, 2007: 34).

The study concluded that having a joint venture itself was not guarantee that knowledge would be provided and a common understanding of the purpose of the ISA was required to foster a commitment to learning.

The structure of the multinational corporation was also identified as a significant factor in the transfer of knowledge by Kasper et al. (2008). In their study of eight MNEs, they were able to illustrate the negative effects of centralization and significance of communities of practice on knowledge sharing. The research concluded with the importance of encouraging knowledge sharing through communities of practice and reiterated the significance of networks of interpersonal relationships in this process (Kasper et al., 2008: 65).

As a result of the many challenges associated with knowledge management, many large multinationals have seen the need for a proactive approach to organizational learning and knowledge transfer. An example of what this involves can be seen in Case Study 9.5 on Hewlett Packard.

 Case Study 9.5   Hewlett Packard's learning communities

This overview of knowledge management at Hewlett Packard explains the importance of communities of practice or learning communities (LCs) for staff to share, expand, and exchange knowledge and to develop individual and organizational capabilities. While the article suggests that the LCs have no regional or organizational boundaries, it later goes on to explain the importance for the LCs of regular face-to-face meetings, combined with teleconferences and intranet communication, discussion forums, virtual classrooms, etc.

> LCs mostly meet once every two weeks or once a month and participation varies between five and forty people. Besides the face to face meetings, LCs also employ mailing lists and LC forums on the intranet for quick and easy access and exchange of information and explicit knowledge.
>
> (Kohlbacher and Mukai, 2007: 15)

> The regular meetings and discussions of the LCs help employees to share current information, news on important issues and their expert know-how on certain topics, as well as their experiences, success and failure stories, and best practices. Thus, LCs also provide a space and a context for education of its members and for the solution of concrete problems as well as their pro-active prevention.
>
> (Kohlbacher and Mukai, 2007: 15)

The article concludes that HP's LCs are all different, depending on their context, purpose, and location; second, that face-to-face communication and sharing rich tacit knowledge predominates; and third, that 'HP's knowledge orientation, KM organization and the coordination of LCs foster knowledge creation, sharing, and organizational learning at the communities' (Kohlbacher and Mukai, 2007: 16).

Summary

This chapter began with a discussion of theory linked to training and development and its wider context and link to strategy. It then gave an example of how human capital theory is applied in a national context. The chapter also indicated that culture affects perceptions of appropriate leadership style and outlined the various roles of expatriates and the types of training provided. Learning styles were also briefly discussed, leading to the concept of the learning organization.

However MNEs face challenges when providing training and development and sometimes they fail to address the needs of expatriates. While stressing the importance of CCT at the pre-departure stage, the evidence shows that expatriates and their spouses also need more support while on assignment. It is suggested that more planning is required for expatriate appointments, for their training, and for their future careers.

Experiential training for global managers can be a key part of their training but some potential subsidiary managers (HCNs) may face cultural difficulties during training at headquarters, as inpatriates, with acceptance by staff there. Some reasons why women are not selected for training and for international assignments have been suggested.

The second part of the chapter opened with an introduction to knowledge management and its traditional link to the roles of expatriates as PCNs and global managers. It argued that knowledge transfer and knowledge sharing in multinational organizations are complex processes, which do not happen automatically. The many factors that prevent knowledge transfer include organization structure, culture, and expatriate willingness. Particular challenges with knowledge transfer are found in international strategic alliances. However, organizations can manage this process, particularly through communities of practice or learning communities. The research indicates that this process needs support from the centre. While expatriates have a role to play in the process of knowledge transfer, it is evident that this resource is not being fully exploited and that a fuller understanding of the links between training, expatriation, knowledge management, and career management are required. More attention needs to be paid to developing learning communities and encouraging participation in these to ensure individual and organizational learning and knowledge sharing.

Review questions

1. To what extent do you think the emphasis on CCT for expatriates is justified?

2. What other forms of training and development would you advocate for expatriate employees?

3. How should potential global managers be trained? Is experiential training effective? Would you recommend regional or global training, and why?

4. What can be done to ensure that more women have opportunities for expatriate training and overseas assignment opportunities?

5. Why might some expatriates be unwilling to share knowledge with their subsidiary employees?

6. What can multinational organizations do to encourage knowledge sharing and knowledge transfer?

7. To what extent should multinational organizations control knowledge management and centralize information?

8. How can the difficulties of knowledge sharing be avoided in international strategic alliances?

9. How can learning communities be developed today, especially with the use of the internet? Consider how this idea might be used in your organization.

10. In your own experience of training and development, what factors made the learning experience effective? Have any of the issues raised in this chapter been similar to your own experience?

Further reading

Abbott, G.N., Stening, B.W., Atkins, P.W.B., and Grant, A.M. (2006) Coaching expatriate managers for success: adding value beyond training and mentoring, *Asia Pacific Journal of Human Resources*, 44(3): 295–317.

An interesting discussion on how professional coaching could be an additional effective way to support expatriates.

Bonache, J. and Zárraga-Oberty, C. (2008) Determinants of the success of international assignees as knowledge transferors: a theoretical framework, *International Journal of Human Resource Management*, 19(1): 1–18.

This article considers the characteristics of the knowledge transfer mechanism in MNCs and the range of factors that influence the success of international assignees as knowledge transferors.

Kupka, B. and Cathro, V. (2007) Desperate housewives—social and professional isolation of German expatriated spouses, *International Journal of Human Resource Management*, 18(6): 951–68.

A plea to MNEs to support women who have often given up their own careers to go overseas with their husbands. The article explains how much more could be done to support expatriate wives.

Tarique, I. and Caligiuri, P. (2009) The role of cross-cultural absorptive capacity in the effectiveness of in-country cross-cultural training, *International Journal of Training and Development*, 13(3): 148–64.

The paper strongly develops the case for further CCT in the destination country as a viable way to increase cultural knowledge.

Varma, A., Toh, S.M., and Budhwar, P. (2006) A new perspective on the female expatriate experience: the role of host country national categorization, *Journal of World Business*, 41: 112–20.

This article explains the preference for American female expatriates in India over their male counterparts, with interesting cultural justifications.

Bibliography

Abbott, G.N., Stening, B.W., Atkins, P.W.B., and Grant, A.M. (2006) Coaching expatriate managers for success: adding value beyond training and mentoring, *Asia Pacific Journal of Human Resources*, 44(3): 295–317.

Argyris, C. (1982) *Reasoning, Learning, and Action: Individual and Organizational*, San Francisco, CA: Jossey-Bass.

— and Schön, D. (1978) *Organizational Learning: A Theory of Action Perspective*, Reading, MA: Addison Wesley.

Ashton, D.N. (2002) Explaining change in national HRD strategies: the case of three Asian tigers, *European Journal of Development Research*, 14(1): 126–44.

Black, J.S. and Mendenhall, M. (1990) Cross- cultural training effectiveness: a review and a theoretical framework for future research, *Academy of Management Review*, 15: 113–36.

—, —, and Oddou, G. (1991) Towards a comprehensive model of international adjustment: an integration of multiple theoretical perspectives, *Academy of Management Review*, 16: 291–317.

Bonache, J. and Zárraga-Oberty, C. (2008) Determinants of the success of international assignees as knowledge transferors: a theoretical framework, *International Journal of Human Resource Management*, 19(1): 1–18.

—, Brewster, C., and Suutari, V. (2001) Expatriation: a developing research agenda, *Thunderbird International Business Review*, 43(1): 3–20, online at http://onlinelibrary.wiley.com/doi/10.1002/1520-6874(200101/02)43:1%3C3::AID-TIE2%3E3.0.CO;2-4/abstract (accessed 26 December 2012).

Brookfield Global Relocation Services (2010) Global relocation trends survey 2010, online at http://knowledge.brookfieldgrs.com/content/insights_ideas-2012_GRTS (accessed 29 May 2012).

Caligiuri, P. and Colakoglu, S. (2007) A strategic contingency approach to expatriate assignment management, *Human Resource Management Journal*, 17(4): 393–410, online at http://chrs.rutgers.edu/publications/ (accessed 26 December 2012).

—, Phillips, J., Lazarova, M., Tarique, I., and Burgi, P. (2001) The theory of met expectations applied to expatriate adjustment: the role of cross cultural training, *International Journal of Human Resource Management*, 12(3): 357–72.

—, Lazarova, M., and Tarique, I. (2005a) Training, learning and development in multinational organizations, in H. Scullion and M. Lineham (2005) *International Human Resource Management, A Critical Text*, Basingstoke: Palgrave, p. 77.

—, —, and — (2005b) Systematic process of designing effective cross cultural training process, adapted from Fig 4.2, Training, learning and development in multinational organizations, in H. Scullion and M. Lineham (2005) *International Human Resource Management, A Critical Text*, Basingstoke: Palgrave, p. 83.

Colakoglu, S., Tarique, I., and Caligiuri, P. (2009) Towards a conceptual framework for the relationship between subsidiary staffing strategy and subsidiary performance, *International Journal of Human Resource Management*, 20(6): 1291–308, online at http://chrs.rutgers.edu/pub_documents/Towards_a_conceptual_framework-_staffing_strategy-subsidiary_performance[1].pdf (accessed 20 May 2012).

Curado, C. (2006) The knowledge based view of the firm: from theoretical origins to future implications, Working Paper 1/2006 ISEG, Instituto Superior de Economia e Gestao, Universidade Técnica de Lisboa, Department of Management Working paper Series 0874-8470 online at http://www.repository.utl.pt/bitstream/10400.5/725/1/working%20paper%20-%20FINAL.pdf (accessed 20 May 2012).

Dodgson, M. (2009) Asia's national innovation systems, institutional adaptability and rigidity in the face of global innovation challenges, *Asia Pacific Journal of Management*, 26: 589–609.

Earley, P.C. (1997) Intercultural training for managers: a comparison of documentary and interpersonal methods, *Academy of Management Journal*, 30: 685–98.

Evans, D. (2007) An exploratory review of global leadership: the example of French and British leadership styles, *Journal of Leadership Studies*, 1(1): 28–33.

Evans, P., Pucik, V., and Barsoux, J-L. (2002) *The Global Challenge, Frameworks for International Human Resource Management*, New York: McGraw-Hill Irwin.

Garavan, T.N. and Carbery, R. (2012) A review of international HRD: incorporating a global HRD construct, *European Journal of Training and Development*, 36(2/3): 129–57.

GlaxoSmithKline (GSK) (2010) Esprit GSK global MBA development programme, online at http://www.gsk.com/careers/postgraduates.html (accessed 16 December 2012).

Graf, A. (2004) Screening and training inter-cultural competencies: evaluating the impact of national culture on inter-cultural competencies, *International Journal of Human Resource Management*, 15(6): 1124–48.

Grant Thornton IBR (2011) Proportion of women in senior management falls to 2004 levels, Grant Thornton, *International Business Report 2011*, online at http://www.internationalbusinessreport.com/Press-room/2011/women_in-senior_management.asp (accessed 20 May 2012).

Gryger, L.Saar, T., and Schaar, P. (2010) Global survey on building organizational capabilities: McKinsey global survey results, *McKinsey & Company Quarterly*, March.

Guthridge, M. and Komm, A. (2008) Why multinationals struggle to manage talent, *McKinsey & Company Quarterly*, May.

Harvey, M., Speier, C., and Novicevic, M.M. (2001) Strategic human resource staffing of foreign subsidiaries, *Research and Practice in Human Resource Management*, 9(2): 27–56.

Harvey, M., McIntyre, N., Thompson Heames, N., and Moelle, M. (2009) Mentoring global female managers in the global marketplace, *International Journal of Human Resource Management*, 20(6): 1344–61.

Harzing, A.W.K. (1995) The persistent myth of high expatriate failure rates, *International Journal of Human Resource Management*, 6(May): 457–75.

— and Christensen, C. (2004) Expatriate failure: time to abandon the concept?, *Career Development International*, 9(7): 616–26.

— and van Ruysseveldt, J. (eds) (2004) *International Human Resource Management*, 2nd edn, London: Sage.

Hashim, F. and Abu Bakar, A.R. (2007) Learning from foreign partners through international alliances in Malaysia, *Malaysian Management Review*, 43(2): 23–38.

Hocking, J.B., Brown, M., and Harzing, A.-W. (2007) Balancing global and local strategic contexts: expatriate knowledge transfer, applications, and learning within a transnational organization, *Human Resource Management*, 46(4): 513–33.

Hofstede, G. (1991) *Cultures and Organizations*, Maidenhead: McGraw-Hill.

Honda Dreams Fund (HDF) (2011) online at http://autobizz.com.my/forum/forum/General-Chat/2542-Honda-Dreams-Fund-scholarship-open-for-application.html (accessed 20 May 2012).

— (2012) announcement, online at http://www.honda.com.my/aboutus/annoucement (accessed 20 May 2012).

House, R.J., Javidan, M., Hanges, P., and Dorfman, P. (2002) Understanding cultures and implicit leadership theories across the globe: an introduction to project GLOBE, *Journal of World Business*, 37: 3–10, online at http://www.thunderbird.edu/wwwfiles/sites/globe/pdf/jwb_globe_intro.pdf (accessed 20 May 2012).

Human Resources Development Fund (HRDF) (2012) online at http://www.hrdf.com.my (accessed 20 May 2012).

Husted, K. and Michailova, S. (2002) Diagnosing and fighting knowledge sharing hostility, *Organizational Dynamics*, 31(1): 60–73.

Hutchings, K. (2005) Koalas in the land of the pandas: reviewing Australian expatriates' China preparation, *International Journal of Human Resource Management*, 16(4): 553–66.

International Labour Office (ILO) (2004) R195 Human Resources Development Recommendation, concerning human resources development: education, training and lifelong learning recommendation, Geneva session of the conference: 92, date of adoption 17 June 2004, online at http://www.ilo.org/skills/lang–en/index.htm (accessed 26 December 2012).

Irving, J.A. (2010) Educating global leaders: exploring intercultural competence in leadership education, *Journal of International Business and Cultural Studies*, 3: 1–14, online at http://www.aabri.com/manuscripts/09392.pdf (accessed 20 May 2012).

Jie Shen (2005) International training and management development: theory and reality, *Journal of Management Development*, 24(7): 656–66.

— and Darby, R. (2006) Training and management development in Chinese multinational enterprises, *Employee Relations*, 28(4): 342–62.

Jokinen, T., Brewster, C., and Suutari, V. (2008) Career capital during international work experiences: contrasting self-initiated expatriate experiences and assigned expatriation, *International Journal of Human Resource Management*, 19(6): 979–98.

Kale, D. (2010) The distinctive patterns of dynamic learning and inter-firm differences in the Indian pharmaceutical Industry, *British Journal of Management*, 21(1): 223–38.

Kasper, H., Hühlbacher, J., and Müller, B. (2008) Intra-organizational knowledge sharing in MNCs depending on the degree of decentralization and communities of practice, *Journal of Global Business and Technology*, 4(1): 59–68.

Kealey, D.J. and Protheroe, D.R. (1996) The effectiveness of cross-cultural training for expatriates: an assessment of the literature on the issue, *International Journal of Intercultural Relations*, 20: 141–65.

Kohlbacher, F. and Mukai, K. (2007) Japan's learning communities in Hewlett-Packard consulting and integration, challenging one-size fits all solutions, *The Learning Organization: International Journal of Knowledge and Organizational Learning Management*, 14(1): 8–20.

Kolb, P., Osland, J., and Rubin, L. (1995) *Organizational Behaviour: An Experiential Approach*, 6th edn, Englewood Cliffs, NJ: Prentice Hall.

Kowske, B.J. and Anthony, K. (2007) Towards defining leadership competence around the world: what mid-level managers need to know in twelve countries, *Human Resource Development International*, 10(1): 21–41.

Kupka, B. and Cathro, V. (2007) Desperate housewives—social and professional isolation of German expatriated spouses, *International Journal of Human Resource Management*, 18(6): 951–68.

Lee, L.-Y. and Li, C.-Y. (2008) The moderating effects of teaching method, learning style and cross-cultural differences on the relationship between expatriate training and training effectiveness, *International Journal of Human Resource Management*, 19(4): 600–19.

Lineham, M. (2005) Women in international management, in H. Scullion and M. Lineham (eds) *International Human Resource Management, A Critical Text*, Basingstoke and New York: Palgrave Macmillan, pp. 181-201.

Lucas, L.M. (2006) The role of culture on knowledge transfer: the case of the multinational corporation, *The Learning Organization*, 13(2/3): 257-75.

Lucas, R., Lupton, B., and Mathieson, H. (2006) *Human Resource Management in an International Context*, London: Chartered Institute of Personnel & Development (CIPD).

McDonnell, A., Lamare, R., Gunnigle, P., and Lavelle, J. (2010) Developing tomorrow's leaders—evidence of global talent management in multinational enterprises, *Journal of World Business*, 45(2): 150-60.

McKenna, S. and Richardson, J. (2007) The increasing complexity of the internationally mobile professional, issues for research and practice, *Cross Cultural Management: An International Journal*, 14(4): 307-20.

Metcalfe, B. and Rees, C. (2005) Theorizing advances in international human resource development, *Human Resource Development International*, 8(4): 449-65.

Minbaeva, D. and Michailova, S. (2004) Knowledge transfer and expatriation in multinational corporations, the role of disseminative capacity, *Employee Relations*, 26(6): 663-79.

OECD (2012) Reviews of vocational education and training—learning for jobs, online at http://www.oecd.org/edu/highereducationandadultlearning/learningofrjobs.htm (accessed 26 December 2012).

Reiche, B.S., Harzing, A-W., and Kraimer, M.L. (2008) The role of international assignees' social capital in creating inter-unit intellectual capital: a cross-level model, *Journal of International Business Studies*, 40: 509-26.

Reid, M.A., Barrington, H., and Brown, M. (2004) *Human Resource Development, Beyond Training Interventions*, 7th edn, London: Chartered Institute of Personnel & Development (CIPD).

Saka-Helmhout, A. (2007) Unravelling learning within multinational corporation, *British Journal of Management*, 18(3): 294-310.

Scullion, H. and Lineham, M. (eds) (2005) *International Human Resource Management, A Critical Text*, Basingstoke: Palgrave.

Selmer, J. (2010) Expatriate cross-cultural training for China: views and experience of 'China Hands', *Management Research Review*, 33(1): 41-53.

Sparrow, P. and Hiltrop, J-M. (1994) *European Human Resource Management in Transition*, London: Prentice Hall.

Tarique, I. and Caligiuri, P. (2009) The role of cross-cultural absorptive capacity in the effectiveness of in-country cross-cultural training, *International Journal of Training and Development*, 13(3): 148-64.

Tayeb, M. (2004) *International Human Resource Management, A Multinational Company Perspective*, Oxford: Oxford University Press.

Tung, R.L. (2004) The model global manager?, *Organizational Dynamics*, 33(3): 243-53.

United Nations Development Programme (UNDP) (2006) Knowledge services and learning, a UNDP capacity development resource, conference paper #3, working draft, November 2006, Capacity Development Group, Bureau for Development Policy, UNDP, online at http://www.undp.org/capacity/knowledge.shtml (accessed 23 November 2010).

— (2010) UNDP and Honda provide scholarships in Malaysia, online at http://www.honda.com.my/hdf_about.html (accessed 26 December 2012).

van der Heijden, J.A.V., van Engen, M.L., and Paauwe, J. (2009) Expatriate career support: predicting expatriate turnover and performance, *International Journal of Human Resource Management*, 20: 4831-45.

Varma, A., Toh, S.M., and Budhwar, P. (2006) A new perspective on the female expatriate experience: the role of host country national categorization, *Journal of World Business*, 41: 112-20.

Vidal, Ma E. Sánchez, Valle, R. Sanz, and Aragón, Ma I. Barba (2007) The adjustment process of Spanish repatriates: a case study, *International Journal of Human Resource Management*, 18(8): 1396-417.

Waxin, M-F. and Panaccio, A. (2005) Cross-cultural training to facilitate expatriate adjustment: it works!, *Personnel Review*, 34(1): 51-67.

Welch, D.E., Welch, L.S., and Worm, V. (2007) The international business traveller: a neglected but strategic human resource, *International Journal of Human Resource Management*, 18(2): 173-83.

World Trade Organization (WTO) (2010) Trade related technical assistance programmes (TRTA) information, see WTO homepage, Trade topics, Building trade capacity, online at http://www.wto.org/ (accessed 26 December 2012).

 Visit the Online Resource Centre for web links, interactive glossary, and more:
http://www.oxfordtextbooks.co.uk/orc/crawley

Diversity management in an international environment

 Learning Outcomes

After reading this chapter you will be able to:

- appreciate the concept of a diverse workforce marked by differences between an organization's employees
- explain the particular relevance of managing diversity for multinational companies
- outline the essence of 'diversity management' in relation to the alternatives of managing employee differences by use of discriminatory policies and practices or by equality management
- identify the challenges facing MNEs intending to introduce diversity management policies and practices in overseas subsidiaries
- critically assess the claims made for diversity management compared with its actual practice.

Introduction

This chapter draws our attention to the notion of diversity within a workforce, emphasizing the *differences* that exist between an organization's employees and suggesting the potential benefits of harnessing such a distinctive combination of qualities. In an organization where such diversity is readily accepted, each individual is respected and their contribution valued.

Workforce homogeneity

At the same time we need to be aware that some organizations are marked by a discernible *lack* of difference between their staff, especially when we focus our attention on those attributes that are more visible, such as gender, ethnicity, age, and disability. In such organizations differences can be greatest between those who are employees of the company and those who are not. Consequently, workforce diversity may well be viewed more negatively and employees that are seen to be 'different' from the mainstream can experience less favourable treatment. Such discrimination might be reflected in one group being favoured (unfairly) over another in relation to jobs, promotion, pay, and other rewards. Here, similarity and workforce homogeneity are preferred to workforce diversity. Hence, employees that differ from the dominant group may be viewed disapprovingly on the basis of their common characteristic, such as age, gender, or ethnicity.

MNEs and workforce diversity

While not all companies have a diverse workforce, multinationals invariably do, since they employ people across—and from—a number of countries. However, this does not mean that they necessarily value this diversity and, focusing on the overseas companies of multinational organizations, we can distinguish between three main types of choice available to management on how it treats its workforce. These are:

- **discriminatory management;**
- **equality management;**
- **diversity management**.

Discriminatory management in the MNE

In deciding how to manage diversity, the MNE might choose *discriminatory management*, favouring one group over others. For example it might adopt an ethnocentric approach and assign Parent Country Nationals to head up its subsidiaries. Alternatively, a polycentric approach would see the company favouring Host Country Nationals and appointing them to run its overseas operations. Typically, such decisions are portrayed as the outcome of what is considered best for the business. As such they are not necessarily viewed as unfair to employees by those making these decisions, even though they entail discriminatory treatment against a particular group.

Equality management in the MNE

However, where unfairness and inequity surface as an issue to be resolved, those who manage the MNE might seek to ensure some equality of treatment and a balanced representation between categories of employees by following an 'equal employment opportunity' philosophy. Thus, based upon concerns over unfairness and a need for social justice, *equality management* (EM) initiatives are introduced to tackle practices construed as discriminatory and to rectify any imbalance in, for example, management posts held by host country and expatriate staff or between the proportion of men and women.

Diversity management in the MNE

Latterly, however, certain multinationals have proclaimed their enthusiasm for *diversity*. They expect differences between individual employees to be positively valued throughout the organization. Consequently, they introduce initiatives that promote a culture of 'inclusion' and respect for all.

Ideally, *diversity management* (DM) should *build on* EM measures. First, EM measures are intended to promote equal employment opportunities and to eradicate unfair discrimination and treatment dealt out to minority groups (defined in terms of their lack of power and influence in the company, rather than their numbers). Then, following a diversity philosophy, all members of the workforce should see each other first and foremost as human beings who possess distinctive qualities that should be recognized 'on merit', irrespective of gender, age, nationality, culture, and other specified characteristics.

MNEs that practise DM might also be expected to adopt a geocentric approach to human resource management. A geocentric orientation does not differentiate between employees on the basis of their nationality or culture. 'The only culture that matters is that embodied in the multinational company itself which, in demoting nationality per se, will espouse the value of the diversity of skills and insights that national differences can bring' (Walsh and Doughty, 2009: 381). Hence, arguments in favour of diversity are sustained by a business case that appreciates the value of gathering together a wealth and multiplicity of employees' disparate as well as similar contributions. Indeed, organizations worldwide have invested in diversity programmes 'to attain outcomes such as better utilizing talent, increasing creativity and better serving demographically diverse customers' (Syed et al., 2010: 144).

Moreover, for the DM approach to have credibility across the organization, the MNE can be expected to nurture multicultural teams and to have a top management line-up that is international in composition. These set a practical example and send a message that DM is more than a proclamation of policy emanating from corporate headquarters.

Challenges to diversity management

At one level DM 'evokes various colourful metaphors of harmonious coexistence of elements of difference inside the confines of organizational boundaries' (Kamp and Hagedorn-Rasmussen, 2004, cited in Jamali et al., 2010: 167). However, while the geocentric claims made for DM in an MNE appear to be persuasive, they have not gone uncontested. Neither can we ignore the challenges and contradictions faced by MNEs within their foreign subsidiaries. For example, rather than welcoming the celebration of employee differences, the transfer of a DM initiative overseas might be viewed by those in the host country as the imposition of the MNE's own national or corporate value system. This is because the rationale for DM has its origins in the USA, leading to a US-centric approach that may be at odds with the employment culture and institutions of the host country (Syed and Özbilgin, 2009).

Paradoxically, therefore, the supposed adoption of a geocentric approach through a DM intervention can be interpreted—by those on the receiving end—as the ethnocentric implementation (even imposition) of a parent company's directives or instructions. For example an MNE's insistence on equal treatment regardless of a person's age, gender, religion, disability, or nationality, etc. may be at odds with a particular country's norms and traditions, which uphold the correctness, morality, and merit of certain inequalities.

Managing workforce diversity in the MNE

Organizational attitudes towards workforce diversity range from intolerance to tolerance and even appreciation (Joplin and Daus, 1997, cited in Shen et al., 2009: 235). Applying this insight to

Figure 10.1 Approaches to managing workforce diversity

Figure 10.1 above, we can suggest that the diverse composition of a multinational workforce can be managed in broadly three ways.

- Where the organization is predominantly *intolerant* of employee diversity, management is more likely to adopt a discriminatory set of practices, which favours members of a particular group of employees to the detriment of another.
- Where an organization is *tolerant* of diversity, management may strive to combat the unfair treatment and exclusion of certain categories of employee by EM processes, adopting equal employment opportunity policies and practices.
- Where individual differences are both recognized and actively *appreciated*, management can promote a DM culture that treats all staff on merit and aims to secure the inclusion of the whole workforce.

Figure 10.1 conveys the possibility that MNEs will move progressively from discriminatory management towards DM. Whereas EM seeks to combat the negativity and unfairness of discriminatory management against underprivileged groups, DM can build upon these EM foundations by its more inclusive and meritocratic policies.

However, as we begin to explore the practice rather than the intent of managing diversity in MNEs, we may discover certain shortcomings. For example, if it is shown that DM is simply about respecting individual differences and that it overlooks the role of EM in tackling the organization's inequalities (e.g. of gender, nationality, and ethnicity), it is unlikely to deliver a truly diverse work-force, which is meant to contribute more effectively to the business (Jamali et al., 2010: 170). In other words, 'diversity and celebrating differences are of limited added value if the structure and culture of organizations remain fundamentally unchanged' (Jamali et al., 2010: 181).

Discriminatory management: an MNE in Nigeria

Before examining more thoroughly the essential nature and challenges of DM in multinational organizations, let us reflect on Case Study 10.1, which charts the developments of an MNE's new hotel in Nigeria and its progress from what appears to be a form of discriminatory management.

 Discussion Activity 10.1

Read Case Study 10.1 (Part One) below. In what way is the appointment of a multinational group of departmental heads indicative of a geocentric approach to managing diversity?

This multinational's decision to call on its own in-house international expertise was almost certainly motivated by its practice of relying on 'company men' with proven capability, to

Case Study 10.1 (Part One)   By Choice Hotels (BCH) Group: staffing a new hotel in Lagos, Nigeria

The 'By Choice Hotels' (BCH) Group is a well-established American multinational company that has its headquarters in Los Angeles, California, from where it oversees the management of its five-star hotels located in 100 countries worldwide. Governed by a strategy of organic growth, BCH's senior management team has turned its attention to Africa and particularly towards those nations that can support demand for five-star accommodation. Its latest project is a new, purpose-built hotel in Lagos, a metropolis of over fifteen million people in oil-rich Nigeria. Lagos is the centre for Nigeria's economic and financial activity, and home to its largest port, which exports crude oil worth 90 per cent of the nation's foreign exchange earnings.

BCH has a prestigious global brand and reputation for providing outstanding service to business and tourist clients, and is able to charge premium prices. The new By Choice-Lagos hotel has 600 guest rooms, including 300 standard rooms from US$650, 200 executive rooms at US$800, and 100 suites at US$1000 per night. The demand for such a product was borne out by market research, which highlighted international business executives as the main customer base. As a five-star hotel, By Choice-Lagos has a selection of restaurants and bars; sports and recreation facilities; a business centre; over twenty function rooms providing banquet, meeting, and conference facilities; and room amenities that convey international standards of hospitality.

However, the hotel's general manager is well aware that 'in the hospitality business, most important are the employees and the service they provide'. To this end, By Choice-Lagos recognizes the value of continuous training and improvement of both skills and attitude for its amenable but inexperienced Nigerian staff. The company has to make sure its clients experience the seamless qualities of five-star service throughout their stay. So management has implemented various programmes for its employees to ensure they understand what quality service is, what the guests expect, and how they can 'exceed the guests' expectations'. Some of this training is delivered by the general manager himself, a German with over twenty years' service in many countries with BCH. The rest is delivered by his seven departmental heads, all of whom have been selected for Lagos by group headquarters in the USA. All are steeped in the BCH's strong corporate culture and have long experience of establishing BCH Group hotels in a variety of host countries. Interestingly, they represent six different nationalities, comprising Asian, American, and European countries. In addition, the hotel's master chef is French. All of these expatriates are men aged between forty-eight and fifty-four years.

deliver the group's five-star service in what was seen as a lucrative but challenging location. From this we can deduce that individuals were ostensibly chosen on merit rather than on the basis of nationality. This certainly fits one notion of being geocentric. However, in terms of managing diversity, we might observe a rather narrower interpretation of 'merit', since the selection of these expatriate managers excluded females, Host Country Nationals, and anyone under forty-five years old.

In this sense, By Choice-Lagos would seem to be applying *discriminatory management* practices against women, Nigerians, and younger candidates. Such an observation was unlikely to bother BCH's management, who were concerned to act in what they considered to be 'the best interests of the business'. Indeed, when establishing its Lagos hotel, BCH's management was reassured that the Nigerian workforce was adequately educated, spoke good English, and was likely to be appreciative of a position within a prestigious western multinational. Moreover, the relatively modest salaries on offer to local candidates would be considered generous in Lagos.

Case Study 10.1 (Part Two)   Early success at By Choice-Lagos—
jeopardized by diversity issues?

Three years after opening its new hotel in Lagos, BCH's corporate executives are very pleased with
how well this hotel has performed. Securing an average occupancy rate of over 80 per cent and
able to maintain its premium price structure, the hotel has consistently delivered high profits to its
American owners and has hitherto maintained the brand's international standing. Much credit has
been given to the hard work and experience of the hotel's expatriate managers; and their efforts in
training the local staff and in encouraging them to share in the sense of excitement of establishing
their city's leading luxury hotel.

However, human resource problems are beginning to emerge. In part these can be related to
the company's discriminatory approach to its employment practices. The satisfaction of local staff
has appeared to falter. Their high levels of performance and relatively low rate of turnover can no
longer be taken for granted. Staff now seem to be acquiescent rather than committed in their work.
Moreover, the expectations and aspirations of a significant number have changed. Talented and
capable staff are now seeking career development and management appointments, but feel their
enthusiasm and ambitions are not being recognized. Unsurprisingly, there is some resentment against
the vastly better rewards given to their expatriate 'betters'—and the first signs of Nigerian staff moving
to competitors and taking with them transferable, marketable skills.

At the same time the hotel's head of HR is under pressure from corporate headquarters to cut back on
expatriate remuneration. Fortunately, perhaps, the Group's policy of moving its managers to new locations
has meant that several expatriate managers are being relocated and others are quite keen to follow.

Potential repercussions of discriminatory management

In such circumstances, issues raised by BCH's discriminatory management might seem non-
contentious. However, several years down the line, employee attitudes can change in ways
that might jeopardize the business, as we can now see.

 Discussion Activity 10.2

   a   To what *extent* are the mounting grievances from the Nigerian staff related to the company's
ethnocentric approach to workplace diversity?

   b   BCH Group has no formal policy on managing diversity, so what can the hotel's general manager
do to help rectify the discriminatory management experienced by Nigerian staff?

Although the company had appointed a team of managers from diverse nationalities, it has
shown a clear preference for expatriate appointments over Host Country Nationals for management positions. This can be confirmed by an initial management view that local staff
would be suitable only for *operational* tasks such as those in reception, reservations, house-
keeping, security, maintenance, restaurants, and bars. Similarly, the support functions of the
departments of marketing, sales, purchasing, accounting, and HR, are each headed by an
expatriate, with administrative roles taken by well-educated Host Country Nationals.

In this respect the hotel's senior management initially viewed its Nigerian staff from an
ethnocentric viewpoint, based upon an outlook that assumed the 'superiority' of a western

approach to business in general and hotel management in particular. The ensuing divide between expatriate and local staff was to a great extent the source of the discontent felt and then voiced by the hotel's Nigerian employees.

Over time, however, expatriate managers came to appreciate the capabilities and drive of their more talented local staff—and encouraged and helped them to develop management skills. But it was only recently, with expatriates moving on and managerial positions beginning to open up, that the general manager could offer these opportunities to Nigerians. Moreover, his choices for promotion meant that he was able to increase workforce diversity in terms of gender, age, and nationality: increasing the proportion of managers who were women, under thirty-five, and Nigerian.

However, such appointments were made on the pragmatic basis of recognizing employees' capabilities and potential. They were certainly not informed by reference to EM policies designed to reduce employment inequalities. Should this really matter? It may well do in Nigeria, a country with over 200 recognized ethnic groups, the chief ones being the Hausa in the north, the Igbo in the south-east, and the Yoruba in the south-west, which includes Lagos. Most importantly, as well as speaking their own languages these groupings are generally marked by religious affiliations. Most Hausa are Muslim, the Igbo mainly Catholic, and the Yoruba typically non-Catholic Christians.

These kinds of division might not be an issue in a society tolerant of difference. However, a study of Nigeria's ongoing 'communal and ethno-religious clashes' reveals bloodshed and slaughter with a loss of lives numbering thousands (Okafor, 2007). Such violence is relatively widespread and, 'the violent communal and ethno-religious clashes that have swept across the nation ... are too numerous to mention' (Okafor, 2007: 36). In Lagos, this has involved ethnic and religious clashes between local Yoruba and Hausa, who were regarded as 'migrants' even though their families had lived there for more than 100 years. These clashes led to over 1000 dead on one occasion and more than 100 on another (Okafor, 2007). While these are not everyday incidents, they do reveal the cleavages between and among individuals and groups, characterized by mutual suspicion and an uneasy coexistence.

Equality management: implications for an MNE in Nigeria

Features of society such as those observed in Nigeria clearly have implications for managing a diverse workforce. They also raise questions concerning the extent to which *equality management* interventions in the workplace can effectively help management to address these aspects of local difference.

Perhaps we can catch a glimpse of the possible implications of these tensions within Nigerian society by travelling forward to the present day, when the general manager of the By Choice-Lagos hotel and his heads of department are Nigerian. This will enable us to explore the rationale of EM interventions and to consider the extent to which they might appeal to managers in their efforts to manage a diverse workforce.

 Discussion Activity 10.3

Read Case Study 10.1 (Part Three) below. In what ways is the hotel practising discriminatory management? Would an EM policy help matters?

Case Study 10.1 (Part Three) Religious and ethnic tensions in Nigeria: implications for By Choice-Lagos?

The By Choice-Lagos hotel is managed very successfully by its Nigerian management team, who have acquired the knowledge, skills, and experience in delivering the international standards established by their expatriate predecessors. Made up of roughly equal numbers of male and female staff, the hotel now seems to have a workforce that more closely reflects local diversity.

However, all managers are from the Yoruba tribe and follow the Christian faith. Only a handful of Hausa are employed, none of whom is earmarked for promotion. In view of the ethno-religious intolerance in the country, this is perhaps not surprising.

The previous discriminatory behaviour by expatriate managers against Host Country Nationals has been replaced by similar behaviour by Yoruba managers against members of other ethnic groups, notably the Hausa. Thus, one form of ethnocentric discrimination (nationality) has been replaced by another one (ethnic allegiance), such that preferential treatment in recruitment, promotion, and privileges, is based on ethnic affiliation (Ituma and Simpson, 2009).

As we have seen, Nigerian society is deeply structured along ethnic lines and an organization's Nigerian decision makers are typically more favourably disposed towards individuals of similar ethnic background. This reflects a lack of trust between ethnic groups and a desire by the dominant tribe to protect its own interests. Thus, where a Yoruba, Hausa, or Igbo is in charge of recruitment and employment, they are most likely to fill any openings in their organization with a member of their own tribe or ethnic region, irrespective of whether or not there is a more qualified person from another ethnic group (Ituma and Simpson, 2009: 741). Here ethnic considerations outweigh economic rationale, resulting in the exclusion of many talented and capable individuals.

Arguments in favour of employing a diverse workforce

At the By Choice-Lagos hotel, management's adoption of EM interventions—by implementing and monitoring equal employment opportunity policies and procedures—should help to redress the disadvantages instigated by Yoruba managers and experienced by those minority groups. This counts as a *social justice reason*. At the same time an EM initiative would widen the pool of talent made available to the hotel and help it appoint the best qualified candidates for each job. This is considered a *business reason*. Moreover, by taking steps to minimize unfairness and remove barriers against marginalized groups, the hotel would be seen as complying with the Nigerian government's intention and laws to reduce ethnic tension. This would be in keeping with EM thinking and establish a hotel workforce more representative of the linguistic, ethnic, and religious diversity of the nation.

This combination of reasons: social justice, business, legal, and human resourcing, might seem to offer a strong justification for an MNE deciding to introduce non-discriminatory policies in order to employ a heterogeneous workforce. Indeed, where control for HR resides in the hands of parent country rather than local managers, it is more likely that EM and DM processes will be implemented. In Nigeria, for example, foreign-owned banks have insisted on employing customer-facing staff who are representative of the nation's ethno-religious diversity. In line with mainstream thinking on employing a diverse workforce, retail banks are keen to signal to their customer base that they are not limited to serving one particular segment or group of society. In so doing, they are not only recruiting from a wider pool of talent, they are also appealing to a greater number of clients.

Maintaining a homogeneous workforce

In view of what we now know of the significance of ethnicity within Nigeria, it is understandable why the By Choice-Lagos hotel's Yoruba managers might continue to discriminate in favour of their own tribal members. In their minds, recruiting more widely from other groups will only make things worse by stirring up tensions within the organization. In the country's northern hotels a similar view will be held by Hausa managers towards those from the Yoruba and Igbo tribes.

Managing diversity in different nations

So, on balance should the MNE insist on establishing EM policies throughout its worldwide network of hotels? Based on our interpretation of diversity at By Choice-Lagos, it will not be easy for corporate headquarters to insist on the same degree of compliance expected in its American and European hotels, where anti-discrimination interventions on the grounds of race or ethnicity may be significantly more robust. Indeed, the likelihood of a multinational successfully transferring its home country version of EM (or DM) to an overseas subsidiary is open to question. Its corporate definition as to what is 'fair' and 'unfair' treatment of employees might not be accepted elsewhere: an issue we have seen only too clearly in relation to ethnicity in Nigeria.

The above point can be developed in relation to homosexuality. BCH Group hotels in the United States and Europe, for example, need to comply with legislation that makes discrimination on the grounds of sexual orientation illegal. By contrast, in Nigeria it is homosexuality that is illegal.

Hence, we can conclude that interpretations as to how we manage diversity differs between nations. In one context (such as the USA) employees who are gay are meant to be treated no less favourably than employees who are heterosexual. In another context (such as Nigeria) homosexuals are vilified, based on a belief that being gay is unnatural: a view that is sanctioned and promoted by fundamentalist Muslim and Christian teachings.

It is this degree of disparity between societies that raises serious doubts as to whether MNEs can standardize and successfully transfer EM initiatives globally. Indeed, as we have seen, obstacles to tackling inequalities can also arise from *within* the MNE itself. The organization's own managers may well hold discriminatory attitudes and practise discriminatory behaviour, which they may believe to be entirely correct and proper.

The nature and 'normality' of unequal treatment: an MNE in Zambia

From our discussion above, it would appear that aspects of *discriminatory management* are perceived as quite normal and quite acceptable by those who practise it. However, it would

also be useful to consider the nature and implications of such acts of discriminatory management. We do so by listening to host country employees' reactions to the way they are managed by their Chinese expatriate managers in Zambia, a landlocked country of twelve million
people in Southern Africa.

 Discussion Activity 10.4

> What evidence is there that the Chinese managers' approach to their Zambian workforce is
> discriminatory? To what extent do you regard this treatment as no more than the outcome of simply
> recruiting local people to do local work?

The comments of its Zambian workers reveal the perceptions they have formed about this
MNE's approach to diversity as practised by its Chinese expatriate managers. This behaviour is viewed as discriminatory to the extent that the Chinese occupy all of the project's
management and technical roles, whereas the Zambians make up all of the manual labour
force, receiving lower pay and experiencing poorer conditions of work. At one level this bias
(leading to exclusion) might depict the unsentimental business logic adopted by the management decision makers in serving their own self-interests and those of the organization.
In this instance, the technical and organizational skills required for key positions have led
to the appointment of Parent Country Nationals; and the manual jobs are given to the local
workforce. 'Not only are they significantly cheaper to employ, such staff are attractive to the
management if they are perceived to be malleable and conveniently recruited, trained, and
retained (at least in the short term)' (Walsh and Doughty, 2009: 367).

However, a further interpretation is that such treatment is the result of *more* than a detached, economic decision. The dominant group of Chinese expatriates seems to exhibit an

---

 Case Study 10.2 Discriminatory management in Zambia: China
Henan International Corporation

China Henan International Corporation (Chico) has overseas offices in over twenty countries in Asia,
Africa, and Europe, and has completed more than 300 engineering projects in these countries. Its
latest contract is with the Zambian government to rebuild 300 km of a major road network; and Chico
has sent a team of civil engineers and managers from China, the parent country, to supervise the
project through to completion.

The company has employed local men to do the manual work: either as labourers—chosen for their
physical capabilities—or to drive the huge trucks and road-building equipment. Drivers were selected
on the basis of their driving licence and record, and how well they performed in a short driving test.
As the unemployment rate in Zambia is 50 per cent and 85 per cent of the country's workforce are
employed in (low-paid) agriculture, the company had no shortage of willing applicants. This meant
that the Chinese managers were able to take advantage of their relatively powerful position as
employer and adopt an autocratic and 'hire-and-fire' approach when it suited.

We can gain an insight into this by recounting the following observations voiced by the Zambian
workforce, as they eat their lunch and complain that it is always the same bad diet of small fish and
cabbage. More reflectively, workers suggest that this is indicative of their superiors' attitude towards
them. 'We are doing the job for them so that they can benefit, but they don't respect us as much as we
expect. We are not trusted at all; they can't leave you alone; they don't regard us Zambians as people'
(BBC Four, 2010).

ethnocentric orientation, in which their home culture is regarded as superior to that of the host culture. The Zambian workforce is evaluated unfavourably against the standards and expectations of the parent country and categorized as low-skilled, untrustworthy, and requiring firm handling. It is very much a case of 'them' and 'us'.

We can deduce that the expatriates' discriminatory treatment is 'against' the local workforce and is supported by a combination of (a) their culturally biased attitudes; and (b) decisions and behaviour they consider managerially neutral, in that they are 'acting in the best interests of the company'. An insistence on the impartiality of this business rationale might persuade the expatriates that they are not treating Host Country Nationals unfairly. However, those on the receiving end realize that they are treated less favourably because of who they are, in that 'they don't regard us Zambians as people'.

 Stop and Think

We have learned that the basis for discriminatory behaviour against a workforce of a different nationality or ethnic group is as much to do with the decision maker's cultural bias or prejudicial attitudes as it is with their making a decision for impartial, business reasons.

The concept of **social categorization**, which relates to social identity theory, enables us to stop and think how discriminatory behaviour can be understood as part of a *psychological process* (Tajfel, 1982). People typically place others into categories, labelling a group (e.g. 'Zambian labourers') in a way that says things about them.

This generally automatic process can also be linked to 'comparison' in that people compare their own group category (e.g. 'Chinese managers') with other groups and tend to form biases against the 'out-group'.

In turn this enables a form of self-esteem through 'identification' with one's own and superior 'in-group', a perception that is likely to be reinforced by the explicit division between management and workers ('them' and 'us') within the organization.

These psychological concepts relate to prejudice and describe inter-related cognitive processes, to which we can add that of **stereotyping**.

Such psychological processes help to explain the behaviour of the Chico's Chinese expatriates. One might conclude, therefore, that for them to move towards an authentic acceptance and appreciation of people's diversity, there would need to be a significant adjustment across all three areas: social categorization, comparison, and identification.

Tackling the unequal treatment of HCNs: an MNE in Azerbaijan

Chico's management of its Zambian operation seems very different from the efforts we can now observe at 'Verve Oil' in its operations in Azerbaijan. Verve, a major European multinational company operating in five continents, has invested billions of dollars in oil-rich Azerbaijan.

In line with its production agreement with the government of Azerbaijan, Verve has a target of employing 90 per cent of its workforce from the local population. Accordingly, this MNE has sought to reduce its considerable reliance on expatriate staff by recruiting and training Host Country Nationals. However, this has proved to be an immense challenge, especially in locating suitably qualified and experienced people to undertake the range of technical and managerial jobs in the industry's specialist fields of engineering, exploration, and drilling.

Consequently, 'Verve-Azerbaijan' (Verve-Az) continues to employ several hundred international staff, including many in its senior management team. Even so, the employment of HCNs has increased substantially. The newly appointed CEO is an Azerbaijani and there are now over 2000 local employees, making up 85 per cent of the workforce. In addition, the localization of its workforce has meant considerable savings on expatriate salaries for 'Verve-Az', though in the shorter term this has had to be offset against significant investment in training and development for the company's less experienced successors, the HCNs.

Another advantage of tackling the unequal treatment of HCNs through the employment of locals has come through the increased number of Azeri staff in the HR Department of Verve-Az. Over a period of four years HCNs have replaced a dozen expatriates, whose numbers have been reduced to three. The current head of HR, who is an expatriate, believes that the locals' knowledge of the host country context and culture makes them best placed to perform HR roles. In turn, the company has supported these local HR staff through a two-year part-time educational programme, giving them a CIPD professional qualification. This has provided substance to the MNE's commitment to these less experienced local appointees, increasing both their competence and their confidence.

Once, senior line managers used to insist on working with HR expatriates. Now, the same managers (expatriate and local) appreciate that their Azerbaijani HR Advisors are 'among the best they have ever worked with'.

The treatment of HCNs: Verve-Az and Chico

From the above example, we might conclude that Verve Oil's decision to address its unequal treatment of HCNs and appoint local staff to its HR department was primarily motivated by business and work-performance reasons, related to governmental influence and economic savings. Moreover, the company's prolonged stay in Azerbaijan helps to justify the amount of time and money invested in host country employees.

By contrast, it would seem financially imprudent and unrealistic for Chico to appoint Zambian locals to professional jobs. The road-building project was relatively short term and would not have warranted the levels of investment spent by the oil company. Also, the relevance of local knowledge for the role of HR specialist is unlikely to have the same significance for that of a road-building labourer. Moreover, the homogeneity of the Zambian workforce might actually be advantageous to their work performance, in terms of ease of communication and sharing of know-how on their routine tasks (Rowley et al., 2010: 187).

However, the above analysis might not give the whole story behind the appointment of Azerbaijani HR staff. In particular, it may seriously undervalue the role played by Verve Oil's global policies on DM, which are intended to promote greater awareness of the value of employee difference throughout its business units worldwide. As such, the company's global DM policies may have encouraged sceptical members of Verve-Az staff to show more tolerance to those well-educated, English-speaking, Azerbaijani females who had replaced expatriate staff in the HR department.

Case Study 10.3   Verve Oil: statements on diversity

- We try hard to ensure our selection and assessment processes are free from bias and that Verve Oil offers everyone access to opportunity, regardless of background, age, religion, ethnic origin, nationality, disability, sexual orientation, gender identity, or marital status. We do not tolerate harassment or discrimination in our workplaces.

- We are committed to a culture of diversity and actively embed inclusion across the organization. It is through the talents of different people that we will succeed as a business. It helps us attract, develop, and retain outstanding skills and talents. By valuing the differences among us and having a respect for different views and employees' personal needs, we strive to establish a platform for creativity, innovation, and problem solving.

Equality management *with* diversity management: global policies at Verve Oil

Verve Oil certainly promotes the importance of diversity worldwide. For example its website recognizes that its 75,000 workforce are naturally diverse in terms of gender, race, nationality, and culture. Consider Case Study 10.3, which is a précis of the company's official statements on equality and diversity.

 Discussion Activity 10.5

Comment on the view that Verve Oil's statement on workforce diversity in Case Study 10.3 indicates a combination of both EM and DM approaches.

The messages contained in the first paragraph are typical of an EM approach, whereas the second paragraph reveals a DM approach. EM is designed to avoid *unfair disadvantage* against specific *groups* (e.g. women) and to promote *equality of status and opportunities*, bolstered by *compliance with rules* that forbid discriminatory behaviour. In one sense, therefore, EM tends to emphasize *similarity*, since it groups people together in relation to a characteristic that they share, such as nationality. It is also concerned with *sameness* in that the need to right the wrongs suffered by various *categories of people* implies a move towards making everyone the same (Rowley et al., 2010: 183).

These features associated with EM contrast with DM, which tends to emphasize *difference* between *individuals* and to focus our attention on *enabling* individuals to make a *contribution* to the organization through their *distinctive and valued qualities*. Moreover, the organization is adding to the *business case* for diversity by promising enhanced levels of problem solving, creativity, and innovation. Interestingly, such a claim may be overstated. Studies conducted in organizations showed 'an increased number of conflicts and stereotyping within groups as a result of workforce diversification' (Rowley et al, 2010: 186).

Whatever the merits of a diverse workforce, we can suggest that Verve Oil has adopted EM measures in order to move away from any behaviour that discriminates against minority groups. In so doing the company intends its staff to be more tolerant of employee diversity. From this foundation, Verve Oil has then aspired to progress to a DM approach. This requires employees and managers to develop a mindset that positively values workforce diversity, by embracing a culture of inclusiveness across the organization.

We can also conclude that Verve Oil combines EM and DM approaches, at least in terms of its formal statements (i.e. at the level of rhetoric). This should not surprise us, as the two approaches are 'often considered as interdependent' (Rowley et al., 2010: 186). DM focuses on valuing individual differences, while EM aims to ensure that specific groups are not discriminated against. It follows, therefore, that DM should go 'beyond embracing and accepting differences, to modifying organizational practices and policies to challenge discrimination ... facing and dealing with notions of stereotyping, prejudice and institutional and interpersonal discrimination' (Kamp and Hagedorn-Rasmussen, 2004, cited in Jamali and Abdullah, 2010: 122). The message is that the effective management of workforce diversity requires EM *with* DM. Such a conclusion is signposted in Figure 10.1.

Diversity management *without* equality management

However, it seems that not all companies regard EM and DM practices as complementary. Instead, they may well choose to concentrate on one rather than the other. For example DM may be seen to operate on its own—without the support of EM. Such an arrangement has been robustly criticized as being used by companies to detract from, weaken, or avoid EM's concerns over discrimination against certain groups. This is because, in practice, many organizations with DM policies do not 'go beyond diversity awareness and diversity training' and produce a 'lip-service commitment' to the management of diversity that 'may be used to prioritize soft, rather than hard equal opportunity practices' (Wrench, 2005, cited in Jamali and Abdallah, 2010: 123).

Creating a diverse workforce in the MNE

While Verve Oil certainly stipulates mandatory training in 'diversity and inclusion' for its 6000 senior leaders, it also adopts other methods. Its 'global diversity council' provides a steer for the establishment of 'diversity plans and targets', which are tailored to each business unit, like Verve-Az. The council also lends support for 'affinity groups' by providing access to company resources such as funds, rooms, and webspace.

Formed on the basis of a shared, 'protected' characteristic, Verve has several global affinity groups. Its 'Women's International Network' builds on local women's networks that exist in several regions, including Azerbaijan. Its 'Pride Connection' affinity group is for the 'lesbian, gay, bisexual, and transgender community'. Other groups are based in particular countries: the 'Grey Association' in the USA brings together older workers and 'Multi-National Plus' is a UK-based group for ethnic minority employees.

Corporate support for affinity groups and their network of contacts is based on the belief that Verve's business interests are facilitated by 'removing barriers, welcoming diversity, and enabling all employees to achieve personal fulfilment in their careers'. However, the essential nature of DM, which is to promote a mindset amongst staff that celebrates individual difference, may appear to be at odds with Verve's designation of staff into special groups. This is because workers are perceived in terms of their membership of a group based upon a shared characteristic, such as gender, ethnicity, age, or sexuality. So, for example, in place of the unique qualities of 'Irina Mammadova' we have an 'Azerbaijani, married female with two young children'. Thus, the encouragement of difference and inclusion is perhaps ill-served by a reliance on mechanisms that emphasize a group's distinguishing characteristic.

On the other hand, identification of groups that are seen as disadvantaged and in need of 'protection' is considered key to the company's EM agenda. If we conclude, therefore, that the effective management of diversity is to *combine* EM and DM, we might also agree that the aim is to 'nurture appreciation of demographic, ethnic and individual differences through cultural change, followed by modification of organizational procedures and practices to foster more hospitable and hence more productive work environments' (Jamali et al., 2010: 168).

Methods for managing diversity in MNEs

As a starting point, Kossek et al. (2006: 53) suggest that EM and DM initiatives need to increase the numerical representation of historically excluded groups, thus creating a diverse workforce, which should then participate fully in organizational decision making and be included in every aspect of organizational life.

So, what practices can MNEs use to deliver these outcomes? Kossek et al. (2006: 55–7) offer an overview of these 'strategies', of which the following is a synopsis:

- Categories of people that have been previously under-represented or excluded from the organization (e.g. women or ethnic minority groups) can be part of a wider pool of talent, attracted through recruiting efforts that target particular groups or by tapping into the network of current employees.
- The inclusion and involvement of minority groups into a more diverse workforce can be sustained by the use of formal and informal mentoring programmes and by encouraging support groups.
- A cultural change programme can promote the importance of diversity in the organization through frequent communication, supported and reinforced by: awareness training for all staff, performance evaluation of managers' achievement of diversity goals, and employee attitude surveys that incorporate diversity issues.
- Varied perspectives within the workforce can be utilized—for problem solving and innovation—by setting up diverse teams and providing them with training and resources, as well as implementing team-based recognition and rewards for successful contributions.
- Employees can be offered cross-cultural, skill-building opportunities, including developmental assignments that expose employees to multiple cultures.
- In relation to EM concerns, the company can: 'monitor recruiting, hiring, promotion, and compensation systems for compliance and equity'; adopt processes that demonstrate a 'zero-tolerance of harassment and discrimination'; and provide 'flexible benefits that address a broad range of employee work and family needs' (Kossek et al., 2006: 55).

- Finally, the company can enhance its reputation as an employer by advertising its approach to diversity through a variety of channels, including its website and targeted media. In turn this should underline the methods outlined above.

From the foregoing list, it seems that the MNE can call upon an array of methods for transferring its policies and practices on managing diversity to its overseas subsidiaries. However, what may be more problematic are the *targets* for these diversity interventions. Is it gender, age, ethnicity, sexuality, nationality, disability, or all of these? We have already suggested how some societies take exception to having an MNE dictate its version of what is right and fair in the workplace.

Verve Oil has sought to address the issue of national sensitivities by additionally devolving accountability to each subsidiary. According to its policy document, this means that each subsidiary 'can focus on the very different diversity challenges it faces, from providing the right conditions for more women to advance into senior positions, to safeguarding and promoting rights of minorities in multi-ethnic communities'. As such, each subsidiary is required to devise a diversity plan, which includes its specific targets.

However, this approach would seem to imply that the MNE can achieve only limited diversity, dependent upon how receptive countries and regions are to change. We saw this at By Choice-Lagos hotel. Similarly, a Nigerian subsidiary of Verve Oil would be less likely to tackle the tribal divisions that exist there, even though Verve's global policy would interpret this as critical for the promotion of the rights of ethnic minorities.

Challenges and limitations of managing diversity in an MNE

Our exploration of managing diversity seems to reveal the *challenges* facing MNEs—and also the *limitations* inherent in attempts by MNEs to transfer their idea of diversity to a subsidiary outside the parent country.

In essence, when an MNE transfers its ideas of a diverse workforce to another country it is seeking to create an organizational oasis or haven within a *potentially* inhospitable, unreceptive, even hostile, environment. From this perspective, the ideal outcome would be that, whatever the situation outside the organization, a subsidiary's workforce is a representative one, avoiding unfair disadvantage against specific groups (EM). Its employees should also be able to act in accordance with notions of valuing the distinctive qualities of individuals (DM).

Thus, the MNE is not usually motivated by trying to change the host society, although its actions could be seen as an implied criticism of that society. It simply seeks to treat its workforce differently from the way that the host society treats its population. It does so because it is seen to make good sense, both morally and for the business.

However, MNEs would do well not to underestimate the challenges and structural barriers it may face, both within that society and within its own workplace. Indeed, Sippola and Smale (2007: 1913) warn that at best MNEs can expect only surface-level changes, since DM initiatives are unlikely to produce the 'required shifts in organizational and individual attitudes and behaviours'.

We can now test this supposition by exploring India, a society that poses particular problems. In so doing we concentrate on *gender*, which is 'an important dimension of diversity, not least because of the fact that women constitute half the world's population and have been historically a victim of patriarchal stereotypes and gender discrimination' (Syed et al., 2010: 145).

Managing gender inequalities: MNEs in India

In some respects countries such as India might appear to offer an encouraging setting for an MNE's diversity initiatives. After all, India is portrayed as one of the world's fastest developing, modernizing, and globalizing states, which can be seen in its burgeoning cities, expanding businesses, and an increasingly affluent consumer class.

India is also host to a growing number of global companies. Many have set up contact centres there and found its young Indian graduates, male and female, to be very competent employees. Moreover, the nation has relatively strict and clear equal employment opportunity (EEO) laws, including those that prohibit unfair discrimination on the grounds of gender. In addition, the state is obliged to minimize inequalities in income, status, and opportunities, including equal pay for equal work for both men and women (Ali, 2010: 40).

However, it would appear that contact centres are perhaps the exception when it comes to establishing a more diverse workplace. Indeed, women account for no more than 20 per cent of the MNE workforce in India. Nationally, women make up only a quarter of workers in formal employment, with the largest proportion in manufacturing. However, this comprises only 10 per cent of total female employment, since 75 per cent work in the informal and less regulated sector of agriculture and fisheries. The overall ratio of female-to-male earned income is 0.31 (HDR, 2008) and women comprise just 3 per cent of senior professionals and managers (Ali, 2010: 33–4). Gender gaps appear in education too, indicating the existence of discrimination in building those capabilities that would equip women to compete for jobs and earnings. Most recently, the female-to-male ratio for enrolments in tertiary education is 0.70 (HDR, 2008, cited in Ali, 2010: 36).

In summary, according to Ali (2010: 47) women 'occupy a lower rank, earn lower wages and have little recognition of their significant contribution to family, society and to the economy'. Hence, the challenge to any MNE seeking to combat such inequalities through global equality and diversity policies within its subsidiaries is likely to be considerable.

This is because Indian society exhibits standards of behaviour that are gender-based, which men and women are expected to carry over into the work environment. It is a patriarchal society, which is characterized by women's obedience to men, in conjunction with 'each man's obligation to support his wife and children' (Ali, 2010: 35). Hence, women are seen as dependent on men. They are also 'expected to be chaste and especially modest in all actions' (Ali, 2010: 35), a view bolstered by an allegiance to religious traditions and rules.

This is not to say that women are inevitably unaware or passively accepting of their 'place' either in the home or at the workplace. People are capable of taking some responsibility for their own course of action, working within and around such constraints. Certainly, the university-educated younger generation is showing signs of departure from some traditions, including that of marriages arranged by their parents. This may mean that these kinds of employee are likely to be more receptive to an MNE's ideas of gender equality and respect for individuals' different qualities.

Fundamental obstacles to gender equality

Yet the Indian context presents fundamental obstacles (Syed and Özbilgin, 2009). This is be-cause a belief in the inferiority of women appears deep-seated and buttressed by the caste system. By tradition a person inherits his or her family's rank and is assigned to a preordained place in society.

Even though officially illegal, the caste system persists. Thus, marriages are arranged ac-cording to the respective positions of the man and woman in the caste system. So entrenched is this practice that 'the killing of young couples who challenge the wishes of their families is not uncommon in rural India where the centuries-old traditions of caste and tribe remain little diluted' (*The Independent*, 2010).

However, one might presume that such 'honour killings' are less common in the major cit-ies. Paradoxically, though, with

> rapid economic changes in India, young people no longer live with their parents and they're meeting and falling in love in large cities. Many are from different castes, which is creating conflict with their elders in their families and villages.
>
> (Sinha, 2010)

Such honour killings are certainly an extreme step and probably most remain unreported. This helps explain the public horror that greeted the brutal murder of a young man and his bride-to-be that took place in the city of Delhi. The couple were bound, beaten with metal bars and given electric shocks, allegedly by the young woman's father and uncle, because the man she wanted to marry was from a different caste (*The Independent*, 2010).

Such extreme cases might seem unrelated to the ambitions of MNEs striving to deliver gender equality within their companies, but they represent the tip of an iceberg that can be an overwhelming obstacle to those EM and DM interventions designed to end the unfair dis-crimination of women as employees. Further evidence on the enormity of this 'iceberg' lies in a report for the charity ActionAid, which states how

> deeply entrenched discrimination against women has led to the survival rates of baby girls hitting an all-time low. With parts of society regarding girls as little more than economic and social burdens, families are going to extreme lengths to avoid having daughters.
>
> (Kelly, 2008)

The primary research covered more than 6000 households across five states in North-Western India. Under 'normal' circumstances, it concludes, there should be about 950 girls for every 1000 boys, but in three of the five states, that number was below 800.

One might suggest that such trends are less likely among more prosperous and better edu-cated Indians, whose children will typically form the workforce for the MNEs. Yet, research shows that ratios of girls to boys were declining fastest in comparatively prosperous urban areas. In one site in the Punjab state there were just 300 girls to every 1000 boys among higher caste families. Avoiding having a daughter is for some women a rational choice—and wealthier families now use ultrasound scans and abort female foetuses, despite the existence of a 1994 law banning gender selection and selective abortion.

We can see that Indian woman from all backgrounds are put under intense pressure to produce sons. We might conclude, therefore, that this level of social conformity to a system and culture—that predominantly views girls as a burden rather than an asset—raises serious questions as to the extent that MNEs can successfully transfer their equality and DM practices to India.

Managing diversity in practice: an MNE in Finland

One would rightly expect there to be fewer issues for MNEs when transferring EM and DM policies and practices to a more westernized context. Yet research into a well-known British MNE by Sippola and Smale (2007), which charts developments over two years, reveals some interesting insights into the dynamics between the company and its subsidiary in Finland. As our next case scenario is an elaboration of their study, the name of this British MNE has been altered (to 'Prolix').

The company operates in more than 100 countries and employs over 100,000 people. One of its subsidiaries, 'Prolix-Finland' (P-Fin), was established in 1911 and employs around 1700 people across 400 service outlets. In the past two years this particular subsidiary was selected, along with several other European operations, to be part of its MNE's first ever DM initiative.

When compared with India, Finland appears to be a country that would be very receptive to EM and DM interventions, since it combines a political ideology with a legislative structure that promotes the equality of its citizens. More specifically, employment laws prohibit direct and indirect discrimination in working life on the grounds of gender, national or ethnic origin, religion, age, health, disability, sexual orientation, and belief or opinion. Moreover, Finland is especially noted for having minimal gender inequalities—and organizations employing over thirty people are legally required to have a gender equality plan.

On the other hand, in spite of legal provisions against ethnic minority discrimination, Finland has been criticized for unfair treatment of its immigrants, with close to a third of this group being unemployed. One explanation for this is that the Finnish population generally lacks multicultural experience. Foreign citizens represent only 2 per cent of a population of five million, and the remaining majority are drawn together by sharing a Finnish ethnicity and language—and their Lutheran religion (Sippola and Smale, 2007: 1904–5).

In addition, Finns find it difficult to come to terms with a person's sexual orientation and exhibit a tendency to discriminate against those who are not heterosexual. Hence, 'whilst gender equality was considered to be a non-issue, the cognitive and normative shifts required to discuss openly the issues of sexual orientation and ethnicity were shown to be a slow and, at times, painful process' (Sippola and Smale, 2007: 1913). The issue of sexual orientation is perhaps related to the typically reserved nature of the Finnish people; while that of ethnicity is likely to result from organizations having a workforce consisting almost entirely of Finns.

 Discussion Activity 10.6

In relation to Case Study 10.4 (Part One) below, critically consider:

a   the positive features of Prolix's centralized interventions and methods designed to bring about DM in P-Fin;

b   the possible challenges from within P-Fin to this approach.

Case Study 10.4 (Part One) Managing diversity: interventions at Prolix-Finland (P-Fin)

At the outset, Prolix adopted a global approach to managing diversity, seeking to stamp its own version on chosen subsidiaries and to deliver a cognitive and behavioural shift in its individual employees and managers. Hence, the company adopted a *top-down* approach, outlining its DM philosophy, policy, and broad plans (of targets and common performance indicators), centrally determined by a corporate-level 'Diversity Council' and 'Diversity Steering Group', leaving little room for local digression.

Prolix also devised a *number of methods* to underline and deliver its prescribed form of DM in P-Fin.

People-based integration is the responsibility of carefully selected local Diversity Co-ordinators. Among other things, they make sure all P-Fin's managers attend a standardized one-day training session on 'Diversity Awareness', which is delivered at Prolix's European headquarters. Some managers are also required to go on a three-day, intensive course.

Information-based methods of integration use the internet for publicizing Prolix's company-wide commitment to DM, as well as the corporate intranet to give access to relevant information, training materials, and self-assessment tools. All of these are written only in English.

Formalization-based methods of integration focus on Prolix's efforts to get P-Fin managers to use, in their staff appraisals, global performance criteria that now comprise 'diversity' and 'inclusiveness'. The idea is that staff should see that decisions about individuals' rewards and bonuses are related to DM. This is emphasized by Prolix's use of staff surveys on 'Diversity and Inclusiveness' and by an annual 'Diversity Assurance Letter' from P-Fin's own CEO, which reveals how far agreed targets have been met.

Prolix's package of global interventions can certainly act to signal the company's intentions and commitment in achieving DM in its Finnish subsidiary. However, it may come as no surprise that such edicts are perceived locally as an external, largely Anglo-Saxon set of imposed interventions. In addition, the local staff are critical of the absence of anything written in the Finnish language. They also highlighted that there was no incentive for employees to refer to the intranet. Consequently, *information-based* integration might be regarded as less effective.

Rather more potent perhaps are *formalization-based* methods of integration, notably in the inclusion of diversity criteria in the appraisal process. Moreover, P-Fin's own training programmes have been adapted to include a diversity perspective. Yet the initial emphasis on *global* standards means that P-Fin's *local* HRM processes still contain no written guidance on diversity.

Another major concern, voiced by P-Fin's CEO, is that the assortment of formalized diversity tools and mechanisms serves to increase the level of bureaucracy. Designed to enable a change in the attitudes and behaviour of staff, these systems were regarded as especially onerous for this relatively small subsidiary.

 Discussion Activity 10.7

In relation to Case Study 10.4 (Part Two) below, why is it that, even with a balance of *globally standardized* and *locally adapted* DM interventions, Finnish managers and employees still show a tendency to discriminate against those minority groups with a different ethnicity or sexual orientation?

Case Study 10.4 (Part Two)   Managing diversity: outcomes at Prolix-Finland (P-Fin)

Prolix's headquarters' management came to appreciate that they faced a constant battle to win the hearts and minds of local management. As a result, they concluded that centralized instructions and interventions would be ultimately unsuccessful and that on balance some element of *local adaptation* should help matters.

In due course the actual targets and means of implementing DM policies at P-Fin have been routinely modified to suit host country priorities. In this way, DM practices have subsequently stemmed from a combination of globally standardized and locally adapted systems.

Yet the most recent evaluation is that P-Fin has demonstrated no more than *ceremonial adoption* of diversity. It has efficiently implemented company policies and practices, but has yet to internalize a belief in the positive value and use of a truly diverse workforce.

First and foremost, whatever approach is adopted people do not always find it easy to change their traditional and deep-rooted attitudes and behaviour, especially if beliefs about certain minority groups are shared and reinforced by members of the majority group to which they belong. In this case, the company's Finnish managers and employees tend to hold negative views towards foreigners and towards those whom they perceive as not heterosexual. So there appears to be no compelling reason why P-Fin's efficient following of headquarters' policies and practices should develop into local employees changing their beliefs simply because they have been invited to contribute to the DM initiatives.

Moreover, an enhanced degree of decentralized decision making can actually offer an opportunity for P-Fin to use its autonomy to its own advantage. In this case, Finnish management and employees can resist those areas for diversity that they had previously not acknowledged: namely discrimination over foreign workers and the need to respect a person's sexual orientation.

Hence, while P-Fin had moved beyond compliance with equality legislation (EM) and was beginning to show signs of valuing differences, it did so to satisfy headquarters. Consequently, in spite of a combination of central and local management inputs, the subsidiary remained 'some way off the desired ingrained behaviours and practical application of diversity and inclusiveness principles' (Sippola and Smale, 2007: 1911).

Managing diversity in practice: American MNEs in Europe

The above analysis points to the likely resistance from foreign subsidiaries to an MNE's DM initiatives. Such a conclusion is shared by Ferner et al. (2006), based upon their study of nine American MNEs operating in one of four host countries: Germany, Spain, Eire, and the UK. They found that global policy tended to focus on gender diversity. Thus, in contrast to Prolix, policies on ethnicity, sexual orientation, and disability, were much less prominent. Moreover, where such policies did exist, MNEs gave their subsidiaries considerable discretion in applying them. Although subsidiaries were required to have a diversity policy, it was left to host country managements to specify their precise content.

Whether in spite of the leeway granted to subsidiaries or because of it, Ferner et al. observed negative, even hostile, reactions of overseas subsidiary management to international diversity policies. They found:

- a strongly held perception that 'diversity' was an American obsession. In Spain and Germany especially, managers did not even accept that diversity was an issue and were hostile to the notion itself (Ferner et al., 2006: 161);

- host country subsidiaries were 'critical of what they saw as the inflexible way in which the diversity agenda was applied', being set requirements that they regarded as irrelevant to the local context (Ferner et al., 2006: 161);

- it was felt that such policies were counterproductive to the business, especially when they were seen to conflict with local legislation.

In short, subsidiary managers often saw the diversity policy of their particular MNE as 'inflexible, too insistently applied, driven by domestic preoccupations and at odds with ... legislative traditions' (Ferner et al., 2006: 162). At the same time, subsidiary managers were perceptive enough to show some degree of engagement with the policy, in order to satisfy headquarters. However, in so doing, 'lip service was paid to the diversity agenda, while shaping it to local needs and priorities' (Ferner et al., 2006: 164).

One tactic employed was that of 'displacement', which often meant accepting a diversity policy in principle, while pointing to practical constraints that prevented implementation. Thus, local managers could indicate a need to comply with local legislation or highlight when diversity would be counterproductive to business goals (Ferner et al., 2006: 163).

An alternative tactic was for subsidiary managements to 'distract headquarters' attention from aspects of diversity policy they were not keen on to those that they felt happy with implementing' (Ferner et al., 2006: 164). For example although German managers were among those hostile to the very idea of diversity, it suited one German subsidiary to stress *nationality* as a key dimension of its diversity strategy. This was because its need for low-skilled and low-cost labour was best served by targeting immigrant labour. Thus, monitoring and reporting on the nationality of its workforce to MNE headquarters emphatically demonstrated compliance with corporate policy (Ferner et al., 2006: 170).

Summary

Early in this chapter we indicated the American origins of schemes for managing diversity. US MNEs, with their international workforces, have led the way for other MNEs seeking to transfer diversity practices to their overseas operations. From this perspective these initiatives might be interpreted as 'largely an expansion of domestic policies driven by specific US concerns' (Ferner et al., 2006: 171). It also helps explain why there has been 'a lack of fit' between certain areas of diversity and host country contexts, 'provoking considerable resistance from subsidiaries' (Ferner et al., 2006: 171).

Such reasoning seems to concentrate on the distinctive characteristics of an MNE, with tensions between its central headquarters and overseas operations. However, this would be to neglect those aspects of managing diversity related to 'human nature'. Thus, even where organizational and societal environments might be regarded as highly supportive of workforce diversity, not everyone in the MNE will be equally disposed towards adopting appropriately tolerant attitudes and behaviour. For EM and DM schemes to be truly successful, therefore, they must break the barriers of human prejudice, which are typically unthinking and anchored in cultural traditions. In short, they must modify people's attitudes and behaviour so that unfair treatment is eradicated, diversity is genuinely valued, and inclusion is consistently practised.

Whereas IHRM literature is conventionally concerned with the challenges of cross-cultural management, as discussed throughout Chapter 4, the diversity perspective suggests that differences (as well as similarities) across the workforce can actually be beneficial to achieving the goals of the organization. This moves us on to *diversity management* (DM), whereby the MNE justifies its deliberate harnessing of workforce differences by reference to the 'business case'. Rather surprisingly, though, DM can be viewed as a close relation of *discriminatory management*—in that both seek to manage staff differences in a way that is seen as best for the business.

However, as suggested above, there will be situations where deliberate discriminatory behaviour against certain categories of worker results from management prejudice. Where such treatment is considered to be unfair and widespread, governments have often sought to protect those who appear disadvantaged. As a result, MNEs have been obliged to comply with each nation's laws, which are designed to curb unjust discrimination. In so doing, MNEs are said to engage in *equality management* (EM) practices. Thus, whereas DM tends to result from a voluntary decision of the MNE to encourage and support an ethos of valuing individuals' difference, EM is typically an MNE's response to state legislation.

While our analysis has enabled us to differentiate between DM and EM, it has also led us to conclude that to be effective DM needs to *build on* EM. This is based on the argument that when DM is designed to *replace* EM, DM's emphasis on respecting each individual's qualities can be at the cost of not securing a presence and fairness for those groups who are disadvantaged.

Finally, it should be evident that our analysis has highlighted the problematic nature of the efforts of MNEs to manage workforce diversity. We should point out, however, that there are supporters of DM who may prefer to focus attention on the benefits of DM to the business. These 'apologists' are to be found predominantly in publications written for a management practitioner audience. Nonetheless, for a reasonably balanced managerial account, the factsheets produced by the CIPD (2011a and 2011b) can be recommended.

Review questions

1. While not all business organizations will have a diverse workforce, multinationals invariably do. Why is this?

2. What are the potential business benefits that have been attributed to those multinational organizations that value and actively encourage workforce diversity?

3. Under what circumstances might a multinational company practise 'discriminatory management' in its treatment of employees in order to promote its business interests?

4. In what sense does a multinational organization's 'equality management' approach emphasize the prevention of unfair discrimination against its employees?

5. What can a multinational organization do to successfully implement a 'diversity management' approach that aims to promote and harness individual differences among employees?

6. Thinking of what we mean by 'discriminatory management', 'equality management', and 'diversity management', respectively, which of these organizational approaches is (a) tolerant; (b) intolerant; and (c) appreciative of workforce diversity?

7. Why might an MNC's efforts to implement EM and/or DM policies and practices in its overseas subsidiary be met by resistance by those affected?

8. In what way is an ethnocentric approach that favours Parent Country Nationals over local employees a form of 'discriminatory management'?

9. In what way is an MNC's use of 'diversity management' strengthened by its employing a geocentric approach to human resource management?

10. To what extent does an MNC's management of its workforce's diversity require a combination of EM and DM approaches in order for it to be effective?

Further reading

Astill, J. (2010) A village in a million, *The Economist*, Xmas Edition, 18 December.
 This perceptive article on life in an Indian village highlights the long-held and deeply embedded inequalities built on the traditions of caste and gender—and the slow, inexorable change occupying the cities of this vast industrializing nation. This depiction of a day in the life of an Indian village gives substance to the significance of a society dominated by inequalities. As such it puts into stark perspective the challenge such a system will have for employers who are intent on promoting equality and DM in their multinational organizations, often populated by villagers who migrate to work in the cities.

Blaine, B. (2007) *Understanding the Psychology of Diversity*, London: Sage.
 Written at an introductory level this text covers those psychological processes that offer an explanation of prejudice against minority groups. It features chapters on concepts such as categorization, stereotyping, sexism, racism, and social stigma. It provides, therefore, insights into the obstacles facing those organizations striving to implement DM.

Foster, C. and Harris L. (2005) Easy to say, difficult to do: diversity management in retail, *Human Resource Management Journal*, 15(3): 4–17.
 This article conveys the inherent difficulties organizations can face in implementing DM policies, even in the UK, where there is a perceived move 'to encouraging and managing diversity in order to gain wider business and societal benefits' (p. 5). The authors' study of a high-street retail company identifies the role of line managers as pivotal in implementing diversity initiatives, but this often means managers doing what is most expedient and giving greater priority to other aspects of their work. Barriers to successful implementation included the managers' views that DM presented conflicts and complexities and the lack of a shared understanding about the precise meaning of the concept.

Mor Barak, M.E. (2011) *Managing Diversity: Towards a Globally Inclusive Workplace*, 2nd edn, Thousand Oaks, CA: Sage.

Based on years of research into workforce diversity from a global perspective this compendious text develops from the author's view that a workforce is likely to be more satisfied, committed, and productive if individuals feel included in their organization's decision making and communication networks. Hence, those employees who feel socially excluded because of a certain characteristic that is perceived as making them different (e.g. ethnicity, gender), are less likely to perform as well. With this in mind, the author examines DM (i.e. where the organization values and utilizes the diversity of its workforce) as a means of reaping the benefits of a globally inclusive workplace, drawing on examples from a number of countries and international organizations.

Noon, M. (2007) The fatal flaws of diversity and the business case for ethnic minorities, *Work Employment Society*, 21(4): 773–81.

This article presents a critical analysis of DM and challenges the popular belief in its business benefits, including reservations held by managers themselves. It contends that the emergence of DM has potentially been at the expense of EM and suggests that such a development is likely to be unhelpful for disadvantaged employees, such as those from ethnic minorities.

Bibliography

Ali, F. (2010) A comparative study of EEO in Pakistan, India and Bangladesh, in M. Özbilgin and J. Syed (eds) *Managing Gender Diversity in Asia: A Research Companion*, Cheltenham: Edward Elgar.

Astill, J. (2010) A village in a million, *The Economist*, Xmas Edition, 18 December.

BBC Four (2010) *Storyville: When China Met Africa*, transmitted 21 June.

Blaine, B. (2007) *Understanding the Psychology of Diversity*, London: Sage.

Chartered Institute of Personnel and Development (CIPD) (2011a) Diversity in the workplace: an overview, CIPD Factsheet, online at http://www.cipd.co.uk/hr-resources/factsheets/diversity-workplace-overview.aspx (accessed 30 March 2012).

— (2011b) Diversity and international management, CIPD Factsheet, online at http://www.cipd.co.uk/hr-resources/factsheets/diversity-international-management.aspx (accessed 30 March 2012).

Ferner, A., Morley, M., Muller-Camen, M, and Susaeta, L. (2006) Workforce diversity policies, in P. Almond and A. Ferner (eds) *American Multinationals in Europe: Managing Employment Relations Across National Borders*, Oxford: Oxford University Press.

Foster, C. and Harris, L. (2005) Easy to say, difficult to do: diversity management in retail, *Human Resource Management Journal*, 15(3): 4–17.

Human Development Report (HDR) (2008) *Fighting Climate Change: Human Solidarity in a Divided World*, New York: UNDP Publications.

The Independent (2010) Indian couple electrocuted for daring to marry outside caste, 16 June, p. 27.

Ituma, A. and Simpson, R. (2009) The 'boundaryless' career and career boundaries: applying an institutionalist perspective to ICT workers in the context of Nigeria, *Human Relations*, 62(5): 727–62.

Jamali, D. and Abdallah, H. (2010) Diversity management rhetoric versus reality: insights from the Lebanese context, in M. Özbilgin and J. Syed (eds) *Managing Gender Diversity in Asia: A Research Companion*, Cheltenham: Edward Elgar.

—, Abdallah, H., and Hmaidan, S. (2010) The challenge of moving beyond rhetoric: paradoxes of diversity management in the Middle East, *Equality, Diversity and Inclusion*, 29(2): 167–85.

Joplin, J.R.W. and Daus, C.S. (1997) Challenges of leading a DIVERSE workforce, *Academy of Management Executive*, 11(3): 32–48.

Kamp, A. and Hagedorn-Rasmussen, P. (2004) Diversity management in a Danish context: towards a multi-cultural or segregated working life, *Economic and Industrial Democracy*, 25(4): 525–54.

Kelly, A. (2008) *Disappearing Daughters*, London: ActionAid UK, online at http://actionaid.org.uk/doc_lib/disappearing_daughters_0608.pdf (accessed 3 April 2012).

Kossek, E.E., Lobel, S.A., and Brown, A.J. (2006) Human resource strategies to manage workforce diversity, in A. M. Konrad, P. Prasad, and J. M. Pringle (eds) *Handbook of Workplace Diversity*, Thousand Oaks, CA: Sage, pp. 54–74.

Mor Barak, M.E. (2011) *Managing Diversity: Towards a Globally Inclusive Workplace*, 2nd edn, Thousand Oaks, CA: Sage.

Noon, M. (2007) The fatal flaws of diversity and the business case for ethnic minorities, *Work Employment Society*, 21(4): 773–81.

Okafor, E. (2007) Sociological implications of communal and ethno-religious clashes, in new democratic Nigeria, *Studies of Tribes and Tribals*, 5(1): 35–46.

Özbilgin, M.F., Mulholland, G., Tatli, A., and Worman, D. (2008) *Managing Diversity and the Business Case*, London: CIPD.

Rowley, C., Yukongdi, V., and Wei, J. (2010) Managing diversity: women managers in Asia, in M. Özbilgin and J. Syed (eds) *Managing Gender Diversity in Asia: A Research Companion*, Cheltenham: Edward Elgar, pp. 183–209.

Shen, J., Chanda, A., D'Netto, B., and Monga, M. (2009) Managing diversity through human resource management: an international perspective and conceptual framework, *International Journal of Human Resource Management*, 20(2): 235–51.

Sinha, S. (2010) Rise in brutality is traditional society's revenge on modern life, *The Independent*, 16 June, p. 27.

Sippola, A. and Smale, A. (2007) The global integration of diversity management: a longitudinal case study, *International Journal of Human Resource Management*, 18(11): 1895–916.

Syed, J. and Özbilgin, M. (2009) A relational framework for international transfer of diversity management practices, *International Journal of Human Resource Management*, 20(12): 2435–53.

—, Burke, R.J., and Acar, F.P. (2010) Re-thinking *tanawwo* [diversity] and *musawat* [equality] in the Middle East, *Equality, Diversity and Inclusion*, 29(2): 144–9.

Tajfel, H. (ed.) (1982) *Social Identity and Intergroup Relations*, Cambridge: Cambridge University Press.

Walsh, D. and Doughty, D. (2009) Human resourcing in international organisations, in J. Leopold and L. Harris (eds) *The Strategic Management of Human Resources*, Harlow: FT Prentice Hall, pp. 289–347.

Wrench, J. (2005) Diversity management can be bad for you, *Race and Class*, 46(3): 73–84.

 Visit the Online Resource Centre for web links, interactive glossary, and more:
http://www.oxfordtextbooks.co.uk/orc/crawley

11

Corporate social responsibility and ethics

⊙ Learning Outcomes

After reading this chapter you will be able to:

- understand the main concepts in CSR and ethical issues for international business
- appreciate the complexities of the meaning of right and wrong in different cultural contexts
- provide examples of CSR challenges and ethical issues faced by international managers
- explain the role of international organizations and NGOs in encouraging CSR in MNEs
- discuss the various ways MNEs can improve their CSR performance
- understand the usefulness of codes of practice and CSR reporting.

Introduction

This chapter will provide an overview of the meaning of **corporate social responsibility** (CSR) and its relationship with the subject of ethics to provide a backdrop for a discussion and examples of dilemmas that multinationals and their expatriates face in managing international business.

The importance of **codes of ethics** and the growing interest in CSR as part of business school education and in organizations arose perhaps first with the Union Carbide disaster in Bhopal, India, in 1984 when a gas leak from a factory producing pesticides resulted in more than 2000 deaths, blindness, and ongoing health problems for 200,000, and devastation for the whole community. With this tragedy, the responsibilities of overseas business were first brought to the public's attention. More recently as a result of the corporate corruption scandals of the 1990s and earlier this century (such as those at Enron and Arthur Anderson, Shell, BAE Systems, and accusations of exploitation of overseas employees by Nike, Gap, and others) even more attention has been given to corporate responsibility in the areas of finance, corruption, the environment, and employment. While multinational organizations benefit from globalization, questions are being asked about the impact they have on the communities in which they operate.

The financial crisis of 2008–9 has also put the spotlight on the irresponsible behaviour of large banking corporations and more recently on their continued payment of high salaries and bonus payments to senior managers, despite the obvious management, financial, or operational failures that occurred while these managers were in charge.

In addition, multinational organizations, while operating globally, are constantly faced by new ethical challenges, different cultural norms, new industries, and more public scrutiny. Actions taken by individuals on behalf of organizations need to be justified. Justifications tend to be made on the basis of ethical theories that prescribe morally correct ways of behaving (Crane and Matten, 2010: 86).

Corporate social responsibility

CSR is a broad term, which suggests that business has a responsibility to the society of which it is a part. This implies that business has a direct responsibility to all its stakeholders. Big business is now also expected to come up with solutions to some of society's social and environmental challenges. The concept of CSR arises from society's values and beliefs. These are based on ethics or the fundamental principles of human conduct. These moral principles are extended and applied to the corporation in business and employment ethics. Business ethics in an academic context is 'the study of business situations, activities and decisions where issues of right and wrong are addressed' (Crane and Matten, 2010: 5). For organizations, business ethics refers to acceptable business behaviour, frequently laid down in guidelines or codes of conduct that are applied to business activities, strategy, operations, and employment relationships.

However, the significance and meaning of CSR differs between developed economies and emerging ones. The strength of government institutions and their ability to enforce laws that control the activities of business and employment may determine how MNCs' subsidiaries approach CSR in developed and emerging economies (Yang and Rivers, 2009).

This chapter focuses on the wider context of business ethics, since expatriate employees of MNEs are likely to come into contact with a wide range of ethical issues in international business, including those related to employment.

While some actions of both people and organizations are governed by law, other actions are the result of free choice. For example people and organizations cannot, by law, embezzle company funds, but at the same time they can decide between various options how best to spend those funds. Some actions, while not governed by law, are constrained by the commonly shared ethical values of a society. For example the distribution of wages between senior executives and other staff will tend to reflect the values of society, so that in the USA the difference in salaries between the bottom and top of the organization may be larger than they are in Europe. This is influenced by the values of European society in which, in general, a more egalitarian approach to reward in business is found.

Ethics as the basis for corporate social responsibility

Differing attitudes to what is morally right or wrong arise from our values and principles. Actions and decisions taken in business today need to be justified to stakeholders and to be seen to be ethical. Ethical principles can be looked at from two extremes: ethical absolutism or ethical relativism.

Ethical absolutism claims that there are external, universally applicable moral principles, so that right and wrong are objective and rationally determined (Crane and Matten, 2010: 86).

Ethical relativism claims that morality depends on the *context* and that it is *subjective*. There is no absolute right and wrong; this depends on the person making the decision and the culture. It is argued that morality is culturally determined (Crane and Matten, 2010: 87). This is an important viewpoint for international business, as is shown in the Siemens Case Study 11.2.

These two extreme points of view may not be very helpful for making business decisions, since there needs to be some consensus by international bodies about the limits of acceptable business behaviour.

Different perspectives on ethics: Anglo-American and European

In addition to the two approaches to morality and ethics mentioned above, perspectives on business ethics in Europe differ from those in Anglo-American societies. Very briefly, the Anglo-American approach takes an individualistic perspective on morality, while the European ethical theories focus on the design of institutions in the economic system as the main influence in developing and applying theory.

Second, the American literature does not question the capitalist system, while the European approach questions the ethical justification of capitalism. Third, there is some difference between northern Europe, Sweden, Germany, and the Netherlands, where there is a higher degree of pluralism of moral conviction and values (including secular and other philosophical approaches), which are strongly debated, compared to the USA, where the focus is the application of morality to business and the domination of Christian-based values is widely accepted (Crane and Matten, 2010: 89). Furthermore, there are many more approaches to morality arising from other religions such as Islam, Buddhism, and Hinduism, as well as the culture of contemporary China. It is these differences in values and perspectives on morality that make it complex to find a universal concept of right and wrong and that bring challenges to managers in MNEs.

However, it is possible to consider the justification for action or decisions and judgements and whether they are right or wrong, by taking either of two approaches: consequentialist or non-consequentialist.

Consequentialist ethics considers the intended outcome of actions, their aims or goals, to determine whether they are morally right or wrong. The two main theories in this category are egoism and utilitarianism.

The **Egoism** theory says that 'an action is morally right if the decision maker freely decides in order to pursue either their (short-term) desires or their (long-term) interests' (Crane and Matten, 2010: 93). In the business context, this theory has been adapted to incorporate the concept of **Enlightened Self-interest**. In this case an action is taken if it will serve one's own interest in the long term. For example organizations might support local transport services by providing them with subsidies. As well as a generous gesture, in the longer term it helps their employees arrive at work on time, thus serving their own interests.

The **Utilitarianism** theory maintains that:

'an action is morally right if it results in the greatest amount of good for the greatest amount of people affected by the action', (Crane and Matten, 2010: 94). This view is commonly accepted in the Anglo-Saxon world, having been made popular originally by philosophers and economists Jeremy Bentham (1748–1832) and John Stuart Mill (1806–73).

Non-consequentialist ethics considers the *underlying principles* and motivation of the decision maker, including the rights and duties of the individual, to determine whether the action is morally right. The theories associated with this approach normally applied to business ethics are 'ethics of duties' and 'ethics of rights and justice'.

Ethics of duties is a viewpoint developed by Kant (1724–1804), who believed that morality and right and wrong were questions of external, abstract, unchanging principles, or moral laws. He thought of people as moral actors capable of making rational decisions regarding right or wrong.

As such decisions should always be based on the categorical imperative, comprising three parts (1) consistency (everyone can follow the same principle); (2) there is human dignity and respect; and (3) it can be followed consistently by everyone (Crane and Matten, 2010: 97–8). *Stakeholder theory* has probably been derived from these ideas and is discussed in more detail later in the chapter.

Ethics of rights and justice

Ethics of rights is based on the ideas of the philosopher John Locke (1632–1714) and the concept of 'natural rights', originally defined as rights to life, freedom, and property. Today, these include rights to freedom of speech, conscience, consent, privacy, and fair legal process. A definition of natural rights claims: 'Natural rights are certain basic, important, inalienable entitlements that should be respected and protected in every single action' (Crane and Matten, 2010: 100).

These rights have been incorporated into the United Nations Universal Declaration of Human Rights (1948) and the Charter of Fundamental Human Rights of the European Union (2000). Today, basic human rights include a right to life, liberty, justice, education, fair trial, fair wages, and freedom of belief, association, and expression. International businesses as corporations are frequently judged in terms of how far their policies and practices respect these rights. As a result, organizations are increasingly incorporating references to these rights into their Codes of Practice, *Mission Statements* and *Corporate Responsibility Reports.*

 Discussion Activity 11.1

Consider how far your country supports human rights. Does it recognize the United Nations Declaration of Human Rights? Is there any situation when a government should curtail individual freedom or freedom of speech or association? Do multinational organizations in your country respect human rights?

Ethics of justice refers to individual rights that exist within a specific social context; they need to be respected equally and fairly. The issue of justice needs consideration. 'Justice can be defined as the simultaneously fair treatment of individuals in a given situation with the result that everyone gets what they deserve' (Crane and Matten, 2010: 104).

Some of the difficulties associated with justice systems and ensuring fair procedures and outcomes are illustrated in the report 'Reality of Rights' from the Corporate Responsibility Coalition (2009), which among other cases, details the problems faced by Bangladeshi garment makers, discussed in Case Study 11.1 below.

Case Study 11.1 Bangladeshi garment makers

The following issues are extracted from the report, 'Reality of rights: barriers to accessing remedies when business operates beyond borders'.

The average wages received by Bangladesh's workforce are currently ranked as the lowest in the world. Half of all Bangladesh's garment exports are destined for the European market, including the UK—major UK retailers such as Asda, Tesco, and Primark buy tens of millions of pounds worth of clothing produced by Bangladeshi workers each year.

UK retailers manage this by means of 'arm's length' off-shore purchasing relationships with local companies and foreign manufacturers in Bangladesh. The power wielded by these large UK buyers over the terms of purchasing contracts is used to impose very demanding requirements for low prices and fast turn-around times on orders, which fuels strong downward pressure on factories within Bangladesh to achieve competitiveness, often at the cost of workers' rights.

UK business practices contribute to sustaining extremely low wages among workers, the majority of whom receive an average monthly wage of less than £25. Workers are typically required to work 10–16 hour days, in violation of both existing Bangladeshi law and International Labour Organization (ILO) conventions. Workplace health and safety is an additional major problem in much of the sector. Over the past decade, at least thirty cases of factory collapses and fires have occurred, leaving hundreds of workers dead, and thousands injured.

The denial to most garment workers of freedom of expression is another major problem in the sector, constituting a direct violation of core civil and political rights. Trades unions are illegal in the export processing zones, while harassment, sexual abuse, and physical violence are used to prevent workers trying to organize.

Although there are some avenues of redress, these are not effective because of an under-resourced judicial system and understaffing of the factory inspectorate. For example in 2006 there were only four safety inspectors and three health inspectors, who were responsible for 11,665 premises.

In addition various agencies in Bangladesh give the export sector priority over protection of workers' rights because of its strategic importance, as well as the direct involvement of a number of politicians who own garment-making factories.

Confronted with systematic violations of their human rights by UK companies and their local business partners, Bangladeshi workers can, in theory, pursue their grievances by means of a range of formal and informal avenues at local and international levels. However, access to appropriate remedies by workers has been limited because of the cost, complexity, length of the process, and lack of judicial resources. Action has to be taken against local factory owners, not end buyers such as Asda, Tesco, or Primark. According to the report 'the capacity constraints and repressive environment confronting the union movement in Bangladesh seriously complicates access barriers for many workers'.

Adapted from: 'Reality of rights: barriers to accessing remedies when business operates beyond borders', May 2009, the Corporate Responsibility Coalition (CORE, 2009) (with kind permission of the Corporate Responsibility Commission)

 Stop and Think

Think of countries such as Bangladesh, where wage levels enable clothes to be produced more cheaply.

1. Would you be willing to pay more for your clothes if you knew they were coming from countries with better employment conditions? If so, how much more?

2. What are the main factors preventing change to the conditions of workers in Bangladesh?

3. Which approaches to ethics are relevant when examining the situation in the Bangladeshi garment workers case?

Case Study 11.1 raises questions regarding where the responsibility for these conditions lies. Some organizations such as War on Want and Labour Behind the Label (LBL) are now acting to fight this type of exploitation by bringing the issue to the attention of consumers at the end of the supply chain. As part of its campaign 'Love Fashion, Hate Sweatshops', War on Want is demanding that the UK government regulate UK retailers' business practices to ensure overseas workers are guaranteed a living wage, decent working conditions, and the right to join a trade union (War on Want, 2011). The organizers believe that change can only be brought about through 'government regulations that protect the rights of workers supplying UK companies' (War on Want, 2011). (The issue of justice in reward is also considered in Chapter 7, 'International reward management', in the section *Organizational justice*, and in Chapter 14, 'The dark side of international employment', in the section *The role and responsibility of multinationals.*)

While the case of the Bangladeshi garment workers was discussed in the context of the ethics of justice, we now consider another form of ethics that may result in behaviour considered unethical by others. The chapter now continues with an explanation and example of an aspect of international business that has brought considerable debate, that of **ethical relativism**.

Ethical relativism

The Siemens scandal was one of the most high-profile cases in recent years of bribery and wrongdoing with international dimensions. The author suggests that 'relative ethics' may have been used by executives to justify their behaviour when they were 'conforming' to locally acceptable behaviours, by using bribes and kickbacks.

Universal ethics versus ethical relativism

On what basis do people make ethical decisions or judgements? People make judgments based on three factors: the action being evaluated, the prevailing norms of acceptability, and the person's value judgements about these (Boddy, 2008: 151). For these reasons different people will come up with different value judgements. However, there is an additional factor, which managers overseas may use to justify actions taken. It is suggested that the basis upon which people make ethical decisions differs depending on their cultures. Thus the term 'ethical relativism' has arisen. This means that ethical judgements cannot be made independently of the culture in which the issue arises. This view has become a convenient way to justify participating in business deals involving bribes, slush funds, and backhanders. This causes difficulties for individual managers who morally cannot support such activities. These situations are becoming more problematic for international managers because of laws in the USA, such as the *Foreign Corrupt Practices Act (1977)*, which, as its name implies, extends responsibility for corruption to outside the USA, and laws in Europe that hold companies responsible for such actions, even though they take place outside their jurisdiction. Legislation such as that of the Council of Europe, Civil Law and Civil Law Convention on Corruption (1999) and the establishment of OLAF (European anti-fraud office), as well as the OECD Convention on Combating Bribery of Foreign Public Officials in International Business Transactions (1999), together facilitate action to combat international corrupt practices (EU Legislation Summaries, 2009).

The combined strength of all this legislation is illustrated in the Siemens case, December 2008, which came about as a result of cooperation between various investigating agencies in the USA, Europe, and countries implicated in the case. This case is a clear example of the lack of CSR shown by a large European company in its business dealings overseas.

 Case Study 11.2 Siemens

In December 2008 Siemens AG pled guilty, in action taken under the US Foreign Corrupt Practices Act, of circumventing and failing to maintain adequate internal controls and failing to comply with the books and records provisions of the Act. Under this law:

> 'it is a federal crime for US citizens and companies traded on US markets to pay bribes in return for business'.

According to Joseph Persichini Jr, Assistant Director in Charge of the FBI's Washington Field Office, Siemens and its three subsidiaries had to pay a substantial fine, of over 450 million US dollars, in combined criminal fines. Siemens, through its subsidiaries, was found guilty of having paid bribes and kickbacks to officials for contracts in Iraq, Argentina, Venezuela, and Bangladesh between 1998 and 2007. In the Department of Justice press release it stated: 'Today's filings make clear that for much of its operations across the globe, bribery was nothing less than standard operating procedure for Siemens.'

'This pattern of bribery by Siemens was unprecedented in scale and geographic reach. The corruption involved more than US$1.4 billion in bribes to government officials in Asia, Africa, Europe, the Middle East, and the Americas', said Linda Chatman Thomsen, Director of the SEC's Division of Enforcement, US Department of Justice (2008a).

In connection with the cases brought by the Department, the SEC, and the Munich Public Prosecutor's Office, Siemens AG will pay a combined total of more than $1.6 billion in fines, penalties, and disgorgement of profits, including $800 million to US authorities, making the combined US penalties the largest monetary sanction ever imposed in an FCPA [Foreign Corrupt Practices Act] case since the act was passed by Congress in 1977.

The Department and the SEC closely collaborated with the Munich Public Prosecutor's Office in bringing these cases. The high level of cooperation, including sharing information and evidence, was made possible by the use of mutual legal assistance provisions of the 1997 Organization for Economic Cooperation and Development Convention on Combating Bribery of Foreign Public Officials in International Business Transactions, which entered into force on 15 February 1999.

(US Department of Justice Report, 2008b; European legislation summaries, 2009a, 2009b)

In the Siemens case, it is clear that many managers who were involved in these practices were influenced by the *prevailing ethical attitude* in the regions in which they operated, while accountants and others behind the scenes helped to make the payments possible. Employees were acting in accordance with prevailing cultural norms and were aware that the business deals they were seeking could probably only be obtained if such payments were made, thus demonstrating the application of *relative ethics*.

However, international law has now demonstrated that this is no longer acceptable. Some might regard such legislation as 'ethical imperialism' as it seeks to impose the standards and laws of the USA or Europe on countries generally outside their jurisdiction.

While fines may be a deterrent to this type of activity and send a clear warning to corporations, the sentencing of senior executives to jail terms sends a message to those who might be tempted to bribe others. Enst Keil von Jagemann and Wolfgang Rudolf admitted to 'being accessories to misappropriation and corruption', thereby assisting in a €1.3 billion worldwide web of bribery. However, they were only sentenced to two years and nine months respectively, in suspended sentences, and fined (DW-World, 2008).

Other sources that provide further information on the Siemens scandal and subsequent trials include the *New York Times* (2008), and the *Washington Post* (2008).

Discussion Activity 11.2

In the Siemens case, the company was made to pay substantial fines for its activities. In addition there were subsequent cases in which executives were sentenced to jail terms.

1. What are the difficulties associated with finding the people ultimately responsible for the illegal activities in large multinational organizations?

2. Do you think fines alone will in future prevent organizations from paying bribes for business?

Siemens and the future

According to Becker (2009: 19) Siemens has subsequently taken some important steps to minimize the effects of the scandal on its reputation. It admitted its wrongdoings, appointed an outsider as CEO, employed a chief compliance officer to oversee the anti-corruption measures and a directorate at managing board level. The company took internal legal action against 500 employees and dismissed 30 per cent of these. Siemens consolidated its anti-corruption regulations and undertook company-wide ethics training, while employing external compliance consultants to take clean-up measures. The company pressed charges and sought damages against eleven top managers, including a former chairman and the former CEO (Becker, 2009: 19). Becker uses the example of Siemens to illustrate how the company is trying to make a new start with moral leadership at its core.

He asserts that moral leadership is embedded in organizations and that corporations are moral persons, and as such, ethical principles help define the corporate mission, determine obligations, and set guidelines for the organization's policies and practices. He concludes that 'leadership is grounded in the personal morality and authenticity and the solid structures of corporate ethics, it can only succeed when leaders walk the talk' (Becker, 2009: 7).

Similarly, Caldwell et al. (2011) propose a theory of ethical stewardship for HR professionals. This is a theory of organizational governance in which:

'leaders seek the best interests of stakeholders by creating high trust cultures that honor a broad range of duties owed by organizations to followers'(Caldwell and Karri, 2005; Pava, 2003, cited in Caldwell et al., 2011: 173). In order to do this, they suggest that HR professionals need to raise the standards of their performance and adopt the qualities of transformative leaders. The article goes on to explain the many facets of transformative leadership but concludes that 'adopting the standards of ethical stewardship and the best practices of leadership may be a daunting challenge for HRPs' (Caldwell et al., 2011: 179).

While calls for such changes in the world of HRM are to be applauded, the reality of international business operations reveals situations that enable organizations to continue to utilize relative ethics as well as other means to operate unethically, as the next section illustrates.

Relative ethics and international transparency

According to Meschi (2009) international organizations face uncertainty where there is bribery and government corruption. 'According to transaction cost theory, government corruption is a critical factor of environmental uncertainty. From the viewpoint of foreign firms, any additional environmental uncertainty in emerging economies contributes to increasing transaction costs' (Meschi, 2009: 245).

In countries with high levels of government corruption it is very difficult for international managers and executives to avoid corruption, since it is often endemic to the whole business system. If managers have a universal perspective, their ethical perspective will not change, regardless of the country they are in. However, if a manager accepts the view that local cultural norms need to be incorporated into decision making, he/she is adopting a *relative* rather than universal view of ethics, adjusting it to suit the local culture Thus managers working overseas may be tempted to make decisions that are acceptable in that country but that would not be acceptable at home or under international law.

Various forms of 'bribery' are endemic in Asia; even for a routine process 'coffee money' may be paid to junior civil servants to facilitate approval of permits or visas. This form of bribery is done with the connivance of local administrators, accountants, or company secretaries (Crawley, author's personal observation). However, when the payments extend to the top echelons of government, questions about transparency and fairness arise in terms of contracts awarded and kickbacks paid. As a result the perception of corruption increases, which is illustrated in Transparency International's Corruption Perception Index. Malaysia is steadily dropping in position and in 2010 it was at number 56 (TI, 2010) and at number 60 in 2011 (TI, 2011).

The Transparency International Corruption Perception Index gives a clear indication of how difficult it is to do business in most countries in Asia without meeting corrupt officials or having to pay bribes. The exception is Singapore, which ranked number 1 in 2010 with a score of 9.3 points. Hong Kong managed to rank 13, while Thailand was behind Malaysia with a ranking of 78; Indonesia was ranked 110. Other Asian countries were even further down. For comparative purposes, the UK ranked number 20 and the USA number 22. You are advised to go to the website for further information on how the results are obtained (TI, 2010). Factors such as these lead to business environments of uncertainty and may be used as indicators of risk when doing overseas business. (See Chapter 2, 'The wider context of IHRM', section *International risk*, for further discussion of this topic.)

 ### Discussion Activity 11.3

1. Find out where your country ranks on the corruption perception index by checking the Transparency International website. Look at the map and results by country. Go to: http://www.transparency.org/policy_research/surveys_indices/cpi/2010/results.

2. What are the reasons for your country's position on the TI Corruption Perception Index?

3. What factors have enabled Singapore and Hong Kong to have relatively high (good) rankings on the index?

Having considered two cases where corporations have not behaved in an ethical manner through involvement in bribery or unjust treatment of employees, we now consider why CSR is important for all stakeholders of the organization.

The business case for CSR and the stakeholder perspective

CSR and ethics are increasingly being discussed in the context of the organization's responsibilities towards all its stakeholders, including those stakeholders in their overseas businesses. Stakeholder theory maintains that businesses need to satisfy all their stakeholders in order to be effective. In fact, Freeman (1984, cited in Blowfield and Murray, 2008: 160) maintained that 'managing stakeholders was essential to the very survival and prosperity of the enterprise'.

Stakeholders include customers, employees, suppliers, contractors and the local community, government, and anyone who comes into contact with the organization or is affected by it in any way.

Four types of social responsibility have been identified: economic, legal, ethical, and discretionary (Carroll, 1979, cited in Blowfield and Murray 2008: 21). These explain the ways that businesses manage their relationship with wider society and imply that organizations have obligations to the society that they serve, even though these may not always be legally defined. While in the past Friedman (1962, cited in Blowfield and Murray, 2008: 23) had contended that companies' only social responsibility was to maximize profit for its shareholders, this view is highly contested today.

Companies today are being held responsible for a wide range of corporate responsibility issues in addition to compliance with the law, including: philanthropy, environmental sustainability, animal and human rights, workers' rights and welfare, market relations, and corporate governance (Blowfield and Murray, 2008: 24, Box 1.3).

Organizations are also subject to the influence of **ethical investors** and pressure groups who may hinder the implementation of management decisions by giving the organization negative publicity, taking direct action such as boycotting goods, threatening or taking legal action, and taking action to prevent planning permissions or licences from being granted (Boddy, 2008: 158). Socially responsible investing is a process in which shareholders consider a company's internal operating behaviour (including employment policies) as well as its external practices before deciding to invest, or even withdraw investments from MNCs, thus attempting to influence their CSR behaviour (Yang and Rivers, 2009: 163). Given all these pressures, it is clear that acting in an ethical manner is in the organization's best interests.

According to Edwards et al. (2007: 2): 'CSR codes appear to be a principal way in which MNCs seek to achieve a degree of consistency across their operations and/or a degree of legitimacy in their external environment.'

Most MNCs in the UK have corporate codes that include CSR and have international scope. About 20 per cent of these have been negotiated with an international trade union or works council. However, MNCs with headquarters in the USA are likely to have a code that has probably not been negotiated with workers (Edwards et al., 2007: 8). Criticism has been levelled at MNCs in the past for the fact that they only have codes of conduct because of pressure from governments and other stakeholders. Murphy (2005: 3–4) explains the purpose as follows:

> [T]hese codes of conduct seek to promote socially-responsible MNC conduct, largely in the developing world, so as to prevent harm or mistreatment of persons or things caused by MNC operations (e.g. the existence of unhealthy working conditions in an MNC factory).

However, this is not the central concern of the MNC. According to Murphy (2005: 8) codes of conduct are often developed under pressure from other members of society. He suggests that they may be more effective if they were introduced in cooperation with governments and other stakeholders, while the companies could be empowered within some 'bounds of justice, fairness and equity'.

The international manager has to ensure that the activities he/she oversees comply with the highest standards of ethical behaviour. However, in order to do this, each manager needs to understand the company's policy on CSR and the extent to which it defines his/her respon- sibilities in relation to overseas laws and more problematically, the overseas customs and culture. Expatriate managers may have a wide range of different responsibilities and have to interact with local government officials, their own employees, local customers, or suppliers. They are constantly confronted with new ways of doing business, affected by local culture, institutions, and practices. These may include invitations to dinner, drinking sessions, Karaoke sessions with 'hostesses' included, lavish gifts at Christmas or Chinese New Year. It is sometimes difficult for new executives or managers to know how and where to draw the line in terms of giving and accepting gifts. Not everything can be defined in codes of conduct and in many instances it is up to the individual executive to make the final decision on ethical behaviour.

Actions to illustrate that they are responsible corporate entities are often taken by organi- zations because to do so is in their own best interests. Their activities are increasingly being scrutinized by organizations such as the Corporate Register (http://www.corporateregister.com/). This scrutiny has led to more organizations ensuring that they adopt policies; improve their level of socially responsible behaviour by leading by example; adopt codes of ethics, create formal ethical structures and reporting mechanisms, including an ethical audit; or work to be included in the FTSE4Good Index. Thus they may make CSR their mission; focus on meeting customer needs; behave responsibly as part of their strategy; or act responsibly to avoid nega- tive publicity (Boddy, 2008). At an international level the expected behaviour of multinationals in this respect is outlined by the 'OECD Guidelines for Multinational Enterprises', which is supported by many governments committed to encouraging enterprises to observe a set of principles and standards for responsible business conduct (OECD, 2011).

The OECD (2011) Guidelines include specific paragraphs related to the management of human capital, including training and development and treatment in accordance with the principles of human rights. OECD also attempts to fight bribery through its anti-bribery con- vention (OECD, 2009). It is also supported today by the International Standards Organisation (ISO) and its ISO 26000 Standard (Frost, 2011). According to the ISO website:

> ISO 26000 was developed to respond to a growing world need for clear and harmonized best practice on how to ensure social equity, healthy ecosystems and good organizational govern- ance, with the ultimate objective of contributing to sustainable development ... ISO 26000 gives guidance on SR. It integrates international expertise on social responsibility—what it means, what issues an organization needs to address in order to operate in a socially responsible manner, and what is best practice in implementing SR.

(Frost, 2011)

CSR and HRM

Who should take responsibility for CSR? Some suggest that CSR is the responsibility of the HR department because it is linked to employment conditions, wages and salaries, fairness in process and practice of appraisal, employee development, redundancy issues, employee relations, diversity issues, and work-life balance concerns. Caldwell et al. (2011) suggest it should be HR professionals, in line with the concept of the Society for Human Resource Management (SHRM), in a role of ethical stewards.

According to the Chartered Institute of Personnel and Development (CIPD), UK, HR has significant responsibility for both policy and practice of CSR in organizations and to some extent the CIPD appears to see itself as a champion of CSR, or at least as adopting CSR as its own domain of interest. It offers information and training on CSR to its members, making the assumption that this is its role, as it states in its CIPD Corporate Responsibility Fact Sheet (CIPD, 2011):

The role of HR in CR may take a number of specific forms including (in summary):

- helping ensure that, as a minimum, statutory obligations are met—taking responsibility for the key systems and processes ... such as the employer brand, recruitment, appraisal, retention, motivation, reward, internal communications, diversity, coaching, and training;

- training and educating employees on their social and environmental responsibilities;

- integrating these values into the culture of an organization;

- influencing attitudes and behaviour change with line managers and the top team;

- using the positive aspects of CR in respect of the employer brand in recruiting, motivating, and retaining highly skilled people.

The CIPD viewpoint is that

> CR offers HR professionals many opportunities to make a strategic contribution to their business. This may involve reviewing existing policies and practices on issues such as internal communications, remuneration practices, recruitment, induction, health and safety, diversity, or training. CR can become an instrument of change in an organization's behaviours, attitudes, and performance and this is where the HR function can make its greatest contribution to the success of CR initiatives.
>
> (CIPD, 2011)

While it seems clear that HRM needs to accept that CSR is a concept that should be incorporated into its policies and activities, the way to achieve this is quite complex, given the role of HR professionals and the context of their work. HR professionals work as agents of management, with conflicting stakeholder interests to appease, informed by a utilitarian environment of the capitalist economic system, within a liberal democracy that champions the rights of individual freedom over and above the responsibilities for society as a whole, with few moral, religious, or corporate guidelines to turn to. Peter Ackers summarizes the dilemma facing would-be supporters of 'employment ethics' when he urges us to recognize:

> the crucial distinction ... is between employment ethics as a public relations facade and rationalisation for what business already does out of short term economic interest; and employment ethics as an active commitment to employees above and beyond this. For managers can and should play a crucial role in the construction of socially responsible business organisations at the heart of a decent society. This would require a pluralist institutional framework which placed the long term employment and wages and conditions of employees alongside other stakeholders at the heart of the business organisation. In these circumstances we could speak meaningfully of social partnership, loyalty and commitment. Within a framework of relationship capitalism, managers could regain their professional autonomy and integrity, as public servants with a stakeholder ethos, rather than handmaidens of private capital ... Although the rhetoric of HRM contains elements that appeal to ethical principles, it fails to meet its promises.
>
> (Ackers, 2006: 442)

Another point of view, this time concerning the practicalities of HR's role in promoting an ethical organization, comes from Australia. Segon (2010: 22) suggests that HR professionals are not qualified for the task of overseeing the ethics function in organizations. In the Australian context, he suggests that, based on research into the postgraduate training of HR professionals in Australia, they do not have the expert knowledge or capabilities to carry out the functions of ethics officers.

Lam and Khare (2010: 4), however, suggest that HR is 'suitable to lead and/or play a coordinating role in various aspects of CSR'. Lieber (2010: 105) too supports this view, suggesting a wide-ranging role for HR professionals, including actively participating in creating and implementing a code of conduct, communicating the organization's ethical values, and rewarding ethical behaviour. But more significantly, Lieber suggests that HR should be responsible for training employees at all levels in the organization, on the code of ethics as well as other ethics-related policies and subjects. The training should be adjusted to suit the level of employee; and where the company has overseas offices, the training should be translated as required. While no mention is made of the training of HR professionals themselves, the article does suggest the use of 'due diligence in contracting with outside training vendors'. (Interestingly, the author of this article is a lawyer and compliance training solutions provider.)

Lam and Khare (2010) suggest a specific process for adopting CSR, with HR taking the lead, justified because they are responsible for leadership and employee influence, organizational culture, and behaviour. In addition, they argue that major aspects of CSR already fall within the HR remit, including the effective use of human capital and its development, which contribute to sustainable development, equity, and distributive justice. They also believe that CSR should 'begin at home' and employees are the key to contacts with other stakeholders. As CSR requires a major philosophical and behavioural change, HR should act as the key change agent and utilize its role in 'work design, training, performance and rewards management ... as ways "to facilitate the change"' (Lam and Khare, 2010: 5).

The paper goes on to provide some practical suggestions to support these ideas. It also asserts that HR's involvement in CSR will assist HR 'to raise its strategic profile and have a deeper, broader, positive influence on employees and humanity overall' (Lam and Khare, 2010: 13)

Line managers also, regardless of whether they have had training in ethics and codes of practice or not, need help to make ethical decisions. An approach is presented by Hosmer (2008, cited in Katiyar et al., 2010: 2) in a framework of ethical management that provides guidelines to managers to make morally responsible decisions. Katiyar et al. (2010: 3) suggest that Hosmer's framework is applicable to a wide range of business decisions, including those made in IHRM. They link the ideas with those of Pfeffer (1998) on the seven factors necessary to produce high-commitment and high-trust management systems. The article shows, with specific corporate examples, the links between decisions on IHRM policies, the morality of these decisions, and Pfeffer's factors. They 'identify how international HRM issues are heavily impacted by ethical implications and suggest five propositions (associated with Pfeffer's factors) to assist HR Managers to be more effective' (Katiyar et al., 2010: 4–5). In conclusion, the article re-asserts the value of combining a high-trust work culture with moral management decision making (Katiyar et al., 2010: 9).

CSR in MNC subsidiaries

While the HR department may wish to claim responsibility for CSR, in international business the MNC subsidiary operates at some distance from the parent company headquarters and HR department. There are numerous social and organizational factors that may impact on CSR decisions by managers when overseas (Yang and Rivers, 2009: 155). The impact of stakeholders and institutions in the CSR decisions of MNC subsidiaries is evaluated in detail by Yang and Rivers (2009: 155–63), who provide a model to depict the range of factors that influence these decisions. This includes consideration of the degree of strength of formal institutions in the host countries, especially in emerging economies, where these are often weak. They highlight the challenges faced by MNCs from developed countries in aligning their CSR approach with local practices in emerging markets such as China, where CSR is just beginning. They recognize the 'institutional duality' of MNC subsidiaries, which have to conform to host country pressures by adopting local practices and parent company pressure in their practices and strategy. Yang and Rivers note the significance of weak institutions (in emerging economies) for CSR practices of MNCs' subsidiaries and argue that: 'subsidiaries, which operate under a legislative regime that has few laws or where laws are not enforced, such as those in emerging economies, will be less inclined to adapt to local CSR practices' (Yang and Rivers, 2009: 159).

In other words, they may not even conform to basic employment laws, or health and safety legislation.

This is borne out by research conducted in Africa, in the extractive industries, which illustrates the failure of MNEs in Nigeria, South Africa, and Zambia to manage ethically, citing tensions over pay, employment of expatriates in place of locals, negotiation rights, and employee wellbeing (Eweje, 2009: 207). The behaviour of Chinese investors in Africa is also widely criticized in this regard, in a paper by Jawahir Adam, and detailed research in a book by the African Labour Network, on Chinese investments in Africa from a labour perspective (Adam, 2010; Yaw Baah and Jauch, 2009).

Yang and Rivers (2009: 157) consider the relative strength of stakeholder groups such as NGOs, consumers, and employees in developed countries compared with that in emerging economies, with examples of the power of pressure groups to influence corporate behaviour in developed countries. For example consumer behaviour, in boycotting the purchase of Shell petrol in Europe in the 1990s, resulted in the company agreeing not to sink the Brent Spar oil platform (Yang and Rivers, 2009: 159).

Employee power is greater too in developed countries, especially in times when the labour market is tight, but employees can also influence organizations to utilize more progressive 'labour relations policies, safety standards, and job security' (McWilliams and Siegel, 2001, cited in Yang and Rivers, 2009: 156). However, in emerging economies employees are often 'deemed to be expendable' and have little power over the behaviour of their employers. MNCs' subsidiaries recruitment policies respond to the context and take the power of prospective and current employees into account (Yang and Rivers, 2009: 162). Shareholders, particularly shareholders with a CSR interest such as groups of 'socially responsible investors', are having increasing influence on the CSR policies of MNCs in developed countries as well as their activities overseas (Yang and Rivers, 2009: 163).

Finally, the authors suggest that the degree of dependence of the subsidiary on the parent company for vital resources will affect the degree to which they adapt to local practices. More reliance by the subsidiary on the parent will result in less local adaptation (Yang and Rivers, 2009: 161). While this article considered some very important influences on the actions taken in subsidiary companies, the international expatriate manager is often responsible for taking policy decisions on the ground, in the host country, and dealing with the consequences. Some of the practical challenges are now discussed.

International employment and CSR

Expatriates who are sent overseas are confronted with different and difficult cultural, social, and environmental contexts and need a foundation or at least support from their head office on how to behave, basically in the form of a code of practice. They also need:

- legal experts to refer to for difficult situations with regard to fairness of employment practices, such as long hours, discrimination against women, or other diversity issues;
- guidance on issues of employment opportunities or conditions when they are contrary to human rights;
- support when factory operating conditions may cause pollution or include less than safe working conditions;
- an opportunity to speak up when they are surrounded by employees earning less than a living wage;
- the support of the head office HR department when facing these challenges.

However, at the same time, the ethical dilemma facing HR professionals is discussed in a thought-provoking article by Wright and Snell (2005: 181):

> The HR profession has reached a critical juncture in its history. We are being asked to be business partners, and business-driven, yet we frequently face situations where our historic values conflict with short-term decisions made in the business.
>
> We seek to be business partners, but if we take the shortcut by sacrificing our values and integrity for a 'seat at the table' we may actually end up playing a significant role in the demise of our organizations. Instead, HR Leaders require the vision and courage to integrate the different value systems in an organization for its long-term viability.
>
> (Wright and Snell, 2005: 181)

Thus both the HR profession and the expatriate may be facing a similar dilemma. They may be aware of their roles as business partners focused on the bottom line but may question this in the face of the reality of overseas business operations. These often exist purely to exploit the benefits of cheap labour abroad, sometimes at the expense of jobs at home. Alternatively they may have to supervise work in poor working conditions, with fewer safety requirements. This raises a further question regarding the role of expatriates in terms of the support they receive from their own headquarters, and the CSR of organizations to their own expatriate employees, illustrated in Case Study 11.3.

Case Study 11.3   Expatriates and localization policies

An interesting scenario facing international managers is their responsibility for training and developing local employees so that they can play a greater role in the business. The process of localization sometimes faces obstacles because of the attitudes of expatriates to the process and their lack of willingness to 'work themselves out of a job', because of difficulties in finding another job (Selmer, 2004: 1097). Selmer's research investigates a variety of reasons why expatriates may not support or put into practice the localization process in China, citing their own inability to perform this role, or the fact that this task is not included in their goals and objectives. In some cases, such as joint ventures, the expatriates disagreed with the need for localization, indicating that expatriates were required to protect the interests of the expatriate joint venture partner (Selmer, 2004: 1102). Others felt that, as senior managers, the process of localization was not part of their job specification and that they did not have the time or skills to take on this additional role, which would not be assessed in their performance review (1099). Other expatriates were unsure of other how their careers might progress in the organization if they trained local people to take on their roles. They therefore made excuses about the local readiness or need for localization in order to protect their own positions (1097). All of these issues could be regarded as a failure by international organizations to fully understand the needs of their own expatriates. At the same time, the IHRD should be responsible for developing adequate policies and allocating appropriate people to take on the task of training local Chinese employees (1104). By failing to do this they were preventing local employees from having the opportunities they felt they deserved.

The findings indicate that despite the reluctance of some expatriate managers to train locals, the process of localization was not impeded, partly because some foreign firms had introduced localization as a business policy (Wong and Law, 1999; Worm et al., 2001, cited in Selmer, 2004: 1102).However, the findings also indicate that 'there may be good reasons for expatriate managers to be hesitant' about localization in China, and 'there may be an optimal level of localization because expatriates play roles crucial for the performance of foreign operations' (Selmer, 2004: 1102–3).

Adapted from: Selmer (2004)

 Discussion Activity 11.4

1. Why do you think expatriates might want to stay in their overseas posts?

2. Why is localization important for the local employees?

3. Why are organizations and some expatriates sometimes hesitant about promoting localization plans?

HR departments' responsibilities to expatriates

On the other hand IHRDs have also been accused of failing in their duty or CSR to their own expatriates by not providing adequate support for them to carry out their duties in difficult environments such as China. Seak and Enderwick (2008: 1311) have conducted research into how New Zealand expatriates in China were managed by their home employers. Their research concludes that:

> In expatriate selection, this study has identified the importance of cross-cultural competencies, cross-functional abilities, cross-cultural communication and training skills in managing successfully in China. It is recommended that the selection of candidates focus[es] on a potential expatriate's possession of these critical skills and abilities.

Further, responses to the research of New Zealand expatriates in China found that

> training, support, care, and provision for expatriates and their families' needed to be improved. Pre-departure training and incumbent support offered are seen as inadequate. The personal needs of expatriates are not well supported by the parent organization, with much of the limited support provided targeting relevant business functions in China. Despite its obvious importance, parent organizations do not appear to place much value on the de-brief process and continuous communication with their expatriate managers.
>
> (Seak and Enderwick, 2008: 1311)

The findings in this research are not unusual. Expatriates generally receive little useful pre-departure training. Support for themselves, their wives and families once overseas is also often very poor, except perhaps in the largest organizations. (This topic is discussed further in Chapter 9, 'Training, development, and knowledge management', in the section *Cross-cultural training.*)

Support for integrating CSR into corporate policy

As a result of the negative publicity associated with international business and CSR, multinational organizations are gradually beginning to respond and incorporate CSR into their mission statements and codes of practice. They are increasingly adding a corporate responsibility report or audit to their annual financial report. Organizations such as the Corporate Register UK and CSR Europe work to increase CSR awareness and to encourage organizations to incorporate CSR into their policies. CSR Europe has produced a guide for organizations on how to implement CSR through collaboration with stakeholders: *Proactive Stakeholder Engagement; Practical Guide for Companies and Stakeholders* (CSR Europe, 2012).

Similarly, the Corporate Responsibility Coalition is a voluntary organization that works towards better governance of organizations in terms of rights of workers, duties to communities and the environment through their operations (CORE, 2009). Another organization, Corporate Register, carefully monitors the corporate responsibility reports of large organizations to evaluate how far they are meaningful and truly address CSR issues (Corporate Register, 2012). The organization publishes reports and provides 'expert reviews' of these on its website. These evaluate the content and recommend improvements in terms of depth of issues covered, topics not covered, and detail missing. The reviews provide an interesting insight into how organizations often avoid complete reporting on controversial issues. As a result of the activities of such organizations, multinationals are being urged to take a more responsible attitude in their operations.

The United Nations Global Compact also tries to assist multinationals in ensuring that their business is conducted in ways that benefit economies and societies everywhere. It is a 'strategic policy initiative for businesses that are committed to aligning their operations and strategies with ten universally accepted principles in the areas of human rights, labour, environment and anti-corruption' (UN Global Compact, 2012).

The Global Compact is endorsed by chief executives, has 8700 corporate participants from over 130 countries, and is the largest voluntary corporate responsibility initiative in the world. The ten principles, their justification, and examples of how they can be applied to business can be found on their website.

Despite attempts by the United Nations and all the other organizations mentioned above to promote the adoption by businesses of the principles of CSR, including anti-corruption measures, research indicates that some multinationals still regard government corruption in emerging economies as an opportunity (Meschi, 2009). A summary of some of the ideas in this research is provided in Case Study 11.4.

Case Study 11.4 Taking advantage of corrupt governments

This research considered 171 European firms operating in emerging Asian economies, mainly in China, India, Malaysia, and Indonesia, and the changes in their international joint venture (IJV) equity stakes from 1996 until 2007. It looked at how government corruption affected these investments and showed contrasting responses to increased corruption. Some firms find this threatening and divest or limit their presence in the country. Others, however, view government corruption as an opportunity that allows them to overcome the 'liability of foreignness' and to influence government decisions to their advantage, through their involvement with joint venture partners (Meschi, 2009: 242).

International corporations are able to operate in these scenarios by setting up IJVs. It is the local partner, with its knowledge of political stakeholders and government officials plus its social networks and connections with the government, that provides protection to the foreign partner. The article suggests that 'foreign firms trade ownership, control and profit of IJVs in emerging economies for information, protection and external legitimacy' (Meschi, 2009: 245).

While foreign firms may encourage local partners in the corruption process, when corruption becomes public they may claim they knew nothing about it and thus protect their corporate image and reputation. Thus foreign companies become more dependent on the IJV partner as an asset while corruption increases. They are willing to keep the IJV stable or turn it into a wholly owned subsidiary, to protect themselves or escape from environmental uncertainty (Meschi, 2009: 246).

This finding was linked to the extent of government corruption as measured by organizations such as the Economist Intelligence Unit, Transparency International, and other Political Risk Service scores. Other factors, including country experience and experiential learning of foreign partners, affect such decisions.

The decision to exit or to acquire the IJV has different antecedents and is affected differently by government corruption (Meschi, 2009: 254).

As a foreign firm becomes more knowledgeable and experienced in a country, it may become less dependent on the local IJV partner (Meschi 2009: 258–9).

The paper concluded that government corruption in emerging Asian economies was linked to the likelihood that foreign partners will terminate the IJV; however, results differ depending on the corruption measure used. Second, this is affected by the foreign partners' country experience, which in turn moderates the relationship between government corruption and changes in the equity stake in the IJVs (Meschi, 2009: 241). Thus the value and use of IJV partners working in collaboration with corrupt governments to shield foreign partners from risk was valid.

This research provides an interesting insight into the activities of international companies and their relationships in IJVs. It indicates that, when overseas, there will always be ways to hide non-ethical activities, which are contrary to CSR.

Adapted from: Meschi (2009)

Note: This case provides only partial coverage of information from the original research article.

Discussion Activity 11.5

1. What insights about corporate responsibility and behaviour can you derive from this case?
2. If you were working in a multinational organization, would you be willing to work in a country with high levels of government corruption?

See throughout Chapter 5, 'Understanding IHRM: the institutional approach', for more details of how institutional factors impact on IHRM.

The positive side of CSR

To add a more positive note to this chapter, multinational organizations are gradually responding to their CSR. There is evidence of this in their mission statements, codes of practice, and annual reports.

For example the coffee industry has come under fire for sourcing coffee at prices that are unsustainable for the growers and industry as a whole. As a result, organizations such as Fair Trade have made efforts to ensure growers receive a fair price and that multinationals do not price themselves so low that supplies will be threatened as growers turn to other crops (Fair Trade, 2012). For example Starbucks, as part of its 'shared planet' campaign states: 'We're committed to buying and serving the highest-quality, responsibly grown, ethically traded coffee to help create a better future for farmers and a more stable climate for our planet' (Starbucks, Malaysia, 2009).

The company says that by 2015, 100 per cent of the coffee it buys will be responsibly grown and ethically traded. In 2008 Starbucks bought 77 per cent of its coffee this way, to almost the value of £300 million (Starbucks, Malaysia, 2009). In addition, its CSR report for 2007 acknowledges previous adverse publicity and perhaps less than ethical behaviour when it states:

> The foundation of everything we do at Starbucks is our Mission Statement and Guiding Principles. Although we haven't always been perfect, we have always been dedicated to being the kind of company that is trustworthy and authentic. Being transparent and openly sharing our successes and challenges through our Corporate Social Responsibility Annual Report is an important part of our strategy. Another component is our support of the 10 universal principles of the United Nations Global Compact.
>
> Howard Schultz, Chairman, President and Chief Executive Officer, Starbucks (2009)

While recent corporate efforts to embrace CSR remain under scrutiny, at least there seems to be a willingness to consider more than the bottom line. However, we can never be sure how far such website statements are part of the companies' public relations campaigns. The results and effectiveness of these policies and mission statements is a story yet to be told.

This chapter has discussed a variety of international management CSR challenges, from bribery to exploitation, the responsibilities of the head office HR department in supporting expatriates to the role of IJVs in collaboration with corrupt governments. It now concludes with an example of the type of dilemma an MNE can face.

Dilemmas facing MNEs operating in different countries

While the United Nations Commission on Human Rights has adopted a comprehensive list of 'Norms on the responsibilities of transnational corporations and other business enterprises with regard to human rights' (UNHCR, 2003), the reality facing MNEs on the ground is that their codes of practice may be at odds with local tradition, laws, or practices.

While MNEs may try to utilize standard codes of practice in their activities overseas, the culture and institutions of each country may also dictate a variety of ways of operating. Local employment practices are dictated by local laws and cultural traditions and it is these that often predominate. Imposing or even suggesting alternative 'fairer' ways of operating may be regarded as **cultural imperialism**. Thus good intentions can be misconstrued, and the transfer of HR practices is often a slow process of adaptation rather than complete adoption (Faulkner et al., 2002; Zhu et al., 2007).

Finally, further issues related to CSR and many aspects of international business, are included throughout Chapter 14, 'The dark side of international employment'.

Summary

The chapter began with an introduction to the meaning of CSR and discusses various aspects of ethics as the basis for CSR today. It has shown the links between CSR and business ethics. It has illustrated the different approaches taken to discern right from wrong and the problems associated with coming to a common understanding of ethical behaviour in different cultures.

The chapter illustrates the lack of ethical business practices in the first case study, on Bangladeshi garment workers. It then considers the difference between the concepts of universal ethics and ethical relativism. The consequences of adopting the relativist approach are shown in the second case study example of legal action taken against Siemens.

The business case for CSR and the stakeholder perspective are considered next, as well as the role of HRM in managing CSR. The influences that impact on MNCs and their approaches to CSR are discussed, as well as the relevance of CSR to the management of expatriates.

The case studies have illustrated situations where large corporations have not behaved ethically; how they have been able to hide behind the excuse of ethical relativism; or have passed the responsibility for unfair treatment of employees to local employers, and have used IJV partners to avoid responsibility for corrupt practices. However, the case studies have also shown how the world is beginning to examine corporate behaviour more effectively and that there are organizations working to help businesses to move towards practices that are in line with CSR. While there is still a long way to go to ensure that large corporations are working justly with others across the globe, fortunately there is growing awareness of CSR within and outside the firm; and pressure is constantly being put on multinational organizations, by both stakeholders and independent organizations, to practice socially responsible behaviour and to report on and justify all their activities.

Review questions

1. In the case of the Bangladeshi garment workers, which stakeholders benefit most from this injustice? Who should be held responsible? What can be done to improve the situation?

2. Do you think expatriates have any power to influence the activities of their IJV partners? How can they do so?

3. Can or should expatriates be held responsible for the activities of their IJV partners?

4. According to Peter Ackers, HRM professionals face a dilemma when being asked to focus on the bottom line, which may imply sacrificing their values. In your opinion, how far can HR be a champion of employees while at the same time maintaining its focus on the 'bottom line'?

5. Why does the dilemma in question 4 become even more complex and ethically challenging when managing employees in an international environment?

6. What factors need to be considered by HRDs for the management and training of expatriates in organizations that are trying to localize their operations?

7. What reasons might senior expatriate managers give for their reluctance to train local employees to take over their positions, especially in JV organizations?

8. What factors, do you think, prevent head office HRDs from providing adequate support for expatriates and their families?

9. Explain the difference between consequentialist and non-consequentialist ethics. Explain, with examples, which approach is most commonly used when CSR issues are discussed. Which approach do you favour and why?

10. To what extent do you think organizations such as the United Nations Global Compact, CORE, Corporate Register, etc. contribute to improving the behaviour of MNCs in terms of CSR in their overseas operations?

Further reading

Ackers, P. (2006) Contemporary HRM, ch. 17, in T. Redman and A. Wilkinson (eds) *Employment Ethics*, London: Pearson Education.

This is an excellent chapter outlining the meaning and significance of employment ethics, and it provides a critical review of the role of HRM in ensuring a more ethical work environment.

Bhagwati, J. (2005) *In Defense of Globalization*, Oxford: Oxford University Press.

This book evaluates globalization and provides a readable counter-argument to the anti-globalization writers. It argues that globalization is part of the solution to these problems, not part of the problem.

Blowfield, M. and Murray, A. (2008) *Corporate Responsibility, A Critical Introduction*, Oxford: Oxford University Press.

This is a detailed critical text, which provides an up-to-date overview of the meaning of corporate responsibility, how to manage and implement it. It also evaluates the impact and future of corporate responsibility in the context of globalization.

Crane, A. and Matten, D. (2010) *Business Ethics*, 3rd edn, Oxford: Oxford University Press.
This book introduces business ethics concepts, tools, and theories and applies them to stakeholders. It looks at what is morally right and wrong in business decisions. It considers corporate citizenship, globalization, and sustainability. The text includes numerous case examples.

Kline, J.M. (2010) *Ethics for International Business: Decision Making in a Global Political Economy*, Hoboken, NJ: Taylor & Francis.
This book considers the difficulties associated with making judgements when faced with ethical dilemmas in international business situations. It includes a wide range of real-world examples.

Bibliography

Ackers, P. (2006) Employment ethics, in T. Redman and A. Wilkinson (eds) *Contemporary Human Resource Management*, Harlow: Prentice Hall, Pearson Education, pp. 427–49.

Adam, J. (2010) China and Africa: the role of CSR in this partnership, MHC International Ltd, Monthly Feature, Development & CSR, October (No. 76), online at http://www.mhcinternational.com/images/stories/CSR%20Africa%20and%20China.pdf (accessed 8 July 2012).

Becker, G.K. (2009) Moral leadership in business, *Journal of International Business Ethics*, 2(1): 7–21.

Bhagwati, J. (2005) *In Defense of Globalization*, Oxford: Oxford University Press.

Blowfield, M. and Murray, A. (2008) *Corporate Responsibility: A Critical Introduction*, Oxford: Oxford University Press.

Boddy, D. (2008) *Management, An Introduction*, 4th edn, Harlow: Prentice Hall, Pearson Education.

Caldwell, C. and Karri, R.J. (2005) Organizational governance and ethical systems: a covenantal approach to building trust, *Journal of Business Ethics*, 58(1): 249–59.

—, Truong, D.X., Linh, P.H., and Tuan, A. (2011) Strategic human resource management as ethical stewardship, *Journal of Business Ethics*, 98: 171–82.

Carroll, A.B. (1979) A three-dimensional conceptual model of corporate performance, *Academy of Management Journal*, 4(4): 589–99.

— (1989) *Business and Society: Ethics and Stakeholder Management*, Cincinnati, OH: South Western College Publishing.

Charter of the Fundamental Rights of the European Union (2000) *Official Journal of the European Communities*, online at http://www.europarl.europa.eu/charter/pdf/text_en.pdf (accessed 7 July 2012).

Chartered Institute of Personnel and Development (CIPD) (2011) Corporate responsibility factsheet, online at http://www.cipd.co.uk/hr-resources/factsheets/corporate-responsibility.aspx#link_cipd_view (accessed 8 July 2012).

CORE (2009) Reality of rights: barriers to accessing remedies when business operates beyond borders, the Corporate Responsibility Coalition and the London School of Economics, online at http://corporate-responsibility.org/reality-of-rights/ (accessed 8 July 2012).

Crane, A. and Matten, D. (2010) *Business Ethics*, 3rd edn, Oxford: Oxford University Press.

CSR Europe (2012) *Proactive Stakeholder Engagement: A Practical Guide for Companies and Stakeholders*, online at http://www.csreurope.org (accessed 8 July 2012).

DW-World (2008) Former Siemens board member sentenced for bribery, *Deutsche Welle World website*, online at http://www.dw.de/former-siemens-board-member-sentenced-for-bribery-/a-3817708 (accessed 26 December 2012).

Edwards, T., Marginson, P., Edwards, P., Ferner, A., and Tregaskis, O. (2007) Corporate social responsibility in multinational companies: management initiatives or negotiated agreements? International Labour Organization (International Institute for Labour Studies), online at http://www.ilo.org/public/english/bureau/inst/publications/discussion/dp18507.pdf (accessed 8 July 2012).

EU Legislation Summaries (2009a) Fight against fraud, online at http://europa.eu/legislation_summaries/fight_against_fraud/index_en.htm (accessed 7 July 2012).

— (2009b) A comprehensive EU anti-corruption policy, online at http://europa.eu/legislation_summaries/fight_against_fraud/fight_against_corruption/l33301_en.htm (accessed 7 July 2012).

Eweje, G. (2009) Labour relations and ethical dilemmas of extractive mines in Nigeria, South Africa and Zambia: 1950–2000, *Journal of Business Ethics*, 86 (Supp. 2): 207–23.

Faulkner, D., Pitkethly, R., and Child, J. (2002), International mergers and acquisitions in the UK 1985–94: a comparison of national HRM practices, *International Journal of Human Resource Management*, 13(1): 106–22.

Freeman, R.E. (1984) *Strategic Management; A Stakeholder Approach*, Boston, MA: Pitman.

Friedman, M. (1962) *Capitalism and Freedom*, Chicago IL: University of Chicago Press.

Frost, R. (2011) ISO 26000 Social responsibility— the essentials, International Organization for Standardization, News, 9 March, online at http://www.iso.org/iso/home/news_index/news_archive/news.htm?refid=Ref1558 (accessed 8 July 2012).

Hosmer, L.T. (2008) *The Ethics of Management*, 6th edn, New York: McGraw-Hill.

Katiyar, A., Thomas, K., and Caldwell, C. (2010) Ethical issues in international human resource management: challenges in implementing high performance systems, 1–15 (authors from McNeese State University, Lake Charles, Louisiana, USA).

Kline, J. M. (2010) *Ethics for International Business: Decision Making in a Global Political Economy*, Hoboken, NJ: Taylor & Francis.

Lam, H. and Khare, A. (2010) HR's crucial role for successful CSR, *Journal of International Business Ethics*, 3(2): 3–15.

Lieber, L.D. (2010) HR's role in creating and maintaining a code of conduct to promote an ethical organizational culture, *Employment Relations Today*, Spring: 99–106.

McWilliams, A. and Siegel, D. (2001) Corporate social responsibility: a theory of the firm perspective, *Academy of Management Review*, 26(1): 117–18.

Meschi, P.-X. (2009) Government corruption and foreign stakes in international joint ventures in emerging economies, *Asia Pacific Journal of Management*, 26: 241–61.

Murphy, S.D. (2005) Taking multinational corporate codes of conduct to the next level, *Columbia Journal of Transnational Law*, 43 (2), online at http://papers.ssrn.com/sol3/papers.cfm?abstract_id=627608 (accessed 8 July 2012).

New York Times (2008) At Siemens, bribery was just a line item, *New York Times*, 20 December, online at http://www.nytimes.com/2008/12/21/business/worldbusiness/21siemens.html?_r=3&pagewanted=3&th&emc=th (accessed 8 July 2012).

Organisation for Economic Cooperation and Development (OECD) (2009) OECD convention on combating bribery of foreign public officials in international business transactions, online at http://www.oecd.org/investment/briberyininternationalbusinessanti-briberyconvention/38028044.pdf (accessed 26 December 2012).

— (2011) Guidelines for multinational enterprises, recommendations for responsible business conduct in a global context, online at http://www.oecd.org/dataoecd/43/29/48004323.pdf (accessed 8 July 2012).

Pfeffer, J. (1998) *The Human Equation: Building Profits by Putting People First*, Boston, MA: Harvard Business School Press.

Redman, T. and Wilkinson, A. (2006) *Employment Ethics*, London: Pearson Education.

Seak, N. and Enderwick, P. (2008) The management of New Zealand expatriates in China, *International Journal of Human Resource Management*, 19(7): 1298–313.

Segon, M. (2010) Managing organisational ethics: professionalism, duty and HR practitioners, *Journal of Business Systems, Governance and Ethics*, 5(4): 13–25.

Selmer, J. (2004) Expatriates' hesitation and localisation in China, *International Journal of Human Resource Management*, 15(6): 1094–107.

Starbucks (2009) Starbucks Corporation, *Fiscal 2007, Corporate Social Responsibility Annual Report*, online at http://assets.starbucks.com/assets/ae2f32c159e64a3e96fafd5a9b37ef25.pdf (accessed 7 July 2012).

— Malaysia (2009) *Starbucks' Shared Planet*, Starbuck's leaflet, distributed in Starbucks cafes in Malaysia.

Transparency International (TI) (2010/2011) *Corruption Perceptions Index 2010*, Transparency International, online at http://www.transparency.org/policy_research/surveys_indices/cpi/2010/results, and http://www.transparency.org/cpi2011/results (accessed 8 July 2012).

United Nations Commission on Human Rights (UNHCR) (2003) Economic, social and cultural rights, E/CN.4/Sub.2/2003/12/Rev.2, 26 August 2003, Norms on the responsibilities of transnational corporations and other business enterprises with regard to human rights, 13 August, online at http://www.unhchr.ch/huridocda/huridoca.nsf/(Symbol)/E.CN.4.Sub.2.2003.12.Rev.2.En (accessed 8 July 2012).

United Nations Declaration and Human Rights (1948) Universal declaration of human rights (1948), United Nations, online at http://www.un.org/en/documents/udhr/index.shtml (accessed 7 July 2012).

US Department of Justice (2008a) Press release, online at http://www.justice.gov/opa/pr/2008/December/ (accessed 7 July 2012).

— (2008b) Report, Siemens AG and three subsidiaries plead guilty to foreign corrupt practices act violations and agree to pay $450 million in combined criminal fines, online at http://www.justice.gov/opa/pr/2008/December/08-crm-1105.html (accessed 7 July 2012).

War on Want (2011) Love fashion hate sweatshops, campaign information, online at http://www.

waronwant.org/campaigns/love-fashion-hate-sweatshops/ (accessed 7 July 2012).

The *Washington Post* (2008) Siemens agrees to pay $1.6 billion fines, will settle bribery cases in the US and Germany, by Cary O'Reilly and Karin Matussek, *Washington Post*, online at http://www.washingtonpost.com/wp-dyn/content/article/2008/12/15/AR2008121502926.html (accessed 8 July 2012).

Wong, C.S. and Law, K.S. (1999) Managing localization of human resources in PRC: a practical model, *Journal of World Business*, 34(1): 26–40.

Worm, V., Selmer, J., and de-Leon, C.T. (2001) Human resource development for localization: European multinational corporations in China, in J.B. Kidd, X. Li, and F. J. Richter (eds) *Advances in Human Resource Management in Asia*, Basingstoke: Palgrave.

Wright, P. and Snell, S.A. (2005) Partner or guardian? HR's challenge in balancing value and values, *Human Resource Management*, Summer, online at http://nreilly.asp.radford.edu/wright%20and%20snell%202005.pdf (accessed 8 July 2012).

Yang, X. and Rivers, C. (2009) Antecedents of CSR practices in MNCs' subsidiaries: a stakeholder and institutional perspective, *Journal of Business Ethics*, 86: 155–69.

Yaw Baah, A. and Jauch, H. (eds) (2009) *Chinese Investments in Africa: A Labour Perspective*, Windhoek, Namibia: African Labour Network Research.

Zhu, Y., Warner, M., and Rowley, C. (2007) Human resource management with 'Asian' characteristics: a hybrid people-management system in East Asia, *International Journal of Human Resource Management*, 18(5): 745–68.

 Visit the Online Resource Centre for web links, interactive glossary, and more:
http://www.oxfordtextbooks.co.uk/orc/crawley

12

Managing the employment relationship in international organizations

Learning Outcomes

After reading this chapter you will be able to:

- explain the essential features of the employment relationship and its critical importance to the management of the workforce
- understand how the employment relationship can be analysed by reference to economic, political, legal, psychological, and social dimensions
- outline the range of strategic options for managing organizational employment relations
- recognize the variety of factors that constrain and influence the management of employment relations in multinational organizations
- make informed judgements on the management of the employment relationship across national boundaries.

Introduction

The *employment relationship* is a shorthand term that broadly describes the relationship between an employing organization and its workforce, as employees. It applies, therefore, to MNEs and domestic organizations alike; and the nature and quality of this particular relationship could be said to permeate and influence most aspects of a company's HRM. It will matter, for example, whether relations between employer and employees are experienced positively or negatively.

The employment relationship: approaches to its management

Within an organization are employment relations viewed or experienced as being helpful and productive or as heavy-handed and antagonistic? The former is generally considered as preferable for sustaining employees' contributions towards achieving long-term organizational success. Such thinking recognizes that 'providing information to employees and not only consulting with them on decisions, but also asking them to shape decisions, is the way forward' (Wilby, 2009: 5). Yet there remains for some organizations a default position that treats workers as 'ignorant children who should recognize "management's right to manage" and do as we are told' (Wilby, 2009: 5).

In stark terms, we can gauge management's general approach to employment relations by whether they treat their staff as (a) a valued and valuable resource; or as (b) a commodity that can be used and dispensed with to suit management's priorities. These divergent approaches *to* managing the employment relationship can be linked to **high-commitment** and **low-commitment** HR strategies, respectively. The former is tied to the 'employer seeking a close relationship with workers who become psychologically or emotionally involved with the enterprise'; whereas the latter will 'follow "hire and fire" principles' such that the 'organization-worker relationship is an "arms-length" and calculatingly instrumental one' (Watson, 2009: 27).

The significance of the employment relationship

Whatever approach management adopts, it can be argued that the employment relationship is *all-encompassing* and that its distinguishing characteristics are likely to affect all other aspects of HRM. When it comes to the management of people, whether in an international or a home-based company, the employment relationship can be seen to underpin or lie at the hub of those functions that go to make up the management of the workforce, such as recruiting, training, rewarding, and redundancy. However, the actual impact of the employee–employer relationship, for good or ill, is essentially determined by how well it is institutionalized or established into these HRM practices (Quang et al., 2008).

Yet the relatively invisible and intangible nature of the employment relationship, when compared with these more explicit HRM activities, suggests that it can be unintentionally ignored or taken for granted by management. Typically, therefore, the real significance of the employment relationship for HR activities might only become apparent when, for example, there are perceptions of unfair treatment or differences of opinion between worker and manager. Hence, notions of *trust* and *fairness* (or the lack of these) can impinge substantively on management's human resource practices and on employees' reactions to them.

Choice and constraint in managing the employment relationship

Organizational choices on how to manage employment relationships can incorporate a decision on whether to emphasize relations with employees as *individuals* or as part of a *collective* group (perhaps a trade union)—or a permutation of the two. Additionally, management's choices for multinational organizations are very likely to be constrained by those institutional and cultural factors that are to be found within the contexts occupied by both parent and subsidiary organizations. By way of illustration, will a Japanese MNE setting up a plant in Germany seek to export its own approach from Japan or will it opt for a German version—or might it construct a hybrid form? However, in depicting such employment relations choices, we should be able to take account of how these organizational decisions might differ if the company's foreign location was, for example, the UK or USA instead of Germany. The former are seen as more 'open' economies and thought to offer more freedom of choice compared with Germany's relatively highly regulated system.

Either way, there is an inherent rationale that management's preference should serve the best interests of the business. Yet, irrespective of the particular employment relations strategy adopted by an MNE, there is no guarantee that this will deliver stability or certainty in the relationship between an employer and its employees. The employment relationship is inherently *dynamic*, whether with employees as individuals or as a collective workforce, and it is quite capable of oscillating between periods of mutual cooperation and overt conflict. Thus, we can typically observe a process whereby a disagreement or dispute between the two main parties (as protagonists) is typically resolved through some form of compromise or settlement, but which by no means secures long-term cooperation.

Five dimensions of the employment relationship

The rather abstract nature of the employment relationship might well throw up a number of obstacles to our understanding. However, by embedding our study in real-world contexts, both national and international, it is hoped that the concept—explained through five key dimensions—will 'ring true' and promote a genuine grasp of the subject.

The five dimensions lay emphasis upon the relationship between management and employees, and are:

1. an economic relationship;
2. a political relationship;
3. a legal relationship;
4. a psychological relationship;
5. a social relationship.

To begin examining these dimensions, let us consider the following scenario.

 Case Study **12.1 (Part One)** Entering an employment relationship at Insure-Co.

You are joining a company for the first time, having applied—and been selected—for employment as a call centre operative with Insure-Co. As a new employee with the job title *Customer Service Representative* (CSREP), you have entered an employment relationship with your employing organization. This relationship is one that spells out responsibilities and obligations for both *parties*— employer and employee—and is one that has been formalized by your agreeing to the company's offer letter and contract of employment. This spells out the *terms and conditions of employment*.

In essence you and other new workers will be required to undertake the tasks and duties of the job in question (e.g. telephoning potential customers and selling them insurance cover for a house or car) and to place themselves at the disposal and direction of the employing organization, represented by supervisors or managers. In return for this effort and subordination to management's authority, the employer provides its CSREP employees with an agreed monetary reward and perhaps other benefits, such as entitlement to holiday and sickness pay. At the same time, so that Insure-Co. has appropriate numbers of staff available for when customers can be contacted by telephone, CSREPs are required to follow a schedule of shift working (e.g. mornings, lates, and nights).

Understandably, actual working hours and levels of payment and benefits may differ between CSREPs based in Insure-Co.'s call centre in Bangalore, India, and those in its UK operations. However, all CSREPs—as employees—have formed an employment relationship with their employer.

Discussion Activity 12.1

> Based on this description, can you suggest how we have already identified the employment relationship as having several dimensions: economic, legal, and political (i.e. related to the exercise of power)?

1. An economic relationship

First and foremost, the employment relationship is fundamentally an *economic* one. Quite simply, when would-be employees offer themselves for employment they are *selling* their labour for it to be utilized by the employing organization. Seen from the company viewpoint, individuals are being *hired* for the *capacities* they can bring (Watson, 2009). Thus, in return for a salary and other rewards Insure-Co.'s CSREP employees will supply their employer with a combination of effort, skills, knowledge, and a purposeful attitude, which can be put into effect in carrying out those tasks required of call centre operatives.

The dynamics of labour markets

In common parlance, employment is an economic relationship formed between the *buyers* and *sellers* of labour. This results in employers paying—and employees receiving—an agreed 'price' or wage, which can be affected by the respective levels of *demand* and *supply* in the relevant *labour market*. Thus, for example, Insure-Co.'s decision to relocate some of its operations from the UK to Bangalore in India has been influenced by the latter's more favourable labour market. Management calculated that the Bangalore workforce could carry out the same tasks at a quarter of the price.

At the same time, Insure-Co. has employed several expatriate staff from its UK headquarters to help set up and manage its local Indian workforce. Such experienced employees will occupy a different and more costly labour market. Yet both sets of workers (from parent and host countries, respectively) are governed by the same principles of labour market economics. In short, the deal or exchange agreed between employer and employee should result in a cooperative working relationship, with the employee satisfactorily performing their everyday tasks. However, in a capitalist (profit-oriented) economy, employers seem compelled to enhance their position by minimizing labour costs—while their employees will endeavour to increase their earnings and at the very least preserve their standard of living. Thus, inherent conflicts of interest will exist alongside taken-for-granted levels of management–worker cooperation.

2. A political relationship

The outcome of these competing interests in the form of an agreed deal (or 'terms and conditions' of employment) can depend on the **balance of bargaining power** between employer and employee, which brings us neatly on to the *political* (i.e. power) dimension of the employment relationship. As we have previously stated, this is related to the demand for labour relative to its supply, but in turn this will depend on the capabilities of the two parties to strengthen their respective positions. Historically, workers have joined together in trade unions in order to act collectively. Negotiating on behalf of a united group of all CSREPs is likely to have more impact than if the CSREPs speak out as individuals.

Employers, on the other hand, can seek advantage by, for example, pointing out to their staff the possibility of 'their jobs' being relocated elsewhere. Globalization has given the employer the ability to 'scan the globe to find the highest returns and lowest costs, which usually means the lowest wage rates and lowest taxes' (Wilby, 2009: 4). It was this process that led Insure-Co. to move its UK call centre jobs off-shore to Bangalore, a decision that was strengthened by the absence of trade union membership among its Indian CSREPs.

The managerial prerogative

Also, the scenario confirms that on entering employment the workers agree (in return for payment) to a position of subordination to management. In this sense management has more power, whereby the needs of Insure-Co. are given priority. More explicitly, both sides (employer and employee) recognize and act in accordance with 'management's right to manage', namely the *managerial prerogative*.

At Insure-Co. this means requiring staff to work a shift rota. Moreover, by accepting Insure-Co.'s offer of employment as CSREPs, workers have also 'signed up' to meet certain targets in the number of calls made and customer sales successfully concluded. In so doing they have agreed to carry out tightly defined tasks and to have their work performance monitored. An Automatic Call Distribution System records each individual's length of calls, average speed of answer, and customer waiting times. This provides real-time statistical measures for each CSREP, while a supervisor can also observe what is happening on the shop floor and listen in to telephone conversations.

Employee power?

Thus, in a capitalist system it is the employer that sits in a more powerful position. The company is bigger than any individual. On the other hand, employees enter an employment relationship voluntarily and they can end it in the same way. It should not surprise us to learn, therefore, that the call centre industry is typified by high rates of *labour turnover*, which is measured by the annual aggregate of employees who terminate their employment, calculated as a percentage of the numbers employed. For these staff the inherent sentiment is that they are no longer prepared to accede to the company's authority. Similarly, the call centre industry also exhibits high levels of *absenteeism*, which in the case of CSREPs might be construed as an employee's temporary departure from a job that combines intense demands with low levels of employee autonomy.

The balance of power

For the most part, managers and their workers are unlikely to comment on or draw attention to the political aspects of their employment relationship. Management's right to manage is typically taken at face value, including a customary acceptance of the rules and regulations drawn up by management for ensuring personnel meet the organization's standards of behaviour and work. As a consequence, both sides will tend to cooperate with respect to their mutual work obligations. However, the underlying reality of where the balance of power actually resides may become evident when worker performance or behaviour does not meet the company's standards. In essence, when a company decides it no longer wishes to pay a member of staff because of inadequate performance or because of unacceptable conduct, such as theft or fighting, it may go on to dismiss the individual. This means terminating the individual's contract of employment, an action that also signifies a legal end to the employment relationship.

3. A legal relationship

Employer and employee are parties to a legal relationship that is generally governed by laws specific to their particular location. More specifically, their contract of employment is ultimately governed by the employment laws of a specific country. At Insure-Co. the terms and conditions of employment relating to its CSREPs in India will be regulated by that country's legal provisions. Similarly, the employment of staff based in the UK will be subject to the statutes and case law that apply in the UK.

The contract of employment

It follows, therefore, that central to the employment relationship are those provisions contained within a contract of employment. At Insure-Co. these terms and conditions of employment for CSREPs are to be found in the contents of their offer letter, certain verbal agreements, and in the company's staff handbook. There are also aspects of the contract that are implied, being unspoken but largely understood. Most notably, there is an expectation that any employee will follow reasonable instructions given by an authorized manager, and by the same token that the employer will provide all necessary facilities to enable an employee to do their job effectively (Cushway, 2004: 48).

National employment law

In general, employment laws confirm the contractual obligations placed upon workers and their employer. Such laws might also set out minimum standards required of the employer, designed to help protect employees from the unfettered application of management's right to manage. In the UK, for example, while companies are entitled to terminate an employee's contract, they must do so fairly. Not only must the reason for dismissal be a justifiable one (such as an employee's serious wrongdoing or a persistent inability to perform their job), management's decision must be seen to be a reasonable one, generally reached after a thorough and transparent disciplinary process.

It follows, then, that a multinational's approach to managing the employment relationship of an overseas enterprise will be constrained by the legal system functioning in that particular location. In theory this should not create too many issues, in that the *legal* dimension is supposedly the most transparent of all factors. Yet in practice it can be the most elusive and complicated. Consequently, the confusion and nuances surrounding national employment law, including regulations on contracts of employment and statutory rights, will merit obtaining the services of an employment law specialist (Walsh and Doughty, 2009).

MNEs and host country employment law

Informed decisions can then be made as to the legal constraints placed on management, combined with management's judgements as to (a) the leeway afforded by the legal system; (b) the degree of influence of headquarters over its subsidiary company; and (c) the relative balance of power between management and the workforce. A balance of power that favours management may provide a greater range of options as to how the multinational manages the employment relationships of an overseas enterprise (Walsh and Doughty, 2009). This element of choice suggests the possibility of MNE managements adopting a rational and detached approach in their efforts to shape the way the employment relationship is managed. This may mean a decision to either comply with or to circumvent aspects of a host nation's employment laws.

Insofar as MNE managements adopt an impersonal approach to the employment relationship, their employees, by contrast, are more likely to experience any management decisions personally and even emotionally. As such the employee's response can be helpfully defined in psychological terms.

4. A psychological relationship

Whether an employee's mental reaction to the way the employment relationship is managed is either a conscious or an unthinking one, from the employee's perspective there is a *psychological relationship*, which can be more to do with their own agenda and priorities than those of the organization they have decided to work for. This psychological dimension will impact on an employee's general attitude towards their employment relationship, as well as on their feelings or emotions. To explore this further, consider the second part of the Insure-Co. scenario.

 Case Study 12.1 **(Part Two)**   Employees' psychological relationships with Insure-Co.

Focusing on Insure-Co.'s employment of CSREPs in Bangalore, India, let us consider the personal or psychological responses from two employees, each influenced by their own particular priorities and expectations.

First, Preethi has recently graduated from the local business school and is ambitious to use her qualification as a stepping stone to a successful career in management. She is new to call centre work, but has some idea of what the work entails and is excited about the prospects of working for a western employer like Insure-Co. with good terms and conditions. She is especially interested in the excellent opportunities for promotion, which are based on merit and supported by the company's appraisal system. Preethi is also reassured by the promise of a friendly and supportive work environment. Following her selection interview, she is keen to start and determined to perform to the best of her abilities.

By contrast, Ravi has moved to Insure-Co. from another call centre in Bangalore, attracted mainly by better pay and benefits, and the need for a change of surroundings. Having already experienced the humdrum nature of call centre work and feeling let down about his previous employer's lack of so-called 'promotion opportunities', he sees his employment with Insure-Co. more as a short-term expedient than a career move: a stopgap until something better turns up. He knows, however, that he will not be able to disregard the company's targets for calls made and customer sales completed, but he will not be 'putting himself out' to make an extra effort.

Discussion Activity 12.2

Based on this picture of Preethi and Ravi consider their respective psychological relationships as CSREPs with Insure-Co.

a Briefly, suggest how they might differ, in terms of:

– what they *think* about their employment (the meaning they attach to it);

– what they *feel* about their employment (their emotions).

b How are these thoughts and feelings likely to influence the effort they might apply to their work?

c What factors might have influenced their thoughts and feelings about their employment?

Individuals' psychological relationships

Insure-Co.'s priorities are the same for both Preethi and Ravi. They are both to be employed as CSREPs and, in return for salary and benefits, will be expected to meet their 'side of the bargain' as set out in the terms and conditions of employment. Also, they have both been told about promotion opportunities and how the company encourages a friendly working environment. In relation to the economic, political, and legal aspects they have an identical employment relationship, but it is clear that their perception of this relationship is actually different because of their respective psychological relationships with Insure-Co.

Preethi's psychological relationship with Insure-Co. is quite distinct from Ravi's; and this seems to potentially change the very nature of the employment relationship they hold with the company. First, let us compare what they *think* about their employment.

While Preethi thinks that working for Insure-Co. will give her a worthwhile and well-paid job, she also sees entry to the company as giving her a foothold on the promotional ladder and a career in management. Ravi, on the other hand, has become rather disillusioned by his time working for another call centre. So for him the main attraction of a move to Insure-Co. is an improved income (a 'pull' towards Insure-Co.) and as a way to escape the dissatisfaction he was experiencing in his old job (a 'push' away from his former employer). Indeed, he is already looking beyond Insure-Co., which he sees as no more than a short-term appointment (information he chose not to divulge at his selection interview). This represents the differences between our two CSREPs at a *rational* level, concerned with the meaning they each attach to financial, job, and developmental aspects of their employment.

Based upon the evidence to hand we can perhaps speculate about the *feelings* experienced by them. Preethi is likely to feel more positive, optimistic, and enthusiastic about working for Insure-Co. than is Ravi. She believes that she will enjoy the experience that lies ahead of her. Such a high level of personal commitment should be evident from the way Preethi applies her energies to the job in hand. Ravi, however, seems to be more sceptical about call centre work. Even though he has no reason to believe Insure-Co. is not a good employer, his emotional attachment to his employment is more restrained than Preethi's. Consequently, unless the company is able to change his outlook, Ravi's more detached relationship with Insure-Co. is liable to be reflected in his work effort.

It would appear, then, that the thoughts and feelings of our new recruits shape the way they perform their work at Insure-Co. Preethi has a more committed attitude towards her employment compared with Ravi, who seems more likely to settle for doing enough to comply with Insure-Co.'s requirements, but no more.

A prior orientation to work

With regard to *factors* that might have influenced their thoughts and feelings about their employment, it should now be clear that employees do not passively respond to a job offer; rather, they come to employment seeking to advance their own priorities and aims. In other words they approach a new job with a **prior orientation to work**, which 'predisposes them both to think and act in particular ways with regard to that work' (Watson, 2006: 116). Whereas Preethi's initial work orientation is focused on longer-term promotional opportunities, Ravi is more interested in the money he can earn. As a result, the identical economic, political, and legal relationships they have with their employer are translated into different psychological relationships—made up of meanings and emotions.

A psychological contract

This observation leads us to the conclusion that, as part of their employment relationship with Insure-Co., each of our two CSREPs has a differently perceived **psychological contract** with the company. For the most part, Ravi sees his side of the deal as doing a reasonable job in terms of quality and quantity of work. In return he expects a certain level of pay. By contrast, Preethi perceives her psychological contract as a higher-level exchange between her inputs and rewards. Thus, in return for her willingness to take on extra responsibility and to put in additional effort, she expects her rewards to include more than money. Job satisfaction, agreeable social relationships, status, training, and career development are all important to her.

From this outline we can agree that the psychological contract is a 'subjective perception which differs between individuals' (George, 2009: 10). From Preethi and Ravi's points of view this form of their employment relationship has resulted from their different interpretations of reciprocal exchanges with Insure-Co., which incorporate the promises they believe Insure-Co. made to them.

Of course, we know that promises are made by the prospective employee as well as by the employing organization. There is 'a two-way communication of—and also perception of—the promises made by both sides of the employment relationship' (George, 2009: 18). As such, the psychological contract can be defined as 'the sum of mutual expectations between the organization and the employee' (George, 2009: 4), with the resulting agreements being inherently implicit and not at all formalized in writing. Neither can we expect these matters to be openly discussed, which means that the psychological contract 'only becomes apparent when it is breached, causing feelings of violation' (George, 2009: 3).

This is what happened to Ravi in his previous employment. Having joined the company with a work orientation not dissimilar to Preethi's, he felt badly let down when he did not receive the training and development he thought was promised. Initial feelings of disappointment turned to those of anger and resentment, aimed mainly at his line managers, who seemed to be reneging on this part of the company's promise. Little surprise, then, that Ravi left his employment, signifying an end to the *mutual self-interest* that had bound both parties to their employment relationship. Thereafter, we see Ravi's revised work orientation, which reflected his jaundiced view and scepticism of call centre employers. His new 'mental map' of his psychological contract with Insure-Co. was one that could offer him protection against similar disappointment. Thus, Ravi's psychological contract with Insure-Co. will be very influential in how he conducts himself at work, as will the social relationship he forms with his managers.

 Stop and Think

We have learned that Insure-Co. has employed Ravi and Preethi on identical terms and conditions of employment; and that this is a prerequisite for ensuring the fairness and consistency that help to sustain a stable and cooperative employment relationship with each individual. Yet in spite of the company meeting these essentials, the attitudes of these two employees towards their work remain quite different.

It is the concept of the 'psychological contract' that leads us to stop and think how 'managing' the employment relationship is inherently problematical. Employees should not be seen as passive recipients of management's directions, but as people with their own distinctive reasons and aims for taking up their employment.

Hence, employees who have been subject to the same recruitment and training processes can still end up with different psychological contracts—peculiar to them. Thus, a management's efforts to systematically manipulate workers' behaviour might not deliver the outcomes it anticipates.

5. A social relationship

In general, the dimensions of the employment relationship, including those recognized as psychological, are experienced primarily as interactions between employees and their managers, in their role as representatives of the company's authority. This introduces us to probably the most tangible and perceptible aspect of the employment relationship: the *social* dimension, which is concerned with interpersonal relations and the everyday experience of an employee's continuing transactions with their employing organization. As such, managers can have an important effect on workplace employment relations through their interactions with employees. We can explore this particular aspect through our final visit to Insure-Co.

 Discussion Activity 12.3

Read Case Study 12.1 (Part Three) below. From the viewpoint of the CSREPs, what can they reasonably expect of their immediate managers in the way they are treated by them?

 Case Study 12.1 (Part Three) Employees' social relations with managers at Insure-Co.

We know that working as a CSREP might not be a very intrinsically satisfying experience, especially when 'cold calling' potential customers who may see an invitation to buy insurance as an unwelcome intrusion. However, at Insure-Co. there are promises of a friendly and supportive workplace and opportunities for career development.

In such a challenging environment, the role of the line manager can be pivotal in influencing the actual work experience of CSREPs. In turn this can impact upon each employees' perceived psychological contract and their work performance.

Respect, fairness, and trust

As the basis for cooperative and productive relationships one might expect that managers will treat their subordinates with *respect*, by showing consideration and ideally involving staff in decisions that affect them. They should also be seen to treat them *fairly*. Employees expect equitable treatment, being ever alert to signs of a manager's favouritism, whether this is to do with a change of hours, the allocation of duties, or opportunities for advancement. For the most part, they also like to feel *trusted* by their managers, typically resenting instances of overbearing and obtrusive supervision.

Expectations of respect, fairness, and trust can be added to those we have already identified, to form a more complete list of the employees' side of the psychological contract. In turn, it follows that staff will be expected by their managers to reciprocate appropriately. Hence, respect should be *mutual*, as should consideration and fair behaviour towards others. Trust will also need to be two-way in that staff should not abuse the goodwill shown by their superiors (Rollinson and Dundon, 2007: 18). Yet the reciprocation of such goodwill cannot be relied upon. For example, where workers are shown a high level of trust that they do not deserve, 'management can be regarded as naive (even foolish in an extreme case) by employees, which could cause a cynical attitude to the company ... and ... the risk of a firm being abused by its employees' (Lämsä and Pučėtaitė, 2006: 134).

Trust and distrust

Trust has been recognized as 'the essential lubricant of all on-going relationships' (Rollinson and Dundon, 2007: 16) and of especial importance in the management of employment relations because there is an implicit link between trust and cooperative behaviour. Where employees perceive a manager as trustworthy they are more inclined to follow his lead, based on a belief that 'he will perform an action that is beneficial or at least not detrimental to us', such that they are more likely to 'consider engaging in some form of co-operation with him' (Bijlsma and Koopman, 2003: 535).

We might also take account of research by Tzafrir, which suggests that managers' confidence and trust in their employees can in turn increase employees' 'trusting behaviour, competence and organizational performance' (2005: 1617). In short, when both sides believe they can rely on each other to act 'in good faith' they will feel able to work constructively together, which 'potentially leads to enhanced organizational performance and can be a source of competitive advantage in the long run' (Lämsä and Pučėtaitė, 2006: 130).

However, the very nature of work in call centres conveys an inherent lack of trust in employees by management. CSREPs have very little discretion in the tasks they carry out, a feature that can be exacerbated by the close supervision and monitoring of their work performance. Hence, no matter how well-meaning are management's stated intentions towards staff, a climate of distrust can arouse employees' suspicions of their employer's motives. It becomes especially difficult to establish organizational trust when employees observe that management's words and actions do not coincide (Lämsä and Pučėtaitė, 2006: 137). In such an organizational setting individual managers are likely to be significantly restricted in what they can achieve in promoting positive social relations through their interpersonal skills.

Maintaining positive social relations between management and staff also requires attention to those potential ruptures or cracks in the employment relationship, which might otherwise lead to its acrimonious breakdown. In practical terms this means having transparent and consistent processes in place that can help resolve complaints by either party against the other. This will permit management, the party in formal authority, to (a) receive and respond to employees' *grievances*; and (b) to take steps to resolve *disciplinary* issues over poor employee performance or misconduct.

Such steps might usefully be guided by following and demonstrating the principles of trust, fairness, and respect. To this end companies such as Insure-Co. have grievance and disciplinary procedures to help manage and maintain a satisfactory employment relations climate, even in circumstances when the final resolution to any particular case is a formal decision to terminate the employment relationship.

Managing employees' grievances

For whatever reason, Ravi's *grievance* against his previous employer was ignored and he left his employment, offended at the company's failure to act on its promises. By contrast, his new employer, Insure-Co., has a system for management to listen to and fully consider the merits of any grievance. This includes those against fellow employees, whose respective conducts are ultimately an employer's responsibility. Dependent upon their interpretation of the facts of the case, managers can then seek to resolve the issue in a way acceptable to all parties. However, Insure-Co.'s approach is to encourage its staff to first raise any issue informally with their manager, a step that is intended to help minimize any ill feeling and personal strain, which can occur when pursuing the formal course of action.

Managing disciplinary issues

On the other hand, *disciplinary* procedures are designed to effectively resolve management's concerns over employees' behaviour or work performance. In theory this aims to repair any fracture of the employment relationship and reflects a 'rehabilitative' or corrective approach to both conduct and capability problems (Rollinson and Dundon, 2007). Furthermore, the workforce is 'likely to feel reassured if management's conduct of the disciplinary process is perceived as consistent, fair, and reasonable' (Walsh and Lugsden, 2009: 335). To maintain trust, therefore, management should not be seen as using (or abusing) the disciplinary process to punish offenders as a deterrent to others. Rather, management is advised to adhere to the principles of 'natural justice' if it is to convince employees that the checks and balances of the disciplinary process are being adhered to, ensuring a fair and reasonable outcome.

Discipline and 'justice'

Following the work of Colquitt (2001) on 'organizational justice', management should seek to demonstrate 'procedural justice' through the perceived fairness of the processes used. Applying this to discipline, management would make no specific allegation of a disciplinary breach against an employee unless a prima facie case had been established from a thorough preliminary investigation. Also, if management is to avoid any suggestions of vindictiveness or victimization, there should be a hearing that is seen to be impartial, where the individual should be given the opportunity to put their side of the story and to be represented or accompanied. In relation to 'distributive justice' and the perception of the fairness of the outcomes (Colquitt, 2001), any penalty handed out—ranging from warning to dismissal—should correspond to the severity of the offence, taking into account any extenuating factors.

To promote trustworthy employment relations it is important that employees' suspicions of persecution or unfair treatment by management are allayed. This is especially critical when employees are formally disciplined, because management is following a process in which it assigns to itself the roles of investigator, prosecutor, jury, and judge. It is vital, therefore, that trust is gained by management's attention to impartiality through natural justice and procedural correctness (Walsh and Lugsden, 2009: 336).

Needless to say, individual managers can strengthen this impression by treating employees with respect and sensitivity. This conveys 'interpersonal justice' (Colquitt, 2001). Managers can also achieve **informational justice** in the eyes of employees by taking steps to carefully describe the procedures and to explain the rationale for any decisions made (Colquitt, 2001). Even so, since perceptions of justice are considered to be dependent on subjectivity, there can be no guarantee that employees will always share management's views on what is 'fair' (Colquitt et al., 2001).

Social relationships in multinational companies

The term 'natural' when associated with 'justice' in the workplace implies that its principles will be 'universal' in application, as does a belief in 'fairness' and 'mutual respect'. Such a conclusion is debatable. More certain perhaps is that the *means* required to show fairness and gain respect may not be universal.

National differences of culture are well charted throughout Chapter 4, 'Understanding IHRM: the cultural approach'; and for MNEs a key challenge can be the quality of social relations formed between expatriate managers and host country employees. In short, attention to cultural factors by expatriate managers will help to secure employees' respect. Management's aim is to maintain cooperative employment relations and avoid those negative employee sentiments and actions that may arise from 'showing a lack of respect' through transgressing local norms and expectations. Distress, discomfort, frustration, friction, exasperation, and alienation describe likely employees' reactions to cultural infringements (Walsh and Doughty, 2009: 406). By being sensitive to the local work culture, expatriate managers can avoid such pitfalls, maintain respect, and promote better social relations with their employees. This may appear fairly straightforward, but not if expatriate managers show ethnocentric signs, through their gestures and body language, that convey arrogance, superiority, and aloofness.

Even when these extremes are avoided there may still be issues of cross-cultural discord. As we learn in Chapter 4 (see section headed *Body language, gestures, and rituals*), the American way of communicating is very direct and instrumental, a manner that may cause employees from high-context cultures to feel offended. Similarly, while acknowledging that people vary within cultures as well as between them, Steers et al. suggest that French managers in their work 'are often formal, impersonal and authoritarian' and that in inter-personal relations 'subordinates are routinely criticized' (2010: 108). This would be espe-cially damaging for employees from those Asian cultures, where 'confronting an employee with "failure" is considered to be very tactless and even dangerous' (Schneider and Barsoux, 1997: 141). Accordingly, Asian managers are anxious to preserve harmony and to avoid any unpleasantness or perceptions of rudeness. This is related to the need to 'save face' and to maintain an individual's self-esteem and overall reputation. A loss of face can engender intense feelings of shame and humiliation, which can result in an employee harbouring resentment against the perpetrator and perhaps engaging in forms of resistance against the company (Walsh and Doughty, 2009: 407).

With regard to its Indian employees, Insure-Co.'s expatriate managers can perhaps be guided by Hofstede's assessment that Indian workers are high in terms of Power Distance and low on Uncertainty Avoidance (Walsh and Doughty, 2009: 330). This would explain the CSREPs' general deference towards managerial authority and their relatively relaxed at-titude to changeable work situations. At the same time, employees such as Ravi and Preethi seem more amenable to Insure-Co.'s fairly western style of management. English-speaking graduates like Preethi and Ravi, though upholding the family and religious traditions of the previous generation, have adopted a more modern outlook towards their work and careers. Such an observation of generational differences should suggest treating typologies of national cultures with caution. Hence, it would be better to treat the work of Hofstede, for example, as only a starting point for an analysis of cultural factors affecting host country workers (Walsh and Doughty, 2009: 331).

Strategic options for managing organizational employment relations

An individualistic–unitarist approach at Insure-Co.

From an employment relations standpoint, Insure-Co.'s management will be concerned with maintaining appropriate goodwill and cooperation in each of its subsidiary companies. To this end Insure-Co. has developed 'management by distraction' (not the words the company would choose to use), whereby a weekly disco, team meetings, and a prize draw (open to successfully performing individuals) are designed, some would argue, to anaesthetize staff against the tedious effects of call centre work. The company also operates a scheme that allows managers to nominate high-performing staff for a place on its in-house 'fast-track' management programme, with prospects for team leader and shift leader appointments. Alongside this the company has a non-trade-union regime, allowing its senior management to unilaterally decide upon the 'deal' for wages and benefits in line with local labour market competition.

The management of Insure-Co. would prefer to view its employment relations strategy as an individualistic one, which seeks to gain employees' commitment by communicating with them directly as individuals, each of whom is encouraged to 'buy-in' to the success of a uni-fied organization. This view, which we can identify as *unitarist*, is influenced by a managerial perspective, which emphasizes that management and employees are working for the same ends. They should act with one accord for the success of the company and its staff. As such this particular way of thinking can see no justification for a trade union presence, which is regarded as a threat to a harmonious employment relationship.

A collectivist–pluralist approach

An alternative viewpoint, not shared by Insure-Co. management, recognizes that some workers may choose to become members of a trade union so that it can represent them when their interests are in conflict with those of the company (e.g. over pay or work arrangements). This **pluralist view** is influenced by a perspective that acknowledges that managers and employees have a number of objectives (a plurality), some of which they may disagree over. If managements subscribe to this pluralist perspective, they are more likely to see the advantage of entering discussions with a trade union as the best way to settle a dispute that affects a group of employees. In so doing the company seeks to conclude a lasting agreement with the union, acting *collectively* on behalf of its members. This collectivist arrangement typically depends upon the goodwill of both sides to reach a *compromise*, whereby each might 'give ground' on its initial demands, offering a concession in order to arrive at an acceptable deal.

Alternative approaches

Other strategic options for managing the employment relationship, including *combinations* of the above, are available to organizations. However, the mix of dimensions that go to make up the employment relationship (economic, political, legal, psychological, and social) might reasonably lead us to conclude that all options are probably rather *blunt* instruments for dealing with the permutations and complexities involved. In order to further explore these possible approaches, let us turn our attention to a different industry and examine those approaches chosen by *international airlines*, through studies of British Airways (UK), Southwest Airlines (USA), and Ryanair (Eire).

British Airways: a dual approach?

Employment relations at British Airways (BA) have achieved widespread media attention and coverage (*The Telegraph*, 2011). BA's own account of its predominant approach to employment relations can be found in its annual reports, and below we consider some extracts from the 2008–9 report (British Airways, 2009). During this period BA employed around 40,000 workers, who are referred to as 'colleagues'.

 Discussion Activity 12.4

Read Case Study 12.2 below.

a Over what issues are employees and management at BA most likely to be (i) divided; and (ii) united?

b What evidence is there that BA is using both *collectivist* and *individualistic* approaches to the management of employment relations?

c In what ways might the *collectivist* and *individualist* approaches complement each other? How might they also come to work against one another?

Case Study 12.2   BA's management of employment relations

The way we run our business

To create a really high performing business we need to build an inspiring and rewarding workplace where talented people can work to the best of their ability to meet our customers' needs and our wider responsibility (p. 34).

The workplace

We are reinventing the way we work at British Airways. We are creating a leaner organization with a distinctive, high performing culture through our flagship change programme, Compete 2012 (p. 35).

People and organizational effectiveness

In transforming the way we work, we remain focused on creating a diverse, challenging and rewarding workplace which people across the airline can feel proud to be a part of, despite our expectation that the number of people employed will need to reduce as we seek to streamline our business (p. 38).

Employee relations

We negotiate with a total of three trade unions representing colleagues across the business. We seek to work constructively with colleagues and their representatives to improve productivity and performance ... We continue to work hard to foster good relations with the representatives of our flying community. These relationships will remain key as we tackle the challenges ahead.

Despite the challenges we faced in the early days of Terminal 5, we went on during the year to achieve significant improvements in our operational performance. This was partly down to the agreements we reached for new working practices at the terminal. A major feature of these agreements was direct colleague engagement with the involvement of our recognized trade unions (p. 40).

Engaging our colleagues

We ensure that colleagues are kept well informed about our Company, customers, and industry by using comprehensive internal communications. Face to face communication is our priority and we run regular briefings across the Company so that as many people as possible can meet, question, and share ideas with senior and line managers. We run workshops to support managers in communicating key announcements and also online forums and an online Ideas Exchange to encourage wider dialogue. Other communication channels include a personalized intranet, mobile SMS messaging, video, and a range of Company-wide and local newsletters (p. 41).

BA is regarded as a long-established 'legacy airline' (Bamber et al., 2009a: 636) and not a 'no frills' low-cost operation. So it seems sensible for the company to set its sights on creating (as it states above), a 'really high performing business', placing emphasis upon building a workplace where 'talented people can work to the best of their ability to meet our customers' needs and our wider responsibility'. At the same time the company is well aware of the need to create a 'leaner organization' and to reduce the numbers employed in order to 'streamline our business', which allows it to compete with lower-cost airlines.

Workers may well *share* in management's *unitarist* enthusiasm for building 'an inspiring and rewarding workplace', in which they can be proud to play a part. They are unlikely, however, to respond positively to management's messages on the need for job cuts. On this issue there will be division, as employees fear for the loss of their livelihood.

The challenge for management is how to win employees' cooperation in pursuit of these diverse company goals. Based upon the evidence of its own statements, BA has adopted a *dual* approach. On the one hand, it has used *individualistic* methods by communicating directly with its staff, including team briefings delivered in person by line managers, supported by mass-media channels for supplying information. This is intended to win over employees to the company's plans. Alongside this is BA's *collective* approach. This is conducted through the company's negotiations with elected representatives of trade unions, which the company recognizes as speaking on behalf of BA employees. It is through this process of *collective bargaining* that the company (with 97 per cent union membership) can discuss differences of opinion and reach compromise agreements with the unions over wages and other terms and conditions of employment. This differs from Insure-Co., which has a non-union strategy and whose management makes such decisions unilaterally.

The annual report goes on to suggest that BA manages the employment relationship through an effective combination of (a) reaching collective agreements with the relevant trade unions; and (b) directly engaging with individual employees. Where the latter has been delivered with the unions' involvement, one might assume that these two approaches are indeed mutually beneficial. However, this does not always follow. For example in situations where employees distrust their employer, a move towards direct employee involvement could be perceived as evidence of management's intention to undermine the power of the trade unions, by efforts to marginalize union activities, or by offering employees an alternative to the union.

A model of employment relations strategies

These differing possibilities for management can be appreciated by the use of a model that depicts a company's respective relationships with employees (individualistic) and trade unions (collectivist). This can be seen in Figure 12.1, through which Bamber et al. explore the

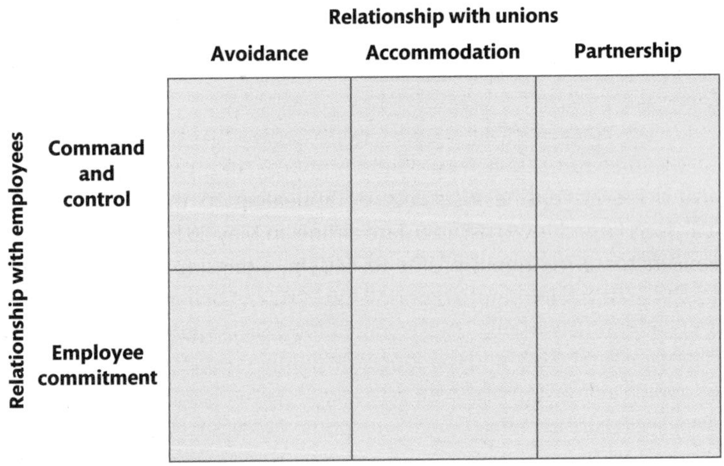

Figure 12.1 Employment relations strategies

Source: Adapted from Walton et al. (1994, cited in Bamber et al., 2009a: 638) by permission of Harvard Business School Press.

employment relations strategies used by international airlines and compare 'two of the largest and most successful new entrants', Southwest Airlines and Ryanair (Bamber et al., 2009b: 637).

Contrasting approaches at Southwest Airlines and Ryanair

Southwest Airlines, founded in Texas in 1971 and operating throughout the USA, has chosen a strategy based on a *combination* of a high-commitment approach to employees and a close *partnership* with its trade union. Unlike *accommodation* with the unions, which means negotiating with them, typically in an adversarial way, *partnership* means promoting 'a cooperative, joint problem-solving atmosphere', where all parties 'work together to achieve common goals' (Watson et al., 2009: 442). Southwest reports that 82 per cent of its employees are represented by trade unions; and relations with each of its ten employee groups (e.g. pilots, flight attendants, and mechanics) are governed by one of ten different collective bargaining agreements (Southwest, 2011). However, in order to move its relations with trade unions beyond that labelled 'accommodation', Southwest Airlines 'implements further formal or informal mechanisms to foster the involvement of employees' interests in decision making' (Bamber et al., 2009a: 639). In turn, the potential conflict between these two dimensions of this strategy is minimized by Southwest's emphasis on building a high-trust regime, which is designed to encourage employees' work productivity and good customer service.

By contrast Ryanair, founded in Eire in 1985, focuses on minimizing wage costs and achieving high productivity by a *combination* of management's *command and control* of employees and the *avoidance* of trade unions. Indeed, for Ryanair, 'avoidance' might be translated into it being 'anti-union', since the company 'aggressively avoids unions via suppression' and leaves workers feeling mistreated and mistrusted (Bamber et al., 2009a: 643). In addition, Ryanair has a policy of staffing its operations through 'the use of contract agencies' (Ryanair, 2011: 100). No less than 72 per cent of its 2344 pilots and 61 per cent of its 5429 cabin crew are contracted from agencies and so are not employees of the airline itself (Ryanair, 2011: 100). This compares with Southwest's 35,000 staff, who are all full-time employees (Southwest Airlines, 2011: 15). This would seem to provide Southwest with a more secure and stable employment relationship, on which to foster the dedication and allegiance of its workers, demonstrated through their reputation for outstanding attention to customer care.

Nevertheless, in spite of their very different approaches, both Ryanair and Southwest Airlines have achieved business success by appealing to their respective customers. Ryanair is Europe's largest low-cost/low-fare airline. In May 2011 the company announced a 26 per cent increase in annual profits to €401m, alongside an 8 per cent increase in traffic and a 7 per cent fall in unit costs (Ryanair, 2011). Similarly, Southwest has become America's largest low-cost carrier, based on its 'mix of low fares and friendly service' (*The Economist*, 2011: 76).

Employment relations under strain at British Airways

In contrast to Southwest Airlines (Partnership-Commitment) and Ryanair (Avoidance-Control), Bamber et al. (2009a: 641) place BA firmly in the Accommodation-Control sector of Figure 12.1.

They conclude from their study of BA's history 1997–2007 that, 'although BA uses the *rhetoric* of partnership with unions ... in *reality* it accommodates rather than partners with unions. Further, it does not seem to be achieving a consistently high degree of employee commitment, rather it seems to practise more of a control approach' (Bamber et al., 2009a: 641). As the authors suggest, it is difficult to maintain a genuine sense of employee commitment and union partnership when there is a continuing emphasis on labour costs and on cutting jobs and benefits. This can have a negative impact on staff's morale and their trust in management.

The company itself seems to confirm this judgement. In its annual report (British Airways, 2010: 39), BA records that over a period of eighteen months its workforce fell by 3800 to 36,832. It also acknowledges that its continued effort to control employment costs through reduced cabin crew numbers increases the risk of a breakdown in negotiations with trade unions, which can disrupt operations and adversely affect business performance.

The company has hard evidence for coming to this conclusion, following twenty-two days of walkouts by a number of its 10,000 cabin crew (represented by their trade union) during almost two years of a hostile dispute over cost-cutting moves by the airline, which included the shedding of jobs and the introduction of new work practices (*The Guardian*, 2011a). In response to the first wave of strikes, management removed employees' substantial travel concessions and instituted disciplinary measures against some union members.

After two years of public drama and rancorous intransigence, an agreement to settle this long-running conflict saw both of these issues resolved, but not the reversal of staff cuts that triggered the initial dispute. The airline said that these long-term structural changes had given it an annual saving of £60m. At the same time the cost to the company of this protracted dispute was put at £150m (*The Guardian*, 2011b). There is also the damage to the reputation of BA with its customers, following considerable disruption to hundreds of thousands of passengers amid the glare of front page news. To engender or renew its employees' commitment to providing a superior customer service, BA needs to restore a constructive employment relationship. However, after such an acrimonious dispute, this would appear to be a major challenge for both 'sides' of the relationship.

Managing employment relations: choice, rhetoric, and reality

From our brief analysis of Insure-Co., BA, Southwest Airlines, and Ryanair, respectively, we can deduce that companies can choose how to manage the employment relationship, with varying combinations of employee and union relations.

The Avoidance–Control option delivers a low-commitment, 'low-road' strategy to employment relations, characterized by 'hire-and-fire' methods for a workforce primarily thought of as a 'commodity'. At the other end of the spectrum, Partnership–Commitment is a high-commitment, 'high-road' strategy that seeks to develop a close and involving relationship with workers, who are regarded as a valued 'resource' and encouraged to engage with the aims of the company (Gittell and Bamber, 2010). This is indicative of a 'hybrid' perspective, with management combining elements of pluralism and unitarism, and of direct and indirect (i.e. representative) forms of employee participation (Watson et al., 2009: 463–4).

Relationship with employees	Relationship with unions: Avoidance	Accommodation	Partnership
Command and control	**Ryanair** 'Insure-Co' (reality)	British airways (reality)	
Employee commitment	'Insure-Co' (rhetoric)		**Southwest airlines** British airways (rhetoric)

Figure 12.2 Managing the employment relationship

Source: Adapted from Walton et al. (1994), cited in Bamber et al. 2009a: 638) by permission of Harvard Business School Press.

We can also distinguish between *rhetoric* (what a company states it does) and *reality* (what it actually does). Insure-Co., for example, would claim to adopt the Avoidance-Commitment permutation. This would represent an alternative non-union strategy through *union substitution*. The company provides high wages and good conditions of employment 'with a deliberate purpose of assuaging the perceived need for a trade union among employees' (Gittell et al., 2004: 169). However, we have also seen how call centre workers experience elements of 'management by control'. So, from this perspective Insure-Co. might be said to have much in common with Ryanair and to share features of Avoidance-Control. More noticeably, perhaps, we have also observed how BA's espoused blend of managing through Partnership and Commitment is more accurately depicted in practice as a combination of Accommodation and Control. Figure 12.2 sets out our conclusions so far.

The management of employment relations in multinational organizations

German MNEs in the UK

Which employment relations approach might an MNE choose for its overseas subsidiary? Tüselmann et al. (2007) undertook a study to examine the actions of German multinationals in the UK, noting that the UK provided the ideal environment for their study 'because it allows companies to experiment with different approaches to employee relations (as) there are fewer regulations that prescribe the form that these approaches should take' (Tüselmann et al., 2007: ix).

Would these companies retain or jettison their parent company methods based on *co-determination*, the German form of social partnership between workers and employers, where both sides seek to arrive at agreements by making joint decisions? In practice, this means collective bargaining on wages and working conditions, involving both unions and employers (Bamber et al., 2009b: 43). The firm-level institution of co-determination is the *works council system*, which gives employees a voice in decisions affecting the running of the company.

From their study of all known German subsidiaries in the UK, based on a postal survey, Tüselmann et al. (2007) emerged with two main findings. First, the German MNEs did *not* use the opportunities of the UK's less regulated employment relations environment to implement non-union approaches based solely on management's prerogative. Second, the German collective approach to employment relations, based on works councils, provided a suitable model and foundation for the MNEs' international operations. Typically, this took the *hybrid* form of adopting more individualistic methods in combination with a works council structure (Tüselmann et al., 2007: 11). In short, they decided upon a Partnership–Commitment model (see Figure 12.1), seeking the complementary involvement of unions and individual employees.

Managing employment relations in overseas subsidiaries

Although the decision makers of MNEs have choices as to how they will manage employment relations in overseas subsidiaries, they are influenced by a variety of factors associated with: the parent company and its home country environment; the subsidiary and its host country environment; and senior management's ideas of what might be considered the 'best practice' management of employment relations. Thus, an MNE might choose between: transferring its current systems to the subsidiary; following the local approach; adopting a combination of both of these; or devising something entirely different.

Although a key feature of MNEs is their ability to transfer employment practices across borders, we cannot assume that this is governed by the 'rational choices made by one group of calculating economic actors' (Edwards et al., 2007: 202). Rather, senior decision makers at corporate headquarters may well find themselves opposed by a subsidiary's managers, who are 'able to draw on their knowledge of local institutions to mould the process of transfer to protect or further their interests' (Edwards et al., 2007: 215). Hence, an employment relations practice that is the subject of transfer to a subsidiary 'may be implemented in full in some countries, partially in others and not at all in others' (Edwards et al., 2007: 215).

US multinationals in Spain: approaches to union avoidance

A study of American MNEs in Spain (Quintanilla et al., 2008) identifies the general dominance of US parent companies over their Spanish subsidiaries. This has resulted from the drive of the MNEs for tight, centralized control mechanisms, which are complemented by the relative malleability of Spanish companies and the receptiveness of host country managers to parent company ways. Hence, in this set of circumstances, any tension between headquarters' control and subsidiary autonomy becomes less likely (Quintanilla et al., 2008: 681).

However, this degree of centralization is not simply imposed by US headquarters. Instead it emerges through a process of negotiation between headquarters and the Spanish subsidiary

(Quintanilla et al., 2008: 683). Even so, when it comes to managing employment relations this power disparity enables headquarters' preferences to prevail. This is in spite of a significant difference between those MNEs that are accustomed to a non-unionized US model and the Spanish system, in which unions play an important role enforced by labour legislation (Quintanilla et al., 2008: 690).

Such a difference would appear to present an institutional constraint upon an MNE's choice of strategic option, yet this has not unduly inhibited them. American MNEs have managed to keep the 'danger of unionization at bay', while still complying with the law that states that it is necessary for companies in Spain to have representatives of the workers and that they should have the choice of whether to be affiliated to a trade union or not. In one MNE, for example, where a trade union was formally recognized, the joint works council effectively had no more than a token role, dealing with routine administrative issues. Management's additional 'preventative measures' have included the tendency to pay well above the market rate, welfare policies that promote employee loyalty, and the use of employee involvement and participation, 'with the aim of avoiding labour conflicts' (Quintanilla et al., 2008: 690).

However, not all American MNEs adopt this welfare or 'high-road', Employee Commitment approach to Union Avoidance in Spain. There are other choices. Consider the following information adapted from a study by Royle (2004) of MNE employment practices in the Spanish fast-food sector.

 Case Study 12.3 Anti-union employment relations: American fast-food companies in Spain

American fast-food giants with subsidiaries in Spain have adopted an anti-union approach, which is typical of their business sector in the USA. These MNEs seem able to undermine the effectiveness of the Spanish industrial relations system, such that their employment practices appear to negate Spain's statutory systems of employee representation.

Unionization is discouraged among employees. Union members are deterred by threats of dismissal, pay reductions, loss of hours, and promotion blockages. By contrast 'loyal' employees are rewarded with pay rises, lighter duties, and promotion. However, most fast-food employees are aged eighteen to twenty-two and in general have little experience of work or interest in trade unions.

Spanish law provides for *workers' committees* in firms with fifty or more employees. This committee is an employee-only body made up of delegates, who are elected every four years from nominations put forward by either unions or groups of individual employees. Where trade unions are involved they normally dominate the elections.

These committees have rights to information on 'economic and financial matters, the type and number of new employment contracts, and absenteeism, accidents, and illness' (Royle, 2004: 60). Workers' committees must also be consulted in advance in areas such as changes in working hours and payment systems; and they may also represent individual employees in cases of discipline and dismissal. They have a duty to ensure the employer complies with the law; and they may also negotiate company-level collective agreements.

The law seems quite clear, but American fast-food companies have proved adept at avoiding or controlling workers' committees, as part of their anti-union strategy. Management fills election lists with its own candidates and makes sure that trade unions find it hard to gain nominations. Any would-be union delegates face threats of dismissal and intimidation.

Discussion Activity 12.5

   a What factors are likely to influence the decision of the MNEs to opt for an anti-union approach?

   b What are the advantages and disadvantages of adopting a 'low-road' (i.e. a command and control) approach to managing the employment relationship?

The factors that may have influenced the anti-union strategy of these American fast-food MNEs are associated with the parent company and country, where a belief in management's right to manage and a fear of the potential power of trade unions combine to create a unitarist philosophy, emphasizing the management of individuals, not the collective. So strong is this view that such companies are prepared to circumvent the host country's laws, by a strategy of 'union exclusion, low trust, low skills, and low pay' (Royle, 2004: 58), which fits into the Union Avoidance–Command and Control part of the model (see Figure 12.1).

These MNEs are household names worldwide and have proved highly successful in their business sector, based upon a low-cost, low-pay strategy, which is seen as complementary to a non-union, Command and Control management of the employment relationship. As Royle suggests, this has much to do with the fast-food sector and its employment of acquiescent workers (Royle, 2004: 68). Moreover, the reliance on low skills requires only employee compliance, rather than employee commitment. Neither is high staff turnover a major issue in those economies marked by unemployment.

Yet as pressures on costs intensify and changes in work practices are needed, an increased strain can be placed upon employment relations. In theory this can lead to expressions of discontent and various forms of industrial conflict. In practice, however, while employees remain unorganized collectively, they are less likely to contest an MNE's resolve.

Summary

The employment relationship is a very simple concept that is central to the management of people in business organizations. Yet paradoxically this very simplicity masks its inherent complexity, as depicted in five of its dimensions. This means that management's efforts to manage this aspect of human resources are problematic. Thus, while this chapter identifies the range of choices open to management, any resultant strategy is likely to be a blunt instrument when seeking to cope with essentially dynamic situations, which can combine (and oscillate between) forms of cooperation and conflict.

Moreover, management choice is constrained or influenced by a range of factors. For an MNE this will involve factors internal to the organization, including the often competing views and preferences of its parent company and subsidiary managements. External factors are linked to the labour market and the resultant balance of bargaining power, as well as to the differences between the MNE's parent and host countries. This can mean that a particularly dominant MNE may try and circumvent local constraints, including national employment laws, in favour of transferring to a subsidiary its own version of employment relations management.

In some instances, however, faced with competing choices of unitarist/pluralist; individualist/collectivist; high-/low-commitment approaches, MNEs may attempt to combine them through a hybrid approach. These strategic approaches can be analysed in terms of an MNE's avoidance, accommodation, or partnership with trade unions. Whatever approach an MNE adopts, contradictions will exist, underpinned by the dichotomous nature of the employer–employee relationship, which encompasses aspects of both common and differing interests—of cooperation and opposition. Moreover, the MNE's precise approach can become clouded when management's rhetoric is shown to be inconsistent with the everyday reality of its policies and practices.

Review questions

1. How do you think treating staff as a 'valued resource' will impact on the employment relationship? What if employees are seen by management as a 'commodity'?

2. With particular reference to the economic and political dimensions of the employment relationship, explain why inherent conflicts of interest exist alongside management–worker cooperation?

3. What do you understand by the 'balance of bargaining power' between employer and employees and how can each side strengthen their respective positions?

4. If the psychological contract is inherently implicit and not formally stated, why is it so important for our understanding of the employment relationship?

5. Thinking of examples that illustrate where a *lack of trust* exists between managers and employees, why is mutual trust of particular importance in the successful management of employment relations?

6. In its conduct of the disciplinary process how can management demonstrate to employees that it is being 'consistent, fair and reasonable'?

7. Applying your answer to Figure 12.1, what might a company do to combine the Avoidance–Commitment approaches for its employment relations strategy?

8. What does it mean for management to seek to resolve conflicts of interest with its employees by unilateral action, consultation, and negotiation, respectively?

9. Thinking of the disputes such as the one involving British Airways cabin crew, to what extent does the use of retaliatory methods by both sides serve to make it more difficult to resolve the dispute and restore goodwill in its aftermath?

10. Thinking of a multinational organization that plans to transfer its employment relations practices to its overseas subsidiaries, why might it find that they are 'implemented in full in some countries, partially in others, and not at all in others' (Edwards et al., 2007: 215)?

Further reading

Edwards, T. (2004) The transfer of employment practices across borders in multinational companies, in A.W. Harzing and J.V. Ruysseveldt (eds) *International Human Resource Management*, 2nd edn, London: Sage, pp. 389–410.

Although it does not deal specifically with the employment relationship, this chapter provides a very clear explanation of the factors that can influence the extent to which multinationals transfer their employment practices to their overseas subsidiaries.

Gennard, J. and Judge, G. (2010) *Managing Employment Relations*, 5th edn, London: CIPD.
Although focusing on the UK, this text provides an up-to-date consideration of the major topics within the subject of employment relations, including employee involvement and engagement strategies. It also covers the practical aspects of managing negotiations, discipline, grievances, and redundancies.

Gittell, J.H. and Bamber, G.J. (2010) High- and low-road strategies for competing on costs and their implications for employment relations: international studies in the airline industry, *International Journal of Human Resource Management*, 21(2): 165–79.
This article helps to further our understanding of the employment relations strategies that can be adopted by organizations, utilizing the figure contained in the chapter and with particular reference to the airline industry.

Hollinshead, G. (2010) *International and Comparative Human Resource Management*, Maidenhead: McGraw-Hill.
Chapter 6 entitled 'International labour relations and employee participation' (pp. 107-36) provides a useful foundation for appreciating variations in 'labour relations' between different countries. It examines trade unions, employers' organizations, collective bargaining, and approaches to employee involvement and participation.

Kahancová, M. (2007) One company, four factories: coordinating employment flexibility practices with local trade unions, *European Journal of Industrial Relations*, 13(1): 67–88.
This article provides very useful case study research into the flexible working practices of production workers in four factories of a Dutch multinational. It explores the employment relations variations in these factories, which are located in Belgium, France, Hungary, and Poland. The interests of management and local unions, and the character of their mutual interaction, are central to the workplace employment practices of each factory.

McKay, S.C. (2004) Securing commitment in an insecure world: workers in multinational high-tech subsidiaries, *Economic and Industrial Democracy*, 25(3): 375–410.
This article complements the analysis in this chapter (from pp. 294-6) on low- and high-road versions of managing the employment relationship. It offers the opportunity to explore the strategies used by three multinational electronics companies in their subsidiaries located in the Philippines. The author traces the connection between distinct approaches to high-tech work reorganization and the types of worker commitment they generate: coerced, purchased, and bargained, respectively.

Bibliography

Bamber, G.J., Gittell, J.H., Kochan, T.A., and von Nordenflycht, A. (2009a) Contrasting management and employment-relations strategies in European airlines, *Journal of Industrial Relations*, 51(5): 635–52.

—, Gittell, J.H., Kochan, T.A., and von Nordenflycht, A. (2009b) *Up in the Air: How Airlines can Improve Performance by Engaging their Employees*, Ithaca, NY: ILR Press.

Bijlsma, K. and Koopman, P. (2003) Trust within organisations, *Personnel Review*, 32(5): 533–55.

British Airways (2009) *Annual Report and Accounts 2008/2009*, online at http://www.britishairways.com/cms/global/microsites/ba_reports0809/index.html (accessed 12 May 2010).

— (2010) *Annual Report and Accounts December 2010*, online at http://www.britishairways.com/cms/global/microsites/ba_reports0910/pdfs/BA_AR_2010.pdf (accessed 13 February 2012).

Colquitt, J.A. (2001) On the dimensionality of organizational justice: a construct validation of a measure, *Journal of Applied Psychology*, 86(3): 386–400.

—, Conlon, D.E., Wesson, M.J., Porter, C.O., and Ng, K.Y. (2001) Justice at the millennium: a meta-analytic review of 25 years of organizational justice research, *Journal of Applied Psychology*, 86(3): 425–45.

Cushway, B. (2004) *The Employer's Handbook: An Essential Guide to Employment Law, Personnel Policies and Procedures*, 2nd edn, London: Kogan Page.

The Economist (2011) Smiles and free peanuts, 6 April, 399 (8736), p. 76.

Edwards, T. (2004) The transfer of employment practices across borders in multinational companies, in A.W. Harzing and J.V. Ruysseveldt (eds) *International Human Resource Management*, 2nd edn, London: Sage, pp. 389–410.

—, Colling, T., and Ferner, A. (2007) Conceptual approaches to the transfer of employment practices in multinational companies: an integrated approach, *Human Resource Management Journal*, 17(3): 201–17.

Gennard, J. and Judge, G. (2010) *Managing Employment Relations*, 5th edn, London: CIPD.

George, C. (2009) *The Psychological Contract: Managing and Developing Professional Groups*, Maidenhead: Open University Press.

Gittell, J.H. and Bamber, G.J. (2010) High- and low-road strategies for competing on costs and their implications for employment relations: international studies in the airline industry, *International Journal of Human Resource Management*, 21(2): 165–79.

—, Kochan, T.A., and von Nordenflycht, A. (2004) Mutual gains or zero sum? Labor relations and firm performance in the airline industry, *Industrial and Labor Relations Review*, 57(2): 163–80.

The Guardian (2011a) British Airways settles cabin crew dispute, 22 June, online at http://www.guardian.co.uk/business/2011/jun/22/british-airways-and-unite-settle-cabin-crew-dispute (accessed 3 August 2011).

— (2011b) British Airways cabin crew dispute resolved, 22 June, online at http://www.guardian.co.uk/business/2011/jun/22/british-airways-cabin-crew-dispute-resolved (accessed 5 August 2011).

Kahancová, M. (2007) One company, four factories: coordinating employment flexibility practices with local trade unions, *European Journal of Industrial Relations*, 13(1): 67–88.

Lämsä, A-M. and Pučėtaitė, R. (2006) Development of organizational trust among employees from a contextual perspective, *Business Ethics*, 15: 130–41.

McKay, S.C. (2004) Securing commitment in an insecure world: workers in multinational high-tech subsidiaries, *Economic and Industrial Democracy*, 25(3): 375–410.

Quang, T., Thang, L.C., and Rowley, C. (2008) The changing face of human resources in Vietnam, in C. Rowley and S. Abdul-Rahman (eds) *The Changing Face of Management in Southeast Asia*, London and New York: Routledge, pp. 185–220.

Quintanilla, J., Susaeta, L., and Sáchez-Mangas, R. (2008) The diffusion of employment practices in multinationals: 'Americanness' within US MNCs in Spain? *Journal of Industrial Relations*, 50(5): 680–96.

Rollinson, D. and Dundon, T. (2007) *Understanding Employment Relations*, London: McGraw-Hill.

Royle, T. (2004) Employment practices of multinationals in the Spanish and German quick-food sectors: low-road convergence? *European Journal of Industrial Relations*, 10(1): 51–71.

Ryanair (2011) *Annual Report 2011*, online at http://www.ryanair.com/doc/investor/2011/Annual_Report_2011_Final.pdf (accessed 3 August 2011).

Schneider, S.C. and Barsoux, J.L. (1997) *Managing across Cultures*, Hemel Hempstead: Prentice Hall.

Southwest Airlines (2011) *Annual Report 2010*, online at http://www.wouthwestonereport.com/2011/#!/people/employees/index (accessed 19 December 2011).

Steers, R.M., Sanchez-Runde, C.J. and Nardon, L. (2010) *Management across Cultures: Challenges and Strategies*, Cambridge: Cambridge University Press.

The Telegraph (2011) BA dispute—a timeline travel chaos, online at http://www.telegraph.co.uk/travel/travelnews/8508691/BA-dispute-a-timeline-travel-chaos.html (accessed 5 August 2011).

Tüselmann, H-J., McDonald, F., Heise, A., Allen, M., and Voronkova, S. (2007) *Employee Relations in Foreign-owned Subsidiaries: German Multinational Companies in the UK*, Houndmills: Palgrave Macmillan.

Tzafrir, S. (2005) The relationship between trust, HRM practices and firm performance, *International Journal of Human Resource Management*, 16(9): 1600–22.

Walsh, D.A. and Doughty, D.A. (2009) Human resourcing in international organisations, in J. Leopold and L. Harris (eds) *The Strategic Managing of Human Resources*, 2nd edn, Harlow: FT Prentice Hall, pp. 289–347.

— and Lugsden, E. (2009) Parting company: the strategic responsibility of exit management, in J. Leopold and L. Harris (eds) *The Strategic Managing of Human Resources*, 2nd edn, Harlow: FT Prentice Hall, pp. 250–88.

Walton, R.E., Cutcher-Gershenfeld, J., and McKersie, R.B. (1994) *Strategic Negotiations*, Boston, MA: Harvard Business School Press.

Watson, T. (2006) *Organising and Managing Work: Organisational, Managerial and Strategic Behaviour in Theory and Practice*, 2nd edn, Harlow: FT Prentice Hall.

— (2009) Organisations, strategies and human resourcing, in J. Leopold and L. Harris (eds) *The Strategic Managing of Human Resources*, 2nd edn, Harlow: FT Prentice Hall, pp. 6–33.

— Leopold, J., and Watling, D. (2009) Strategic choice in patterns of employment relationships, in J. Leopold and L. Harris (eds) *The Strategic Managing of Human Resources*, 2nd edn, Harlow: FT Prentice Hall, pp. 442–72.

Wilby, P. (2009) Go forth and organise, in *Trade Union Guide 2010* (supplement, *New Statesman*, 14 September).

 Visit the Online Resource Centre for web links, interactive glossary, and more:
http://www.oxfordtextbooks.co.uk/orc/crawley

13 Global talent management

 Learning Objectives

After reading this chapter you will be able to:

- explain the differences between global talent management and IHRM
- discuss the complexities of identifying 'talent'
- describe typical approaches to talent management
- identify and discuss threats to effective and fair talent management strategies.

Introduction

In 1997, Ed Michaels and colleagues at McKinsey & Company wrote about 'the war for talent'. By 'war' they meant that organizations that were growing and expanding into new national and geographic markets were competing with each other for high-quality, high-performing employees. The idea that organizations were competing for talent caught the imagination of business leaders and, latterly, of academics. Seeing good employees as talent opened up new ways of thinking about labour markets and new discourses grew around the high performers that organizations wanted to attract and retain which forced, or at least obliged, HRM practitioners to rethink their human resource strategies to match and respond to the new love of 'talent'.

The basic idea and guiding principle is that talented employees make disproportionate or differential contributions to organizations. A sort of Pareto effect is assumed; that 20 per cent of employees deliver 80 per cent of the organization's value added. As such, the strategic imperative to sprinkle talent across an organization has attracted a big following. Indeed, a recent paper on talent opened with 'Talent management has emerged as one of the key strategic issues facing managers in the twenty first century' (Mellahi and Collings, 2010: 143). This chapter first looks at definitions of talent and talent management, contrasting talent management with IHRM. The idea of a talent philosophy is discussed before factors surrounding the fair recognition of talent in organizations are considered in detail.

Talent management and multinational enterprises

Talent strategies of one sort or another can exist in any type of organization but there are grounds for thinking that talent management is more important in multinational enterprises (MNEs) (McDonnell et al., 2010).

- International managers, i.e. with the knowledge and skills to operate across cultures and borders, are critical to MNE success.

- Finding and retaining international talent is difficult in a context of increasing MNE activity.
- The competences required of good international managers are more complex and scarcer than those required in domestic organizations.

These propositions are interesting but debatable and arguably serve the interests of those who work with MNEs. Good managers are surely critical to organizational success in all types of organizations; are MNEs really in a different position?

 Discussion Activity 13.1

Is talent management more important in international businesses than in large domestic businesses?

With increasing foreign direct investment and cross-border activity there would appear to be a growing need for managers who can function both internationally and locally. Added to this are high levels of economic growth in some regions, such as the Gulf and China, fuelling demand for expatriate workers in spite of government policies to employee locals (e.g. Saudization). It follows therefore that human resource practices need to match trends in international business activity. Selection, development, and reward practices, among others, need to be able to add value to operations that are increasingly international.

The extent of interest in talent management can be gauged from a recent survey of North American companies (ADP, 2011), which found that most (89 per cent of companies with over 5000 employees) used some form of performance metric to evaluate themselves in terms of development, reward, succession planning, and performance management. Metrics include, for example, measures of leadership and morale, performance review outcomes, and employee retention. Thirty-two per cent felt that their metrics were 'extremely' or 'very' effective in measuring progress towards talent goals. Fifty-eight per cent said they had a formal talent plan particularly covering attraction, development, and performance. However, of this 58 per cent, most saw their talent goals only 'pretty closely' or 'moderately' aligned to the company's business objectives. Only 12 per cent felt they were 'completely aligned'.

In sum, narratives surrounding talent are about sustained and above-average employee performance; they are about high-potential employees making big contributions, leading change, and about promotability. Interest in talent is fuelled by surveys reporting that organizations have trouble recruiting the skill sets that they feel are needed for international operations (Towers Watson, 2011; World Economic Forum, 2011).

What is talent management?

Lewis and Heckman (2006) put forward three views of talent management. First, that talent management is little more than a re-labelling of conventional human resource management practices. In this context, selection, development, and other HRM practices focus on high-performing employees, but otherwise there is little differentiation between talent management and HRM practices applied to all employees. The second view is that talent management embraces the creation of talent pools (i.e. groups of employees labelled as talented) that are targeted for succession planning and career development in the organization. This second variant differs from the first in that it singles out the stars of the present and future and links them to key positions.

The third, broader approach to managing talent is unashamedly elitist in its philosophy. Here, talent is identified to match mental models (of knowledge, skills, competences) held by top management. Talent is then managed through differential selection, development, appraisal, and reward strategies into key or pivotal roles where talent is presumed to make a strategic difference. The star performers have different identities and experiences from the majority. They have better access to power networks and enjoy the sexiest projects and assignments to work on. This elitist approach has a dark side, namely the differential treatment of employees who in their regular appraisals are rated as below average and who may find themselves on 'improve or out' approaches to performance management. This third view is the one that begins to clearly differentiate talent management from traditional approaches to HRM.

Immediately we can see that talent and talent management are strongly related to organizational context. A profit-seeking multinational operating in forty countries will surely see talent and manage it in a different way from a public authority delivering services to a local community. While there may be similarities in the meaning of talent in each organization, the different cultural and institutional contexts will shape how talent is perceived and managed. For instance public organizations in the UK are very sensitive to equality and will build talent strategies around such sensitivities. Private organizations, while wanting to see that their strategies are fair, could be more bullish about giving differential treatment to small proportion employees (Swailes and Orr, 2008).

Definitions

If talent management is different from IHRM then it needs a definition that sets it apart. While there is no single, universally accepted definition, to be different talent management needs to embrace several anchor points; describing talent, identifying key roles, assessment of performance and potential, career development, succession planning, and retention. Collings and Scullion (2008: 102) define global talent management as 'the strategic integration of resourcing and development at the international level which involves the proactive identification and development and strategic deployment of high-performing and high-potential strategic employees on a global scale'.

Farndale and colleagues (2010) add to this the importance of retaining 'high-value' employees. The importance of retention is captured in the definition given by Tarique and Schuler (2010: 124):

> [G]lobal talent management is about systematically utilizing IHRM activities (complementary HRM practices and policies) to attract, develop and retain individuals with high levels of human capital (e.g., competency, personality, motivation) consistent with the strategic directions of the multinational enterprise in a dynamic, highly competitive, and global environment.

Of interest in these and other definitions is the use of 'high' in reference to employee performance and potential. The meaning of 'high' has to be left to each organization to decide for itself, but it is usually taken to mean the top few per cent of employees at particular levels, as judged through a performance appraisal and review system.

Discussion Activity 13.2

> Talent is usually taken to mean 'high' potential and performing employees. How would you define 'high'? From your experience of work, how inclusive or elitist would you be?

Some differences between IHRM and global talent management are shown in Table 13.1.

Talent philosophy

Talent management is about the way core HRM practices are used. It involves a philosophy of what it takes to be 'talented', how talent is distributed in a workforce, how best to deploy talent, and how core practices should be configured to implement the philosophy. Borrowing from the idea of reward philosophy and strategy (see section headed *Reward philosophy and strategy*, in Chapter 7, 'International reward management') organizations should develop a philosophy that guides and shapes their talent strategies. A talent philosophy covers:

- how the organization defines talent in terms of skills, behaviour, knowledge, and competences;
- where and how the organization looks for talent levels and functions;
- how talent is assessed, e.g. in appraisals, and given opportunities to contribute to the organization.

Philosophies should cover how inclusive or elitist the organizational approach will be and how it will respond to the people that its systems identify as showing high performance and potential. Given the possible pitfalls of talent strategies such as glorifying an elite group

Table 13.1 Talent recognition and distance

Comparator	International HRM	Global talent management
Stakeholder focus	Wide focus to include interests of all internal and external stakeholders.	Narrow focus on actual and potential employees.
Range of practices	All HRM remits are covered, including employee relations, health and safety, and organizational structure.	Narrower focus on HR architecture to attract and retain high-performing people.
Scope	Coverage of all employees and all jobs.	Commonly focused on a minority of stars ('A-listers') and key strategic roles but can be more inclusive, depending on the philosophy. The focus may shift in response to temporary skills shortages or problems in particular locations.
Purpose	Optimization of HR practices on an international scale.	Maximizing the contribution from a small group of employees in 'key' roles.

Case Study 13.1   Talent management in Cargill

Founded in 1865, Cargill now produces and markets products and services in the food, agriculture, and industrial sectors worldwide. About 140,000 people are employed in 65 countries and total revenue for 2011 was US$120 billion. Cargill employs about 1300 people in research and technical specialist roles to keep the company at the forefront of scientific knowledge. Several career paths are available, including European and US Graduate Programmes, Law, Strategy and Business Development, and Research and Development.

The company gives a good insight into the management competences it is looking for. MBA graduates recruited to the Strategy and Business Development stream are asked to show integrity, conviction, and courage. Specifically, the company looks for:

- learning capacity interpreted as the curiosity to learn more than is taught, adaptability, and conceptual strength;

- execution capacity, which is a 'keen sense of priorities', 'relentless determination', ability to develop others, motivation for excellence, optimism, and compelling communication;

- knowledge of the business and its operating environment and leading change;

- behaviours that 'discuss, decide and champion', 'demonstrate respect, candour and commitment', value differences, and leverage insights gained from customers.

These are presumably the attributes that are assessed when talent decisions are made. People accepted onto the programme complete a 12-month field assignment in one of the business areas, one to two years as a business analyst 'teaming' with senior executives on a range of strategic projects, followed by project team leadership for up to 18 months, where skills are refined and global networks enhanced; finally, frontline leadership as part of the team running a Cargill business.

Cargill has a centralized talent management team that works with international businesses to identify and measure talent. A major talent review exercise is carried out every two years. Talent is placed into different pools. Next generation leaders are those who have the potential to run a major business area. Emerging leaders are those who could become general managers. High-impact performers are those whose departure would adversely impact on the business. Employees in the talent pools undergo formal and informal development. There is a high-performance Leadership Academy with structured modules. Formal programmes are linked to work-related projects and assignments. Coaching and mentoring systems are also used to support learning.

Sources: http://www.cargill.com and 'Talent Management: Understanding the Dimensions', Chartered Institute of Personnel and Development (CIPD), 2006.

and alienating a majority of employees (Pfeffer, 2001), the philosophy should recognize the major contextual impediments to talent recognitions (for example geographic distance) and the organization's commitment to minimizing biasing factors in talent identification.

Assumptions behind talent management

To understand talent management and to look at it critically it is useful to bring to the surface the assumptions on which it is based. These are as follows.

1. Organizations can describe talent in terms of knowledge, skills, competences, and behaviour that distinguish high potential and performance.

2. Talented employees can be fairly identified through line management structures.

3. Employees identified as talented deliver higher relative performance, contribution, and value added than the 'not yet talented'.

4. Talent can be managed and deployed into pivotal roles in organizations that contribute more to organizational success than other roles. (Talented people in key roles are unique value-adding resources.)

5. Talent is scarce (the supply of knowledge and skills in labour markets lags behind demand from employers).

Normative approaches

There is no shortage of normative, managerialist approaches to talent management advising employers on how to manage their stars (Berger and Berger, 2003; Davis, 2007; Turner, 2007; Tyson and Smith, 2006). However, while any well-developed IHRM systems involve structured selection, development, appraisal, and reward processes of some sort, the question remains, to what extent are they effective in relation to managing talent? In a talent context the devil lies in the detail of the approaches used and how robust and uncompromising they are. For instance many organizations use performance appraisal but, of these, how many use an approach that genuinely and fairly identifies talent and does something about it when it is found? Weak appraisal schemes lead to organizations having no clue who their talent is, where it is, or where they need it. Collings and Mellahi (2009a, 2009b) saw talent management as:

1. identifying key roles that make big impacts on sustainable competitive advantage;

2. creating a talent pool to fill the key roles;

3. developing a differentiated HRM architecture through which people are slotted in to key roles.

They put forward three stages to strategic talent management. The first step requires identification of key positions; the roles that have big impacts on sustainable competitive advantage. This calls for organizations to know what and where these roles are—but how do they do this? Job evaluation is one method but that is only likely to rank jobs in terms of strategic impact if impact is one of the evaluation criteria. Competent managers should know which jobs in their organizations are critical, but we are quickly caught up in the problems of bias and organizational politics. Boudreau and Ramstad (2005) introduced the idea of talent segmentation, which is a way of segmenting roles in terms of impact. There is, however, no easy and objective way of doing this reliably.

The second stage, creating a talent pool, requires identifying people, insiders and outsiders, who deliver high performance and/or who are deemed to have the potential for future promotion—often big promotion. Once the high performance, high potentials are identified they need slotting in to key jobs as by nature they will be anxious that their career expectations are met. Jobs may need to be found and created to satisfy and use particular talents where no job in the normal organizational structure is available for them. The decision processes that lie behind a person's inclusion in a talent pool are an under-researched topic and there is much to learn about how inclusion shapes careers and identities. Systems are also needed to refresh the talent pool and inclusion today is no guarantee of inclusion tomorrow. How does relegation from the pool influence individual identity and career development?

The third aspect is the creation of differentiated HR architecture (Lepak and Snell, 2002). In the same way that new buildings can be beautiful or grotesque, then so can the ways that HR practices are designed and connected to each other. Configurations of HR practices can also be beautiful or grotesque—or somewhere in between. The idea of differentiated architecture is that it should respond to the ways employees are differentiated and how they should be managed differently. Groups might be differentiated, for example, in terms of those occupying key roles who contribute through intellectual and conceptual skills, people identified as having high potential for greater responsibility, and employees who carry out relatively low-skilled, routine operations. The ways that each group is developed and rewarded may need to be quite different and a 'one-size-fits-all' approach to IHRM runs the risk of not optimizing the contribution of the different groups by treating them all the same.

 Case Study 13.2   PriceWaterhouseCoopers

PriceWaterhouseCoopers is one of world's top consultancies advising organizations on finance and accounting, taxation, strategy, people management, and business recovery, among other fields. PWC employs about 160,000 people in around 150 countries. The organization has to stay at the leading edge of financial and management practices and has to embed professionalism in all its transactions with clients worldwide. Given the differing nature of the types of consultancy provided it is common for staff to specialize in an area, such as taxation. Senior staff, however, need a more rounded appreciation of how organizations work.

PWC takes on graduate junior professionals each year in a Level 1 talent pool. Staff in the pool undergo a structured development programme extending over four years. During this time, they experience a range of projects, which helps them assess the areas in which they want to specialize. PWC uses a framework of seven core competencies against which employees are measured in terms of talent and future leadership potential. Technical skills are taken for granted. Over and above technical skills, behavioural, people-management skills are important. The traditional approach to development had been based around fixed-term secondments, but a different approach is now used in which employees move around PWC to benefit from a range of placements. This approach provides a better match between the development that individual employees are looking for and PWC's need to expose staff to different parts of the business. At senior levels, managers have access to mentoring schemes; not just one mentor but several, depending on the situations that need discussion. Data on talent are produced for top management.

For the highest flyers, PWC runs a 16-week intensive programme in Washington DC where future leaders meet to focus on leadership and participants also benefit from mentoring and support arrangements. PWC also runs a programme consisting of five modules and an eight-week assignment aimed at creating a global network of responsible leaders. Although about half the workforce is female, only about 15 per cent of partners are women. In 2006 PWC created a Gender Advisory Council aimed at improving opportunities for women in the organization.

Sources: Turner, Talent: strategy, management, measurement. research into practice, CIPD, 2007, with additional information from http://www.pwc.com

Talent management—the dark side

Although talent management has a big following it is not without problems, some of which are considered below.

Unbridled talent

There have been some spectacular corporate failures where suspicion falls on the so-called talented and the ways they were managed. In the recent financial crisis some suspicion falls on the so-called talented working in financial institutions that designed and sold products of such complexity to each other that they became unviable when property prices began to fall. The lesson from this episode is that talent needs a firm hand of responsible leadership and adherence to principles of corporate social responsibility (CSR), at least when national economies and the investments of people are at risk. If a manufacturer or retailer becomes extinct due to its over-indulgence of 'talent' and profligate management, then better-managed organizations will evolve to fill the niche it vacates. But such risks cannot be taken at national

---

 Case Study 13.3 Enron

Back in 1998, a top Texas-based utility company called Enron was managing talent. A new Chief Executive in his first week challenged his HR director about graduate recruitment in the company. Not satisfied with what he was told, changes were made to how and where the company recruited people such that, 'he has transformed Enron into one of the most exciting companies in the world driven largely on the strength of a very different breed of Enroners'. Enron had become an employer of choice for the world's best MBA graduates.

You may be wondering ... 'where have I heard of Enron before?' The answer is that it became a spectacular corporate collapse in 2001 leading to massive losses for its shareholders, trials and convictions of former executives, and the collapse of Arthur Andersen, its financial auditor, which at the time was one of the world's top accounting companies.

Enron had become synonymous with talent and talent management in the spirit of *The War for Talent* espoused by McKinsey & Company. Paul Dinte of IIC Partners considered that the end of Enron 'heralded the end of the First War for Talent'. This interesting idea leads to questions about what that first war was like. Indeed, one could argue that the analogy of war in this context when first introduced was unhelpful in glamourizing talent and then triggering and encouraging the aggressive, competitive behaviours that led to concerns about corporate behaviour.

Enron fell because of highly irregular accounting procedures that gave the impression that the company was in good financial health when it was not. While this cannot be blamed directly on its talent strategies, the collapse has hopefully led to much greater concern at government level and among business leaders about ethical management and responsible leadership. It is not enough to recruit talent and give it a free hand in creating deals and products, which is a plausible explanation for the recent financial crises. If there is a second war for talent then its battleground is hopefully in more responsible boardrooms played out by generals who are more conscious of how they handle their troops.

Sources: Bartlett, C.A. and Ghoshal, S. (1998) Play the card right to get the aces in the pack, *Financial Times*, 28 July, 1998, p. 14.

Dinte, P. (2011) The war for talent: the fact overtakes the fad, available at http://www.iicpartners.com

or societal level—both UK and US governments have made it clear to banks that a return to the ways of the recent past will not be tolerated.

Dysfunctional culture

Jeffrey Pfeffer (2001) put forward several criticisms of talent strategies that relate to the possible effects on organizational culture.

- overemphasizing and/or over-rewarding individual performance, which runs the risk of undermining team efforts and of creating unhelpful internal competition between employees;
- glorifying the contribution of the 'talented' and thereby alienating employees not labelled as talented—feelings of alienation are likely to lead to reduced motivation and withdrawal;
- creating a self-fulfilling prophecy in which the 'talented' are given the best development opportunities and then praised for their achievements, while those excluded from the best opportunities, and as such not able to develop knowledge and skills so well, are labelled as relatively poor performers;
- creating an elitist culture in which a majority of 'untalented' employees are cynical towards the talented.

Top management will need to draw on its talent philosophy and practice to prevent these unwanted and damaging outcomes.

Headquarters–subsidiary distance

Mellahi and Collings (2010) put forward two perspectives on why global talent management might be compromised in MNEs. The first perspective draws on agency theory, which can be used to frame the relationship between a headquarters (HQ) organization and its subsidiaries. Subsidiary performance will be judged by HQ, so the subsidiary will influence some control over the information that gets back to HQ. This could include suppressing information about talented employees because the subsidiary management does not want them to be transferred to another location. Why should a high-performing manager be identified if their transfer would not help the future performance of the subsidiary? If agency theory does correctly describe the situation, then it raises implications for MNEs to design global talent strategies that minimize subsidiary influence over the identification and movement of talent. Mellahi and Collings (2010) also suggest that agency effects will be influenced by national cultural factors. In high Power Distance cultures, for example, employees who feel their high performance or potential is not being fully leveraged may be reluctant to question the decisions of subsidiary managers, as doing so could lead to loss of face and reputation.

Overlaying the likelihood that talent decisions are satisficing, there is the problem of proximity or social distance. Employees in subsidiaries are further away (socially and geographically) from the principal organization in the same way that employees on the first floor are separated from executives on the tenth floor. The closer, socially and geographically, people are, then the more likely they are to have contact with each other. There comes a point when

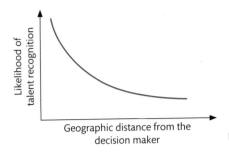

Figure 13.1 Talent recognition and distance

employees are simply off the radar that sweeps the landscape for talent. This effect is illustrated in Figure 13.1.

The second perspective comes from the idea of **bounded rationality** (Simon, 1979). This says that people do not make perfectly rational decisions; rather, their rationality is bounded, limited, and constrained. Top managers cannot obtain or access complete and perfect information, so decisions are made on partial information. Clearly, the decision on whether an employee is 'talented' and to what extent they are is a complex decision process laden with subjective information about performance.

> Limited by their cognitive ability to access, process and make judgements about complex talent management data, managers at the centre focus on limited cues in forming heuristics based decisions about talent management before terminating the search for more pertinent information.
>
> (Mellahi and Collings, 2010: 147)

The use of heuristics (short-cuts) creates a situation where managers 'satisfice' and make decisions to their satisfaction, but these may not necessarily be based on full information or be fair.

Identifying talent

While there is no shortage of normative advice, there is much less critical analysis concerning why some people end up in talent pools and others do not. Yes, performance appraisal ratings play a part but they are fraught with bias, and across an MNE a single appraisal system can be interpreted and administered in different ways reflecting local cultural values (Kostova and Roth, 2002). Makela et al. (2010) put forward three propositions to help understand why people are, or are not, included in MNE talent pools.

1. The likelihood of inclusion decreases as institutional and cultural distances increase. This is based on the argument that decision makers remote from the source will be less trusting of decisions made in different cultural contexts. Would a South Korean MNE trust decisions made in its German subsidiary about German nationals more than its own decisions about Korean nationals who work closer to home?

2. Homophily (liking something that is similar to oneself) increases the likelihood of inclusion in a talent pool and could be based on gender, race, language, religious views, technical background, values, and type of education, among other factors. People with similarities to

decision makers may be more visible to the decision maker and so more likely to be included in decisions. Stereotyping may also function if, for example, a decision maker feels that people from a particular country are lazy—then people from that country face greater prospects of exclusion. Conversely, if a decision maker has a Harvard MBA, then s/he may favour others who have attended top US business schools.

3. Likelihood of inclusion in a talent pool increases with proximity to MNE networks. This proposition assumes that employees who are 'out of sight' by virtue of not being in organizational networks connecting to the decision makers are also 'out of mind'. Employees on the outside or edges of networks will struggle to be included simply because decision makers do not know they exist.

Proposition 1 (above) can be seen as a perceptual filtering problem. A subsidiary employee's performance is an outcome of the opportunities they get, which are influenced by the relationship with the subsidiary. An HR system will lead to judgements of performance and potential, usually through a formal appraisal rating. Personal relations with the subsidiary manager influence the rating given and additional information communicated about the employee to HQ. HQ will then interpret information from the subsidiary, comparing the individual against information received about other employees. Geographic and social distance clouds the HQ decision. The main implication of this situation is to alert MNEs to the many factors that dilute talent decisions such that they are at least recognized when talent strategies are designed and implemented. The 'on-line' aspects of identifying talent such as data from performance ratings are only one part of the process. 'Off-line', i.e. the softer aspects of identifying talent, also exist and need attention to reduce these discriminatory effects (Makela et al. 2010).

Building on Makela et al. (2010) and their three threats to inclusion above, several other problems can be identified.

Person–organization fit

Behaviour at work reflects the coming together of an individual's competences (broadly defined), their aspirations, and the work environment in which they have to function. Stemming from Lewin's (1935) work on personality, interest in the interactions between people and environments has led to interest in person–vocation fit, person–organization fit, person–team fit and person–job fit (Kristof, 1996; Kristof-Brown et al., 2005). Organization fit occurs when an employee's personality, values, goals and aspirations, intellectual needs, and attitudes are matched by the culture, challenges, and rewards provided by a workplace. There is also a resource-matching aspect in that the employee's resources in terms of available time and their competences need to match what the organization wants from them if high fit is to occur. Organization fit splits into supplementary and complementary fit. Supplementary fit occurs when a person brings characteristics similar to those already held by others. Complementary fit occurs when a person brings characteristics that are lacking and so completes what is needed (Cable and Edwards, 2004).

Vocational fit is based on the premise that different jobs have different intellectual and cognitive demands (Holland, 1997). The gravitational hypotheses (McCormick et al., 1979) propose that, across a career, people gravitate towards jobs that provide a good fit with their intellectual abilities. Of course, there are social and economic reasons for job changes, but the theory explains why some people work in the same place for forty years whereas others have a range of jobs and careers, rising and falling in hierarchies as they move around. While good person–vocation fit would be a logical predictor of superior performance, its influence seems likely to be mediated by more local influences such as organization culture and fit with the team and the job.

Person–team fit is of interest because of the increased use of teamwork by organizations. Although the incidence of real teams and teamwork remains low (Benders et al., 2001) the large amount of group-work and teamwork that is undertaken requires people to act out team roles. Incompatibility between people and their roles leads to poor person–role fit. Job fit can be seen in two ways: the extent to which the abilities of a person meet the demands of a job (demands–abilities); and the extent to which the attributes of a job meet the desires of a person (needs–supplies). Fit between demand and abilities occurs when the job holder has the technical knowledge and skills to perform effectively. Needs–supplies fit occurs when a person's desires, for example for greater involvement in a some aspect of work to get new learning, are met.

We suggest that sustained, above-average performance needs a high level of person–organization fit to underpin it. High fit, however, would not in itself be a cause of high performance as some, perhaps most, employees will fall into comfort zones in which their rewards for average performance are meeting their needs. Rather, it is the absence of high fit that would prevent sustained high performance occurring.

In a talent context, how is P–O fit assessed and developed? Matching begins to occur when potential applicants interpret corporate literature and experience the organization in selection processes such as interviews and assessment centres. From the organization's side, a candidate's knowledge, skills, and abilities are used to predict person–job, fit whereas values and personality are used to judge P–O fit, with both types of fit used in selection decisions (Kristof-Brown, 2000).

After selection, new starters acquire the knowledge they need through socialization, e.g. how to behave in particular situations and knowledge of the primary beliefs, assumptions, priorities, and stakeholders (Cooper-Thomas et al., 2012). Feelings of fit are enhanced when employees are given systematic, sequential information about career progression (Cable and Parsons, 2001). If information is received in a haphazard way feelings of fit are more likely to dissipate. The use of role models, experienced insiders, and mentors also enhances perceptions of fit in new employees by allowing new starters to explore how they could react in situations. Without this form of socialization employees are prone to uncertainty and vulnerable to forming views of situations that are more likely to lead to feelings of reduced fit (Cable and Parsons, 2001). The implications are that structured and thought-out socialization does enhance perceived fit, although how beneficial this is to organizations in terms of stimulating longer tenure and higher individual performance is less clear.

So far P–O fit has been discussed from the employee's viewpoint, i.e. the employee's perceptions of how well they fit. But what does the organization think? What is the 'actual' fit in the mind of the organization's talent decision makers? Cooper-Thomas and colleagues (2004), for instance, found that socialization in the first four months of a new post influences perceived P–O fit but not actual fit. Talent management can be considered in terms

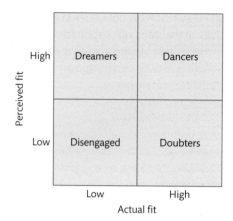

Figure 13.2 Talent fit matrix

of a 2 × 2 matrix that maps perceived and actual fit (see Figure 13.2). Regardless of the criteria on which fit are judged, when both perceived and actual fit are high, then the views of the individual and the organization converge and the conditions for being 'earmarked' as top talent exist. Using common talent vocabulary, people who fit into this quadrant are the 'stars' or A-listers, although here they are called dancers. They are dancers because they are performing for their judges, displaying their talents and charms around the 'organizational pole'. For the dancers, there are plans for development, postings, and promotion, which are a logical outcome of this combination of perceived and actual fit.

Employees who fall into the quadrant where actual fit is high but perceived fit is low are labelled as doubters. For these employees, organizations need to take the initiative and go out of their way to have adult conversations with them about their aspirations. The term 'adult' here is used to mean frank but fair exchanges of views and without prejudice about how things are. The aim should be to assure employees that they are valued, that the organization wants to keep them, and that it will work to create opportunities. Increased socialization could be appropriate. Sometimes managers have to step in and do things for people; this is one of those situations. The aim should be to turn doubters into dancers.

Perhaps the most difficult situation to manage occurs when actual fit is low yet perceived fit is high. In this scenario the employee has favourable impressions of themselves that are not reciprocated by the talent decision makers. Here they are labelled as dreamers. They may be misinterpreting what the organization values or have naive impressions of the value of their own contributions. Employees in this position will struggle to break through this impression barrier to be seen as future talent. Doing so is very difficult without major changes to reporting relationships, as they may have been 'written-off' by their line management. However, assuming that their basic performance is good enough to maintain employment, then it would be necessary to have adult conversations in an appraisal context that bring to the surface what the organization is looking for and why it thinks it is not seeing those qualities. Development aimed at changing employee attitudes and behaviour to bring about better fit could then be initiated.

Of course, actual fit in this model is not actual in any real or lasting sense. It is fit with a set of values and beliefs as perceived by one or more others making evaluations at a point in time. If, say, an employee's line manager changes, then their actual fit with espoused values and beliefs could be seen in a different light. This could work to the benefit of people previously seen as not fitting well as their actual fit is reinterpreted favourably; or to the detriment of people previously seen as fitting well but who are not seen as fitting well with the new order. Employees in this latter category may be moved aside or 'let go'. Another way of converting a low actual fit and a high perceived fit scenario is to move the employee to another area of the organization where different values and beliefs exist and that may suit them better.

The fourth quadrant captures those employees trapped in a situation where both actual and perceived organization fit are low. Here they are labelled the disengaged, as the conditions are created for at best a form of disengaged tenure if performance is good enough to keep the job. Unfortunately, this scenario is not unusual and is perhaps the most common, since most employees are not on talent lists and do not enjoy much, if any, internal promotion.

It would be a useful exercise for talent strategists to assess the proportions of their employees who fall into each of the four quadrants. In a typically elitist approach to managing talent we suggest that dancers make up about 10 per cent, dreamers 10 per cent, doubters 20 per cent, and disengaged 60 per cent—but those figures are purely illustrative and are provided simply to provoke discussion. Very different figures could be produced across, for example, a multinational manufacturer and professional consultancies.

 Stop and Think

Using the concepts above on person-organization fit, how would you assess if you had to identify your own 'fit' in your current organization; which would you be, a 'dancer, dreamer, doubter, or disengaged'? What could you do to change/improve your assessment? Would you want to? Is there anything you could do to improve your 'fit'?

 Case Study 13.4   Using older worker talent at Bosch

An interesting twist on talent comes from the Bosch Group, which is a global supplier of technology and services to the automotive, industrial, consumer, and buildings industries. They provide, among other products, systems for vehicles, electrical components, and power tools. There are over 300 subsidiaries and regional companies. Income in 2011 was €51 billion across Europe, Asia-Pacific, and America. To manage workflow and workloads, Bosch is accessing a network of former employees; people who have retired or who have left but who are 'in good standing'. When a business area identifies a need, a Bosch Management Support (BMS) company matches the customer's requirements with the expertise available in the network. If contracts are agreed, BMS handles the financial transactions between customer and specialist. The scheme makes good use of the long experience held by former employees and was honoured by the UK Human Capital Awards for being an innovative way of engaging the skills of an ageing population. The scheme recognizes skills shortages in engineering on an international scale and differs from the usual talent approach of focusing on young and current employees.

Source: Pollitt, D. (2009) Bosch builds a talent bank of ex-employees, *Human Resource Management International Digest*, 17(5): 9–10

Gender typing

One of the recurring suspicions hanging over talent management concerns is its suscep-tibility to political influences and gendered decision making. This is worrying given that identifying promotability is central to talent strategies. Gender typing in jobs is well known (Powell et al., 2002) and management is prone to be seen as a masculine activity with its rhetoric of tough decisions, results orientation, and forcefulness. These characteristics are stereotypically associated more with men than with women, for whom stereotyping points to concerns for upholding harmony and good relationships. There are routine reminders of the statistical imbalance that shows far more men in top management posts than women (BoardWomen Monitor, 2008). While there are several explanations for this, it is worth con-sidering whether the performance of women at work might be seen in a different light from that of men.

Lyons and McArthur (2007), for instance, found that the evaluation of leadership ability among top managers is gendered; evaluators are much more conscious of women being women; and discourses around what leadership is are masculine. Beehr et al. (2004) identified four routes to promotion: exceptional performance; reliable performance; personal charac-teristics; favouritism and luck. Their research found that people accepted the promotions of others when they believed they were based on performance, but if other reasons were perceived then feelings of injustice arose, with all the negative connotations that accompany them. For instance employees are likely to react adversely if they believe colleagues are being promoted for reasons of affirmative action or favouritism.

Women are also less likely to use impression management techniques to influence promotion decisions, according to Singh et al. (2002). They proposed that women were less likely to ingratiate themselves with others and play organizational politics and that they put greater trust in fair systems to recognize and promote them fairly on the basis of high performance. In contrast, a survey of American public relations managers found no differ-ences in the upward influence tactics used by men and women, which suggests that such differences that are observed could be explained by situational variables such as amount of power (O'Neil, 2004).

Evidence of a performance/promotion bias against women was found by Lyness and Heilman (2006), who studied the performance appraisals of over 400 higher managers in a US financial services organization. They found that women in 'line' jobs, e.g. produc-tion, were rated less well than men and also less well than women in 'staff' jobs, such as support services like human resources. They concluded that gender stereotyping of management and what makes a good manager was a more likely explanation for the results than true differences in ability, and that women were held to 'stricter standards for promotion'. There is also the 'motherhood penalty' as classic career models shaped over the ages by men place a virtue on gaining technical knowledge in early career in preparation for senior responsibility in one's thirties and forties. Although never explicit, women may be less likely to win promotion if there is a feeling that investments that go with it are less likely to come to fruition because of motherhood. The international post-ings often associated with senior posts may also require a level of mobility that further disadvantages women.

Influence

Talent spotting means finding employees who can influence others. Influence, like power, stems in part from the position a person holds, the power invested in that position, and through the resources that accompany it. But we can see in organizations that people occupying the same position differ in the amount of influence that they have. This is not just influence over the people who work for them, but upwards influence as well. One explanation for this stems from personality (Anderson et al., 2008). Investigating the 'Big 5' personality dimensions, Anderson and colleagues found that in a team-oriented consultancy working on brand and corporate image, extraversion was a strong predictor of influence over and above position. In an engineering department providing technical support services that was built around individual completion of tasks, extraversion was not a predictor of influence, but conscientiousness was.

This finding suggests that aspects of personality are linked to influence but that different personality characteristics prosper in different organizational settings and professional cultures. Given that personality is relatively stable, this further suggests that finding talent, and finding people who fit, is partly down to people finding a place where their natural expressions are valued. It also supports the use of personality assessment in organizational selection, although that further requires that organizations know the personality profiles they are looking for and have evidence, not wishful thinking, that certain personality profiles are more likely to associate with influence and fit than others.

Liking

Liking, or interpersonal attraction, is a potential source of bias in talent spotting, as there is ample evidence of biasing effects in appraisal (Lefkowitz, 2000; Varma and Pichler, 2007). Liking of subordinates associates with higher performance ratings (Lefkowitz, 2000) and one source of liking is perceived similarity. Straus et al. (2001) found that appraisal decisions are influenced by perceived personality similarities, although not by actual similarities. Attitudinal similarity is another source of liking and this also influences performance ratings over and above technical ability (Bates, 2002). Furthermore, there are suggestions that dissimilar attitudes have a bigger repulsion effect than similar attitudes have an attractor effect on liking outcomes (Singh and Ho, 2000). Another tactic used to engender liking is impression management by subordinates targeting supervisors. Wayne and Liden (1995) defined impression management as 'those behaviors individuals employ to protect their self-image, influence the way they are perceived by significant others, or both' (Wayne and Liden, 1995: 232); they found that demographic similarities (gender, race, age) between appraisers and appraisees and impression management influence ratings by impacting upon supervisors' liking of subordinates. Against this, Varma and Pichler (2007) found that while liking does influence performance ratings, raters are able to separate liking from performance such that the overriding influence on ratings is actual performance. Questions remain therefore about the size of the effect that liking has on appraisal ratings.

People find it difficult to separate judgements of success and failure in a person from their like or dislike of them (Avison, 1980). Liking may lead to a person's failures being explained using external factors. Disliking may lead to a person's successes being explained through

Case Study 13.5 Managing talent: UK and French perspectives

Boussebaa and Morgan (2008) illustrate how British and French conceptions of management differ such that efforts to develop a transnational talent strategy failed completely. The companies are not identified but referred to as B and F, respectively. B-group was a large home improvement retailer with operations in Asia and Europe. B-group acquired a controlling stake in F-group and B was concerned about underperformance of the newly acquired French business. One approach to improving things was to develop an integrated talent management strategy—exceptional French and British managers were to experience the same development systems. This involved shared systems for training, appraisal, and career development.

B-group's approach was to identify young employees who could be future leaders. There were two strands; high-potential identification and high-potential development. Future stars were identified through appraisals and then through assessment centres. Those who performed well were to be segregated into a talent pool with carefully managed professional development. But the French would have none of this. There were disagreements about how potential could be measured. The French perspective was that assessing potential was irrelevant because all their managers who had gone through the *grande école* system had potential. In France, the *grandes écoles* are at the top of the higher education tree and have long played a big role in producing managers. 'These schools act as an homogenizing force, imbuing students with an elitist ethos and providing them with a distinctive shared identity and a strong sense of belonging to a higher, nobler class that is associated with intellectual ability, privilege and social status' (Boussebaa and Morgan, 2008: 27). Holding a *diplome* is enough to set people apart as holders feel they constitute a management elite with the right to manage. It is the *grands écoliens* that usually rise into top management.

While there are 'top' business schools in the UK, there is no equivalent to the French system. The right to manage comes through experience and results. While UK schools teach business administration, this is not the same as developing people so that they become better managers. The British side saw the French approach as backward, whereas the French had no interest in adopting the British appraisal-based approach. French managers felt they had already qualified for higher management and did not want to compete in a talent competition with the British. There were also clashes over the content of development programmes. The British emphasized practice and 'what works', compared to the French, who wanted more intellectual and theoretical insight. French managers dismissed the training programmes as 'psuedo-science' as well as 'simplistic and naive'. British approaches were seen as too keen to put things into practice at the expense of thorough discussions about planning and preparation.

After several years of trying, it was clear to the British that an integrated system was not going to happen. They spoke of clearing out the senior management of the French firm so that control could be regained.

The case shows that talent in the French company was not something to be assessed and measured. Rather, it was something that was developed in the *grandes écoles* through intensive and highly competitive teaching and learning. The British framework imposed on the French was completely oblivious to this massive institutional difference. How dare a lowly placed HR manager make an evaluation of a *grand écolien*?

In the end, the British company abandoned the idea of creating a cross-national management group and resorted to financial controls as a way of controlling the French company. So long as financial targets were met, the methods by which they were met had slipped off the agenda. The case reveals how difficult it can be to integrate national cultures where there are marked differences in social and institutional structures.

Source: Boussebaa, M. and Morgan, G. (2008) Managing talent across national borders: the challenges faced by an international retail group, *Critical Perspectives on International Business*, 4(1): 25–41

external factors rather than the person's competences, whereas their failures may be attributed to internal factors such as lack of social skills or lack of organization.

One aspect of being liked is the amount of information that we disclose to others. People who give away intimate details are liked more than people who give away less. People disclose more to people that they like; and people like others that they have disclosed information to (Collins and Miller, 1994). However, this does not follow a linear pattern, as increasing information about others also leads to less liking. Liking develops until evidence of dissimilarity is found; that is, when information is revealed that one party dislikes (Norton et al., 2007). After a point of dissimilarity is reached, further information is more carefully interpreted so that information that might previously have been seen as neutral is seen as unwelcome. For instance a manager may initially like what an employee reveals about his/her attitudes to work and to colleagues. But if the employee later reveals information about themselves or attitudes that clash with the manager's values, then liking will diminish. The implication for those who want to be in talent pools is to appreciate the values of those who they would impress, and to be economical in what they reveal to them. The break point in the non-linear nature of disclosure leading to liking can come early or late in a relationship. In a first conversation information can be revealed that leads to a state of disaffection, or an affective relationship could exist for years before information is revealed that leads to disaffection.

Another source of affect comes through propinquity, which is the amount of exposure that people have to each other. People who encounter each other more often than others are more likely to form liking or loving relationships. People working in adjacent offices have higher propinquity than people working in offices in other buildings on the same site. Although strong and fair appraisal should identify high performers even if they are hidden away from top managers, employees with little exposure to top management are less likely to be liked and may miss out on the benefits that liking brings.

Organizations concerned about minimizing biasing effects arising from interpersonal affection can use appraisal feedback from multiple raters (e.g. 360-degree). Fletcher (1999) concluded that gender differences had impeded the selection, appraisal, and promotion of women but that multi-source performance appraisal (360) helps to create a more level playing field. In addition, using objective criteria to rate performance and training raters to make them aware of similarity biases helps to alleviate biasing effects (Straus et al., 2001).

Summary influences on talent recognition

Figure 13.3 draws together influences on the identification of talent in organizations. From a starting point where each employee displays an actual level of performance at a particular time, the actual/potential performance will be influenced by the opportunities that they are given and that they take, their innate characteristics and abilities, their fit in the organization, and the influence their colleagues have on their performance. This actual performance will have a direct influence on the line manager's appraisal of potential and performance; but that will also be influenced by the employee's impression of management tactics and their level of information disclosure with the appraiser. Appraisal ratings impact upon talent reviews, which may be formal or very subjective exercises. Talent reviews will also be influenced by the organization's imagination and stereotypes of talent, geographic and cultural distances,

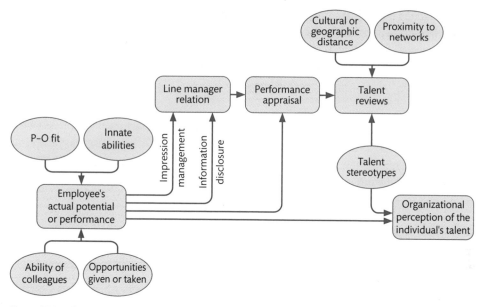

Figure 13.3 Influences on the identification of organizational talent

and proximity to decision networks. Employee reaction to talent review outcomes will impact on individual performance but will be moderated by the employee's ambitions and their self-assessment of their own talent potential.

Summary

Talent management provides a rich arena for advances in practice and for researchers to understand how talent strategies work. This chapter has identified a wide range of threats to fair and equitable talent management on an international scale. Developing talent strategies that minimize impacts of the biasing factors identified in this chapter presents a major challenge to organizations.

Review questions

1. What factors make one job more 'key' or more strategic than another?
2. Thinking of an organization that you are familiar with, how well do you think it identifies and manages talent in its workforce?
3. What is talent and how are the 'talented' differentiated from the majority of a workforce?
4. How might the notion of talent differ across different sectors?
5. Is talent management in MNEs more complex or important than in domestic organizations?

6. To what extent do you agree that about 80 per cent of the value an organization creates is generated by about 20 per cent of the workforce?

7. How might your views in question 6 be influenced by the type of business that you are considering?

8. How could a multi-national organizational evaluate the effectiveness of a talent programme?

9. If employees are deemed 'talented' in one organization, what factors might influence the transferability of their talents if they were to leave and work for other organizations?

10. If an organization runs a talent management programme, how might employees not be selected for the programme react?

Further reading

Bhattacharya, C.B., Sen, S., and Korschun, D. (2008) Using corporate social responsibility to win the war for talent, *MIT Sloan Management Review*, 49(2): 37–44.
   This article provides an insight into the links between attracting talent and corporate social responsibility.

Groysberg, B., Nanda, A., and Nohria, N. (2004) The risky business of hiring stars, *Harvard Business Review*, May: 92–100.
   This article provides a rare consideration of why talent sometimes does not transfer from place to place.

Iles, P., Preece, D., and Chuai, X. (2010) Talent management as a management fashion in HRD: towards a research agenda, *Human Resource Development International*, 13(2): 125–45.
   For a recent review of talent management, see this article.

McCracken, D.M. (2000) Winning the talent war for women, *Harvard Business Review*, Nov/Dec: 159–67.
   See this article for an account of how one company tackled gender unfairness.

Ready, D.A. and Conger, J.A. (2007) Make your company a talent factory, *Harvard Business Review*, 85(6): 68–77.
   This article shows how two companies ran their talent programmes.

Bibliography

Anderson, C., Spataro, S., and Flynn, F. (2008) Personality and organizational culture as determinants of influence, *Journal of Applied Psychology*, 93(3): 702–10.

Automatic Data Processing (ADP) (2011) *Talent Management 2011: Perceptions and Realities*, Roseland, NJ: ADP.

Avison, W.R. (1980) Liking and the attributes of causation of success and failure, *Journal of General Psychology*, 102: 197–209.

Bartlett, C.A. and Ghoshal, S. (1998) Play the card right to get the aces in the pack, *Financial Times*, 28 July, p. 14.

Bates, R. (2002) Liking and similarity as predictors of multi-source ratings, *Personnel Review*, 31(5/6): 540–52.

Beehr, T.A., Nair, V.N., Gudanowski, D.M., and Such, M. (2004) Perceptions of reasons for promotion of self and others, *Human Relations*, 57(1): 413–38.

Benders, J., Huijgen, F., and Pekruhl, U. (2001) Measuring group work: findings and lessons from a European survey, *New Technology, Work and Employment*, 16(3): 204–17.

Berger, L.A. and Berger, D.R. (2003) *The Talent Management Handbook*, New York: McGraw-Hill.

Bhattacharya, C.B., Sen, S., and Korschun, D. (2008) Using corporate social responsibility to win the war for talent, *MIT Sloan Management Review*, 49(2): 37–44.

Boardwomen Monitor (2008) European Professional Women's Network, online at www.europeanwn.net/index.php?article_id=561 (accessed 19 December 2012).

Boudreau, J.W. and Ramstad, P.M. (2005) Talentship, talent segmentation and sustainability: a new HR decision science paradigm for a new strategy definition, *Human Resource Management*, 44(2): 129–36.

Boussebaa, M. and Morgan, G. (2008) Managing talent across national borders: the challenges faced by an international retail group, *Critical Perspectives on International Business*, 4(1): 25–41.

Cable, D.M. and Edwards, J.R. (2004) Complementary and supplementary fit: a theoretical and empirical integration, *Journal of Applied Psychology*, 89(5): 822–34.

—— and Parsons, C. (2001) Socialization tactics and person–organization fit, *Personnel Psychology*, 54(1): 1–23.

Chartered Institute of Personnel and Development (CIPD) (2006) *Talent Management: Understanding the Dimensions*, London: CIPD.

Collings, D.G. and Mellahi, K. (2009a) Strategic talent management: a review and research agenda, *Human Resource Management Review*, 19(4): 304–13.

—— and —— (2009b) The barriers to effective global talent management, the example of corporate elites in MNEs, *Journal of World Business*, 45(2): 143–9.

—— and Scullion, H. (2008) Resourcing international assignees, in M. Dickman, C. Brewster and P. Sparrow (eds) *International Human Resource Management: A European Perspective*, London: Routledge, pp.87–106.

Collins, N.L. and Miller, L.C. (1994) Self-disclosure and liking: a meta-analytic review, *Psychological Bulletin*, 116: 457–75.

Cooper-Thomas, H., van Vianen, A., and Anderson, N. (2004) Changes in person–organization fit: the impact of socialization tactics on perceived and actual P–O fit, *European Journal of Work & Organizational Psychology*, 13: 52–78.

——, Anderson, N., and Cash, M. (2012) Investigating organizational socialization: a fresh look at newcomer adjustment strategies, *Personnel Review*, 41(1): 41–55.

Davis, T. (2007) *Talent Assessment*, Aldershot: Gower.

Dinte, P. (2011) The war for talent: the fact overtakes the fad, online at www.iicpartners.com (accessed 1 April 2012).

Farndale, E., Scullion, H., and Sparrow, P. (2010) The role of the corporate HR function in global talent management, *Journal of World Business*, 45(2): 161–8.

Fletcher, C. (1999) The implications of research on gender differences in self-assessment and 360 degree appraisal, *Human Resource Management Journal*, 9(1): 39–46.

Groysberg, B., Nanda, A., and Nohria, N. (2004) The risky business of hiring stars, *Harvard Business Review*, May: 92–00.

Holland, J.L. (1997) *Making Vocational Choices: A Theory of Careers*, Englewood Cliffs, NJ: Prentice Hall.

Iles, P., Preece, D., and Chuai, X. (2010) Talent management as a management fashion in HRD: towards a research agenda, *Human Resource Development International*, 13(2): 125–45.

Kostova, T. and Roth, K. (2002) Adoption of organizational practice by subsidiaries of multinational corporations: institutional and relational effects, *Academy of Management Journal*, 45(1): 215–33.

Kristof, A. (1996) Person–organization fit: an integrative review of its conceptualizations, measurement and implications, *Personnel Psychology*, 49: 1–49.

Kristof-Brown, A.L. (2000) Perceived applicant fit: distinguishing between recruiters' perceptions of person–job and person–organization fit, *Personnel Psychology*, 53(4): 643–71.

——, Zimmerman, R.D., and Johnson, E.C. (2005) Consequences of individuals' fit at work: a meta-analysis of person–job, person–organization, person–group and person–supervisor fit, *Personnel Psychology*, 58: 281–342.

Lefkowitz, J. (2000) The role of interpersonal affective regard in supervisory performance ratings: a literature review and proposed causal model, *Journal of Occupational and Organizational Psychology*, 73: 67–85.

Lepak, D. and Snell, S. (2002) Examining the human resource architecture: the relationships among human capital, employment and human resource configurations, *Journal of Management*, 28(4): 517–43.

Lewin, K. (1935) *A Dynamic Theory of Personality*, Selected Papers, New York: McGraw Hill.

Lewis, R.E. and Heckman, R.J. (2006) Talent management: a critical review, *Human Resource Management Review*, 16(2): 139–54.

Lyness, K.S. and Heilman, M.E. (2006) When fit is fundamental: performance evaluations and promotions of upper-level female and male managers, *Journal of Applied Psychology*, 91(4): 777–85.

Lyons, D. and McArthur, C. (2007) Gender's unspoken role in leadership evaluations, *Human Resource Planning*, 30(3): 24–32.

McCormack, E., DeNisi, A., and Shaw, J. (1979) Use of the position analysis questionnaire for establishing the job component validity of tests, *Journal of Applied Psychology*, 64: 51–6.

McCracken, D.M. (2000) Winning the talent war for women, *Harvard Business Review*, Nov/Dec: 159–67.

McDonnell, A., Lamare, R., Gunigle, P., and Lavelle, J. (2010) Developing tomorrow's leaders—evidence of global talent management in multinational enterprises, *Journal of World Business*, 45(2): 150–60.

Makela, K., Bjorkman, I., and Ehrnrooth, M. (2010) How do MNCs establish their talent pools? Influences on individuals' likelihood of being labelled as talent, *Journal of World Business*, 45(2): 134–42.

Mellahi, K. and Collings, D.G. (2010) The barriers to effective global talent management: the example of corporate elites in MNEs, *Journal of World Business*, 45: 143–49.

Michaels, E., Handfield-Jones, H., and Axelrod, B. (1997) *The War for Talent*, Harvard Business School Press.

Norton, M.I., Frost, J.H., and Ariely, D. (2007) Less is more, the lure of ambiguity, or why familiarity breeds contempt, *Journal of Personality and Social Psychology*, 92(1): 97–105.

O'Neill, J. (2004) Effect of gender and power on PR managers' upward influences, *Journal of Managerial Issues*, 16(1): 127–44.

Pfeffer, J. (2001) Fighting the war for talent is hazardous to your organization's health, *Organizational Dynamics*, 29(4): 248–59.

Pollitt, D. (2009) Bosch builds a talent bank of ex-employees, *Human Resource Management International Digest*, 17(5): 9–10.

Powell, G.N., Butterfield, D.A., and Parent, J.D. (2002) Gender and managerial stereotypes: have the times changed? *Journal of Management*, 28: 177–93.

Ready, D.A. and Conger, J.A. (2007) Make your company a talent factory, *Harvard Business Review*, 85(6): 68–77.

Schweyer, A. (2004) *Talent Management Systems*, Toronto, ONT: Wiley.

Simon, H.A. (1979) Rational decision-making in business organizations, *American Economic Review*, 69(4): 493–513.

Singh, R. and Ho, S.Y. (2000) Attitudes and attraction: a new test of the attraction, repulsion and similarity–dissimilarity asymmetry hypotheses, *British Journal of Social Psychology*, 39: 197–211.

Singh, V., Kumra, S., and Vinnicombe, S. (2002) Gender and impression management: playing the promotion game, *Journal of Business Ethics*, 37(1): 77–89.

Straus, J.P., Barrick, M.R., and Connerley, M.L. (2001) An investigation of personality similarity effects (relational and perceived) on peer and supervisor ratings and the role of familiarity and liking, *Journal of Occupational and Organizational Psychology*, 74: 637–57.

Swailes, S. and Orr, K. (2008) Talent management in the UK: public/private sector differences and implications for reward, in M. Vartiainen et al. (eds) *Reward Management—Facts and Trends in Europe*, Lengerich: PABST Publishing, pp. 275–93.

Tarique, I. and Schuler, R.S. (2010) Global talent management: literature review, integrative framework and suggestions for further research, *Journal of World Business*, 45: 122–33.

Towers Watson (2011) *Leading Through Uncertain Times: The 2011/2012 Talent Management and Rewards Study*, *North America*, New York: Towers Watson.

Turner, P.A. (2007) *Talent: Strategy, Management, Measurement*, London: CIPD.

Tyson, S. and Smith, P. (2006) *Talent Management*, London: Hodder Arnold.

Varma, A. and Pichler, S. (2007) Interpersonal affect, does it really bias performance appraisals? *Journal of Labor Research*, XXVIII(2): 397–412.

Wayne, S.J. and Liden, R.C. (1995) Effects of impression management on performance ratings: a longitudinal study, *Academy of Management Journal*, 38(1): 232–60.

World Economic Forum (2011) *Global Talent Risk—Seven Responses*, Geneva: World Economic Forum.

 Visit the Online Resource Centre for web links, interactive glossary, and more:
http://www.oxfordtextbooks.co.uk/orc/crawley

14 The dark side of international employment

Learning Outcomes

At the end of this chapter you will be able to:

- discuss the meaning of migrant labour and why it is perceived to be a problem
- understand the effect of worldwide migration on labour markets
- appreciate how migrant workers are being employed indirectly by multinational enterprises in the global supply chain
- show how migrant workers may be unfairly treated or exploited in various occupations
- explain the significance of temporary staffing agencies in the employment of migrant labour
- provide examples of how migrant workers are employed in a variety of countries.

Introduction

This chapter addresses, albeit briefly, an issue that is rarely included in a textbook on international human resource management (IHRM); that is, the growth of migration and the contribution of migrant labour to both western and developing economies. The 'dark side' refers to the exploitation and ill-treatment of employees, particularly migrant workers, across the world. The focus will be on legal migrant workers, but clearly many of the scenarios covered will also apply to marginalized workers, minority groups, and illegal migrants too.

Agriculture, construction, manufacturing, and the service sector across the world require low-skilled employees, and particularly employees willing to work in the difficult, demeaning, demanding, dirty, or dangerous occupations, which are shunned by local populations.

Despite different demographics across the globe, there are similarities in the challenges facing migrant labour and for the managers of organizations employing them. An examination of salary levels and working conditions among Bangladeshi garment workers illustrates the ways migrant labour is exploited, while further investigation shows the difficulties migrants face with lack of representation or opportunity to protest, usually for fear of losing their jobs (Macdonald, 2009: 17).

This chapter will look at migration to and from different regions of the world and will outline the dominant types of migrants and employment and particular problems encountered in these regions. The extent to which multinational organizations are involved in these operations, often through outsourcing contracts or sub-contracting arrangements, will be considered to show that this aspect of IHRM cannot be simply pushed aside, as something beyond HR's reach or responsibility. The term 'migrant worker' will be used in this chapter for simplicity. A section below on 'terminology' will explain the classification of migrant workers in more detail.

Scope of the subject

Migration occurs both within and between countries. Perhaps the largest recent migration within a country has occurred in China, as millions of workers from the poorer interior regions have flocked to the fast-expanding cities of the coastal states to work in construction and manufacturing, retail, and services during the past ten to fifteen years. In 2008, it was estimated by the National Bureau of Statistics, Boxun, that the rural migrant worker population had reached 140 million (Scheinson, 2009).

Within continents such as Africa there are as many as 13 million migrants, and 35 million within Asia, while it is estimated that there are 31 million within Europe. The scale of migration and the importance of remittances sent back to the home countries by migrants are shown in a short video available online (*The Economist*, 2009).

However, many Asians also travel outside Asia. Hugo estimates that there are as many as 20 million Asian migrant workers worldwide, with 8.7 million of these working in the Middle East (Hugo, 2005b: 10; Castles and Miller, 2009). Estimates vary, however. The ILO suggests that there is a total of about

> 100 million migrant workers worldwide, 20 million in Africa, 18 million in North America. Similarly there are 12 million in Central and South America, 7 million in South and East Asia, 9 million in the Middle East and 30 million in Europe.
>
> (Asian Migration News, 2005, cited in Hugo, 2005b: 2)

Clearly the accuracy of statistics depends on what is being counted. Statistics may include immigrants who settle in a country, both legal and illegal migrants, refugees, asylum seekers, and other migrants such as some women who accompany husbands, who are not themselves migrant workers.

According to the Global Commission on International Migration (GCIM), international migration contributes to the destination countries by filling gaps in the labour market and brings social, cultural, and intellectual dynamism to those societies. Immigration also contributes to the economic development of the countries they leave behind through the remittances they send back (GCIM, 2005: 23). It should not be forgotten, however, that migration also constitutes a huge brain drain for many developing countries, particularly in sectors such as health care, where nurses and doctors from all over the world are leaving their home countries for better opportunities abroad. However, research by Goldin et al. (2011, reviewed in *The Economist*, 26 May)) suggests that overall, the gains vastly outweigh the losses. They suggest that the brain drain actually helps poor countries, since the 'prospect of migration spurs people in poor countries to acquire marketable skills'; savings from and working abroad can provide contacts and funds for investment on return; and that migrants create jobs for the natives, for example IT entrepreneurs from India in the USA (Goldin et al., 2011).

The chapter continues with a discussion of why migrant labour is perceived to be an international problem; the difference between migrant workers and expatriates; the relevance and significance of migrant workers to IHRM and global supply chains; and the role and responsibility of multinationals in the use of migrant workers. It will then explain some of the challenges facing migrant workers.

The migrant labour problem

Migrant labour is widely recognized as a policy issue that needs to be tackled by governments (OECD, 2009: 2). Because of **globalization** there is a need for low-skilled labour across the world, but governments seem to be unwilling to adjust immigration policies sufficiently to support the needs of employers. As a result there is a combination of both legal temporary migration and illegal migration in nearly all developed and developing countries.

The OECD suggests that most governments favour high-skilled immigration but that they also need to recognize the demand for low-skilled migrants in some occupations and sectors (OECD, 2009: 3). Despite the downturn, businesses across Europe face a 'chronic shortage of engineers, technicians, craftspeople and medical staff'. According to the European head of Manpower there are four million unfilled jobs in Europe (Thiel, 2010). Failure to recognize this is illustrated in immigration laws, which make legal migration a complex process in all de- veloped and developing countries. Other authors suggest that the mismatch between more liberal trade policies and stricter migration policies results in more illegal migration to meet the demand for unskilled labour (Castles, 2004).

Similarly, a recent OECD report says:

> There is a growing recognition that offering limited possibilities of legal entry for low-skilled jobs when there is strong demand for such jobs may create a fertile ground for irregular mi- gration and that enforcing such a policy may be difficult and expensive.

> (OECD, 2009: 3)

Most countries address this problem by allowing the temporary entry of low-skilled workers. However, the OECD report suggests that these labour needs may in fact be permanent and as a result it is in the interests of both the immigrant and employer to maintain the employment relationship. It recommends that countries try to reduce irregular migration and illegal employ- ment and redirect them into legal channels to ensure better outcomes for the immigrants and their children. According to OECD Secretary-General, Angel Gurria (2009): 'Migration is not a tap that can be turned on and off at will'. 'We need responsive, fair and effective migration and integration policies—policies that work and adjust to both good economic times and bad ones. We also need to ensure that the benefits of migration are shared between sending and receiving countries.'

Castles (2004) also suggests why migrant labour is perceived as problematic and why it is an issue that is politicized in the west, especially by right-wing groups.

> Migration is seen as a crisis because it is symbolic of the erosion of nation-state sovereignty in the era of globalization. It is becoming increasingly difficult for states to control their borders, since flows of investment, trade, and intellectual property are inextricably linked with move- ments of people. Elites generally benefit from trans-border flows. It is the groups who feel threatened in their security by economic restructuring and social service cuts that generally oppose migration most vocally. The visible presence of migrants in Northern cities symbol- izes wider changes in economy, culture, and society.

> (Castles, 2004)

The social consequences of migration is an issue that cannot be addressed here; however, some discussion of these concerns can be found in the Eurofound report on the *Quality of life in Europe 2003–2007*, in the section on Social Tensions (Eurofound, 2009) and numerous other publications.

Public discomfort at the presence of large numbers of migrant workers can result in social unrest as local employees see wages reduced and foreign workers given preference for jobs. Governments are in conflict with employers' groups who wish to keep labour costs low and favour the presence of more compliant migrant workers, while governments wish to reduce the number of temporary migrants. Trade unions see their influence drop as local workers are replaced by migrant workers who are less likely to join unions and who have limited power to negotiate wages and conditions of employment because of the nature of their temporary contracts. Agents for migrant workers have little interest in the needs of the workers and tend to focus on the commissions they can obtain for the supply of cheap labour combined with the placement and other fees they can extract from the workers, legal or otherwise. This combination of factors results in the almost inevitable exploitation of migrant workers, as is explained below in Case Study 14.1.

 Discussion Activity 14.1

Do migrant workers come to your country and if so, why? What do you think is the effect of migrant workers on your country's economy? Who recruits the migrant workers? What is the proportion of legal migrant workers to illegal migrants in your country? What does your government do to control or restrict migrant workers?

In order to fully understand the literature on this subject it is important to understand the terms used to describe different types of workers and people from overseas. An overview of the terminology follows.

Terminology and types of migrant workers

There is a need to distinguish between the different types of immigrants, migrants, and expatriate employees. The terminology is often confusing and the topic is often politicized and used to raise alarm by the popular press in the UK. For example *asylum seekers* (who do not usually have a right to work in the UK) are often confused with *refugees*, who do. They may be confused with *illegal immigrants* and, more recently these people may even be confused with *potential terrorists* in the UK and the USA. Similarly in Spain, people without legal immigration papers, the *sin papeles*, have become the object of political debate, with some local authorities trying to deny them access to local social services (Gonzales, 2010). As in other countries with a sudden increase in foreigners in the local job market, there are claims that migrant workers are denying locals opportunities for jobs while there is increasing stress on health, education, and other social services, because of the growing numbers of immigrants and migrant workers, especially in the cities.

In HRM, there is specific terminology applied to types of expatriate such as PCNs (Parent Country Nationals), or TCNs (Third Country Nationals), or HCNs (Host Country Nationals who work in their own countries). *Self-initiated expatriates* is the term used for employees who have made their own arrangements to move and live overseas, and these may also be referred to as **local hires**. Local hires may also include **immigrants** (this applies strictly to people who leave one country to settle permanently in another), **migrants**, *foreign labour, or aliens*, usually employed temporarily on work permits for two to five years, often recruited through agents, sometimes in large groups for factory work in Asia. These may also include professionals such as nurses and IT engineers and analysts, some executives or technically qualified people, and teachers from overseas, but predominantly they comprise lower-skilled or unskilled labour. Detailed reports on national policy issues posed by migrant workers can be found at Migration Information Source (2012) and the UK Border Agency (2012).

Patterns of migration in the EU

The pattern of migration within the enlarged European Union has changed during the past few years, with many migrants from the Eastern European countries searching for work opportunities in the West. Somerville et al. (2009) state that about 700,000 workers from Eastern Europe have settled in the UK since 2004, the majority of whom are Polish. More than half of the 1.5 million people from 'new' European countries have now returned home and are contributing to their own countries' growth. (More details of migration to the UK are given in Case Study 14.1 below.) The special features of this new type of migration, which occurred

 Case Study 14.1   UK's New Europeans

According to Sumption and Somerville (2010) 'UK's New Europeans', this group of East European immigrants is unlike previous groups who have settled in Britain, for a number of reasons. They receive low wages, are employed in unskilled occupations despite having high levels of education, and often have precarious housing arrangements. They lack support networks and they are vulnerable to exploitation.

Compared with the UK population they are relatively young and receive lower wages than their counterparts, despite being more highly qualified. Unlike previous groups of migrants who have come from further away, these migrants appear to make 'circular' visits to the UK and may be employed on short, seasonal contracts. There is considerable uncertainty about the duration of their stay. Statistics show that the number of immigrants tends to increase in the summer when there is seasonal work in agriculture and tourism. In terms of finding work, these immigrants have had to rely on their own social networks (partly because of poor English skills) and often depend on specific agencies for finding employment, which has determined where they have found work.

Research by Eade et al. (2006) suggests that the these new immigrants are a heterogeneous group in terms of immigration strategy and intentions; some of whom come to work for short periods of two to six months, such as students; others stay longer, perhaps to earn income for a project at home; others are ambitious and wish to progress, so come with the intention to stay; while others come with an open mind, willing to look for career opportunities in either country, the largest group.

This group of immigrants may be disadvantaged by utilizing private agencies to search for work. Agency work in the UK is often temporary and agencies are typically used by low-skill industries in which there is little opportunity for upward mobility. While agency work does allow the opportunity to change jobs, it does not improve the long-term prospects of a much better job. These workers are often exploited by employers or agents who fail to pay wages, fail to pay the minimum wage, or make disproportionate deductions for housing (Sumption and Somerville, 2010). However, these immigrants have reportedly integrated successfully into the UK job market but into low-skill jobs.

Adapted from: Sumption and Somerville (2010)

in the UK, are now outlined in Case Study 14.1, to show how these migrants are particularly vulnerable to exploitation and shoddy treatment.

Local HR departments are responsible for the employment of such low-skilled migrant workers, but normally they are under pressure to keep staff costs down; using such workers contributes to the company's bottom line. HR departments work within the company's overall employment strategy and often do little more than ensure that all legal requirements are met, in terms of work permits and social security payments. Codes of conduct that are applied and are more than a statement of intentions could improve the treatment of migrant workers (Kaptein, 2010). However, the solution to equity or similar issues comes at corporate level, combined with tighter employment legislation at a national level, and regulation systems to ensure that minimum wage and other requirements are met.

Terminology in the USA

In the USA, the term **resident non-immigrant** covers foreign nationals granted *temporary* entry into the USA. It is used to describe both students and labour employed temporarily in the USA, is particularly associated with agricultural work, but includes workers in 'speciality occupations', which means they are professionals, including doctors, many people in IT, including engineers and systems analysts, and sometimes programmers, who obtain H1 Visas (Monger and Barr, 2008). (See Case Study 14.3, America's high-tech sweatshops, below.)

In the USA people who are employed on a temporary basis are eligible to apply for **immigrant status**. If successful, they are lawfully admitted for permanent residence and employment in the USA. This is often referred to as having a Green Card. After five years with this status, a USA immigrant can apply for citizenship. However, as is the case in some other countries, these immigrants, also referred to as 'aliens', do not have the right to bring their spouses or dependants to live in the USA during this five-year period, while those on shorter, temporary work visas sometimes do have this right.

Terms used to describe immigrant or migrant labour are not always used accurately in the public domain, particularly in the popular press, and vary between countries. Short-term, seasonal migrant workers, migrant workers employed on annual or two-year work permits, and immigrants who are likely to settle in a country comprise distinct groups.

Illegal immigrants

Illegal immigrants are often employed illegally or on the fringes of legality; these are the people most likely to be exploited or abused. They include people who have entered a country illegally, as well as those who have entered legally on tourist or student visas and overstayed. There are also many ways in which people who are not legally allowed to work in a country manage to work around regulations and find employment. They develop their own network and become integrated into the community. For example in the UK, especially in London, there are thousands who manage to obtain some documents, by borrowing or renting other peoples' papers and thus have a National Insurance number and pay tax and social security deductions, yet are illegally in the country (Vasta, 2008: 10). There are ongoing efforts by government agencies to ensure that employers and illegal workers are punished. Examples of their 'successes', including arrests of restaurant workers without work visas, or people who have entered the country illegally, can be found in the news articles section of the UK Border Agency website (UK Border Agency, 2011). However, these illegal workers are perhaps the easiest to exploit or to employ with less than favourable conditions.

Modern-day slavery

Finally, one group which will not be discussed in depth in this chapter is that comprising those who are *trafficked* against their will, such as women and girls who are trafficked and tricked into working in prostitution, or people considered chattel, or caught in generational debt bondage arrangements.

There is also a form of human trafficking that is more difficult to identify and estimate. According to the International Labour Organisation (ILO):

> The majority of human trafficking in the world takes the form of **forced labour**, according to the ILO's estimates. Also known as **involuntary servitude**, forced labour may result when un-scrupulous employers take advantage of gaps in law enforcement to exploit vulnerable workers.
> US Department of State 2009

> Forced labour is a form of human trafficking that is often harder to identify and estimate than sex trafficking. It may not involve the same criminal networks profiting from transnational sex trafficking. Instead, it may involve individuals who subject workers to involuntary servitude, perhaps through forced or coerced household or factory work.
> (US Department of State, 2009).

The findings of the Trafficking in Persons Report are a sensitive issue for many Southeast Asian governments, which are likely to suffer cuts in US assistance if they are unresponsive to calls to fight trafficking. Countries such as the Philippines and Singapore are now off the 'watch list' and are included in Tier 2 countries. This means they still do not fully meet standards on human trafficking but are making efforts to do so. Malaysia, Thailand, Vietnam, and China however, are all on the Tier 2 'Watch List' (US Department of State, 2011).

The Trafficking in Persons Report explains the main forms of trafficking and how even *legal migrant workers* can become trapped into forms of work that are effectively slavery. While this topic cannot be discussed at length here, it is worthwhile bearing in mind that exploita-tion of migrant labour, especially where this involves threats, coercion, and lack of freedom, constitutes slavery. Many of the legal migrants discussed below *may* fall into this category. (For further information on this topic, see the further reading at the end of this chapter.)

For the rest of this chapter the term 'migrant worker' will be used to encompass all types of legally employed immigrant or foreign workers. Where a different term is used, a reason will be given.

 Discussion Activity 14.2

What types of businesses are the major employers of migrant workers in your country? Are they paid the same rates as natives of your country? To what extent, if at all, do you think immigrants and migrant workers are exploited? Why does this happen?

The difference between an expatriate and a migrant worker

There are many differences between the expatriate sent abroad by his/her organization and the migrant worker. The migrant worker does not have the cushion of an employer to return to at the end of the assignment. His or her job and work permit may or may not be renewed for another contract period. The migrant worker has few if any benefits associated with the employment contract, other than the basic accommodation that is sometimes provided. Social security and health benefits are usually minimal. The migrant worker is not expected to adjust or fit into the society in which he/she works, but is almost a non-person, there to fill a job role, rarely considered part of the society in which he/she works. The migrant worker's adjustment to the new culture is rarely considered a factor in his or her ability to perform well. The performance of migrant workers is not frequently evaluated in any formal way, except when renewal of a visa is under discussion.

In the case of migrant workers on temporary work permits, there is rarely any hope of long-term settlement in that country, even though they often work in a country for up to ten years. Despite this, in some occupations the worker has considerable personal contact with the local population as part of his/her work role, for example if employed as a domestic or care worker, in the health care, retail, or hospitality sectors; but the degree to which this relationship extends into friendship with local people varies. In parts of Asia, local arrogance, racial discrimination, and caste differences can result in all but minimal interaction between these groups of migrant workers and local people. In many situations in Malaysia, the migrant worker will interact almost exclusively with other migrant workers of the same type or nationality, and may have accommodation provided, such as shared housing or dormitories with other migrants, and little free time to interact with anyone else. Unlike expatriates, migrant workers are rarely allowed to bring spouses or dependants to the destination country.

Relevance of migrant workers to IHRM

Immigrant and migrant workers constitute a significant element in supporting the economies of many developed and developing countries. They may be employed directly, or indirectly through agencies, and consequently often contribute to the functioning of the global supply chain of multinational organizations. They are often employed by contractors and subcontractors of multinational organizations, as out sourcing and off-shoring have increasingly been used to move operations, or to obtain supplies and services, from overseas. Additionally, migrant labour makes a significant contribution to local organizations, both large and small, facing labour shortages, particularly in the agriculture and food manufacturing industry, hospitality, health, and IT sectors, which increasingly rely on migrant workers.

While the adjustment of expatriates, from the West to the East or from one culture to another, and from more to less developed countries, is discussed at length in the IHRM literature, there is little discussion of other migrant workers. They are not included as a topic of IHRM and have generally been excluded from mainstream IHRM journals and textbooks. Why is so little attention paid to such a large number of employees worldwide? An occasional mention may be found under the topic of diversity management, international employee representation, and more recently within the context of outsourcing, where the costs and benefits are now being questioned in the context of managing outsourcing quality and contracts (Sissons, 2006: 248; Goel et al., 2008: 32–5). The reason for this omission can be partly explained by looking at the main difference between an expatriate and a migrant worker. The *expatriate is clearly the responsibility of the headquarters* of the organization, while *migrant workers, at the local or subsidiary site, are generally of local concern*, left to be managed by local HR managers.

IHRM discourse is usually restricted to the issues surrounding expatriate employment, but fails to address the major issue of managing a much larger international workforce at other levels in the organization. As today's multinationals are directly and indirectly employers of large numbers of workers from across the globe, it is the author's view that the scope of the subject needs to be extended. HR managers, both in the UK and across the world, are already responsible for many more international employees than 'expatriates', and clearly there is a need for more discussion and debate on the diversity issues that this implies, as well as the need for more interaction between managers handling national and international HRM.

The human resource departments (HRDs) and line managers of companies employing migrant workers handle both administrative complexity and diversity issues, often on a much larger scale than an MNE HQ, which handles relatively few expatriates. The legal status and local immigration requirements for work permits in all countries are often complex and involve tedious processes. Sometimes these activities are subcontracted by HR departments to other local agencies or contacts within government departments, which specialize in providing these services; arrangements with temporary staffing agencies (TSAs) vary by country (Rubery, et al., 2010: 86; Hugo, 2005b). According to the ILO (2009) the economic crisis has resulted in the loss of jobs by many migrant workers and a return to their home countries, as well as a reduction in remittances sent home by others. The impact of the crisis varies in depth by country and sector. In addition, 'Little information also exists regarding the employment conditions of migrant workers, who may be willing to take precarious work conditions and pay cuts rather than face unemployment' (ILO, 2009: 2).

Society may exhibit racist attitudes towards its migrant workers (Vasta, 2006; Sumption and Somerville, 2010). Thus, their employment raises issues of justice in the management of diversity as well as migrant workers' representation rights, unionization, and other employment rights such as leave, overtime pay, and health care (Human Rights Watch, 2011; Rubery et al., 2010). Migrant workers are generally treated less favourably by managers and co-workers than are native workers, illustrating the lack of awareness and training in diversity as well as racial discrimination in many instances (EHRC, 2010; Rubery et al., 2010: 93).

There are failures by employers of migrant labour to manage the performance of these workers and pay sufficient attention to their wellbeing. This includes failure to manage safety and health, stress and adjustment issues, as well as poor management of their pay and conditions of work and also the existence of corporate social responsibility (CSR) codes (Edwards et al., 2007: 9; Rubery et al., 2010: 94). The lack of consideration for the welfare of migrant workers seems to suggest a view that there is a neverending supply of people from poorer countries who are easily replaced and whose welfare, training, and development have little importance. However, conditions vary between countries and depend on local laws and terms of contracts. The national institutional factors that impact on migration and the outsourcing of work in European countries, with some specific case examples from the IT/call centre industry, elderly care, and IT outsourcing are discussed in depth by Rubery et al. (2010: 89–95). The article includes not only an overview of institutional differences and the resulting policies but also the impact on work organization and terms and conditions of employment of these policies, as well as efficiency and equity issues raised by the cases. (See discussions throughout Chapter 5, 'Understanding IHRM: the institutional approach', for more on the impact of institutional issues on employment.)

While it has been indicated that responsibility for the migrant worker falls under the remit of the local HRM, it is also important to know how these migrants come to be employed in the company. We now consider the role of temporary staffing agencies in this process.

The role of temporary staffing agencies in outsourcing and migration

In an analysis of the effect of institutional factors and varieties of capitalism on migration and outsourcing, Rubery et al. (2010: 83–6) illustrate how migration differs between countries because of these factors, and include discussion of the significant role of TSAs. The massive growth of TSAs across the world is illustrated in their global turnover figures estimated to have been US$83.2 billion in 1996 and US$228 billion in 2006 (Rubery et al., 2010: 85). These agencies facilitate the migration and placement of workers across the globe. They enable 'employers to tap into an external source of labour without incurring the costs and risks of direct international recruitment and enable workers to locate a source of employment' (Rubery et al., 2010: 83). While an elite group of twenty agencies from the USA, Western Europe, and Japan accounts for 40 per cent of the global market, it is the

> small and medium sized agencies that are more likely to be involved in the direct mobilization of migrant workers across borders ... All types of agency, from transnational to SMEs, are, however, involved in placing migrant workers when they arrive at their final destination.
>
> (Rubery et al., 2010: 83-4)

The reasons for organizations to use TSAs can vary and the opportunities, for example to offer lower terms and conditions, depend on the national context.

> In many jobs, however, less skilled workers will be employed on lower terms and conditions than directly employed staff ... Migrant workers are particularly likely to be used to reduce the costs associated with long and flexible hours of work, that is by being excluded from unsocial hours premia.
>
> (Rubery et al., 2010: 87)

An additional role of the TSAs is to increase employment flexibility. According to Rubery et al. (2010: 89), TSAs, through their institutional presence, are changing the structure and operation of labour markets. They are involved in industry associations and lobby to increase their activities, publicizing their role in promoting flexible employment practices. However, the fact that TSAs operate most in areas where there are opportunities to change the terms and conditions of employment provides evidence that 'employers are motivated to use TSAs to reduce labour cost not through smarter working but through reduced rewards for work'

(Rubery et al., 2010: 89). However, the article cautions that the lower wages for temporary workers can also generate indirect costs in terms of higher employee turnover, thus requiring higher training costs or loss of quality standards. (For more information on issues related to reward, see discussions throughout Chapter 7, 'International reward management'.)

In the USA, the role of the Federal Government in controlling the conditions of migrant workers has been raised in research by Kerwin and McCabe (2011). They claim that while the US law sets significant standards such as minimum wage, overtime pay, child labour, safe and healthy workplaces, and antidiscrimination for legal employees, it needs to extend core labour protection to unauthorized workers. However, budgetary limitations at both federal and state levels 'constrain the ability of enforcement agencies to carry out their mandates'. They also state:

> The fact that many unauthorized immigrants work in jobs not covered by these standards places them in jeopardy, drives down wages and working conditions for other employees, and undermines the US labor standards enforcement system as a whole. Strengthened and well-enforced standards could safeguard vulnerable workers, while ensuring that scofflaw employers do not benefit at the expense of companies that are complying with the rules.
>
> (Kerwin with McCabe, 2011: 3)

They also argue that Congress should increase penalties for violations of labour standards to promote compliance.

The use of outsourcing agents and their responsibilities has recently received publicity in Malaysia (Malaysia has approximately two million legal migrant workers and an estimated two million illegal ones, in a total population of 29 million.) There has been discussion about whether the outsourcing agent for the 'imported migrant workers' can be considered the employer, rather than the company that actually provides the work. In a legal case between a Japanese MNE and a human rights activist, Charles Hector Fernandez (Hector, 2011), who was defending Burmese migrant workers facing deportation, the Japanese MNE asserted that 'migrant workers (who) were not the company's responsibility because they were supplied by an outside firm and not placed on the company's direct payroll'. Hector maintained that

> the company should indeed be regarded the migrant workers' 'actual employer' as they (the employees) are directly under the company's control and doing work for them during working hours. The company must be responsible for all the workers working in their factory.
>
> (Hector, 2011)

This case raises important issues regarding the country's laws with regard to the employment relationship and the ultimate responsibility for the welfare of migrant workers. The case was 'settled' in August 2011, but without clarity regarding the key issue in the case, of who is ultimately the employer of the migrant workers.

The CNN Press Room (2011) also exposed another Malaysian outsourcing issue in October 2011, regarding Cambodians working in an MNE. Although their wages and employment conditions were subsequently improved, the staff were still unable to return home. They were trapped by their debt to the outsourcing agency that had 'technically' employed them.

These cases lead us to the next part of the chapter, the role and responsibility of multinationals.

The role and responsibility of multinationals

International outsourcing companies often supply labour to multinationals and large organizations offering facilities management, which includes cleaning, catering, engineering, landscaping, and support services. These companies employ large numbers of low-skilled workers to service their contracts across the globe and have to maintain low labour costs to achieve high margins. Migrant labour inevitably supports their operations. At the same time, the agriculture, food processing, hotel, and tourism industries are also dominated by large multinational groups that depend on agency staff for their seasonal and constantly changing needs. The hospitality sector, for example, is suffering from declining standards of service worldwide as a result.

What is the role of the multinational organization in the employment and possible exploitation of migrant or other overseas workers? While most often the responsibility is indirect, multinationals bear considerable responsibility for this phenomenon. According to a report on overseas textile workers employed to supply clothing to Britain's stores, the rate of pay given to overseas workers needs to be raised substantially.

The authors, Labour behind the Label (LBL), state that the employees are not paid a living wage and explain:

> Wages are low because they are kept that way through a global competition that engages workers, factories and whole countries in a race to the bottom—a race where the winners are those that can produce as quickly, cheaply and flexibly as possible.

> (LBL, 2009: 1)

and

> 'Wages in the garment industry are not low because of poor productivity. They are low because the structure of the industry creates intense competition between brands and retailers, governments, employers and workers'

> (LBL, 2009: 9).

This report goes on to provide examples of what UK high-street retailers are doing, or not doing, towards raising the wages of their garment workers to a living wage. The majority of garment workers are women and girls and many may also be migrant workers, depending on the country in which they are employed.

In recent years some steps have been taken to rectify the situation through the establishment of the Fair Labor Association (FLA) and the establishment of Codes of Conduct, which are applied to affiliates. The FLA conducts regular audits of affiliated multinationals' subcontractors' factories both in the USA and overseas. These audits cover compensation and working hours, abuse and harassment of workers, freedom of association, and health and safety and are published on its website in its Independent External Monitoring (IEM) Reports or Tracking Charts (FLA, 2012). However, the FLA can only evaluate multinationals that are affiliates and clearly there are many others who would rather remain unknown. The FLA and its supporters have made it clear that it is no longer acceptable for global businesses to deny responsibility for its employment activities further down the supply chain. (For more information on CSR and MNEs, see discussions throughout Chapter 11, 'Corporate social responsibility and ethics'.)

A recent example of the work of the FLA occurred with their identification of poor labour conditions, mostly low pay and excessive hours, in Foxconn factories in China making Apple i-Pads (BBC News, 2012a, 2012b). However, recommendations regarding cooperation between workers and managers seem unlikely to be implemented given the cultural environment and Power Distance that exists in China. There needs to be more understanding by the FLA of the realities of a work environment, often governed by fear, in the context of a highly undemocratic society. The suggestion by some reporters of 'empowering the workforce' in an environment where workers are not represented by 'real' trade unions is also somewhat unrealistic (see discussions throughout Chapter 4, 'Understanding IHRM: the cultural approach' for more information on culture and HRM).

In the UK, the Gangmasters Licensing Authority (GLA) works closely with major supermarket chains and the food industry to ensure that their suppliers in agriculture, food processing, packaging, and fisheries do not use illegal labour or exploit migrant labour (GLA, 2011). What can MNEs do to prevent the use of debt-bonded labour or other forms of slavery practised by their distant subsidiaries' outsourced operations?

According to Hemphill and Lillevik (2011): 213) the MNE can take action at the organizational and individual level to ensure the improvement of working conditions through a comprehensive HRM plan, supporting the ethical framework of the Global Ethic Manifesto. They stress the importance of the 'moral individual' and managerial decision maker within the social system of the organization, and their values and level of integrity. The manifesto, which supports the global compact, includes CSR as a fundamental principle.

Wieland (2009, cited in Hemphill and Lillevik, 2011: 222) identifies how 'organizational values can be disseminated via a Values Management System (VMS), to ensure ethical compliance at all organizational levels', within a strategic HRM context. However, to extend such values across the organization's subsidiaries all over the world will be a challenging process for any company.

The chapter now continues with some examples of migrant labour issues that occur in different regions of the world, with reference to the direct or indirect role of MNEs.

Migrant workers in the UK, USA, and the Middle East

Migrant workers in the UK

The UK, like other western European countries, has seen considerable changes in workforce demographics in the past five years. This is mainly as a result of the enlargement of the EU.

According to a research paper by the Migration Policy Institute:

> Eastern European migrants have worked mainly in low-paid jobs in sectors such as hospitality and catering, administration, and construction. In 2008, only 12 percent of Eastern European immigrants worked in highly skilled occupations, and more than half worked in 'routine' ones.
>
> (Sumption and Somerville, 2010: 16; Somerville et al., 2009)

(An example of this was given in Case Study 14.1, UK's New Europeans.)

 Stop and Think

1. Care of the elderly is a growing problem in the west. How are the elderly cared for in your country? For example is it usual or acceptable to place elderly parents in a special home?

2. Who is going to care for *your parents* when they become old? Who will you be able to ask for help with the care of your elderly relatives?

In the UK, migrant workers are mainly employed in agriculture, food processing, factory work, hotel and catering, domestic, and social care. The key findings from research by Oxfam on care workers are presented in Case Study 14.2 below.

The impact of poorly managed care services impacts both the lives of the elderly and migrant workers, many of whom are now affected by the five-year rule visa restrictions related to minimum qualifications for care workers. Thus the availability of care workers will be further

---

 Case Study 14.2   Care workers in the UK

Recent research by Oxfam has revealed 'clear indications of the exploitation of workers by gangmasters in the care, hospitality, and construction sectors'. As a result, further calls have been made for the protection of workers, particularly of workers from overseas, in social care, who according to Oxfam are being similarly exploited (Poinasamy with Fooks, 2009).

As the population of Western Europe ages, increasing numbers of carers will be required for the elderly in care homes or in their own homes. According to Poinasamy with Fooks (2009), there are already 1.5 million workers in the adult social care workforce in the UK. Much of this work has been privatized by local authorities to private care agencies. The jobs of care workers are associated with low pay and low status, so that it is difficult to attract UK workers. As a result, nearly one-fifth of workers in this sector are migrants, recruited by gangmasters and agencies. The research indicates that these care workers experienced significant abuse and exploitation at work. According to Poinasamy with Fooks (2009: 2), the experience of care workers typically involves:

> excessive hours, extreme pressure to work overtime, an expectation that the worker will be constantly on call, spurious deductions taken from pay for petrol and other expenses, and non-payment of holiday and sick pay—all whilst workers are being paid no more than the minimum wage.

These findings are supported by Kelayaan, which also researched the treatment of migrant workers in domestic care (Gordolan and Lalani, 2009: 8). This research found that migrant domestic workers:

> frequently suffer from abuse (sexual, physical, and emotional), discrimination, low pay (or none), exceptionally long working hours, social isolation, and mental health problems arising from the extreme conditions of their employment. Many experience very poor working conditions, such as having to sleep on floors and not being provided with bedrooms, and being given no time off, sick pay or access to healthcare.

The exploitation of migrant workers in care homes has often come about as a result of 'collusion between overseas recruitment agencies and contract and training agencies in the UK and the care home' (Poinasamy with Fooks, 2009: 6).

The principal violations of employment rights included coercion and intimidation, excessive hours and pressure to work overtime, problems with wages, denial of holidays or sick pay, accommodation issues, contract and self-employment problems, and deception regarding the terms of recruitment.

The report comments: 'The lack of an effective employment rights enforcement regime which proactively investigates employers to uncover abuse and exploitation, clearly allows unscrupulous employers to exploit vulnerable care workers' (Poinasamy with Fooks, 2009: 11).

The two reports by Oxfam and Kelayaan make a strong case for more protection for migrant workers and all workers in the care sector in the UK, by extending the remit of the GLA to cover care workers.

Adapted from: Poinasamy with Fooks for Oxfam (2009); Gordolan and Lalani (2009)

The copy on page 336 is adapted by the publisher from *Who Cares? How best to protect UK care workers employed through agencies and gangsters from exploitation, 2009,* with the permission of Oxfam GB, Oxfam House, John Smith Drive, Cowley, Oxford OX4 2JY, UK www.oxfam.org.uk. Oxfam GB does not necessarily endorse any text or activities that accompany the materials, nor has it approved the adapted text.

restricted. At the same time reports of inadequate elderly home care are being published. An inquiry by the Equality and Human Rights Commission (EHRC) has found that 'Care of older people in their homes is so poor their human rights are being overlooked'. It had uncovered worrying cases of neglect and lack of respect for older people's privacy and dignity and concludes that there are major problems in the home care system (BBC News, 2011).

Rubery et al. (2010: 98–9) have also noted that:

> It is not clear, however, that the recipients of care will receive both continuity and quality of care until the more fundamental problems of valuing care work as a profession are resolved. It may still be the case that care workers will include migrant workers, but without professionalizing the work, the problems of casualization and insecurity in the quality of the delivery of care are likely to continue.

Some suggestions for improving this situation are made in the recommendations of the Oxfam report. In addition, the EU Directive regarding agency workers, which came into effect in October 2011, provides agency workers with the same rights as other staff if they have worked for the same employer for at least twelve weeks (EU, 2011).

Migrant workers in the USA

The USA is a land that was founded on the hard work of migrant settlers and since the eighteenth century has been a land that encouraged people from all over the world to come and settle to make a living.

Today, the USA's migrant workers are not a homogenous group. They come from a diverse range of countries, with different intentions. The largest group comes from Mexico and in recent years a large proportion has also come from India, with the Mexicans being predominantly employed in agricultural work, while the migrants from India are found predominantly in the IT sector.

In 2008, the increase in workers from India rose to 12 per cent of the total number of resident non-immigrants in the USA, equal to the number of Mexicans in that category (Monger and Barr, 2008). 'The leading countries of citizenship for **H1-B admissions** (Workers in Speciality Occupations) in 2008 were India (38 percent), Canada (5.7 percent), and the United Kingdom (4.7 percent).'

In the USA migrant labour working in agriculture and especially seasonal work is recognized as being among the poorest paid in the USA. Agricultural workers, often illegal workers, face uncertainty, low wages, exploitation, and often lack representation.

Other migrant workers in the USA who face exploitation include domestic workers, construction workers, and more recently workers in the IT industry, employed by 'body

 Discussion Activity 14.3

In this case, the employees from India were relatively highly skilled and yet they were still misled by agents and sweatshop owners.

To what extent should the end-users of these employees (i.e. the large multinationals, banks, and insurance companies) be held responsible for the poor treatment of these employees? What can be done to reduce this type of exploitation? What does this case tell you about the dangers for multinationals of sub-contracting work to agencies?

shops'—small agencies that recruit staff directly from India in order to subcontract them to large multinational clients. The plight of these workers is outlined in Case Study 14.3 below.

Migrant workers in the Middle East

The development of the Middle East in the past ten years has only been made possible by the hundreds of thousands of temporary migrant workers (sometimes called inpatriates) from

---

 Case Study 14.3 America's high-tech sweatshops

Visa fraud is a big issue facing the USA. Recently, a court case in New Jersey brought to light a typical scenario of visa fraud in the IT industry. The case illustrates how temporary migrant workers are being employed sometimes illegally and often unfairly by large multinationals, through 'body shops', set up to indirectly supply their 'clients' with contract workers.

According to a report in Business Week (Hamm and Herbst, 2009) on America's high-tech sweatshops, low-profile companies recruit workers from abroad to provide tech support and programming and other services to US corporations. While some of these companies work within the law, others commit visa violations by charging the applicant exorbitant fees for the visa, siphoning off their pay, or paying them the incorrect rate for the area in which they work. In some cases no work is provided once the visa has been obtained.

This has occurred as large companies have outsourced their tech systems and back-office operations to firms that recruit workers from India on temporary work visas. These companies are known as 'body shops' because of their role. As a result, prominent American companies end up doing business with 'tech service outlets', which may violate visa laws.

Individuals have alleged that they were underpaid, suffered from delayed payments, and postponed health benefits, or have not been paid at all after working for large international banks as contract employees. Since several layers of companies are involved, the client may have no way of knowing how his 'employees' are being treated.

The legal scenario is complex since the visa system 'ties into a human supply chain that reaches halfway around the world'.

The article concludes that foreign workers cannot wait for the US government to tackle the issue of high-tech sweatshops; rather, they are taking matters into their own hands by setting up websites to discuss their experiences with various companies, thus warning future potential victims of the scams related to H-1B visas (Hamm and Herbst, 2009). In September 2010, the fees for H-1B visas were increased significantly, partly to deter the entry of so many IT migrants being exploited in this way (Bierce and Kenerson, 2010).

In support of the fee changes, Senator Schumer said:

> Congress does not want the H1-B program to be a vehicle for creating multinational temp agencies where workers do not know what projects they will be working on or what cities they will be working in when they enter the country ... But if they are using the H1-B visa to run a glorified international temp agency for tech workers in contravention of the spirit of this program, I and my colleagues believe they should have to pay a higher fee to ensure that American workers are not losing their jobs because of the unintended uses of the visa program that were never contemplated when the program was created.

(Bierce and Kenerson, 2010)

Adapted from: Hamm and Herbst (2009); Bierce and Kenerson (2010)

Asia, mainly Bangladesh, Pakistan, India, and the Philippines, who have worked on construction sites, in health care and as domestic labour. In addition these countries have relied on highly skilled expatriates from the West to develop their oil, health, financial, and business sectors. Saudi Arabia launched a Saudization policy in 2004 and other Gulf States are following suit (Pakkiasamy, 2004; Emiratisation, 2010).

The lack of qualified locals combined with the lack of opportunities to work for women in these Islamic states makes localization something that will only be achieved in the long term. This is exacerbated by the reluctance of local workers to do the available jobs. The demand for low-skilled workers and domestic workers is unlikely to decline in the short term.

Despite the attraction of relatively well-paid work opportunities in the Middle East, newspapers frequently report on the maltreatment and poor working conditions of migrant workers. During the recent global recession, it is the migrant workers who have been left without work first, as the construction sector was the first hit. Often workers are sent home without pay before their contracts have been completed (Kerr, 2009; Malik, 2009). Even in the good times, the treatment of migrant workers has been harsh.

According to the Trafficking in Persons Report (US Department of State, 2009):

> Men and women from Bangladesh, India, Sri Lanka, Nepal, Pakistan, the Philippines, Indonesia, Sudan, Ethiopia, and many other countries voluntarily travel to Saudi Arabia as domestic servants or other low-skilled laborers, but some subsequently face conditions indicative of involuntary servitude, including restrictions on movement, withholding of passports, threats, physical or sexual abuse, and non-payment of wages.

According to Nesrine Malik (2009) of *The Guardian*,

> Usually employed in a semi-formal manner with large companies, Asian workers in United Arab Emirates fall within a vacuum of employment law and social welfare and hence become the first casualties of a recession. Usually indebted to their agents or 'sponsors', i.e. those who have purchased visas on their behalf, and bereft of passports or identification documents confiscated by their employers, they now inhabit a 'grey economy' ... As freedom of movement is denied, a situation has developed where workers are forced to remain and take itinerant cash-in-hand jobs, undercutting other workers by eschewing basic provisions such as healthcare in a grim race to the bottom.

> (Malik, 2009)

The role of multinationals in the Middle East

The role of multinationals in the employment or mistreatment of unskilled labour in the Middle East is difficult to illustrate directly. However, it is clear that the massive construction projects often awarded to international companies or consortia and financed by international banks are the main users of migrant labour. The recent debt crisis in Dubai has revealed the link between their development projects and international finance as it impacted strongly on international stock markets (Oteify and Walid, 2009). As such the massive building corporations, construction companies, contractors, project management companies, and finance companies need to take some responsibility for the employment environment they have created and within which they are so happy to operate.

The large hotels, office complexes, airports, and facilities management companies in the Middle East also employ domestic workers, women from the Phillipines, Indonesia, Thailand, and China to work as cleaners on their premises. (The author has seen groups of cleaners from the Philippines in Doha airport, for example, as well as Bangladeshi, Indian, and Nepalese staff working in the airport's other food and retail outlets.) It is often multinational organizations that own or manage these types of major facilities.

 Discussion Activity 14.4

Why are job opportunities so attractive for migrant labour in the Middle East? What other factors in the Middle East culture and religion make it especially difficult for women to work there? Would you like to work there? Explain your reasons why/why not.

Summary

The chapter begins with an overview of the scope of the chapter and identifies the main types of migrants and their employment problems. It introduces the view that multinationals are often indirectly involved in the employment of migrant labour and need to take some responsibility for these employees. Migrant workers seem to have become an essential element of the 'flexible workforce' promoted in the name of efficiency for multinationals across the world. But it is clear also that the availability of migrant workers offers an opportunity for not only lower costs, but exploitation. As long as there are substantial differences in standards of living between East and West, there will be opportunities for moving work abroad or using cheaper or migrant labour at home or overseas, relying on the desperation of many to work for something, rather than nothing.

The extent of worldwide migration and the reasons why it is perceived to be a problem are examined next, citing globalization, the needs of employers, and unrealistic government polices as being responsible for this negative perception.

The gradual loss of manufacturing opportunities in the West because of the growth of Asia is causing havoc in labour markets in Europe and America. Yet western-based multinationals are still encouraged to lower costs by investing overseas, in countries without labour protection, with minimal regulation of the environmental costs, health and safety, or concern for CSR. However, governments ultimately have to ensure that minimum labour standards are adhered to and that labour is not exploited or forced into a system of modern-day slavery.

Migration issues in general and the importance of having a Green Card in the USA are outlined. The way in which illegal immigrants in the UK manage to find some form of legality, by borrowing national insurance numbers, is also revealed. A brief discussion of modern-day slavery and human trafficking is included, since there is often an overlap between illegal migration and extreme forms of exploitation with slavery.

The key differences between an expatriate's position and that of a migrant worker are then identified in terms of security, conditions of work, and place in society.

The relevance of migrant workers to IHRM due to their increasingly important contribution to global supply chains is reiterated. The significant and extensive role of local HR and line managers in administration and diversity management for numerous migrant workers is mentioned in comparison with the relatively limited headquarters HR role of managing a much smaller number of expatriates.

The impact of different national regulations on migrant workers and the importance of TSAs in outsourcing and migration are discussed, including their role in promoting flexibility and reducing labour costs. In this context the lack of enforcement of labour standards in the USA among unauthorized workers is raised. The role of outsourcing agencies for MNEs in Malaysia is also cited.

The role and responsibility of multinationals in the employment of workers at the end of the supply chain is discussed next, including reference to the living wage campaign for retail workers supplying the UK. The roles of the FLA and the GLA are included. Examples of some migrant worker issues in the UK, the USA, and Middle East are outlined, with examples of each and a discussion of the involvement of MNEs.

The chapter concludes with calls for more monitoring of the activities of multinationals to prevent exploitation across borders and a more humane approach by governments towards their migrant workers. The study of IHRM must include the management of migrant workers and the whole international workforce to truly reflect the full scope of work of both domestic and international HR managers across the world. Migrant workers deserve to have lives and work where they are treated with dignity. The study of IHRM cannot continue to ignore the management of all these international employees.

Review questions

1. What is the difference between an immigrant and a migrant worker? Why is this distinction important in the discussion of labour markets?

2. The OECD suggests that governments in their immigration policies are not responding to the needs of the labour markets across the world. In your opinion, what do governments need to do? What changes should be made to policies on migration and immigration in your country?

3. Why is migrant labour problematic? Why are there so many illegal immigrants in many western countries?

4. To what extent do you think multinational organizations are responsible for the employment of migrant workers? What would you suggest should be done to improve the conditions of migrant workers?

5. Employers favour the use of migrant workers for a number of reasons. What are the reasons for this?

6. Explain the reasons why sectors such as agriculture and tourism will always need temporary workers or a flexible workforce. In your opinion, should different sectors of the economy have different regulations regarding the use of temporary or migrant labour? Why/why not?

7. To what extent is the availability of migrant labour responsible for lowering wages in your country. Does this have to be the case? How can the government regulate this?

8. Some people suggest that the presence of migrant workers is threatening their culture. How would you reply to this?

9. In what ways do HR managers need to improve their knowledge and understanding of diversity issues in your country? How can diversity training improve the management of a workforce from a variety of countries and cultures?

10. Consider two of the cases in this chapter and explain the similarities and differences exposed in the treatment of migrant workers.

Further reading

Bach, S. (2010) Staff shortages and the utilization of migrant labour: the case of healthcare, in B. Anderson and M. Ruhs (eds) *Who Needs Migrant Workers? Labour Shortages, Immigration and Public Policy*, Oxford: Oxford University Press.
> Chapter 4 is relevant.

Emmott, B. (2008) *Rivals: How the Power Struggle Between China, India and Japan Will Shape Our Next Decade*, Orlando, FL: Harcourt.
> An excellent analysis of the political and economic power shifts towards Asia that are occurring now. The author shows how our future may be dominated by three Asian giants. The book considers how the competition between these three powers will affect the West. It considers the tensions and danger zones, as well as benefits of the competition between these rising powers.

Rubery, J., Simonazzi, A., and Ward, K. (2010) Exploring international migration and outsourcing through an institutional lens, in *Globalisation, Labour Markets and International Adjustment*, Essays in honour of Palle S. Andersen, Bank of International Settlements (BIS) Papers, No. 50 January 2010, online at www.bis.org/publ/bppdf/bispap50i.pdf (accessed 20 July 2012).
> Chapter 4, on international migration and outsourcing, is relevant.

Skinner, E.B. (2008) *A Crime so Monstrous: Face-to-face with Modern-day Slavery*, Edinburgh: Mainstream Publishing.
> The plight of modern-day slaves is also described in detail in this recent book.

Somerville, W., Sriskandarajah, D., and Latorre, M. (2009) United Kingdom: a reluctant country of immigration country profile, migration information source, *Migration Policy Institute*.
> An excellent overview of the UK's immigration policies and the current demographics related to the immigrant population (online at http://www.migrationinformation.org/Profiles/display.cfm?ID=736 (accessed 22 July 2012).

US Department of State (2011) *Trafficking in Persons Report*, online at http://www.state.gov/g/tip/rls/tiprpt/2011/ (accessed 20 July 2012).
> This report provides an excellent overview of the topic and is recommended reading for anyone wishing to have a better understanding of modern-day slavery.

Bibliography

Bach, S. (2010) Staff shortages and the utilization of migrant labour: the case of healthcare, in B. Anderson and M. Ruhs (eds) *Who Needs Migrant Workers? Labour Shortages, Immigration and Public Policy*, Oxford: Oxford University Press.

BBC News (2011) Older people cared for at home lacking basic rights, 20 June, online at http://www.bbc.co.uk/news/health-13813460 (accessed 21 July 2012).

— (2012a) Apple hit by China Foxconn Report, 30 March, online at http://www.bbc.co.uk/news/technology-17557630 (accessed 12 July 2012).

— (2012b) A rare look at Apple's production line in China, 21 February, online at http://www.bbc.co.uk/news/technology-17121978 (accessed 12 July 2012).

Bierce and Kenerson, P.C. (2010) US increases visa fees by $2,000 for H1-Bs and $2,250 for certain L's: Sen. Schumer leaps from 'Chop Shops' to 'Body Shops', Chuck Schumer's warning to Body Shops: reform or else!, *Outsourcing Law*, 14 September, online at http://www.outsourcing-law.com/2010/09/u-s-increase-visa-fees/ (accessed 18 July 2012).

Castles, S. (2004) Confronting the realities of forced migration, Refugee Studies Centre, University of Oxford, Migration Information Source, Migration Policy Institute, online at http://www.migrationinformation.org/Feature/display.cfm?ID=222 (accessed 12 July 2012).

— and Miller, M.J. (2009) Migration in the Asia-Pacific region, Migration Policy Institute, online at http://www.migrationinformation.org/Feature/display.cfm?ID=733 (accessed 12 July 2012).

CNN Press Room (2011) CNN Freedom Project: Dan Rivers investigates bonded labor in Southeast Asia, 4 October, video, online at http://cnnpressroom.blogs.cnn.com/2011/10/04/cnn-freedom-project-dan-rivers-investigates-bonded-labor-in-southeast-asia/ (accessed 22 July 2012).

Eade, J., Drinkwater, S., and Garapich, M. (2006) *Class and Ethnicity: Polish Migrants in London*, London: Economic and Social Research Council.

The Economist (2009) Videographic on international migration and remittances, 19 October, online at http://www.economist.com/blogs/freeexchange/2009/10/video_of_the_day_1 (accessed 21 July, 2012).

Edwards, T., Marginson, P., Edwards, P., Ferner, A., and Tregaskis, O. (2007) Corporate social responsibility in multinational companies: management initiatives or negotiated agreements?, Geneva: International Institute for Labour Studies, ILO, online at http://www.ilo.org/public/english/bureau/inst/publications/discussion/dp18507.pdf (accessed 21 July 2012).

Emiratisation (2010) Information portal for the Emirates, highlighting news on policy and job opportunities, online at: http://emiratisation.org/about-us-2 (accessed 21 July 2012).

Emmott, B. (2008) *Rivals: How the Power Struggle Between China, India and Japan Will Shape Our Next Decade*, Orlando, FL: Harcourt.

Equality and Human Rights Commission (EHRC) (2010) Eastern European migrant employment patterns reviewed, Equality and Human Rights Commission, 17January, online at http://www.equalityhumanrights.com/news/2010/january/eastern-european-migrant-employment-patterns-reviewed/ (accessed 21 July 2012).

Eurofound (2009) European Foundation for the Improvement of Living and Working Conditions, *Second European Quality of Life Survey—Quality of life in Europe 2003–2007*, Luxembourg: Office for Official Publications of the European Communities.

European Union (2011) EU Directive on Agency Workers, online at http://www.eurofound.europa.eu/eiro/2010/11/articles/UK1011019I.htm (accessed 21 July 2012).

Fair Labour Association (FLA) (2012) Tracking charts, online at http://www.fairlabor.org/transparency/tracking-charts (accessed 21 July 2012).

Gangmasters Licensing Authority (GLA) (2011) What we do, online at http://gla.defra.gov.uk/Who-We-Are/What-We-Do/ (accessed 21 July 2012).

Global Commission on International Migration (GCIM) (2005) *Migration in an Interconnected World: New Directions for Action, Report of the Global Commission on International Migration*, 5 October, online at http://www.unhcr.org/refworld/docid/435f81814.html (accessed 12 July 2012).

Goel, A., Moussavi, N., and Srivatsan, V. (2008) Time to rethink offshoring?, *McKinsey on Business Technology, IT Management*, 14(Winter), online at http://www.mckinsey.de/downloads/publikation/mck_on_bt/2009/mck_on_bt_14_offshoring.pdf (accessed 20 July 2012).

Goldin, I., Cameron, G., and Belarajan, M. (2011) *Exceptional People: How Migration Shaped Our World and will Define Our Future*, Princeton, NJ: Princeton University Press, reviewed in *The Economist*, Migration, the future of mobility, book review (26 May), online at http://www.economist.com/node/18741382 (accessed 29 October).

Gonzales, M. (2010) Zapatero repudia 'el truco' de Vic contra los 'sin papeles' (Zapatero rejects the 'gimmick' of Vic against the 'undocumented migrant labour'), 21 January, online at http://elpais.com/diario/2010/01/21/espana/1264028402_850215.html (accessed 20 July 2012).

Gordolan, L. and Lalani, M. (2009) Care and Immigration: migrant care workers in private households, online at http://www.kalayaan.org.uk/documents/Kalayaan%20Care%20and%20Immigration%20Report%20280909%20e-version.pdf (accessed 20 July 2012).

Gurria, A. (2009) Launch of the International Migration Outlook, Speech by OECD Secretary-General during the press conference organised for the launch of the International Migration Outlook, OECD Paris, 30 June, online at http://www.oecd.org/document/63/0,

3746,en_21571361_44315115_43214335_1_1_1_1,00.
html (accessed 12 July 2012).

Hamm, S. and Herbst, M. (2009) America's hi-tech
sweatshops, *Businessweek*, 12 October, online at http://
www.businessweek.com/magazine/content/09_41/
b4150034732629.htm (accessed 21 July 2012).

Hector, C. (2011) Malaysian human rights defender
in court over support for outsourced migrant
workers, 7 March, online at http://goodelectronics.
org/news-en/malaysian-human-rights-defender-in-
court-over-support-for-outsourced-migrant-workers
(accessed 20 July 2012).

Hemphill, T.A. and Lillevik, W. (2011) Implementing
a moral values foundation in the multinational
enterprise, *Journal of Business Ethics*, 101: 213–30.

Hugo, G. (2005a) *Migration and Society: Diversity
and Cohesion*, Geneva: Global Commission on
International Migration (GCIM), online at: http://iom.
ch/jahia/webdav/site/myjahiasite/shared/shared/
mainsite/policy_and_research/gcim/tp/TP6.pdf
(accessed 29 October 2012).

—— (2005b) *Migration in the Asia-Pacific Region*, Geneva:
Global Commission on International Migration
(GCIM), online at http://www.iom.int/jahia/webdav/
shared/shared/mainsite/media/docs/wmr/regional_
overviews/ro_asia.pdf (accessed 20 July 2012).

Human Rights Watch (2011) Protecting Asian migrants'
rights: recommendations to governments of the
Colombo process, Human Rights Watch, Migrant
Forum in Asia, CARAM Asia, 19 April, online at, http://
www.hrw.org/en/news/2011/04/19/protecting-asian-
migrants-rights (accessed 20 July 2012).

International Labour Organisation (ILO) (2009)
Fact-sheet on the economic crisis and migrant
workers: regional differences, Global Migration
Group/ILO, September, online at http://www.
globalmigrationgroup.org/uploads/documents/
ILO%20Fact-sheet_2_final.pdf (accessed 18 July 2012).

Kaptein, M. (2010) Toward effective codes: testing
the relationship with unethical behavior, *Journal of
Business Ethics* (2011) 99: 233–51.

Kerr, S. (2009) Dubai's hidden victims of recession, *Financial
Times*, 5 November, online at http://www.ft.com/
cms/s/0/b0c1c53a-c9ac-11de-a071-00144feabdc0.
html#axzz21KI7H7R9 (accessed 22 July 2012).

Kerwin D.M. with McCabe, K., (2011) Labor standards
enforcement and low-wage immigrants: creating an
effective enforcement system, July, Migration Policy
Institute, on-line at http://www.migrationpolicy.org/
pubs/laborstandards-2011.pdf (accessed 18 July 2012).

Labour behind the Label (LBL) (2009) Let's clean up
fashion: the state of pay behind the UK high street,
online at http://www.labourbehindthelabel.org/

images/pdf/letscleanupfashion2009.pdf (accessed 21
July 2012).

Macdonald, K. (2009) *The Reality of Rights: Barriers to
Accessing Remedies When Business Operates Beyond
Borders*, London: The Corporate Responsibility
Coalition/London School of Economics, online at
http://corporate-responsibility.org/reality-of-rights/
(accessed 12 July 2012).

Malik, N. (2009) The virtual slaves of the Gulf States,
The Guardian, 16 November, online at http://www.
guardian.co.uk/commentisfree/2009/nov/16/gulf-
states-asian-workers-rights (accessed 22 July 2012).

Migration Information Source (2012) Country resources,
online at http://www.migrationinformation.org/
resources (accessed 26 December 2012).

Monger, R. and Barr, M. (2008) *Annual Flow Report
April 2008, Nonimmigrant Admissions to the United
States*, April, Washington DC: US Department of
Homeland Security.

Organisation for Economic Co-operation and
Development (OECD) (2009) International Migration
Outlook: SOPEMI 2009, Summary in English, online at
http://www.oecd.org/dataoecd/5/20/43176823.pdf
(accessed 20 July 2012).

Oteify, R. and Walid, T. (2009) Dubai says not responsible
for Dubai world debt, 30 November, *Reuters*, online at
http://www.reuters.com/article/2009/11/30/us-dubai-
idUSGEE5AS0AH20091130 (accessed 20 July 2012).

Pakkiasamy, D. (2004) Saudi Arabia's plan for changing
its workforce, 1 November, Migration Information
Source, Migration Policy Institute, online at http://
www.migrationinformation.org/Feature/display.
cfm?ID=264 (accessed 3 May 2012).

Poinasamy, K. with Fooks, L. (2009) *Who Cares?* How
best to protect UK care workers employed through
agencies and gangmasters from exploitation, Oxfam
Briefing Paper, Oxfam GB, December, online at
http://policy-practice.oxfam.org.uk/publications/
who-cares-how-best-to-protect-uk-care-workers-
employed-through-agencies-and-gan-114060
(accessed 20 July 2012).

Rubery, J., Simonazzi, A., and Ward, K. (2010) Exploring
international migration and outsourcing through an
institutional lens, in *Globalisation, Labour Markets and
International Adjustment, International Migration and
Outsourcing—Essays in Honour of Palle S. Andersen*,
Bank of International Settlements (BIS) Papers, No. 50
January, online at www.bis.org/publ/bppdf/bispap50i.
pdf (accessed 20 July 2012).

Scheinson, A. (2009) *China's internal migrants*, Council
on Foreign Relations, 14 May, online at http://www.
cfr.org/china/chinas-internal-migrants/p12943
(accessed 12 July 2012).

Sissons, K. (2006) International employee representation: a case of industrial relations systems following the market?, in T. Edwards and C. Rees, *International Human Resource Management (HRM) Globalisation, National Systems and Multinational Companies*, Harlow: Pearson Education, pp. 242–61.

Skinner, E.B. (2008) *A Crime so Monstrous: Face-to-face with Modern-day Slavery*, Edinburgh: Mainstream Publishing.

Somerville, W., Sriskandarajah, D., and Latorre, M. (2009) United Kingdom: a reluctant country of immigration, country profile, Migration Information Source, Migration Policy Institute, online at http://www.migrationinformation.org/Profiles/display.cfm?ID=736 (accessed 12 July 2012).

Sumption, M. and Somerville, W. (2010) The UK's new Europeans: progress and challenges five years after accession, Equality and Human Rights Commission Policy Report, prepared for the Equality and Human Rights Commission Migration Summit, 2009 and Migration Policy Institute, online at http://www.equalityhumanrights.com/uploaded_files/new_europeans.pdf (accessed 12 July 2012).

Thiel, S. (2010) Europe's big choice with xenophobia on the rise, Europe must decide: open its doors and prosper, or shut them and pay the price, *Newsweek*, 1 March, online at http://www.thedailybeast.com/newsweek/2010/02/18/europe-s-big-choice.html (accessed 12 July 2012).

UK Border Agency (2011) Sixteen illegal workers discovered in restaurant raids, *News Stories*, 27 July, online at http://www.ukba.homeoffice.gov.uk/sitecontent/newsarticles/2011/july/49sixteen-illegal-workers (accessed 20 July 2012).

— (2012) Policy and law, online at http://www.ukba.homeoffice.gov.uk/policyandlaw/ (accessed 20 July 2012).

US Department of State (2009) *Trafficking in Persons Report, 2009*, online at http://www.state.gov/j/tip/rls/tiprpt/2009/ (accessed 20 July 2012).

— (2011) *Trafficking in Persons Report, 2011*, online at http://www.state.gov/g/tip/rls/tiprpt/2011/ (accessed 20 July 2012).

Vasta, E. (2006) From ethnic minorities to ethnic majority policy: changing identities and the shift to assimilationism in the Netherlands, *COMPAS*, Working Paper No. 26, University of Oxford, online at http://www.compas.ox.ac.uk/publications/working-papers/ (accessed 29 October 2012).

— (2008) The paper market: 'borrowing' and 'renting' of identity documents, Centre on Migration, Policy and Society, COMPAS, Working Paper No. 61, University of Oxford, online at http://www.compas.ox.ac.uk/publications/working-papers/wp-08-61/ (accessed 20 July 2012).

 Visit the Online Resource Centre for web links, interactive glossary, and more:
http://www.oxfordtextbooks.co.uk/orc/crawley

Glossary

360-degree (Three-hundred-and-sixty-degree) or multi-source performance rating system—a performance rating system that uses opinions of not only the line manager but also peers, subordinates, and sometimes customers and suppliers to provide an evaluation of an employee's performance.

Agency costs—internal costs that arise because of problems such as conflicts of interest between the principal and agent. Costs can be reduced if the principal adopts policies that encourage the agent to behave in the common interest. For example the company headquarters may be interested in shareholder value, while the subsidiary manager might be more interested in ensuring his/her own power or wealth.

Agency theory—suggests that in the process of internationalization, MNEs face internal conflicts between MNE headquarters (the principal) and the subsidiaries (the agent) because the two parties have different interests and preferences. For example subsidiary managers may make decisions in their own interests (such as retaining information, and thus retaining some control). This might not benefit the headquarters or the organization as a whole.

Balance of bargaining power—the relative strengths of employer and employees and their respective abilities to influence each other in determining the outcomes of any conflicts of interest, including those over pay and working arrangements. This concept is helpful when seeking to give an explanation for the agreements or compromises reached after negotiations have taken place, bearing in mind the methods used by each side to bolster their positions.

Balance sheet approach for expatriate pay—this approach tries to ensure that expatriates should not lose or gain financially, compared to other home country employees, and that different international assignments should be equally attractive. Reward is adjusted according to cost of living.

Best fit—this approach would suggest that managers need to adopt 'best fit' practices for their organization, when selecting management approaches, taking contextual factors into consideration (see also **comparative/contextual approach**).

Best practice—methods or ways of working that are thought to be the most effective, often having been used in the most successful organizations. It is often suggested that best practices can be used *universally*. The best practices of leading organizations are often identified in the process of benchmarking.

Bounded rationality—this explains that people do not make perfectly rational decisions because their rationality is bounded, limited, and constrained. In other words there is a limit to the information one person can have or obtain at any one time, and as a result they are unable to make completely rational decisions.

Broadbanding—a salary grading system that condenses several narrow bands into fewer broad bands with a bigger salary range. This gives greater freedom to locate employees in a more flexible system and the freedom to increase rewards without the need to promote people in order to give them a pay rise.

Business Process Outsourcing (BPO)—the transfer of some, core or non-core, business processes to an outside provider to reduce costs and improve quality. When the outsourcing provider is in another country it is known as outsourcing **off-shore** or **off-shoring**.

Code of ethics—a set of basic principles that guides decisions and behaviour in an organization. Sometimes also called a *code of conduct* or *code of practice*.

Coercive isomorphism—this refers to pressures that are 'political', or imposed by a more powerful authority such as the organization on which it depends, or the institutions and cultural expectations of the society within which it functions.

Collectivist approach/Collectivism—in the context of employment relations, this approach is intended to win over employees and trade unions to the company's plans. The company negotiates with elected representatives of trade unions and through this process of collective bargaining the company can discuss differences of opinion and reach compromise agreements with the unions over wages and other terms and conditions of employment.

Comparative HRD/HRM—considers how HRM is practised in different countries, including the impact of national institutions and culture on HRM.

Comparative/Contextual approach—an approach that considers factors beyond the firm, including national institutions and culture, as being integral to the study of management and the way it operates in different contexts and countries. This approach would suggest that managers need to adopt **best fit** practices for their organization when selecting management approaches, taking contextual factors into consideration.

Consequentialist ethics—the belief that the intended outcome of actions, aims, or goals determines whether they are right or wrong.

Contextual/comparative approach to HR and management—this approach chooses to explore the cultural and institutional variations that characterize different countries. It is contended that these differences can make it difficult to apply one solution to management issues across the globe. Supporters of this approach would assume that each situation requires the best solution (or **best fit**) for its particular circumstances.

Convergence—the belief that with the spread of globalization, best practices and policies will be adopted by organizations worldwide, until the way of doing business becomes similar, or converges, across the world.

Convergence/divergence debate—the name given to the academic discussion concerning the extent to which organizations across the world are adopting *similar* management approaches and practices. This process of **convergence** results in part from multinationals spreading common practices throughout their subsidiaries. The supporters of **divergence**, on the other hand, suggest that this does not happen, mainly because of the institutional and cultural differences that exist between countries across the globe.

Corporate social responsibility—the belief that business has a responsibility to the society of which it is a part.

Cultural imperialism—the term used to describe an attempt to change behaviours and encourage the adoption of 'western' ways of operating, which may be contrary to local tradition.

Culture shock—the name given to an unpleasant feeling on being confronted with an unfamiliar culture. This state may result in rejection of the culture or a gradual acceptance of the differences experienced. Some degree of culture shock is normal for any person visiting a new country.

Discriminatory management—this process occurs in an organization when either knowingly or unknowingly one group is favoured over another on grounds not related to merit but connected with a feature that differentiates membership of these groups, such as ethnicity, nationality, gender, or age. Hence there will be employees who are excluded from positions within the organization because of a certain characteristic that is perceived as making them different and therefore inferior.

Distributive justice (Colquitt, 2001)—any penalty handed out—ranging from warning to dismissal—should correspond to the severity of the offence, taking into account any extenuating factors

Diversity management—describes organizational initiatives taken by management that emphasize the positive aspects of differences between individuals. The aim is to enhance employees' contributions to the organization by harnessing their distinctive and valued qualities. The rationale that underpins this approach is that proactively promoting workforce diversity within the organization will bring tangible benefits to the business.

Egoism—the view that an action is morally right if the decision maker freely decides to pursue his/her (short-term) desires or (long-term) interests.

Employee value proposition—the unique mix of intrinsic and extrinsic rewards that an employee receives while being a member of the organization. It includes the rewards, benefits, work policies, and practices experienced by an employee in return for their work. The EVP is linked to the organization's mission, values, leadership, culture, and reward philosophy. In the context of employer branding, it is sometimes also referred to as the employer brand proposition.

Employer brand—the idea of the employer brand captures the concept that, from an employee's perspective, some organizations are better to work for than others. Organizations with strong employer brands would have a good reputation as an employer, which might derive from paying relatively well and/ or where working for them has given kudos to the employee and enhances their employability and attractiveness in the labour market.

Enlightened self-interest—to act in a way that will serve one's own interest in the long term.

Equality management—describes organizational initiatives taken by management, which are introduced to tackle practices regarded as unfair in their treatment of employees. Equality management seeks to prevent attitudes and behaviour towards others that are deemed unacceptable within the organization and aims to promote equal employment opportunities.

Ethical absolutism—the view that there are external, universally applicable moral principles, so that right and wrong are objective and rationally determined.

Ethical investors—investors who only invest in organizations that they believe conduct their operations ethically.

Ethical relativism—the belief that morality depends on the *context* and it is *subjective*. Right and wrong depend on the person making the decision and they are influenced by the culture in which the decision is being made.

Ethics of duties—the view that morality and right and wrong are questions of external, abstract, unchanging principles or moral laws.

Ethics of justice—within a specific social context, justice is the simultaneously fair treatment of individuals in a given situation.

Ethics of rights—the belief that ethics should be based on the concept of 'natural rights'. The most basic rights were originally defined as rights to life, freedom, and property.

Evaluator, rater, or appraiser—the person who evaluates the performance of an employee by using some work- or behaviour-based criteria during the performance appraisal process.

Expatriate/international assignee—an employee who is sent overseas or to a subsidiary office to work for a period of time. More specifically, this term usually applies to executives, managers, and technical experts sent overseas to work for one year or more. This person might be a **PCN (parent country national)** or a **TCN (third country national)**.

Explicit knowledge—knowledge that is easy to explain or codify, such as processes, procedures, and that can be transmitted through documentation.

Forced labour—term used to describe all work or service that is exacted from any person under the menace of any penalty. In this situation, the person has not offered him/herself voluntarily for work.

Forced ranking—a system used when compiling performance appraisal results from employees. It obliges raters to allocate a specific percentage of employees to different levels on the rating scale.

Fordist—refers to Fordism, a model of technological progress adapted from scientific management, which combined special tools for low-skilled workers doing repetitive tasks, the assembly line for mass production, with high wages for workers. Henry Ford (1863–1947), used these ideas in the automobile industry, resulting in the term 'Fordism'.

Foreign direct investment (FDI)—direct investment in business operations in a foreign country where the investor often gains a controlling share of the organization. It is often associated with investment in developing countries. As such, it is often used as a tool to measure the development of emerging markets. More accurately, however, it refers to investment in any country, regardless of stage of development.

Gini coefficient—a concept used to express income inequality. The Gini coefficient ranges from 0 to 1, where low coefficients reflect lower inequality. Zero means that there is perfect equality (everyone has the same income); higher scores mean different levels of income inequality. At the highest level, one person has all the income and everyone else has nothing.

Globalization—a term used to describe the recent rapid expansion of business across the world. This involves increasing interdependence between countries' financial and trading systems facilitated through advanced internet communication technologies and increasing cross-cultural influences. It may be perceived as having both positive and negative consequences on both rich and poor nations.

H1-B admission (USA)—a special visa granted to people from all over the world, which allows them to work in the USA as long as they are able to work in a 'speciality occupation', including IT, computing, finance, accounting, engineering, health care, and law, among others. As long as the applicant can find a sponsoring organization, they can be allowed to work for up to six years. The applicant's spouse and children under 21 may accompany them but they cannot work without their own H1-B visa.

Hard & soft HRM—**Hard HRM** or the instrumental approach, considers the rational, quantitative, and strategic aspects of human resource management, with a focus on competitive advantage through measurable performance improvement. Human resources may be seen primarily as costs. **Soft HRM** takes a humanistic approach and sees people as valuable contributors. Their development, collaboration, participation, and trust are recognized. Soft HRM focuses on the integration of HR policies and practices with strategic business objectives.

High- and low-commitment HR strategies—the former strategy is tied to the employer seeking a close relationship with workers, encouraging them to become psychologically involved with their employing organization; whereas the latter will tend to feature hire-and-fire principles and be associated with low-trust relations. The terms 'high road' and 'low road' are also used to describe these approaches to managing the employment relationship, which are typified by their treatment of staff as a 'valued resource' or as a 'commodity' to be directed.

High-performance work systems (HPWS)—an approach to designing organizations that attempts to align systems and structures to the business environment to produce high customer value. HPWSs typically associate with innovative reward and performance management strategies.

Host Country National (HCN)—refers to an employee who works for the subsidiary or partner company of a multinational in the host country and who is a national of the host country.

Immigrant—a person who has left one country to settle permanently in another.

Immigrant status—term used in the USA for a person who is lawfully admitted to the USA for *permanent residence and employment*. This is often referred to as having a 'Green Card'.

Individualism/individualistic approach/ perspective—in the context of employment relations, this is an approach taken by management to communicate directly with its staff, including during team briefings delivered in person by line managers. This is supported by mass media channels for supplying information directly to the employees.

Informational justice—taking steps to carefully describe the procedures and to explain the rationale for any decisions made (Colquitt, 2001).

Inpatriates—host country nationals (**HCNs**) or third country nationals (**TCNs**) who are sent to the headquarters of an organization, usually in the parent country, for a period of time for training. These HCNs are prepared to take over the management of the subsidiary operations in the future.

Internal labour market—exists in a whole organization or part of one, where wages, benefits, and other rewards are determined by organizational policies and procedures. In the past the internal market was comprised of a workforce of almost entirely full-time staff; the organization recruited at the bottom and promoted from within. The proportion of long-serving employees was high.

International assignee/expatriate—refers to an employee who is sent abroad to work for their company. More specifically, this term usually applies to executives, managers, and technical experts sent overseas to work for one year or more.

Involuntary servitude—slavery, peonage, or compulsory labour for the satisfaction of debts.

Isomorphism—refers to the pressure to be similar to other organizations. (There are three types of isomorphism—coercive, mimetic, or normative.)

Learning and development (L&D)—the development of knowledge to achieve goals for both the individual and the organization. It includes the development of both explicit and tacit knowledge.

Line manager—a person who directly supervises the work of an employee and who usually evaluates their work during a performance appraisal. For expatriates, the appraisal might take place in the host country location and could be carried out by a local line manager.

Local hire—a person who is contracted locally according to local terms and conditions, also known as a host country national (**HCN**).

Migrant worker—a person who travels to another country in order to work temporarily.

Mimetic isomorphism—pressures, undertaken in times of uncertainty, to adopt a standard solution or strategy already successfully used by others, including competitors.

Multi-source feedback—a performance rating system that uses opinions of not only the line manager but also peers, subordinates, and sometimes customers to provide an evaluation of the employee's performance; sometimes known as **360-degree** feedback.

Narrow-banding—a salary grading systems in which the difference between the top and bottom of a grade (the band width) is relatively small. Narrow banding gives management tight control over wages but can be frustrating for employees, who rely on promotion to increase their salaries.

National business systems—also known as institutional configurations, industrial orders, or varieties of capitalism. These are the specific configurations that shape and constrain the structure and processes through which business is conducted.

National culture—collectively held values of a group of people from one country that distinguishes them from those of another country.

Non-consequentialist ethics—this approach considers the underlying principles and motivation of the decision maker, including the rights and duties of the individual, to determine whether the action is morally right.

Normative isomorphism—refers to practices that are considered the norm or which are accepted and 'professional' in that environment.

Off-shore/off-shoring—describes a situation in which an organization conducts some part of its business in another country.

One best way—the belief that there are specific methods or ways of working that are most effective, often having been used in the most successful organizations. As a result they become known as **best practice**. It is often suggested that these **best practices** can be used anywhere in the world (or *universally*). The best practices of leading organizations are often identified in the process of benchmarking.

Organizational culture—collection of values, beliefs, traditions, and practices that are shared by an organization's members,

Outsource/outsourcing—to transfer some activity, production, or service to another company or outside provider. Business process outsourcing (BPO) is more specifically the transfer of core or non-core business processes to an outside provider to reduce costs and improve quality. When the outsourcing provider is in another country it is described as **off-shoring**. It also means to transfer some activity, production, or service to another company or outside provider.

Overseas assignment—employment for a period of time in another country.

Parent Country National (PCN)—an employee from the home country of the head office of the organization who has been sent to work overseas and who often represents the interests of the head office.

Performance appraisal, evaluation, or review—formal assessment and rating of individuals by their managers, usually at an annual review meeting.

Performance management—process of managing the work and development of people through setting goals and objectives that support the strategy and needs of the organization.

Performance-related pay (PRP)—a component of reward, based on the belief that an additional reward related to performance targets will raise individual performance. PRP can be linked to the achievement of quantifiable targets, such as profit targets or share price, or to the outcomes of a performance review process. Issues of fairness in measurement of performance and the allocation of PRP provide challenges for HR managers.

PESTLE analysis—analysis of political economic, social, technological, legal, and environmental factors that impact on an organization. These can have a significant impact on business operations.

Pluralist view—perspective that acknowledges that managers and employees have a number of objectives (a plurality), over some of which they may disagree. If managements subscribe to this pluralist perspective, they are more likely to see the advantage of entering discussions with a trade union as the best way to settle a dispute that affects a group of employees.

Prior orientation to work—way in which an individual is *predisposed* to think and feel about their employment, which can be based upon a combination of existing knowledge and the priorities and aims they bring to the workplace. The impact on the employment relationship can be gauged by noting the likely differences between those individuals whose prior orientation gives prominence to the pay they receive, compared with those who seek a job with varied and interesting responsibilities.

Psychological contract—based upon the two-way perceptions of employer and employee, this informal and typically imprecise part of the employment relationship depicts the mutual obligations of each side to the other. It reflects the interpretation of promises and expectations each has of the other, and what they think they should do in return. With respect to everyday workplace relations, the psychological contract may be more influential than the formal contract of employment. However, its precise significance may become apparent only when there is a perception that it has been breached.

Resident non-immigrant—foreign nationals granted *temporary* entry into the USA. This includes students and temporary workers.

Reward philosophy—a statement of the broad beliefs and principles that the organization has about how employees should be rewarded, in line with the organization's vision and mission. These beliefs shape much of the detail of actual reward practices and decisions, for example the combinations of salary, bonuses, and other benefits given to executives.

Reward strategies—statements that explain the long-term objectives of its reward policies and practices and how these contribute towards achieving the strategic goals and the needs of employees. This might include how workforce changes, which may be needed to reach targets, will be rewarded.

Rhetoric and reality—the possibility of difference between *rhetoric*, which is what a company states it does, and *reality*, which is what it actually does. In employment relations, management should be wary of an adverse reaction from employees if they perceive management's behaviour and statements to be contradictory. However, during industrial disputes both sides may choose to use overstated rhetoric if they believe it will advance their arguments.

Small or medium-sized enterprise (SME)—an enterprise that normally has fewer than 250 employees and an annual turnover of under €50 million.

Social capital—the sum of actual or potential resources embedded within, available through, and derived from the network of relationships possessed by an individual or social unit.

Social categorization—psychological process that involves thinking about other people primarily as members of social groups rather than as individuals— and so classifying them in terms of, for example, their nationality, age, gender, occupation, or ethnicity. As a consequence of this perceptual process, there is a tendency to exaggerate the distinctiveness of a group we see as different—and to believe that its individual members are more alike than they actually are.

Social dumping—occurs when an organization moves its productive activities from one country to another country where labour standards are lower or poorly enforced. As a result, the original country loses jobs, but the company benefits from differences in direct and indirect labour costs, constituting significant competitive advantage (see Eurofound for a detailed explanation).

Societal effect—interaction of legal and economic context, organizational forms, HR practices, and business strategies, which leads to different configurations within the same industry, in different countries over time. For example the same industries may evolve in distinct ways in different countries because of this.

Soft HRM see **Hard & soft HRM.**

Stereotyping—embodies an individual's broad description of a certain group of people and represents a set of over-generalized beliefs about its members' behaviours and motives. This concept helps to explain how the process of social categorization is bolstered and reinforced. Thus, for example, based on our stereotypes we believe that members of group 'X' are inherently 'more lazy' when compared to the 'harder working' members of group 'Y'.

Strategic HRM—the pattern of planned human resource deployments and activities intended to enable a firm to achieve its goals.

Strategic international HRM—concerns the processes used by multinational companies to strategically plan, develop, and implement policies and practices for managing people internationally. Strategic IHRM should have the optimum impact on the enterprise's international goals and contribute to the effective operation and profitability of each unit, whatever its context.

Tacit knowledge—knowledge obtained through experience, which is difficult to put into words, or codify, sometimes described as 'know-how'. This knowledge is transferred through the organization by the mobility of people across the organization.

Taylorist management approaches—a top-down management approach in which jobs are broken down into small parts so that workers can be easily trained and controlled. It is also known as *scientific*

management and is based on the ideas of Frederick Taylor (1856–1915). These ideas were adopted by Henry Ford (1863–1947) in the automobile industry, resulting in the term **Fordism**.

Third Country National (TCN)—an employee from a third country, neither the country where the head office is located nor the host country, where the subsidiary or partner company and job is located, who is sent overseas to work at the subsidiary or partner company.

Total reward—a reward package made up of cash remuneration, benefits, development and career opportunities, work-life balance, performance and recognition, and support in a conducive work environment. Total reward is also a reward strategy that is flexible and can be adjusted to changes in the market and employee needs, used to attract, retain, and motivate talent.

Utilitarianism—the view that an action is morally right if it results in the greatest amount of good for the greatest number of people.

Unitary framework/perspective—a managerial perspective that considers the needs of all players in the firm (management and employees) to be the same and ensures that the best interests of all will be achieved by the success of the firm.

Universalist view/approach—supports the idea that there is **one best way** to do things in an organization, which can be applied anywhere in the world, or universally.

Index

354 INDEX